Church and State

Also available from *Continuum*:

The Globalization of Hesychasm and the Jesus Prayer, Christopher D.L. Johnson
A Grammar of the Common Good, Patrick Riordan
Hitler's Theology, Rainer Bucher
The New Visibility of Religion, edited by Michael Hoelzl and Graham Ward
From Political Theory to Political Ideology, edited by Péter Losonczi and Aakash Singh
Politics of Fear, Practices of Hope, edited by Stefan Skrimshire
The Politics to Come, edited by Paul Fletcher and Arthur Bradley
Postsecular Cities, edited by Christopher Baker and Justin Beaumont
Remoralizing Britain?, edited by Christopher Baker, Elaine L. Graham and Peter Manley Scott
What is Political Theology?, edited by Michael Hoelzl and Graham Ward

Church and State
Religious Nationalism and State Identification in Post-Communist Romania

Cristian Romocea

Continuum International Publishing Group
The Tower Building   80 Maiden Lane
11 York Road   Suite 704
London SE1 7NX   New York NY 10038

www.continuumbooks.com

© Cristian Romocea, 2011

All rights reserved. No part of this publication may be reproduced or transmitted in any form or by any means, electronic or mechanical, including photocopying, recording, or any information storage or retrieval system, without prior permission in writing from the publishers.

British Library Cataloguing-in-Publication Data
A catalogue record for this book is available from the British Library.

ISBN: HB: 978-1-4411-6857-3

Library of Congress Cataloging-in-Publication Data
Romocea, Cristian.
Church and state : religious nationalism and state identification in post-communist Romania / Cristian Romocea.
p. cm.
Includes bibliographical references.
ISBN: 978-1-4411-6857-3
1. Church and state–Romania. 2. Christianity and politics–Romania. 3. Nationalism–Romania–History–20th century. 4. Romania–Church history. I. Title.
BR926.3.R66 2011
261.709498'09049–dc22

2010038582

Typeset by Newgen Imaging Systems Pvt Ltd, Chennai, India
Printed and bound in Great Britain

To Oana, Julia, Amanda, and Robert

Contents

Preface		ix
Abbreviations		xii
Introduction		1
Chapter 1	The Orthodox Church in Post-Communist Romania	12
Chapter 2	German Protestantism and Nazism in Third Reich Germany	44
Chapter 3	From Caesaropapism to Religious Nationalism	72
Chapter 4	Nationalist Orthodoxy and the Romanian State	109
Chapter 5	The Marxist-Orthodox Symbiosis	149
Chapter 6	The Theological Error of Nationalism: Barth and Stăniloae	180
Conclusion	Toward a Theology of 'Permanent Revolution'	214
Bibliography		220
Index		243

Preface

The writing of this book has been a fascinating journey, dotted with times of joy and encouragement, anxiety, and frustration. Conceived as a doctoral dissertation, the ideas that have led to the research topic reworked in this book emerged while completing my postgraduate degree in theology at the Evanđeoski Teološki Fakultet (ETF) in Osijek, Croatia. There, amid a society rising out of the ashes of the wars of the former Yugoslavia, I had firsthand experience of the effects of ethnic conflict, war, and its outcomes. I began pondering ways of addressing the role of the churches in relation to war and nationalism. What caused my consternation at the time was the active role the Serbian Orthodox and Croatian Catholic churches played in these wars, encouraging, supporting, and offering religious and nationalist legitimization for their side's criminal military actions, often carried out against unarmed civilians. The proximity of this tragic conflict, the encounter with the shell-ridden towns and grief-ridden war survivors, led me to a moral and spiritual dilemma: What is the value of the Christian church if it provides no defense against ethnic nationalism, violence, and can even become an active participant in genocide?

Nevertheless, many research ideas and worthwhile book projects fail to materialize due to lack of encouragement and support. Fortunately, my desire to explore the relations between church and state in the Romanian context received the constant encouragement of Dr. Peter Kuzmic, rector and founder of ETF, who has remained a model of theological integrity and relevant political activism in the Balkan region. The funding for my research was kindly provided by the Langham Partnership International, which has proved to be not only a grant-making organization but, moreover, a scholarship community of devout, committed, and faithful mentors, friends, and fellow scholars. During the years of researching and writing this book, the example of John R.W. Stott, Langham's founder, has enabled me to develop awareness for relating, in his words, "the ancient Word to the modern world." The yearly Langham consultations in the lovely setting offered by Westminster College in Cambridge, and the chance to share in other scholars' efforts to make theology relevant to today's multifaceted social and political realities, have proved an invaluable source of support and encouragement. I therefore wish to express my gratitude for the support received from Langham's international director, Dr. Chris Wright, and the leadership team, Merritt Sawyer, Paul Berg, and Dr. Howard Peskett.

The Oxford Centre for Mission Studies (OCMS) has been the central hub for all I have done and undergone throughout this research period. A unique learning center in many respects, OCMS has impacted my student life in a special way through the friendly staff and scholars I have been privileged to meet and interact with on a daily basis. Special thanks go to the center's founder, Dr. Vinay Samuel, and to the current director, Dr. Wonsuk Ma, for their supportive attitude and affirmative action in times of need and uncertainty. I also wish to thank my external research supervisor, Tom Gallagher, Professor of the Study of Ethnic Conflict and Peace at Bradford University and an authority on religion as a source of conflict in modern Europe. His expertise on Romanian political and cultural realities has helped me recognize otherwise concealed nationalist ideologies and to focus on the most important challenges facing the Orthodox Church in contemporary society. Prof. Gallagher's expertise in political studies offered a refreshing approach to tackling a theological subject. It also prompted me to embark on a postgraduate course in Politics and International Relations at Cambridge University, as I realized that theologians writing on church–state relations often lack familiarity with political studies. The expertise gained in this process enabled me then to revisit the dissertation manuscript with fresh eyes before publication.

This research would have not been possible without the guidance, encouragement, and great wisdom of my friend, professor, and mentor, Haddon Willmer, Emeritus Professor at Leeds University. Having been instrumental to my intellectual formation since I was still a student in Osijek, Prof. Willmer has opened my eyes to a whole new world in which biblical and theological concerns are faithfully related to social and political realities that meet us in everyday life. His own experience with reconciliation efforts in Northern Ireland, as well as his engagement with German theologian Karl Barth's political thinking as a relevant theology for contemporary churches' struggles, have shaped and greatly expanded my academic horizons. His astute expertise, challenging and incisive engagement, and critique of my ideas and thinking have been constantly balanced by his honesty, devotion, and friendship.

A special thanks goes to Dr. Jonathan Sutton, senior lecturer at Leeds University in contemporary church–state relations and theology in Russia, Bulgaria, Romania, and Ukraine, whom I first met as he sat as my external examiner during the oral defense of my dissertation in Oxford in 2007. His enthusiasm for church–state relations in Eastern Europe, and his knowledge and engagement with Orthodox Christianity, have been crucial to the shaping of the dissertation into what is now this book. Without his advice, suggestions, and encouragement to publish, this book would have not materialized. I also wish to thank a number of friends and colleagues for their sustained support and friendship. Among them, Dr. Lucian Turcescu of Concordia University, Canada, deserves special mention. What makes Dr. Turcescu special is not just his friendship and scholarship, but his unique combination of being an astute Patristic scholar who is equally relevant in engaging with contemporary political issues of church–state relations in Romania. Among various friends you make in life, there are those you call "best friends," and those accolades go to Corneliu Constantineanu, Marcel Măcelaru, and Kosta Milkov. I can say without hesitation that each of them has enriched my life in more than one way, a list that is too long to mention here.

In good Greco-Roman literary tradition, which always left the most important things to come last, my deepest gratitude goes to my wife, Oana. Her companionship, understanding, and encouragement have been essential to the completion of this research and to the publishing of this book, which is dedicated to her and our three children, Julia, Amanda, and Robert.

Abbreviations

ALRC	*Asociația pentru Libertatea Religioasă Creștină* (Christian Committee for the Defence of Religious Freedom)
APADOR-CH	*Asociația pentru Apărarea Drepturilor Omului în România—Comitetul Helsinki* (The Association for the Defence of Human Rights in Romania—the Helsinki Committee)
ASCOR	*Asociația Studenților Creștini Ortodocși din România* (The Romanian Christian Orthodox Student Association)
CSCE	*Commission on Security and Cooperation in Europe*
GDS	*Grupul pentru Dialog Social* (Group for Social Dialogue)
KGB	*Komitet Gosudarstvennoy Bezopasnosti* (Committee for State Security)
NKVD	*Narodnōi Komissariat Vnutrennikh Del* (People's Commissariat for Internal Affairs)
NSDAP	*Nationalsozialistische Deutsche Arbeiterpartei* (National Socialist German Workers' Party)
OSCE	*Organization for Security and Cooperation in Europe*
ROC	*Romanian Orthodox Church*
RSDLP	*Rossiiskaia Sotsial-Demokraticheskaia Rabochaia Partiia* (Russian Social-Democratic Labour Party)
SA	*Sturmabteilung* (Storm-troopers, paramilitary organization of the German Nazi Party)
SDP	*Sozialdemokratische Partei der Schweiz* (Swiss Social Democratic Party)
TDO	Dumitru Stăniloae, *Teologie Dogmatică Ortodoxă* (Orthodox Dogmatic Theology)

Introduction

We live in a religious twenty-first century. Many will be familiar with sociologist Peter Berger's famous "paradigm shift" in the *New York Times* in 1968, when he was forecasting that "[by] the twenty-first century, religious believers are likely to be found only in small sects, huddled together to resist a worldwide secular culture"[1]; only to write in his 1999 volume, *The Desecularisation of the World*: "[T]he assumption that we live in a secularised world is false: The world today, with some exceptions . . . is as furiously religious as it ever was, and in some places more so than ever."[2] Whatever description this century may be given, it is important to recognize that church–state relations and questions about the appropriate interaction between the realms of religion and politics will remain on the agenda.[3]

However, the debate about what role the church should play in culture and public life often gets stuck in a sterile "either/or." Either religion is privatized, or one will end up living in a nationalist and theocratic state. Either Christianity is explicitly recognized as the foundation of nation, culture, and public life, or everyone's life will become irreparably relativized and individualistic. Such antagonistic approaches have been observed particularly in post-Communist societies from Eastern Europe, where democratization and secularization have challenged a religious establishment that for almost 45 years has paid lip service to totalitarian regimes. The established churches have naturally come to fear and distrust secularization and European Union (EU) enlargement, which threaten the deposing of religion from its previously privileged position, both in the public commitments of society and in the recesses of personal subjectivity. In post-Communist societies, democracy has become equated with increasing secularization and confinement of religion to private life, and with pluralization and relativization of belief.

This volume investigates the relationship between the church and the state in post-Communist Romania, exploring venues through which Christian theology can offer a basis for churches' support of a democratic system and liberalism. More specifically, this volume seeks to answer two vital questions in the context of Romanian post-Communist society: Can the Romanian Orthodox Church (ROC) relate in a coherent and rigorous way to the problems of social and political organization in post-Communist Romania without being drawn into the nationalist discourse? What political thinking should theologians encourage in order for the church to have a beneficial role for the whole of society? In dealing with these two questions, this volume employs a comparative treatment of the Romanian Orthodox Church and the Protestant churches in National Socialist Germany. This analysis will help identify certain commonalities, as well as differences, between the totalitarian ideologies of both National Socialism and Communism and their effect on the condition of the church in the state. No two historical circumstances are the same, just as no two ideologies are identical, and for this reason this volume does not pretend to identify in German National Socialism the only possible match for the Marxist Communist ideology encountered by the Orthodox Church in Romania.

Twentieth-century Europe was characterized by an explosion of nationalisms that gave birth to various regimes that all arose within a short space of time (1917–33); among them, the most important were the Bolshevik, the Fascist, and the National Socialist. Whereas this study could draw many useful examples by comparing Romanian Communism with Stalinism, this would not have as great an impact in highlighting the ideological attraction of the church to totalitarianism. The main reason for this limited impact is that Russian Communism has literally been the blueprint for the Communist regime in Romania, the Soviets designing most of the totalitarian apparatus that developed in postwar Romania.[4] This being the case, to compare Romanian and Stalinist totalitarianisms would be comparing two very similar forms of totalitarianism.

Moreover, other volumes that have looked comparatively at the Soviet-type Communism and German National Socialism have shown there is value to such an approach.[5] Authors who have tackled Communism and Nazism comparatively from a "moral theology" viewpoint have been effective in unmasking the lack of opposition and resistance resulting from the moral corruption of these regimes' ideologies.[6] Thus, comparing Romanian Communism with German National Socialism enables an investigation into how the churches' entrapment in and loyalty to the totalitarian regime led to a metamorphosis of the atheist states into political religions. This comparative approach will furthermore present the circumstances for understanding the churches' historical identification with the state, and the detrimental consequences for the churches.

Christianity and Marxism in Eastern Europe

Historically, the Christian churches have struggled to maintain a critical distance from identification with race, nationalism, and their underlying ideologies. Marxist ideology in particular represented a great temptation for the established Christian churches in Communist countries, which maintained close ties with the state. In the case of the ROC, the relationship with the Communist state reached a climax when Marxism and Orthodoxy mixed to form a unique and unprecedented ideological symbiosis.

At the beginning of the twentieth century, the cultural and nationalist influences of ROC theology espoused both idealized versions of a rural past as the embodiment of perfection, and mystical forms of religious nationalism that found expression in xenophobic and anti-Semitic sentiments. The inability to break away from these cultural influences created the basis for a symbiosis between Marxist-Communist ideology and Orthodox theology. As this volume will suggest, the lack of a coherent and uncompromising opposition of the Romanian Orthodoxy to the Marxist-atheist totalitarianism during the twentieth century was the result of a nationalist and ethnic preoccupation among Orthodox theological circles—a preoccupation that could not offer a basis for theological resistance.

Because of this failure, and confronted with the totalitarian excesses of the atheistic Communist regime, Romanian Orthodoxy did not generate a confessional movement. There was no coherent or long-lasting resistance movement, synod, or theological document to expose the Communist regime's infringement of religious freedom and to speak against the suppression of religion. Instead, the Orthodox Church offered an unprecedented theology of the *social apostolate* which, by attempting to encompass elements of Marxist and Leninist ideology, greatly diminished its distinctiveness and prophetic voice and led its clergy and congregations into a controversial relationship with the Communist government.

German Churches and Nationalism

Orthodox Christianity and Marxist Communism were not the only two irreconcilable beliefs that exposed the churches' lack of theological commitment. This volume will draw a comparison between Romanian Communism and German National Socialism as totalitarian regimes. The plight of the Protestant churches in Nazi Germany will therefore inform the investigation into the historical and theological conditions that have given rise to such atypical symbiosis between Orthodoxy and Marxism in the Romanian Communist context.

The example of the German Christians (*Deutsche Christen*) in Third Reich Germany is a telling reminder that even two utterly and fundamentally irreconcilable systems of belief like Christianity and National Socialism could be synthesized. Emerging from the efforts of nationalist-minded Christians to capture the energies of Germany's Protestant churches for the National Socialist cause, the German Christians' movement sought to revive church life through increased emphasis on German culture and ethnicity. Trapped by ethnic nationalism and Nazi ideology dominating the state, the German Christians failed to speak out against the racial discrimination and genocide carried in the name of the *Volk*. The churches identifying with this movement were deceived because they lacked a firm theological foundation that would have enabled them to expose the German people's intoxication with racial purity, the *Volk*, and with their savior, the *Führer*.

Setting the Problem: Church and State in Post-1989 Romania

A comparative investigation of the ideological influences of Nazism and Marxism and their effect on the German and Romanian churches would have little value unless it helped us understand the challenges that churches are facing today. Although more than two decades have passed since the fall of the Communist regimes of Central and Eastern Europe, nationalist temptations reminiscent of the Communist past are still present in post-Communist Romania. Thus, this volume contends that Orthodox nationalism continues to affect church–state relations in post-1989 Romania by virtue of centuries of tradition. Engagement with, and examination of, this tradition will therefore enable us to understand how the implausible symbiosis between nationalism and the Romanian Orthodoxy developed.

In 2006, the Presidential Commission for the Study of the Communist Dictatorship in Romania set out an investigation in order to provide a comprehensive report allowing for the condemnation of Communism as it was experienced in this country. Instituted by President Traian Băsescu, the commission's panel was led by political scientist Vladimir Tismăneanu and examined the activity of institutions that enforced and perpetuated the Communist dictatorship.[7] The findings of the commission, presented before the Romanian parliament in December that same year, are at the center of an ongoing debate in Romanian society not least because the ROC refuses to acknowledge the findings of the report, which identify the collaborationist role played by the Orthodox churches during the Communist period.[8]

The disapproving reaction of the Orthodox hierarchy to the report is consistent with the post-Communist period in which attempts at public repentance concerning the collaboration of various clergy and priests with the totalitarian regime have not been convincing. The same criticism would apply to the reparations the ROC wholly declined or only reluctantly agreed to make in the process of restitution of church buildings and of other properties the Communist regime confiscated from persecuted denominations after World War II and presented to the Orthodox. Another challenge (discussed in chapter 1) refers to the nationalistic inclination of the Orthodox Church, stemming from an established model of church–state relations that resembles the British model. This took the form of constant pressures on the government for constitutional recognition of its dominance, as the national church, over the other denominations. Finally, this volume investigates claims that the ROC continues to struggle with pervasive anti-Western and anti-modernist reflexes that are assumed uncritically and impede constructive dialogue between the church and the state. Such reflexes relate closely to the historical suspicion of Byzantium toward the pragmatic West and which the Communist regime, characterized by deep resentment and distrust toward Western democracy, kept alive.

A contrasting analysis between religiosity and public morality seems to suggest the ROC's poor performance as an agent of spiritual and moral renewal in society. Surveys indicate Romania has enjoyed high levels of religiosity since the fall of Communism. According to the findings of the GfK Custom Research survey 'Religion – A Personal Matter' commissioned in 2004 by *The Wall Street Journal Europe* to assess religious attitudes in Europe, Romania has the highest score for religiosity in Europe.[9] The report stressed that the number of Christian believers in Central and Eastern Europe is above average, at 80 percent, with Romania scoring a top 97 percent of people who think of themselves to be religious. Such high rates are confirmed by the 2002 national census, which showed that 99.6 percent of the Romanian population claims to belong to an officially recognized religious denomination.[10] Concerning the trust people place in state institutions, the Romanian Orthodox Church ranked on the top with 86 percent, followed by the Romanian Army with 69 percent.[11] Also, in terms of daily religious practice, Romania's scores were rivaled only by those of Poland, with high church attendance and trust in the institution of the church.

The predominantly religious proclivity evidenced by these findings is in stark contrast with other surveys, in which Romania figures as one of the poorest countries of Europe as well as one of the leading countries worldwide when it comes to abortion rates, corruption, and internet fraud, as noted by Silviu Rogobete.[12] Based on the 2005 "Country Report on Human Rights Practices," commissioned by the Bureau of Democracy, Human Rights and Labour of the United States Department of State, Romania struggles with widespread corruption among members of the judiciary, and low-level corruption in its law-enforcement agencies, as well as among politicians and civil servants.[13] Thus, it is paradoxical that an Orthodox population with such high rates of religiosity is simultaneously struggling with widespread corruption and immorality at the societal level.

Another topic of concern is growing public activism of the ROC as well as the political manipulation of the church at the hands of social-democratic political bodies that have emerged in the post-Communist era. Reminiscent of the interwar period (between the 1920s and 1940s) when the ROC played a controversial role in the era's "national debate" between those of traditional and those of liberal political affinities, the involvement of the ROC in lobbying post-1989 governments for preferential status for Orthodoxy above other denominations has justifiably raised questions from civil society.

All these aspects have an influence on the identity of the ROC amid a democratic and European society, a pluralist democracy, and a multi-denominational religious milieu. Thus, this volume suggests the historical identification of nationalist Orthodoxy with the Romanian state, and that identification's influences on theology today, are incompatible with the political and cultural direction in which Romanian society is currently moving. As it struggles to relate to current realities, the Orthodox Church denotes incoherence because of its official adherence to the modernization and democratization of society, on the one hand, and its anti-modernism, ethnic nationalism, and historical reliance on the state for benefits and protection, on the other hand.

Summary and Scope of the Study

This volume begins from an evaluation of the current struggles that characterize the ROC as it attempts to relate to the changing cultural and political realities in post-1989 Romania. Thus, it will argue that the ROC continues to be affected by its past of collaboration with the Communist authorities and by the past identification between Orthodoxy and Romanian nationalism. Elaborating on the basis for this assumption, it concentrates on a set of challenges the ROC is facing in contemporary Romania, such as the repentance of the ROC for its Communist collaboration, the restitution of the Greek Catholic Church's buildings, as well as tensions regarding religious pluralism and political activism.

The investigation of the nature of totalitarianism burdening the church in post-Communist Romania leads to a comparative analysis in chapter 2 that surveys the Protestant churches in Third Reich Germany and the development of and role played by Nazi ideology with respect to a shift in the theological focus toward loyalty to culture, race, and supreme leader. The methods and ideologies on which National Socialism thrived, such as nationalism, racism, mythified accounts of nation, and the use of terror tactics, were just as essential for Communist domination, and were instrumental to the political takeover in postwar Romania. The emergence of the German Christians' movement as supporters of National Socialism can be linked with the role played by Protestant theologians of the eighteenth and nineteenth centuries, who developed reductionist dogmas, placed great emphasis on historical continuity, and were unable to dissociate from nationalism.

Similar to the identification of Protestant theologians with German nationalism, the Orthodox Church developed a historical symbiosis with the ruler and the state, as described in chapters 3 to 5. The main factor that enforced the identification between the ROC and the state was the historical self-identity of Romanian Orthodoxy as an organic part of the nation, the people, and the state. Such a legacy is, nevertheless, refuted by Orthodox scholarship that points to the so-called Justinian symphony as a viable model of distinction and collaboration between the religious and the secular realms. Thus, it becomes crucial for the understanding of the ROC's perceived identity in relation to the modern state to examine, initially, their perspective on *caesaropapism*, following a typical

Orthodox theory of culture that assumes an organic succession of historical developments. This will help expose the limitation of the historicist approach in defense of charges of political subordination of the church, especially in the Eastern Orthodox Empire.

While post-Enlightenment nationalism was redefining the role of religion in the nation states, in tsarist and Bolshevik Russia, the tradition of caesaropapism was causing a negative impact on the form of nationalism that emerged as a reaction against it and gave birth to virtual political religions. All the while, the Orthodox Church in the Romanian territories was characterized by a constant mythologization of its own history through the sanctification of origins, religious national heroes, threats to national identity, the social role played by clergy, and the shift in the relationship between the autocephalous Orthodox Church and the united modern state. The ideological influences espoused here marked the interwar period and preceded Communism, when they became incorporated into the extremist ideology of the Iron Guard movement and led to an Orthodox legionnaire, ethnocratic and nationalist ideology.

The development of the social apostolate followed a period of political and cultural changes in postwar Romania, indicating the ROC's inability to achieve a critical distance from the state. The social doctrine emerged in symbiosis between Marxist thought and Orthodox theology, combining elements of both. This led to the Orthodox Church's collaboration with the Communist regime, as illustrated by the church's submission to the totalitarian state apparatus, the support offered by the church to Marxist state propaganda, and the partnership in discrimination against minorities.

In interwar Germany, when the Confessing Church movement stood up against the ideological entrapment of Protestants, the focus of this resistance was on a theology that would undergird political opposition, as described in chapter 6. Swiss theologian Karl Barth's theological opposition to the German Christians' movement, and to Nazism, offered an uncompromising foundation for the Confessing Church's resistance to historical proclivity or political passivity. A similar episode of theological opposition is investigated in the Romanian Orthodox context, but the final contention is that Romanian theologian Dumitru Stăniloae (1903–1993) has not escaped ethnic and nationalist imprisonment. The Orthodox Church's emphasis on the Marxist-inspired social apostolate being too pervasive for theologians to resist, it led to compromise and lack of opposition. An abstract theology of deification has, furthermore, generated passivity toward moral transformation as well as nourishing anti-modern and anti-Western sentiments.

The implications for the ROC's future in a democratic society is weighed in the concluding chapter, which stresses the need for a theology that has moral and practical implications and also nurtures the spirituality of the believers. This chapter also suggests ways of devising a "theology of resistance" that can reject the sacralization or absolutization of any political ideology, including ethnic nationalism. Also suggested is a "theology of permanent revolution" that will offer the Orthodox Church a basis for an affirmative presence in the post-Communist public square.

This volume is about the interrelationship among religion, history, and nationalism. This multidisciplinary approach proposes a theoretical analysis and a dialogue with historians, theologians, clergy, journalists, and political scientists alike. It deals with churches, theological traditions, and denominations, rather than engaging "grassroots" individuals and communities through market research or other forms of quantitative research. However, one approach should not exclude the other. In an essay about the relation between Romanian Orthodoxy and modernity, Iuliana Conovici argued that at times one has to relate to the church officials, whom she called the "interface" of the church, because they are a representation of the inner life of the congregation.[14] To elaborate on this point, a dialogue carried out with Orthodox Church officials is often more productive and can have a lasting impact on the congregation. One of the important ecclesiological distinctions between the Catholic and the Orthodox refers to the role of clergy. In the Roman Catholic Church, the ordained clergy is regarded solely as a representative of Christ before the congregation.[15] The Orthodox Church, however, perceives the minister to be also a representative of the church. In his two-volume *Teologia Dogmatică Ortodoxă*, Stăniloae in fact argued that "without the priest there is no church."[16] Perceived as symbols of Christ, clergy have great authority in Orthodox ecclesiology, even though the disadvantage of such a view is diminished participation of the laity in the liturgical life of the Orthodox Church.[17] For these reasons, the Orthodox hierarchy, regarded as the authoritative voice of the church, can represent an effective channel for communication and dialogue.

In the treatment of historical records, this volume acknowledges that a certain amount of moral shaping of history is inescapable. Robin Collingwood was probably right when he stressed that historians cannot escape imposing a moral framework on their subject of study.[18] However, he added that this limitation compels the historian to acknowledge the insuperability of one's own subjective stance, and openly to integrate it into historiography as a "second dimension of historical thought" rather than naively lull oneself and one's readers into a false sense of dissociated objectivity.[19] The survey of church–state relations presented in this volume attempts to clarify its moral stance openly and critically. As Jürgen Habermas observed, the inescapably political dimension of history necessitates the adoption of a moral stance: "We can only create national self-consciousness out of our better traditions, appropriated not blindly but critically from our history."[20]

Finally, this volume attempts to contribute to what is a highly debated yet scarcely researched topic in post-1989 Romania. There are a limited number of dedicated contemporary studies that have addressed the problem of post-Communist Romanian Orthodox nationalism. The first belongs to Belgian historian Olivier Gillet, who in 2001 published his doctoral dissertation with the title, *L'Église orthodoxe et l'État communiste roumain (1948–1989). Étude de l'idéologie de l'Église orthodoxe: entre traditions Byzantines et national-communisme* (*The Orthodox Church and the Communist Romanian State 1948–1989. A study of the Orthodox Church Ideology: Between Byzantine Traditions and National-Communism*).[21] Gillet used studies and journals written mainly in English, but this volume remains emblematic for the negative reactions received from Orthodox scholars in the field. In fact, the other important study was authored by George Enache, a Romanian Orthodox scholar, who in 2005 published the volume, *Ortodoxie și Putere Politică în România Contemporană: Studii și Eseuri* (*Orthodoxy and Political Power in Contemporary Romania: Studies and Essays*) declaring it a moderate Orthodox response to Gillet's allegedly provocative, inherently flawed, and historically inaccurate account of Romanian Orthodox nationalism.[22] In the same year, Cristian Vasile published the volume *Biserica Ortodoxă Română în primul deceniu comunist* (*The Romanian Orthodox Church during the First Communist Decade*), which looks at the persecution of the Orthodox clergy by the Communist Party in the decade following the war.[23] Another recent study tackling the relationship between the ROC and the state belongs to Lavinia Stan and Lucian Turcescu, respected Romanian academics who although reside and teach in Canada, for over 10 years have published articles focusing on various aspects of Romanian post-communist society and politics. In 2007 they published a volume entitled *Religion and Politics in Post-Communist Romania*, charting the course of the Orthodox Church's involvement in Romanian politics by covering six diverse themes: nationalist identity, the Communist past, Greek Catholic property restitution, the church and elections, religious education, and ecclesiastical views of sexuality.[24] The most recent study belongs to Lucian Leuștean, a Romanian university lecturer in politics teaching in the United Kingdom, whose volume based on newly accessible archival resources is entitled *Orthodoxy and the Cold War: Religion and Political Power in Romania, 1947–65*.[25] According to Leuștean, his study is meant to take Gillet's argument further by emphasizing those factors that helped the church remain socially active during the ROC's collaboration with Communism.[26] While each one of these studies has been engaged in the following chapters, the current volume differs in two significant ways: First, it is a multidisciplinary and comparative approach to Romanian Orthodox nationalism, and second, it allows a theological analysis of nationalism to explain the church's lack of critical distance from the state, but also to suggest ways towards the development of positive church–state relations in Romania.

Notes

[1] Peter Berger, quoted in Rodney Stark and Roger Finke, *Acts of Faith* (Berkeley: University of California Press, 2000), p. 58.

[2] Peter Berger, *The Desecularisation of the World: Resurgent Religion and World Politics* (Grand Rapids: Eerdmans Publishing, 1999), p. 2.

³ One may recall the episode when former British Prime Minister Tony Blair was asked during an interview about his Christian faith, and chief spin-doctor Alistair Campbell interrupted the prime minister's reply to say: "I'm sorry, we don't do God," an intervention which at the time prompted numerous debates on the role of faith in British politics.

⁴ Even before the fall of Communism in Romania, the exiled former secret police chief general I.M. Pacepa wrote about the way in which the Romanian *Securitate* was set up, following the exact model of the Soviet KGB, and in fact the *Securitate's* first chiefs were Soviet secret agents under false Romanianized names. After the fall of Communism, the opening of the secret dossiers confirmed his testimony. Cf. Ioan Mihai Pacepa, *Orizonturi roșii: Amintirile unui General de Securitate* (București: Editura Venus, 1992) also Ioan Mihai Pacepa, *Cartea neagră a Securității*, vol. 2: *Viața mea alături de Gheorghiu-Dej* (București: Editura Ziua, 1999).

⁵ Nick Baron offered a detailed consideration of West German historiographical controversies concerning the interpretation of Nazism as a means for helping elucidate the political and scholarly problem of reinterpreting Russia's Soviet past. It draws useful conclusions suggesting a set of factors hindering consensual cultural development in post-Soviet Russia. Cf. Nick Baron, "History, Politics and Political Culture: Thoughts on the Role of Historiography in Contemporary Russia," in *Cromohs*, vol. 5 (2000). See also Tzvetan Todorov, *Hope and Memory: Lessons from the Twentieth Century*, translated by David Bellos (London: Atlantic Books, 2003); Richard Overy, *The Dictators: Hitler's Germany and Stalin's Russia* (London: Penguin Books, 2004); Henry Rousso, ed., *Stalinism and Nazism: History and Memory Compared* (Lincoln, London: University of Nebraska Press, 2004); Ian Kershaw and Moshe Lewin, eds., *Stalinism and Nazism: Dictatorships in Comparison* (Cambridge: Cambridge University Press, 1997); Slavoj Žižek, *Did Somebody Say Totalitarianism? Five Interventions in the (Mis)Use of A Notion* (London: Verso, 2001).

⁶ Cf. Czeslaw Milosz, *The Captive Mind* (London: Secker & Warburg, 1953). See also John Clark and Aaron Wildavsky, *The Moral Collapse of Communism: Poland as a Cautionary Tale* (San Francisco: ICS Press, 1990).

⁷ "Final Report of the Presidential Commission for the Study of the Communist Dictatorship in Romania" (18 December 2006), [Online] Available at: http://www.presidency.ro/static/ordine/RAPORT%20FINAL_%20CADCR.pdf, accessed December 2006.

⁸ "Contraatac al BOR la Raportul Tismăneanu" in *Ziua*, No. 3811 (20 December 2006).

⁹ GfK Custom Research Worldwide, on behalf of *The Wall Street Journal Europe*, "Religion—A Personal Matter," Nuremberg/Frankfurt, 10 December 2004. [Online] Available at: http://www.marketresearchworld.net/index.php?option=com_content&task=view&id=1356&Itemid=77 , accessed October 2007.

¹⁰ National census conducted by the Gallup Organization, *Metromedia Transylvania*, 2002–04.

¹¹ Institutul Național de Statistică, *Recensământul Populației și al Locuințelor*, vol.1 (București, 2003), pp. 766–95.

¹² Silviu Rogobete, "Between Fundamentalism and Secularization" in *Religion and Democracy in Moldova*, edited by Silvo Devetak, et al. (Timisoara: Brumar Publishing House, 2005), p. 108.

[13] The Bureau of Democracy, Human Rights, and Labor, "Country Reports on Human Rights Practices—2005," (8 March, 2006). [Online] Available at: http://www.state.gov/g/drl/rls/hrrpt/2005/61670.htm , accessed March 2006.

[14] Iuliana Conovici, "L'orthodoxie roumaine et la modernité" in *Studia Politica*, vol. IV, No. 2 (2004), pp. 414–8.

[15] A Roman-Catholic theologian himself, Robertson argues here that the underemphasized role of the priest represents a weakness in Catholic theology. See Ronald Robertson, *Contemporary Romanian Orthodox Ecclesiology* (Romae: Typis Pontificiae Universitatis Gregorianae, 1988), p. 163.

[16] D. Stăniloae, *Teologia Dogmatică Ortodoxă*, vol. 2 (București: IBMBOR, 1978), henceforth TDO, p. 254.

[17] Stăniloae stressed that the priesthood is a confirmation of the real incarnation of the Word of God as the objective mediator before God. As such, the denial of the clergy means doubting the centrality of the Lord's incarnation. Cf. D. Stăniloae, TDO, vol. 2, pp. 251–2.

[18] R.G. Collingwood, *The Idea of History* (Oxford: Oxford University Press, 1961), p. 248

[19] R. Collingwood, *The Idea of History*, p. 248.

[20] Jürgen Habermas, "Concerning the Public Use of History," in *New German Critique*, No. 44 (Spring/Summer, 1988), p. 40.

[21] Translated and published in Romanian as: Olivier Gillet, *Religie și Naționalism: Ideologia Bisericii Ortodoxe Române sub Regimul Comunist* (București: Editura Compania, 2001).

[22] George Enache, *Ortodoxie și Putere Politică în România Contemporană* (București: Editura Nemira, 2005), pp. 7–12.

[23] Cristian Vasile, *Biserica Ortodoxă Română în primul deceniu comunist* (București: Editura Curtea Veche, 2005). Other studies have addressed certain aspects of Orthodox religious nationalism during Communism or focused on particular events or individuals. These sources will be engaged throughout this volume.

[24] Lavinia Stan, Lucian Turcescu, *Religion and Politics in Post-communist Romania* (Oxford: Oxford University Press, 2007).

[25] Lucian N. Leuștean, *Orthodoxy and the Cold War: Religion and Political Power in Romania, 1947–65* (Basingstoke: Palgrave, 2009).

[26] L. Leuștean, *Orthodoxy and Cold War*, p. 5.

Chapter 1

The Orthodox Church in Post-Communist Romania

Introduction

The purpose of this chapter is to describe the challenges facing the contemporary Orthodox Church in post-Communist Romanian society. A contradiction prevails among the Orthodox majority population between the high level of Orthodox religiosity and the low level of morality and commitment to democratic practice, a contradiction that must be perceived within the larger social and political changes taking place after the fall of Communism. The sudden freedom from totalitarian rule meant the churches could finally shape their new identities, both internally and in relation to the state. However, it soon became evident that the path chosen by the Orthodox Church would be controversial. Revisiting the issues surrounding attempts at public repentance and reparations—the ROC's autonomy from the state, understanding of religious pluralism in dealing with other religious denominations, and the controversies surrounding church–state autonomy—will provide further insights into the difficulties the Orthodox Church is facing in the democratic Romanian society.

The attempt of theologians, on the one hand, and secular intelligentsia, on the other, to address church–state relations in an informed way will constitute the subject matter of this chapter in order—it is hoped—to provide insight into the interaction between the Orthodox Church and the Romanian state. This chapter will unveil the incongruity between official pro-democratic statements by some of its clergy and the Orthodox Church's anti-Western and negative perception of the democratic system. The case put forward in this chapter is crucial to the overall argument of this volume because it posits that such discrepancies have roots in the historical identity of the ROC as a national church endowed with special responsibilities toward the state and its people.

Political Identity of Post-1989 Romanian Society

The collapse of Communism in the countries of the Eastern bloc has been perceived as a great liberating event marking the beginning of a new Central and

Eastern Europe. This change brought about the formation of new states and the rediscovery of buried cultural traditions, as well as the resurgence of old ideologies. In Romania, where some argued that the Communist dictatorship was one of the most repressive in the whole of the Eastern bloc, liberation did not come through a nonviolent change of government, but had to be secured with street protests that resulted in hundreds shot and more wounded. Comparable in cruelty to Enver Hoxha in Albania, Kim Il-Sung in North Korea, Mao Zedong in the People's Republic of China, and Stalin in the Soviet Union, Communist dictator Nicolae Ceauşescu's regime was in fact inspired by each one of these grand dictators and, as stated, was probably as cruel as any of them.[1] From all the countries that had gotten rid of Communism by the close of the twentieth century, many expected Romania to become the example of a transition to a democratic society because of the sheer determination and courage shown by the people in bringing a change and attaining freedom from such Communist oppression.

Over two decades later, Romania is lagging behind most other Central and Eastern European countries, struggling to reduce corruption at the societal level, to control a widespread black market, to limit the brain drain and mass emigration, and to convince European Union officials that its commitment to an open economic market is genuine. Analysts have called this a paradox, noting that the most abrupt breakup of the old regime in Eastern Europe has led to one of the least radical transformations.[2] Such evidence only enforces the outsiders' perception of Romania, famously described by Tony Judt as the European "bottom of the heap."[3]

Nonetheless, approximately since the turn of the twenty-first century, positive transformations have begun to take place, offering hope that Romania's political institutions are gradually maturing, and that the social and economic reforms are generating a functioning market economy and a more stable society. Joining the EU in January 2007 represents an impressive achievement in itself, but also presents society with great challenges for continual and effective transformation of the social and economic conditions according to European standards and demands. An important aspect that could significantly influence this process is the need for a change of mentality. In this regard, the Orthodox Church in Romania is often perceived as an institution that retains and perpetuates an irrelevant and outmoded way of social thinking, exhibiting antidemocratic and, oftentimes, intolerant attitudes while at the same time formally supporting the commitment of the society to democracy and European integration.

The Church Following the December Revolution

The events following the December 1989 removal from power of the Communist dictatorship allowed the Romanian churches to gain prominence, with clergy leading public prayers before masses of street protesters in various cities of Romania. The presence of the Orthodox Church's clergy at the formation of the first interim political leadership seemed to indicate the churches would play a positive and active role in the transition of the society from Communist mentalities to democracy. The first steps toward reform and redefinition were taken by a group that included enlightened and well regarded Orthodox clergymen and laity such as Fr. Bartolomeu Anania, Fr. Daniel Ciobotea, Fr. Iustin Marchiș, and Teodor Baconsky, who approached the interim government with the proposal for drafting a religions law and for setting up a group for reflection and renewal within the church.[4]

Thus, after the revolution, the ROC resumed its constitutionally protected social activity in army bases, hospitals, and prisons as well as its philanthropic activity with orphans and the elderly, and providing hot meals, medical assistance, and treatment.[5] With most of the restrictions of the Communist regime against religious associations and organizations now lifted, formerly persecuted Orthodox renewal movements like the Lord's Army[6] and also the Greek Catholic Church[7] were able to regain legal status, while other new associations were formed.[8] A number of rights and privileges were granted the ROC by the new constitution, laws, and emergency ordinances that allowed for rapid development of its infrastructure.[9] Church properties that had been confiscated by the former regime were returned or, where this was not possible, exchanged for others of equal value. Finally, it was decided that the clerical body of the ROC would continue to receive salaries through the Ministry of Religion while activities in support of the church's needs were exempted from taxation.

The new responsibilities of the ROC now included, alongside social and philanthropic activities stipulated by the constitution, a symbolic presence in the public arena. Thus, the Orthodox clergy would offer symbolic legitimization to the opening of the parliamentary session, to official ceremonies, and to other activities organized by institutions of the state. The presence of the Orthodox crucifix and icons in public spaces (parliament, schools, hospitals, courts, etc.) was also reinstated by the new constitution, as were oaths sworn on the Bible—without making such oaths compulsory for other religious denominations.[10]

While such changes were supposed to generate a stable and harmonious relationship between the state and the church, it became evident that the ROC would indiscriminately offer support and legitimization to any government so long as endorsements and privileges continued to come from the state. This realization dawned even on Orthodox intellectuals who decried the church's lack of critical thinking and its deficient social ethics.[11] The Orthodox Church hierarchy's increasing demands included the recognition, in the text of the constitution, of the ROC as the national church, a demand that has generated much debate and is yet to be settled. As Vladimir Tismăneanu has observed, the ROC moved too soon from inconclusive repentance and confession to a resurrection of religious sentiment that revives and fuels nationalist inclinations.[12] Thus, the church's lack of repentance and unwillingness to admit past wrongs and commit to reparations and change became reasons for polemics in society. Given the swiftness with which the ROC hierarchy moved toward taking a demanding posture, the church–state relations were already marred before any attempts at compromise were made. Critics began stressing that an anachronistic Orthodox Church that for 40 years had respected the principles underlying the organization of the Communist Party—and thus is aware of its own guilty conscience toward a people it has ignored and despised—should proceed more cautiously to seek legitimization for merit that may not yet be deserved.[13]

Attempts at Orthodox Repentance

After the collapse of the Communist regime, the hierarchy of the ROC signified that there was a desire for repentance and change among its ranks. The official statements uttered in this period included allusions to public repentance and confessions for the lack of courage in defending the truth, and pleas for forgiveness for concessions made during Communism in order to survive.[14] These ambiguous messages of remorse were followed by some reparations, as clergy who had been defrocked for political reasons were reinstated.[15] Patriarch Teoctist Arăpașu presented his resignation, for "reasons of health," as head of the autocephalous ROC and retired to a monastery.[16] At the same time, under pressure from street protests accusing him of Communist collaboration, Emilian Birdaș, the bishop of Alba-Iulia, quietly resigned from his ecclesiastical position.[17] The example of Teoctist was followed by the Metropolitan Nicolae Corneanu of Banat, who became the first Orthodox bishop to express remorse, clearly and publicly, for collaboration with the Communist regime. In his confession in 1990, Fr. Corneanu declared:

> I could have acted differently, but at the time I thought for the good of the church I had to make compromises with the regime. Now I must confess my sins with all sincerity. I did not fulfill my obligations as a bishop because I did not protest against the regime. . . . I am disgusted for what I did on certain occasions. Many [Greek Catholic] priests and lay people were imprisoned. . . . Even some of my [Orthodox] priests objected against the dictator. I did not protect them. . . . I approved what the administration did. I did not tell them they were wrong. . . . I feel I must free myself of this burden, be sincere about what I had done during the dictatorship and ask pardon, I feel an obligation to speak openly of those years and of the way I acted. . . . If a church [building] belonged to the Greek Catholic it should be returned.[18]

Fr. Corneanu remains the only high official among the Romanian Orthodox ranks who has confessed to having been an informant of the Communist secret police. He is also the only bishop to have acted on his promises and returned, in 1992, a Catholic cathedral and a church and approximately half the Greek Catholic church buildings forcefully acquired by the Communist regime and placed under his diocesan jurisdiction.[19] His reformist perspective, which includes his endorsement of the Romanian Civic Alliance nongovernmental organization, makes Fr. Corneanu the most liberal Romanian bishop.[20] Nevertheless, Fr. Corneanu has been gradually marginalized by the Holy Synod in Bucharest (the ruling council of the Orthodox Church) because of his openness concerning the repossessions.[21]

Such acts of repentance, confession, and reparation were perceived as exceptions from the generally unapologetic attitude of the Orthodox Church clergy toward Communist collaboration. The ROC's dealing with the Communist past, and its lack of repentance for cooperating with the Marxist regime, continue to generate disputes in Romanian society, mainly because the farewell said by the church to Communism was limited to solemn declarations and an idealized discourse shrouded in myths that lacked critical self-introspection.[22]

The starting point of the controversy is the notorious episode of Patriarch Teoctist's self-reinstatement, which attracted much attention at the national level as well as in the international media.[23] His resignation as patriarch of the ROC (for reasons of health) meant the Holy Synod could now choose a successor. However, after a few months of meditation in retreat, and driven by the discovery that, according to the church canon, a patriarch cannot be deposed without his own consent, Teoctist reemerged from the monastery and decided to keep his position and reoccupy his throne.[24]

This sudden change of attitude became a cause of public astonishment when it came to light that, whereas Teoctist was thought to have presented his resignation for reasons of health, it was actually the result of pressure exerted through a petition signed by some 200 Orthodox clergy disappointed with his Communist collaboration.[25] However, within a few months of the petition, a nationalistic current re-emerged within the ROC and demanded the return of the patriarch because supposedly he was the only person capable of keeping the church united in those times of transition.[26] His reinstatement generated an outcry in Romanian society, and numerous clergy and laymen disapproved vehemently of this change of heart. Teoctist showed defiance of the no-confidence vote from those who had made him step down as patriarch, and no criticism was persuasive enough to convince the Patriarchate or the Holy Synod to reverse their decision to reinstate him.[27] These were the first in a long series of Orthodox Church blunders, symptomatic of the unrepentant attitude assumed with regard to collaboration with the totalitarian regime.

The Repossession Saga

The repossession process for private properties, church buildings and places of worship that have been forcefully confiscated and nationalized by the communist regime continues to make headlines in the Romanian and international press.[28] The refusal of the ROC to return church buildings and worship places belonging to the Greek Catholic Church is another example of failed reparations. Confiscated in 1948 by the Communist regime, these buildings were transferred to the Orthodox following the decisions to make Greek Catholicism illegal and to send its entire clergy to prison. With the exception of the buildings returned on Fr. Corneanu's express initiative, many obstacles have been encountered in this reparation process, even in the case of those properties Greek Catholics have won back in judicial courts. The response of the Orthodox Church has more often been to issue threats against the Greek Catholics or to mobilize the Orthodox majority, as was the case with a giant rally in the town of Cluj, carried out under the direct supervision and blessing of Orthodox hierarchy representatives.[29]

This refusal, and the fear tactics employed by the ROC regarding the legitimate demands of the Greek Catholic Church, would not have been possible without the indirect support of the neo-Communist political elite that has governed the country in the decade following the fall of Ceaușescu's regime. As Tom Gallagher has noted, under the political leadership of the Socialist Democratic Party, the parliament passed a law that guaranteed ownership over the confiscated buildings to the current inhabitants of those properties, mostly former Communist activists.[30] Not surprisingly, most political parties in Romania soon realized that an alliance with, and use of, the ROC is beneficial and easily achieved.[31]

When in 1997 the Christian Democratic government came under pressure to deal with the injustices against the Greek Catholic Church, it drafted a law intending to harmonize the restitution process.[32] The drafting of such a law was perceived by the Holy Synod and the Patriarchate to be an "edict" that could affect peace and stability in Transylvania, the Romanian territory with the largest number of Greek Catholics.[33] Even in recent years, Orthodox voices like those of Radu Preda maintain that the Greek Catholic Church exhibits a "retributive and vindictive mentality" in its attempts to regain properties lost in 1948.[34] Despite the fact that in a speech given in 2000 at the Catholic University in Lublin, Teoctist expressed his confidence for the constructive outcomes of the ecumenical dialogue between the ROC and Greek Catholics in Romania, one would expect that the completion of the repossession process should take precedence over ecumenical propaganda.[35]

Nevertheless, the Greek Catholic Church in Romania has often been responsible for exaggerated gestures and attitudes that are unconstructive for a continued dialogue and for a positive ending of this repossession controversy. Some early signs of such unhelpful attitudes have been noted by Webster, who called attention to the exacerbating reactions of Greek Catholic representatives who rushed to appeal to the European Parliament and the United Nations for a political solution to the crisis.[36] Similar concerns were raised when Greek Catholic Bishop Guțiu resorted to celebrating masses in an open-air square, having initially refused the Orthodox offer for the use of the Greek Catholic cathedral (handed over to the Orthodox Church by the Communist regime) at any time of the week except late Sunday mornings, when it was required by the Orthodox congregation.[37]

Notwithstanding this squabbling, the statistics indicate that by 2005, the Orthodox Church had returned fewer than 150 of the almost two thousand Greek Catholic churches, and most of them through the efforts of Fr. Corneanu.[38] Also telling is the fact that it took 10 years for Teoctist to ask for forgiveness for concessions the church made during Communist rule in order to survive, and for causing many believers to suffer because of his lack of courage.[39] Such a long delay could only be understood in light of the former patriarch's deep convictions, expressed during a sermon in 1995 that Communism was somehow permitted by God as a test of the church's faith.[40] These sporadic acts of repentance make even more vital the confession and withdrawal from positions of authority within the church hierarchy of former collaborators who have thus far remained silent.[41] The repentance of the patriarch did not, however, prompt such a withdrawal from the position of authority that he held at the head of the ROC until his death in July 2007.

While individual confession may represent an improvement on the side of the Orthodox Church and an openness that is too little, too late, the real question about the responsibility of the church regarding its past cooperation with the Communist authorities remains unanswered. According to a typology of guilt suggested by Daniel Barbu, Romanian post–Communist society in general, and the ROC hierarchy in particular, are guilty for their "passive obedience."[42] Barbu employed here categories developed by German philosopher Karl Jaspers, who defined passive obedience as political culpability for ethical autism and for silence toward a totalitarian system that used passivity to perpetuate injustice.[43] Alas, it would appear that Jasper's other category, that of "active obedience," defined as moral culpability whereby clergy accepted working or actively cooperating with the regime, is also applicable to Romanian post-Communist society.[44]

Between Autonomy and Separation

A year after the events of December 1989, the ROC declared full autonomy from the Romanian state, banning any interference of the secular state in the election of bishops or in other matters of religious administration.[45] According to the 1991 Romanian constitution, the state's intention was to have a partial separation with the church, based on the principle of autonomy and cooperation.[46] However, as Ioan Ică noted, when it comes to the Orthodox Church the autonomy is not only partial but also relative, as the church continues to stress its status as national, which justifies its reliance on state subsidies and its demands for preferential access to religious education in schools, hospitals, and the army.[47]

To the dismay of the militant Orthodox clergy, the ROC was not even mentioned in the 1991 revised constitution. One of the main contributions the church was expecting from the new constitution and from a religions law was a clause granting official status as national. Around this issue a debate would ensue concerning the implications such a clause would have for non-national religious denominations. As Preda had to admit, this single disagreement concerning a national-religion clause may well be one of the main reasons for the failure of the Ministry of Religions to pass a religions law 16 years after the fall of Communism.[48] The argumentation brought in support of the claim for privileged status includes a historical and cultural self-identity that demands recognition of the important role Romanian Orthodoxy has played as a supporter of the nationalist state.[49] Preda's argumentation in favor of this clause epitomizes the feelings of the Orthodox hierarchy in Romania for whom recognition of this privileged status is simply a matter of subscribing to the principles of proportionality and merit.

The political role assumed by the ROC is based on its self-perception as the only element of social continuity that has survived during the interwar period, through the Communist era, and into post-socialism.[50] This perception adds to the self-positioning of the ROC at the heart of Romanian national identity in order to strengthen the demands for special recognition within the state. The ROC's arguments on this matter are not only insubstantial[51] but also convey nationalist sentiments which, left unchecked, can lead to "phyletism."[52] Furthermore, as has been pointed out to be the case in other post-Communism countries in Europe, this nationalist tendency generates tension between the church and the modern democratic state which, following the French model of separation, refuses the national church formula as an exclusivist position.[53]

Returning to the Orthodox Church's claimed autonomy from the state, the absence of a religions law until December 2006, when a debatable Law on Religious Freedom was rushed through, it meant that legally defined provisions concerning the specifics and nature of this autonomy in the first decade following the fall of Communism were always open to debate.[54] For this reason, the Orthodox clergy has incessantly requested a law that would not simply guarantee, but also define and explicate their national church status. Nevertheless, despite the fact that the revised 1991 Romanian constitution did not specifically mention the ROC, nationalist Orthodox clergy remained hopeful. The constitution stipulated that all religious bodies would answer to the state's organ of control, the Ministry of Religions, which would continue to support the clergy's wages. If this was an indirect recognition of the ROC as an official church of the state, the National Congress of the ROC (held in 1994) clarified its position in Article Two of the Orthodox Church constitution, where its status is described as "national, autocephalous, and united in its organization," thus a national church.[55]

The absence of a clearly defined legal framework for church–state autonomy was used creatively by the ROC hierarchy as it enabled an approach based on individual choice. Thus, while the Synod was able to elect its bishops without state interference, it did not restrict the church from claiming subsidies from the government based on the status of clergy as public workers.[56] To Daniel Barbu, this reflexive reliance on state support is an indication of the church's concealed unwillingness to realize a complete separation from the state.[57] That is not to say that a strict church–state separation is the best model that could be adopted in Orthodox Romania. Nevertheless, such reluctance may signify the church is willing to strengthen the ties with a state that knows it is unlikely for priests, in the position of public workers, to question or critique its authority or competence.

During the first parliamentary elections in 1990, the Orthodox Church forbade the clergy from entering politics and declared its neutrality from any party agenda. However, as Orthodox theology professor Ioan Ică admitted, neutrality did not mean passivity and, as a result, not only did various priests obtain political positions, but the church took upon itself the task of arbitrating their believers' vote—in this case recommending only those political parties whose program supported otherwise loosely defined concepts of "Christian morality."[58]

Such a misunderstood concept of "autonomy" has been admitted by the Orthodox writer and politician Teodor Baconsky, who thinks the church finds it difficult to distinguish between the realms of the spiritual and the political because of the past symbiotic relationship between the church and Romanian nationalism.[59] Thus, the major challenge facing the Orthodox Church today is represented by the legacy of self-identification with the Romanian past and nationalism. In reference to this relationship alone, the ROC is often thought to be permeated more by nationalism and pragmatism than by critical theological reflection.[60]

The Group for Reflection and Church Renewal

It was previously mentioned that the nationalist current within the ROC led to the reinstatement of Teoctist to the top of the Orthodox leadership. The antithesis of this group was represented by the pro-Western, or pro-ecumenical, current of the church in the 1990s, formed around the Group for Reflection and Church Renewal.[61] The initiative to form this group was part of a church renewal movement that gave birth to a number of Orthodox meetings that promoted young clergy to the ROC leadership positions.[62] However, the real alternative was offered by the group itself, which consisted of Orthodox priests and lay intellectuals with an interest in the transformation of the church's hierarchy, an effort aimed especially at those with a past of collaboration with the former regime.[63] Enlisting some of the most reputed names of the day, the group came to include Orthodox theologians like Fr. Dumitru Stăniloae and Fr. Constantin

Galeriu, as well as Fr. Daniel Ciobotea, Fr. Constantin Voicescu, Fr. Iustin Marchiș, and Fr. Bartolomeu Anania from the ranks of the church, and Horia Bernea, Octavian Ghibu, Sorin Dumitrescu, Teodor Baconsky, and others from among the lay intellectuals.

This group was the first voice from within the ROC to address the crucial issue of the relationship between the church and the state—as well as other important aspects pertaining to the new political reality, such as the dialogue between denominations and the problem of ecumenism, as well as stressing the important role played by laity and members of the clergy in the anti-Communist resistance.[64] The role of the group was to act as a consulting agency for the church, and to help achieve a complete break with the past deeds of the church during Communism.[65]

The renewal group was hoping the election of some of its foremost members to high positions in the Orthodox hierarchy would give them greater influence on the church. The election of Fr. Daniel Ciobotea as the Metropolitan of Iași was meant to prepare him to replace Teoctist in the leadership of the ROC, thus effecting a lasting transformation and modernization of the church.[66] With the Holy Synod's election of Fr. Daniel in Moldavia, as well as that of Fr. Bartolomeu Anania as the Archbishop of Cluj, Vad, and Feleac, it was felt that the group had achieved its goals, which dissolved soon after.[67]

The achievement of this group are a matter of interpretation. While religious education was eventually introduced in public schools with great approval from the state, the inter-confessional dialogue remains a sensitive issue for the ROC. Some argued that the group interrupted its activity owing to polemics and tensions generated between its members and the nationalist wing of the church hierarchy.[68] As for the contributions of some members of the group to the renewal of the church, their record is at best controversial.

Patriarch Daniel Ciobotea

The initial plan of preparing Fr. Daniel to replace Teoctist in the leadership of the autocephalous ROC did not work because, despite the protests and his collaboration with the Communist regime, Teoctist remained in good health and maintained an active role heading the affairs of the Holy Synod. When Teoctist passed away in 2007, he was indeed replaced by Fr. Daniel in the leadership of the Romanian Patriarchate, thus fulfilling the wishes of the renewal group.

As a theologian, Fr. Daniel was trained mostly in the West, exposing him to theological diversity and positive interactions with clergy from other Christian traditions. He studied for two years in France at Strasbourg University's Protestant Faculty and spent a similar period at the Catholic Theology Faculty of Albert Ludwig University in Germany. This enabled him to take a balanced view on aspects that are crucial for the role of the church in society and politics. According to Webster, who hails his rise as "meteoric" and sees him as a representative of "a new generation of Episcopal leadership untainted by overt collaboration with the Communist regime," Fr. Daniel possesses a unique understanding of free-market capitalism as a force the Patriarchate must counter with "loyal opposition" on behalf of those not yet ready to become part of this new social order.[69] This loyal opposition is encapsulated in the metropolitan's concept of Christian philanthropy, and based on social thinking that stresses ecclesiology over all other approaches, including moral theology, natural law, and modern rationalistic philosophies or sociological systems.[70] The underlying predisposition to ethics, reflected in Fr. Daniel's argumentation, is not uncommon with Orthodox theologians. His understanding of the sacramental emphasis as a form of reaction to mere social activism is legitimized by the danger any social ethic poses to the transformation of the church into a simple social institution. Thus, he concedes that the only way to avoid a crisis of the church's identity is through an emphasis on a social ethic that centers on the eschatological and mystic-sacramental witness of the church.[71]

However, Fr. Daniel's social ethic is incomplete, as it remains unclear what, according to this sacramental understanding, would be the features of the social involvement of the ROC that stems from such a social ethic. The argumentation remains negative, in that it only stresses what this new ethic *should not* be: "The social commitment of Christians in the world cannot be reduced to the level of ethics, or separated from the spiritual and sacramental life of the church, because authentic social commitment has a sacramental-ecclesial dimension."[72]

Fr. Daniel's activities at the head of the ROC since 2007 have been characterized by an emphasis on ecumenism, physical church building, and militancy regarding the place of religious education in state-run schools' curricula.[73] As hoped by many of his supporters, Fr. Daniel has indeed proved a skilful manager who is modernizing the Orthodox Church, both in terms of economic sustenance and relations with the political elite in Romania.[74] Mihai Neamțu pointed to a number of encouraging signs, such as the church's improved social mission, the development of its media and digital output, and an increase in the number of quality resources published by the Orthodox press.[75] Nevertheless, the same commentator recognizes the need for a rethinking of the church–state relations with an emphasis on economic and political independence, for freedom from electoral games, for ROC support of private initiatives and of a form of capitalism that seeks profit without turning profit into an idol.[76]

In a controversial episode, the National Council for the Study of the Securitate's Archives (CNSAS) deemed that Fr. Daniel had not collaborated with the secret police, although his name appears in the registry of secret services.[77] The council members have reached this conclusion due to a convenient disappearance of his Securitate dossier, apparently destroyed during the events that unfolded in Bucharest on December 23, 1989.[78] While any potentially incriminating files were destroyed, the archives of the Holy Synod of the Orthodox Church remain closed to researchers. Lucian Leuștean rightly noted that as long as the current ROC leadership continues to have deep connections with the Communist past, it will be difficult to have open access to the archival material of the church.[79]

In a traditional institution like the Orthodox Church, change will naturally be a slow and gradual process, but in his first years at the helm of the Patriarchate, Fr. Daniel was expected to have begun addressing the issue of Orthodox collaboration with the Communist regime, the church's nationalist inclinations, the needed dialogue with the intellectuals, and regarding the challenges of modernity. Alas, Cristian Vasile rightly commented that with the exception of some internal changes, the Orthodox Church remains without a much-needed structural change—a change that has to start from a moral cleansing, but that has been particularly hampered by the ROC's archives remaining off limits.[80]

Archbishop Bartolomeu Anania

Archbishop Bartolomeu Anania is one of the brightest theological minds of the Orthodox Church in Romania. Elected to the head of the Archbishopric of Vad, Feleac, and Cluj in 1993, Fr. Bartolomeu was among the initial group that demanded the resignation of Teoctist from the Patriarchate in 1990 because of the latter's collaboration with the Communist regime.[81]

Fr. Bartolomeu was convinced Orthodoxy could bring a moral regeneration to society, with the condition that the church itself first be cured of its moral crisis.[82] However, his proposals were not limited to the cleansing of the church, but also denoted political activism, especially concerning the relationship between the ROC and the state. His controversial suggestions included warning clergy against entering into politics and participating on the electoral rolls of political parties in 1992, as mentioned earlier. In 1996, Fr. Bartolomeu took the opposite route by becoming the herald of the proposal for priestly political involvement as electoral advisers, arguing at the same time that Orthodoxy should have political representation in parliament.[83] Although his claims found support among clergy, such as Bishop Gherasim of Suceava, civil society reacted swiftly to what was perceived to be a rejuvenation of the corporatist model imposed in Romania by King Carol II before World War II.[84]

According to Bogdan Comaroni, despite the bishop's membership in the renewal group, Fr. Bartolomeu could be regarded as the leader of the nationalist wing of the ROC.[85] Thus, in spite of his political activism, most public utterances of Fr. Bartolomeu betray a highly critical attitude toward the process of democratization and secularization that Romanian society has begun. In an interview published in the year 2000, Fr. Bartolomeu declared: "With the exception of the campaigns carried out by a minority of our intellectuals, the problem of secularization does not exist in this country" because in his view this reality characterizes only "Westernized" Europe.[86]

It has been argued that Fr. Bartolomeu's election in the heart of Transylvania, the Romanian territory with the largest number of Greek Catholic churches and believers, was orchestrated by the Holy Synod in view of the theologian's known conservative perspective toward the repossession of the Greek Catholic churches under Orthodox control.[87] Whereas more evidence should be brought in support of such an argument, it is not entirely speculative if one considers that anti-Greek Catholic fear campaigns and rallies initiated by the Orthodox Church in the Transylvanian town of Cluj were carried out with the full knowledge of Fr. Bartolomeu, who has spiritual jurisdiction over that region.

Furthermore, it is a well-known allegation that Fr. Bartolomeu was responsible for cooperation at some level with the Communist regime. Identified in the book, *Red Horizons*, written by a secret-police defector as one of the secret agents sent under the orders of the Communist dictator Nicolae Ceaușescu to compromise the Romanian Diaspora in the United States, Fr. Bartolomeu came under collaborationist accusations in the years following the revolution.[88] His credibility was furthermore questioned owing to his membership in the "Iron Guard" legionnaire movement during his youth, or by his special relationship with Patriarch Justinian Marina, another controversial Orthodox leader who served as head of the church for 30 years during Communism and to whom Fr. Bartolomeu was personal secretary and confidant.[89]

Thus, it is with caution that one has to internalize Fr. Bartolomeu's political openness and support for Romanian modernization and democratization. For him, as for other Romanian Orthodox clergy, "European standards" is a principle that ought to be used pejoratively and with great caution, as it conveys negative meanings for the Orthodox way of life.[90]

Changes to the boundaries of the Transylvanian metropolitanates carried out by the Holy Synod in 2006 have shifted the center of Orthodox activity from the town of Sibiu to Cluj and have resulted in Fr. Bartolomeu becoming metropolitan of a larger portion of Transylvania.[91] These changes resulted in the expansion of Fr. Bartolomeu's influence to include northern regions of Transylvania with large Greek Catholic populations and have raised legitimate questions about the resurgence of Orthodox nationalism.[92] The concerns are that Fr. Bartolomeu will attempt a more conservative approach to the Greek Catholic repossession demands with consequences for interdenominational dialogue or dialogue with secular society.

Andrei Pleșu

Andrei Pleșu is the former minister of foreign affairs (1997–2000), chief editor of the notable publication *Dilema*, and a member of the Group for Social Dialogue (GDS). Although not a member of the Orthodox renewal group, he was instrumental in its formation as minister of culture during 1990 and 1991.[93] Pleșu has had a positive influence on the development of relations between the

ROC and the secular state. Concerning these relations, he asserted that the unquestioned devotion of Romanian society to democracy must be carried out in the company of the Orthodox Church and spirituality, notwithstanding the ideological misconceptions of the contemporary clergy.[94] Pleșu developed his "exteriority versus presence" argument through a critique of the Orthodox Church's emphasis on the exterior, the festivity and triumphalism that permeates its rituals. For him, Romanian society does not need an Orthodoxy that builds new church buildings, but one that becomes involved in the social and moral needs of the people; an Orthodoxy that reflects on its social doctrine in the context of unprecedented social problems facing post-Communist society. Unfortunately, the discussion on these topics in the public arena, initiated by Pleșu, between the ROC and the secular intelligentsia was hampered for the most part by a lack of feedback from the Orthodox hierarchy.

Teodor Baconsky

Teodor Baconsky, an Orthodox layman, former Romanian ambassador to the Vatican (1996–2000), and current Romanian Minister of External Affairs, is a prolific participant in, and contributor to, the discussion concerning the relationship between the state and the Orthodox Church. As a member of the Orthodox renewal group, Baconsky's journey began with an ideological position that assumed Orthodox eschatology is superior to Western individualism and, therefore, church-and-state neutrality, tolerance ,and pluralism—characteristics of liberal democracies—are incompatible with Orthodox holistic tradition.[95] At that stage, Baconsky did not envision a constructive dynamic between Orthodoxy and democracy, and thus supported the reality of a strong, prophetic national Orthodox Church advocated from a "right-wing spirit" ideological position. Gradually, he then came to appreciate European ecumenism and began pondering a positive integration of the values of modernity through an evaluation of the virtues of Western Christianity and deficiencies of the Orthodox Church.[96] With an emphasis on the "urbanity of faith" and on the inevitable transition of Romanian society and churches to the ecumenical and ethical dimensions of the European Community, Baconsky suggested that reconciliation of politics, religion, and society will be achieved when the real and imaginary differences among capitalism, democracy, and Orthodoxy are surpassed and the regressive nationalist and conservatory mentalities become extinct.[97]

A few years later, Baconsky further developed his idea by insisting on three aspects of a new ethic of church action, namely the cooperation between Christian tradition and postmodernism, cooperation between church and state, and the crucial role ecumenism will have to play in this ethic.[98] The same "power of schism" that brings division between the Romanian churches is present in the schizophrenic formalism of the immature community made up of clergy, laymen, and intellectuals, he notes.[99] Baconsky's new proposals convey realism and represent an important transition from the pervasive nationalistic Romanian mentality on the social role of the church in society. A social doctrine of the church would be valuable if it took advantage—in a manner suggested by Baconsky—of the essential commonalities of, on the one hand, democracy, free market, and European openness and, on the other, the churches, civil society, and the political leadership in Romania.

However, Baconsky does not take seriously the nationalist tendencies of the ROC and the change of direction necessary for achieving a durable shift of mentality. Moreover, one of the shortcomings in Baconsky's argumentation is the lack of a critique of modernity and democracy as they are understood and appropriated by the Western world. He has moved too rapidly from a nationalist, rural, and mythical perspective to embrace the positive values of modernity, a condition he coined as "the good's temptation."[100] The positive temptation of all good values inherent in every democracy, which he extols, can easily fall into corruption. In a helpful critique of modernity, another notable Romanian intellectual, writer, and philosopher Horia-Roman Patapievici asks rhetorically: "What is lost when something is won?"[101]

After the anti-Communist revolt, Patapievici, also a member of the GDS, emerged as a convinced advocate of individualism, capitalism, and liberal democracy on the basis of his progressive political patriotism. A fierce opponent of collectivism, rural populism and nationalism fixed on some idyllic past, he proceeded to dismantle the myths of Romania's national history and to critique the flawed relationship of the ROC to modernity and culture.[102] Denouncing the counterproductive populism and anti-intellectualism mentalities of the ROC, Patapievici offers his interpretation of modernity as a form of, rather than a reaction to, Christianity that, he argues, explains why liberal modern individualism is incomplete outside faith in a personal God.[103] The main tenet of his critique is that modernity has to regain the invisible, the Christian tradition, God and his creation.[104] Even though theologically syncretistic, such a critique of modernity is a crucial contribution to the understanding of the common ground shared by modernity and the church.[105] In charging the church to embrace the new modernity, Baconsky does not show awareness of the challenges posed by secularization, universalism, syncretism, or of the collapse of the social values characterizing Western civilization.

Orthodox Views on Church and Society

Having presented the views of the Group for Reflection and Church Renewal on the relations between the church and the state, it is revealing to ponder how other contemporary Romanian Orthodox theologians relate to the interaction between these two realms. It is apparent that the ideological spectrum ranges from radical views on the establishment of a Romanian theocracy to more liberal perspectives that begin to envisage the constructive integration of the church into modern Romanian society. The radical right group has championed a critical and condemning attitude toward modernity and Western civilization, as was the case with the publication of a Fr. Constantin Coman's volume entitled "Orthodoxy Under the Pressure of History."[106] The contributors to this volume display a negative perspective with regard to modernity, while viewing Romanian Orthodoxy to be currently struggling under the pressure of Western secularization and liberalism. Having succeeded in secularizing the Catholic and the Protestant churches in the West, the argument goes, modernity is now aiming to pervert the last bastion of Christianity, which is the Orthodox Church in Eastern Europe. The pragmatic materialism of capitalism and market economic system are viewed as "another Gospel" that attempts to subdue Orthodoxy's spirituality.[107] Among the radical solutions suggested to counter this "pressure of history" is the formation of a federation of Orthodox states that would surpass the national differences among them and would provide a united voice against those influences.[108]

A theological position similar to Fr. Daniel Ciobotea's social thinking has been adopted by Fr. Dumitru Popescu, professor of theology at the Orthodox Theological Seminary in Bucharest, who is concerned with a constructive integration of religion with the modern political and social context. In his work on church and society, Fr. Popescu postulates that Orthodox social thought must avoid the negative consequences of modernity (autonomy and secularism) through a postmodern culture of an "integral Christianity," which could be drawn from a model offered by Trinitarian theology.[109] The dynamic vision of the unity and transcendence of the Trinity would represent the medium for dialogue between Orthodoxy and contemporary society.

Fr. Popescu's optimistic proposal for such an Orthodox Trinitarian approach—in line with modernist theological currents of Orthodoxy in the West—is only slightly tempered by his more negative perception of modernity and its intrinsic values. Although there are merits to his conceptual framework, which allows the integral model to be informed by Trinitarian theology, it is difficult to envisage how this would be compatible with the basic values of autonomy and freedom that constitute a secular society. Defined in these terms, the "integral Christianity" he suggests could only be constituted in a context wherein Orthodoxy takes precedence over the secular state.

A more plausible position has been suggested by the late Fr. Ion Bria, Orthodox theologian and active participant in the ecumenical discussions in Geneva, who insisted that Romanian Orthodoxy must relinquish its triumphalism and historical passivity in relation to social and political thinking.[110] To him, missionary revival, ecumenical witness, and social presence are the tenets of a new social ethic—tenets that are currently absent from the Romanian church's activity. However, Fr. Bria's very accurate and bold critique of the ROC was moderated by a defensive attitude concerning the collaboration of the Orthodox Church during Communism, an inflexible critical stance toward the Greek Catholics in Romania, attempts to justify the pseudo-Marxist social apostolate doctrine, and appropriation of a high theological position that stresses the important contribution Romanian Orthodox spirituality can make to the revitalization of Europe's Christian culture.[111]

In hindsight, these ideological positions on the relationship between the church and society are not uncommon among theologians in any modern society. Their voices represent the position of a church that historically has eschewed secular society, which is perceived to undermine its role as the moral guardian of the nation. The church recognizes limitations in any social or political system, and therefore tends to regard them as utopian visions never to be fulfilled and realized by a temporal form of government.

Left unchecked, however, this religious commitment can often lead to intolerance toward others, reinforcing social and political divisions. Fundamental principles inherent to democracy and modern societies can be traced back to the Christian tradition as it unfolded over centuries: freedom, the individual's dignity, human rights, freedom of conscience, or religious tolerance. A holistic theological reflection can unearth positive aspects that modernity might have to offer, thus exposing deeply embedded resentment toward a democratic or critically adopted pluralistic society. When this reflection is missing, the theologians' discourse becomes antimodern and is counterproductive, leading to a loss of credibility and relevance of the church in society.

Church–State Relations and the Secular Intelligentsia

A survey of the Romanian secular intelligentsia of the post-Communist era will help identify whether their discourse may help theologians and the Orthodox Church relate more coherently to modern, secular society. In the aftermath of the December Revolution, the political landscape was characterized by chaos and confusion; the ad hoc popular revolt was "appropriated" by a neo-Communist reformist group led by interim president Ion Iliescu, while the political opposition was either nonexistent or totally disoriented. The situation was furthermore complicated by waves of violence and fear generated by the miners' raids, the infamous *Mineriade* which became the neo-Communist president's defense against the opposition's attempts to bring about governmental change.[112] Amid these tumultuous times, the GDS became one of the most effective voices of the civil society. The group was crystallized around the circle known as the *Păltinișani*, intellectuals connected with Romanian philosopher Constantin Noica, whose disciples confronted in their writings, directly or subversively, the official Marxist doctrines during Communism.[113] The independent association and the publication *Revista 22* that developed around this circle of intellectuals focused on monitoring the new government concerning the process of democratization and the strengthening of civil society.

As the ROC began to make use of the nationalist discourse, members of the group and other voices from civil society questioned the legitimacy of the church's increasing political demands based on the historical identification of Romanian Orthodoxy and nationalism. In the years to follow, these questions continued to emerge despite a lack of dialogue between the group and the church. The intellectuals' concern was directed at the antidemocratic, nationalist discourse, but also at the growing public activity of the Orthodox Church and its political manipulation in the hands of various political parties or leaders.[114] The underlying logic of these contentions was that the natural solidarity among Orthodoxy, nationalism, and pre-modern traditions resulted in a compelling and dangerous political influence in the form of Orthodox nationalism. This led to radical responses from populist intellectuals who, probably under the influence of revolutionary hysteria, raised fears about the resurgence of a form of Iron Guard fascist movement, or about hidden attempts to set up a theocratic Romanian state.[115]

The perception undergirding these protests was that Orthodoxy represents a threat to Romania's modernization and democratization.[116] The key instrument behind the increase of stability in Eastern Europe was thus thought to be a political limitation of Orthodox domination in countries where these churches represent the majority.[117] More extreme suggestions included the complete removal of the ROC from public life as an ideal solution to the legislative integration of Romania in the EU.[118] The main argument stipulated amid the dispute was that the democratic principles of the Romanian state are under hostile pressure from the Orthodox hierarchy and its institutions, whose structures reject the processes of integration in the EU.

The Revived "National Debate"

The "national debate" of interwar Romania provided the starting point for the post-1989 expressions of these differences between the church and the secular intelligentsia in the country. It was not very difficult to recognize that these disagreements entailed a resurgence of old ambiguities and tensions dominant during the interwar period—as much in Romania as they were throughout Europe—and that these would translate, after Communism, into an exacerbation of the two polarized political options. Nineteenth- and twentieth-century Europe had witnessed the failure of a triumphant modernity that tried to replicate the French Revolution but instead led to the Bolshevik Revolution. Moreover, it attempted to implement the Jacobean state in its two forms, namely individualism as liberal expression and collectivism as a socialist tendency. The outcome of the "Jacobean-totalitarian" state was that it gave birth to the Nazi and Communist states.

In Romania, the clash between left-wing liberals and the nationalists (the national debate) reached its climax during the interwar period.[119] The period of 42 years that commenced with the arrival of the totalitarian political leadership of the Communists prevented Romanian society from coming to terms with the political debate that animated the interwar political landscape. Thus, while in other countries of Europe Christian democracy effected a lasting transformation of the totalitarian ideologies behind fascism and National Socialism that were replaced by post-war democracies,[120] in Romania, as in all other Communist countries in Eastern Europe, these changes were drastically delayed. While in other European countries a milder form of Christian democracy—one that overcame its conservative traditionalism and supported pluralist, republican, and inter-confessional constitutional systems—was reforming the state and its institutions, Romanians were condemned to endure an experiment in totalitarian government that virtually froze any political disputes.

Post-1989 Romania thus witnessed the resurgence of the interwar debates. Nationalist intellectuals revived the "right-wing spirit" of the interwar Orthodox partisans by reediting the works of their "classics," such as Nae Ionescu and Nichifor Crainic, and by setting up cultural foundations and publications like *Anastasia*. Much of the political and ideological opinions of these classical nationalists of interwar Romania were absorbed uncritically and without a reevaluation in light of the broader international political context. Under the umbrella of this nationalist movement, the post-1989 publication *Cuvântul* initiated the section "Orthodox Chronicles," in which the social and political phenomena in Romanian were interpreted from an Orthodox perspective.[121] As Gabriel Andreescu noted, the ideological elements behind this nationalist cultural sphere betray a regressive fixation with an idyllic rural life, excess of ritual symbolism, and lack of ethical interest of an Orthodoxy more concerned with mysticism, authoritarianism, and nationalist demagogy.[122]

The close identification between nationalist political ideology and the ROC, with its negative reaction and condemnation of the challenges of political and religious pluralism, modernity, and the West, led to increasing criticism and concern from Romanian civil society. For Baconsky, there was no doubt that the emerging ideological tension between the church and prodemocratic civil society is almost irreconcilable and has led to a fracture of any constructive dialogue between the ROC and the state in post-Communism, and furthermore provided grounds for increasing polemics among intellectuals.[123]

Although there are grounds for the claim that the alliance between nationalism and Orthodoxy shapes a type of fundamentalism that moves against Romania's present political options (democracy) and commitment (European Union), extreme proposals that seek the removal of the church from public life are unconstructive for a working pluralist society. Such proposals are resonant with French-style secularism, in which the activist social and political influence of churches is regarded as an abuse and as a clear indication of fundamentalism. By playing a deterministic role in the drafting of the limits of religious activity in society, the secular state responds to intolerance with intolerance. Thus, one could agree with Preda that such a political attitude toward the churches in fact conceals the state's own intolerance in its violation of one of democracy's crucial features, that is commitment to pluralism.[124] Nevertheless, the inherent problem with Preda's argumentation is that it concerns less the defending of democratic values and more the voicing of Orthodox fears that their exclusive status as the national church is threatened by religious pluralism. For this reason, there are reservations to Adrian Marino's optimism when he argues that the ROC's official pro-EU integration discourse is an indication that Romania may turn the Orthodox presence to good account.[125] The major challenge is in assisting the Orthodox Church as it internalizes its public discourse and becomes a committed partner to the positive transformation of Romanian society.

The National Cathedral—Orthodox "Marriott"

At the dawn of the twenty-first century, questions are being raised about the Orthodox Church's continuing preoccupation with nationalism. During a national symposium held in 2002, the ROC issued an official statement in which the demand for recognition of "national church" status was reiterated.

> The Romanian Orthodox Church must have its position toward the state defined in the Constitution, in accordance with the status its number of believers confers (majority church), in accordance with the church's contribution in history (national church) and in accordance with today's contributions in its preoccupation with the moral regeneration of the society.[126]

Furthermore, when Fr. Bartolomeu a few years later agreed to the national church clause being dropped from the draft Law on Religious Freedom, the argumentation suggests that its removal from the law text does not change the already self-acknowledged status of the Orthodox Church as national.[127] The accentuated presence of the ROC in the public life worries the intellectual elite, who are justified in reacting against the excessive ritualistic and symbolical presence of Orthodoxy in the public sphere, its nationalist discourse and silent consent to its manipulation in electoral and political propaganda.

The episode of the construction of the Romanian Orthodox national cathedral is illustrative of the continuing nationalist preoccupation of the church in post-Communist Romania. The project has aptly been dubbed the "Orthodox Marriott" by Răzvan Theodorescu, referring to the expensive cost of building a cathedral that would host ten thousand believers in the center of Bucharest.[128] The idea for a national cathedral goes back to the nineteenth century, when the Romanian Kingdom secured its independence from the Ottoman Empire. Intended to show the victory of Orthodoxy over the Muslim Ottomans, the cathedral received strong support but never materialized due to misunderstandings regarding its size and location. The project was revisited in the 1920s, guided by Metropolitan Miron Cristea and benefiting from the support of the crown, but lack of funding meant it was eventually postponed. After the fall of Communism, Teoctist used the seventieth anniversary of the Orthodox Church's independence to propose a new project for the national cathedral, appointing a committee that would work on the design and other technical features of this massive project. Despite criticism from various quarters, in 2004 the municipal council of the capital city approved the church's request to build the cathedral in Carol Park, only to be later moved to the Arsenal Hill (Dealul Arsenalului) behind the House of the People.[129]

As Stan and Turcescu noted, the nationalistic connotations of the name of the new construction are inescapable, implying a theological conception whereby salvation is not an individual act but a national function.[130] Such a nationalist discourse for the cathedral project stands in historical continuity with the Orthodox Church's identification with the state. As if further evidence were required, the cathedral project received not only the blessing of the political elite, including those of President Emil Constantinescu and President Traian Băsescu,[131] but also the active support of nationalist organizations like *ASCOR* (the Romanian Christian Orthodox Student Association) and *Fundația Studenților Ortodocși din București* (Bucharest Theology Students' Foundation).[132] In reaction to these criticisms, Fr. Bartolomeu argued that the nation being a sociohistorical, metaphysical, and theological reality, salvation is obtained collectively and nationally, rather than individually.[133]

Orthodox Churches and Religious Pluralism

In an ostensive statement, political analyst Dan Pavel stressed that a church that finds it as easy to serve under Communism as under democracy, while persecuting the Greek Catholics and Evangelicals with relentless zeal, must be lacking in moral guidance and intellectual reflection.[134] The assertiveness with which the ROC calls itself the national church has long been perceived as unsettling for the minority denominations in Romania, raising concerns about the government's passivity toward this potentially volatile issue.[135] The change of orientation in the last years from *theologia militans* and polemical apologetics to ecumenism and dialogue has been described by some to be a radically positive transformation of interconfessional relations.[136] Yet, the contradiction between official Orthodox statements (expressing commitment to a pluralist society, European Union, and ecumenism) and the actual ideology and policy of the ROC toward other denominations render these ecumenical efforts a matter of cosmetic adjustment. As mentioned in the introduction, since the fall of Communism the Orthodox Church in Romania has come under criticism for its double standard toward religious freedom and dialogue with other denominations. The discrepancy occurs between the official discourse of the Orthodox clergy and the *de facto* situation.

The Western media has publicized over the last couple of years several incidents regarding actions of the Orthodox community against freedom of assembly, or its violence against Evangelical religious communities in a number of villages in Romania.[137] The findings of the 2005 "Report on Human Rights Practices" continue to stress numerous incidents that involve Orthodox clergy prohibiting, or putting political pressure on, the local councils to the detriment of the Evangelical and other minority denominations.[138] These incidents are illustrative of the progress the Orthodox churches have yet to achieve before religious freedom and toleration will become a reality in the society. Therefore, it is worrying that after almost two decades of democracy, Orthodox theologians like Preda insist that the ROC should continue its "virulent propaganda" against the Evangelical denominations in Romania as part of the church's missionary task, drawing at the same time a parallel between these denominations and sectarian and parareligious groups elsewhere.[139]

Although Romania has a democratic constitution that guarantees freedom of religious association, there was hopeful anticipation that the new Law on Religious Freedom would finally protect the minority denominations' rights to exercise their religious freedom. Yet, the draft Law on Religious Freedom and Status of Religious Denominations, presented to Romania's Chamber of Deputies in 2006 was described as preferential toward larger denominations, restrictive and discriminatory against religious groups founded after 1989, and therefore utterly undemocratic.[140] There was evident pressure faced by Romanian politicians when dealing with this important legislation. Despite the fact that the ambiguous language of "religious proselytizing" is discriminatory against the other denominations, state representatives were under constant pressure to define this designation in terms suitable to the Orthodox Church. Moreover, while claiming to support religious freedom that would secure equal rights for all religious groups and organizations according to the constitution, Orthodox representatives have incessantly complained to and pressured the Ministry of Religion for preferential status among the other denominations.[141] The result of these pressures has been highlighted in June 2006 by the Commission on Security and Cooperation in Europe, United States Helsinki Commission (CSCE), an independent U.S. Government agency created in 1976 to monitor and encourage compliance with the commitments to human rights, freedom of press, fair elections, etc., of the Organisation for Security and Co-operation in Europe (OSCE).[142] The Commission's Chairman, U.S. Senator Sam Brownback stressed:

> Romania has made considerable advancements since the Ceauşescu period concerning respect for religious freedom. . . . I am particularly alarmed by reports of amendments that would limit religious-based speech for believers in Romania. The draft legislation should be withdrawn or significantly amended to comply with OSCE commitments.[143]

The troubling aspects of the new draft concern the amendments that criminalize vaguely defined "aggressive proselytizing" with penalties of imprisonment for up to three years that have been approved by the Judicial Committee and the Human Rights Committee of the lower house of the Romanian Parliament.[144] Other limitations besides those on free religious speech include a strict registration system for new denominations and religious organizations, conditions that have been described as the most burdensome in the entire OSCE region. According to the CSCE report of June 2006, approximately one-fourth of the 18 registered religious groups would fail to meet the proposed multitiered system that requires applicant religious communities to wait 12 years before being recognized by the state, and show their membership exceeds 0.1 percent of the population of Romania.[145]

The draft Law on Religious Freedom passed the Romanian Senate in 2005 virtually unchanged despite the fact that more than 80 amendments had been proposed by the Council of Europe's Venice Commission.[146] While all other Romanian religious representatives have criticized and opposed such a discriminatory law, the Orthodox Church representative was the only one in favor. According to Orthodox Bishop Ciprian Câmpineanu, who represented the ROC in this debate, the numerical threshold (minimum percentage of population met to qualify for registration as religious denomination) is important as it limits the potentially numerous variety of denominations that would make it difficult for the Romanian State to manage in case any disputes arise.[147] Such a position illustrates the Orthodox perspective on the role of the state as adjudicator over religious life and is difficult to reconcile with the neutrality and impartiality that should characterize a democratic state in these matters.

In December 2006 the Chamber of Deputies reached, in a matter of hours, parliamentary approval of the controversial Law on Religious Freedom in violation of legal procedures that normally require preparation, debate, and vote on the law.[148] Rushed through in view of the imminent joining of the European Union on January 1, 2007, the passing of the debated law through the Romanian Parliament has been received with street protests by various denominations and NGOs that have been disputing it at the European Court of Human Rights.[149] Approved by the Romanian president on December 27, 2006, the controversial law is considered "Europe's Worst Religion Law" by more than 20 civic associations, including the Institute on Religion and Public Policy in Washington, D.C.[150] The major areas of concern are represented by the law's three-tiered system: state recognition, the powers the law gives to the state and the recognized communities, and the law's stipulations that violate freedom of expression by limiting some religious symbols. The ROC received with enthusiasm the new law, which in Article 13 criminalizes any forms (e.g. religious literature or art) or actions (proselytizing) that would violate or discredit religious symbols.[151]

Conclusion

This chapter has offered a survey and analysis of the current status of church–state relations in post-Communist Romania. The issues discussed here, namely the inconclusive Orthodox repentance and reparations, the debated repossession process, and the ROC's claimed autonomy from the state, suggest that Romanian Orthodoxy continues to exhibit pervasive nationalist and anti-Western tendencies that contradict its supposed pro-democratic and pro-European stance.

Moreover, evidence of the ROC's double standards toward democracy, and its reliance on state protection for national church status are raising questions in relation to the adherence to principles of religious freedom. Owing to the church's historical tradition of church–state identification, it is important to identify and explicate the source of this nationalist inclination pervasive within the ROC. Two important factors seem to impede the performance of the ROC in post-Communist Romania: namely the historical self-perception as possessing a privileged position in the national identity of Romania, and the legacy inherited from the Communist period, when the church encountered the totalitarian pressures of the Marxist-atheist regime.

Notes

1. Cf. Alexander F.C. Webster, *The Price of Prophecy: Orthodox Churches on Peace, Freedom and Security* (Washington, D.C: Ethics and Public Policy Center, 1993), p. 127.
2. Vladimir Tismăneanu, *Stalinism pentru eternitate* (Iași: Editura Polirom, 2005), p. 270.
3. Cf. Tony Judt, "Romania: Bottom of the Heap" in *The New York Review of Books* (1 November 2001). Famous because Judt's article caused a stir in the media and among the intellectuals in Romania. The article has been translated and published along with vehement or supportive responses from the Romanian civil society. Cf. Tony Judt, *România: La fundul grămezii* (Iași: Editura Polirom, 2002).
4. Andrei Pleșu, Petre Roman, and Elena Ștefoi, *Transformări, inerții, dezordini: 22 de luni după 22 decembrie 1989* (Iași: Editura Polirom, 2002), p. 100. Cf. Anca Manolescu, "Grupul de reflecție pentru înnoirea bisericii" in *Dilema*, no. 202 (November 1996), p.11.
5. "Religious cults shall be autonomous from the state and shall enjoy support from it, including the facilitation of religious assistance in the army, in hospitals, prisons, homes and orphanages." *Constituția României 1991*, Art. 29, par. 5.
6. Orthodox Revival movement (1926) under the leadership of Fr. Iosif Trifa in Sibiu.
7. The Greek Catholic Church (derogatorily known as the "Uniate" Church) is a combination between Eastern Orthodox liturgy, ritual, and Glagolitic alphabet but whose doctrines follow Roman Catholicism in recognizing the supremacy of the pope. It emerged in Transylvania at the beginning of the eighteenth century. See chapter 4 for details concerning contribution to Romanian national identity and chapter 5 for their persecution during Communism.

8 In particular we note the creation of *Liga Tineretului Ortodox* (the Orthodox Youth League) as well as ASCOR (the Romanian Christian Orthodox Student Association).

9 For the ROC the period between 1990 and 2003 has been characterized by an exponential increase in the number of churches and monasteries. From 12,389 churches in 1990 the total number by the end of 2003 was 13,800 despite the fact that some of the Orthodox churches counted in 1990 were returned in the meantime to the Greek Catholic Church. Regarding the Orthodox monasteries built in the same period, their number increased from 200 in the 1990s to 570 in 2003. In addition, four Orthodox radio stations were opened, 74 new magazines and newspapers established, 12 new theological colleges were added to the existing 2, and 33 new theological seminaries to the 6 existing in 1990. Florin Frunză, "Biserica Ortodoxă Română și laicizarea" in *Un suflet pentru Europa: Dimensiunea religioasă a unui proiect politic*, edited by Radu Carp (București: Editura Anastasia, 2005), pp. 278–83.

10 *Constituția României 1991*, Art. 82 par. 1–2.

11 Cf. Teodor Baconsky, "Dialog Amânat" in *Dilema Veche*, vol. 43 (5–11 Nov, 2004).

12 Vladimir Tismăneanu and Mircea Mihăieș, *Încet, Spre Europa* (Iași: Editura Polirom, 2000), p. 171. Cf. Mircea Mihăieș, *Masca de Fiere* (Iași: Editura Polirom, 2000), p. 104.

13 M. Mihăieș, *Masca de Fiere*, p. 104.

14 World Council of Churches, "Orthodox Church Admits Mistakes in Romania" in *The Word* (April 1990), pp. 29–30.

15 WCC, *The Word*.

16 A. Webster, *Price of Prophecy*, p. 100.

17 Iuliana Conovici, "Biserica Ortodoxă Română în spațiul public postcomunist" in *Akademia* No. 1/20 (2006), p. 1.

18 Fr. Nicolae Corneanu, quoted in "Pope John Paul II to Romania" (26 March, 2003) [Online] Available at: http://www.hist.edu/roma.html , accessed March 2005. Cf. GDS Prize acceptance speech, 1996.

19 N. Corneanu, *Pope*.

20 For his ecumenical and reconciling perspective see Metropolitan Nicolae Corneanu, *În pas cu vremea* (Timișoara: Editura Mitropoliei Banatului, 2002).

21 Daniel Sârbu, "Legea cultelor: Proiect eșuat" in *Ziua de Ardeal* (3 November, 2001).

22 The official condemnation of Communism was uttered by the ROC on 21 November 1990. The Orthodox Church condemned atheist Communism in abstract terms, referring to it as "an alien enemy of the being of a Romanian people which was Christian from its very birth in history." Cf. Bogdan A. Teleanu, "Condamnarea comunismului de către biserică" in *Ziua* (18 March, 2006), p. 1.

23 Cf. Peter Steinfels, "In Eastern Europe's Churches, Triumph Leads to Uncertainty" in *The New York Times* (22 July, 1990), p. 2.

24 A. Webster, *Price of Prophecy*, p. 100. Cf. A. Mungiu-Pippidi, "Ruler and the Patriarch: The Romanian Eastern Orthodox Church in Transition," in *East European Constitutional Review*, vol. 7, No. 2 (Spring 1998), p. 1.

25 This information was made public by Fr. Gheorghe Calciu, but the Romanian Patriarchate denied the existence of such a petition. Cf. A. Webster, *Price of Prophecy*, p. 100, n. 43.

26 Bogdan Comaroni, "Bătălia pentru Patriarhie" in *Ziua* (7 November 2001), p. 1.
27 In contrast, the demoted Bishop Emilian Birdaş was reinstated as well, this time as Bishop-Vicar of the Bishopric of Arad.
28 In October 2010, the ECHR has suspended all trial cases relating to Romanian property violations for 18 months and ordered Romania to take measures to compensate owners of nationalized houses. 'România, obligată de CEDO să adopte măsuri pentru despăgubirea proprietarilor caselor naţionalizate' in *Gândul Daily*, 12 October 2010. [Online] Available at: http://www.gandul.info/news/romania-obligata-de-cedo-sa-adopte-masuri-pentru-despagubirea-proprietarilor-caselor-nationalizate-7470418 , accessed October 2010.
29 Cătălin Bogdan, "Lupta pentru Patriarhie" in *ID*, Year II, No. 12(15) (December 2005).
30 Tom Gallagher, *Democraţie şi naţionalism în România, 1989–1998* (Bucureşti: All Educational, 1999), p. 338.
31 Cf. Andrei Pleşu, "Poarta cea Largă," in *Dilema*, no. 206 (20–26 Dec. 1996), p. 1.
32 The law proposed the returning of the Greek Catholic churches in towns and villages where there were at least two now-Orthodox former Greek Catholic churches and where a Greek Catholic community still existed. Cf. A. Mungiu-Pippidi, "Ruler and the Patriarch," p. 1.
33 For Bishop Antonie Plămădeală of Ardeal, this law presented by the senate was an "attempt to the very life of the Orthodox Church" while for Bishop Daniel Ciobotea of Moldavia, "a legal support for Catholic proselytising." T. Gallagher, *Democraţie şi Naţionalism în România*, p. 341.
34 Cf. Radu Preda, "Lupta Pentru Patriarhie Continuă," *ID*, Year II, No. 12(15) (December 2005), p. 1.
35 Patriarh Teoctist Arăpaşu, "Mărturisirea valorilor evanghelice," in *Ortodoxia*, LII, no. 304 (2001), pp. 5–10.
36 A. Webster, *Price of Prophecy*, p. 122.
37 A. Webster, *Price of Prophecy*, p. 122.
38 "România respectă dreptul la libertate religioasă" in *BBC Romanian* (10 November 2005). [Online] Available at: http://www.bbc.co.uk/romanian/news/story/2005/11/ printable/051110_libertate_ religioasa.shtml , accessed March 2006. Cf. Cătălin Bogdan, "Insidioasa Intoleranţă" in *ID*, III, no. 1(16) (January 2006).
39 "Romanian Patriarch Asks for Forgiveness" in *BBC News* (15 February 2000). Available at: http://news.bbc.co.uk/1/hi/world/europe/643898.stm, accessed March 2010.
40 Tom Gallagher, *Furtul unei naţiuni* (Bucureşti: Editura Humanitas, 2004), p. 82.
41 Another exception was Fr. Eugen Jurcă, lecturer of the Orthodox Theology Faculty in Timişoara, who in 2001 confessed publicly his lack of integrity and fear of the Communist regime with whom he collaborated silently from within the church ranks. "Am fost turnător din frică, laşitate, ignoranţă şi disperare" in *Evenimentul Zilei*, No. 2665 (26 March 2001).
42 Daniel Barbu, *Republica absentă: Politică şi societate în România postcomunistă* (Bucureşti: Editura Nemira, 1999), pp. 99–100.
43 Jaspers suggested three categories that lead to passive submission, namely political, moral, and criminal culpability. Cf. Karl Jaspers, *Texte Filozofice*, translated by G. Purdea (Bucureşti: Editura Enciclopedică, 1986), pp. 36–9.
44 K. Jaspers, *Texte*.

45 "Romanian Church Seeks to Cleanse Itself" in *Christian Century* (3 April 1991), pp. 357–8.
46 "All religions shall be free and organized in accordance with their own statutes, under the terms laid down by law.... Religious cults shall be autonomous from the state and shall enjoy support from it...." *Constituția României 1991*, Art. 29, par. 3–5.
47 Ioan Ică Jr., "Dilema socială a Bisericii Ortodoxe Române: Radiografia unei probleme" in *Gândirea socială a bisericii*, Ioan Ică Jr., Germano Marani, eds. (Sibiu: Editura Deisis, 2002), p. 543.
48 Radu Preda, "Cultura dialogului sau despre o altă relație biserică-stat" in *Nostalgia Europei: Volum în onoarea lui Alexandru Paleologu* (Iași: Editura Polirom, 2003), pp. 151–2.
49 Cf. Radu Preda, *Biserica în stat: O invitație la dezbatere* (București: Editura Scripta, 1999), pp. 102–26.
50 Dorina Năstase, "Secularizare și religie în integrarea europeană" in *Un suflet pentru Europa: Dimensiunea religioasă a unui proiect politic*, edited by Radu Carp (București: Editura Anastasia, 2005), p. 244.
51 Mircea Mihăieș stressed that the argumentation of the ROC denotes inconsistency with the status of the church as autocephalous, which in principle would enable it to call itself anything. This aspect, Mihăieș continues, is in contradiction with the ROC's stubborn demands for official recognition, and can only point to a hidden agenda, reminiscent of the interwar attempts at linking religion with nationalism. Vladimir Tismăneanu, M. Mihăieș, *Încet, spre Europa*, p. 171.
52 Phyletism is a form of idolatry or exaggerated love for one's nation. The charge that Preda's argumentation denotes a nationalist rhetoric has been observed by Cătălin Bogdan in a 2006 article. Cf. Cătălin Bogdan, "Insidioasa Intoleranță" in *ID*, III, no. 1(16) (January 2006).
53 Năstase makes a comparison between the ROC's demands and common tensions shared by the Polish Catholic Church's claims for recognition as National. C. Bogdan, "Insidioasa Intoleranță."
54 Technically speaking, in the absence of such a law, the stipulations of Decree 177 from 1948 which "allows the state a considerable control on the religious life" were still valid throughout this period. Cf. D. Sârbu, "Legea cultelor: Proiect eșuat," p. 1.
55 A. Mungiu-Pippidi, "Ruler and the Patriarch," p. 1.
56 To those who were hoping that the National Congress of the Orthodox Church in 1990 would ensure the financial autonomy of the church from the state, the church's demand for an increase of the salaries to clergy came as a surprise. Daniel Barbu, *Șapte teme de politică românească* (București: Editura Antet, 1997), p. 164.
57 D. Barbu, *Șapte teme*, p. 119.
58 I. Ică, "Dilema Socială a Bisericii," p. 543. There is not real Christian Democracy in Romania; the parties identifying themselves under this category have party agendas which do not correspond with this label.
59 Teodor Baconsky, *Puterea Schismei: Un portret al creștinismului european* (București: Editura Anastasia, 2001), p. 155.
60 Paul Negruț, *Biserica și Statul: O interogație asupra modelului simfoniei bizantine* (Oradea: Editura Emanuel, 2000), p. 162.

61 These two main currents in the ROC have sometimes been identified as nationalist or traditionalist on the one hand and pro-Western or "ecumenicalist" (i.e. pro-Ecumenism) on the other hand. Cf. Cătălin Bogdan, "Lupta pentru Patriarhie."

62 "Conferinţa naţională consultativă a Clerului Ortodox" (National Consultation of the Orthodox Clergy) held in 1990–1 and "Conferinţa naţională consultativă a Laicului Ortodox" (National Consultation of the Orthodox Laity) held in 1992.

63 Anca Manolescu, "Grupul de reflecţie pentru înnoirea Bisericii (1990–1991)" in *Dilema*, No. 202 (22–28 November 1996), p. 11.

64 Other problems addressed by the group included the development of theological seminaries, the renewal of church administration and the reintroduction of religious education in schools. "Înnoiri în Biserica Ortodoxă" in *Romania Liberă* (14 January 1990), p. 2. Cf. Iuliana Conovici, "Biserica Ortodoxă Română," p. 1.

65 This group had such an effective start that it has been described as an Orthodox replica to the "Group for Social Dialogue" constituted around the publication "Revista 22" and acted as a model and developed the civil society in Romania.

66 According to the Romanian Orthodox tradition, the last four patriarchs were previously metropolitans of Iaşi. Cf. Bogdan Comaroni, "Bătălia pentru Patriarhie," p. 1.

67 In a 1993 speech, Fr. Anania argued that the renewal group ceased because its goals have been met. For him, the main mission of the group consisted of generating calm and clarity in the tumultuous period following the revolution. Cf. Bartolomeu Anania, "File de Jurnal" in *Renaşterea*, Cluj (2003).

68 I. Ică, "Dilema Socială a Bisericii," p. 542.

69 A. Webster, *Price of Prophecy*, pp. 103–4.

70 Daniel Ciobotea, *Confessing the Truth in Love: Orthodox Perceptions of Life, Mission and Unity* (Iaşi: Editura Trinitas, 2001), p. 145.

71 D. Ciobotea, *Confessing*, p. 146.

72 D. Ciobotea, *Confessing*, p. 148.

73 "Patriarhul Daniel semnalează preşedintelui Băsescu eliminarea religiei din legile educaţiei" in *Hotnews.ro* (19 August 2009).

74 "Patriarhul Daniel, managerul în sutană" in *România Liberă* (14 September 2007).

75 Mihai Neamţu, quoted in Mirela Corlăţan, Steluţa Voica, "Schimbarea la faţă a BOR: Patriarhul în blugi Daniel" in *Cotidianul* (29 May 2009).

76 M. Neamţu, quoted in Corlăţan and Voica, "Schimbarea la faţă a ortodoxiei.'

77 "CNSAS: Patriarhul Daniel nu a colaborat cu Securitatea ca poliţie politică" in România Liberă (17 October 2007).

78 As Cazimir Ionescu pointed out, the secret police did not destroy dossiers to protect collaborators but rather as a result of sustained efforts by people or interest groups who worked for the Securitate. Quoted in "CNSAS: Patriarhul Daniel nu a făcut poliţie politică" in *Realitatea.net*, (16 October 2007).

79 L. Leuştean, *Orthodoxy and the Cold War*, p. 6.

80 Cristian Vasile, quoted in Corlăţan and Voica, "Schimbarea la faţă a ortodoxiei.'

81 A. Webster, *Price of Prophecy*, pp. 100–1.

82 Constantin Coman, ed., *Ortodoxia sub presiunea istoriei* (Bucureşti: Editura Bizantină, 1995), pp. 171–83.

83 Vlad Nistor, "Echilibru nepărtinitor" in *Dilema*, no. 284 (10–16 July 1998).
84 A. Mungiu-Pippidi, "Ruler and the Patriarch," p. 4.
85 B. Comaroni, "Bătălia pentru Patriarhie," p. 1.
86 Fr. Bartolomeu, quoted in *Renașterea*, no. 1 (January 2000), p. 5.
87 C. Bogdan, "Lupta pentru Patriarhie," p. 2.
88 Ion Mihai Pacepa, *Orizonturi Roșii: Amintirile unui General de Securitate* (București: Editura Venus, 1992), p. 330.
89 C. Bogdan, "Insidioasa intoleranță," p. 2. For an indepth treatment of Justinian's contribution during Communism, see chapter 5.
90 Fr. Bartolomeu Anania, "România și Europa," in *Renașterea*, no. 9 (September 1998), p. 1.
91 "Proces-verbal al Adunării Eparhiale Extraordinare a Arhiepiscopiei Vadului, Feleacului și Clujului" in *Revista Renașterea* (25 November 2005).
92 Cf. C. Bogdan, "Lupta pentru Patriarhie," p. 2.
93 Cf. A. Pleșu, *Transformări, inerții, dezordini*, p. 100.
94 Andrei Pleșu, *Chipuri și măști ale tranziției* (București: Editura Humanitas, 1996), pp. 169–71.
95 Teodor Baconsky, *Lupta cu Îngerul: 45 de ipostaze ale faptului religios* (București: Editura Anastasia, 1996), pp. 146–51.
96 Cf. Teodor Baconsky, *Ispita binelui: Eseuri despre urbanitatea credinței* (București: Editura Anastasia, 1999).
97 T. Baconsky, *Ispita binelui*, 112–26.
98 T. Baconsky, *Puterea schismei*, pp. 7–9.
99 T. Baconsky, *Puterea schismei*, pp. 7–9.
100 Cf. T. Baconsky, *Ispita Binelui*. The "Good's Temptation" is the translation of the volume's title.
101 Cf. Horia-Roman Patapievici, *Omul Recent: O critică a modernității din perspectiva întrebării "Ce se pierde atunci când ceva se câștigă?"* (București: Editura Humanitas, 2001). Again here, the book's title is revealing Patapievici's approach: "The Recent Man: A critique of modernity from the perspective of the question: What is lost when something is won?"
102 Horia-Roman Patapievici, *Politice* (București: Editura Humanitas, 2002), pp. 56–64.
103 H-R Patapievici, *Politice*, pp. 23–47.
104 H-R Patapievici, *Politice*.
105 H-R Patapievici, *Politice*. Patapievici is discontented with the anachronistic metaphysical image of premodern traditional Christianity, and therefore reluctant to see an important role for the church in society because in a renewed modernity God the Invisible does not need an institutional incarnation. For him, the only indication of the presence of God in this new modernity is the presence of a Holy Spirit totally autonomous and dissociated from the Father and the Son.
106 C. Coman, *Ortodoxia sub Presiunea Istoriei*, p. 180.
107 C. Coman, *Ortodoxia sub Presiunea Istoriei*, pp. 1–143.
108 C. Coman, *Ortodoxia sub Presiunea Istoriei*, pp. 249–50.
109 Cf. Dumitru Popescu, *Hristos, Biserică, Societate* (București: Editura IBMBOR, 1998).
110 Cf. Ion Bria, *Ortodoxia în Europa: Locul spiritualității române* (Iași: Editura Trinitas, 1995), p. 1.

111 Cf. Ion Bria "Confessing Christ Today" in *International Review of Mission*, vol. LXIV (1975), pp. 66–94. See also Ion Bria, *Romania: Orthodox Identity at a Crossroads of Europe* (Geneva: AC Publications, 1995); *Liturghia după Liturghie* (București: Atena, 1997); "Romanian Orthodox Theological Education" in *Catholic World*, no. 237 (January-February, 1994), pp. 17–23; "Evangelism, Proselytism, and Religious Freedom in Romania: An Orthodox Point of View" in *Journal of Ecumenical Studies*, vol. 36 No. 1–2 (Winter-Spring, 1999), pp. 163–83.

112 Cf. A. Pleșu, *Transformări, Inerții, Dezordini*. For an analysis of the miners' raids, see Ruxandra Cesereanu, *Imaginarul violent al românilor* (București: Editura Humanitas, 2003), pp. 209–398.

113 Vladimir Tismăneanu, *Stalinism pentru eternitate, O istorie politică a comunismului românesc* (Iași: Editura Polirom, 2005) p. 274.

114 Andrei Pleșu, "Poarta cea Largă" in *Dilema* No. 206 (20–26 December 1996).

115 A. Mungiu-Pippidi, "Ruler and the Patriarch," p. 2. Cf. Alina Mungiu, *Românii după '89: Istoria unei neînțelegeri* (București: Editura Humanitas, 1995), pp. 148–50. For an analysis of Mungiu's "inverted" populism see Mircea Boari, "Elitism maximal și mentalitate antidemocratică" in *Polis*, vol. 4 (1995), pp. 183–7.

116 Ioan P. Culianu, "Dușmanii capitalismului" in *Mircea Eliade* (București: Editura Nemira, 1995), pp. 169–74. Cf. "Ku Klux Klan Ortodox" in *Meridian* (May-June, 1990), p. 64.

117 Gabriel Andreescu, "Relații internaționale și Ortodoxie în estul și sud-estul Europei," in *Studii Internaționale*, No. 4 (1998), pp. 25–31.

118 G. Andreescu, *Relații internaționale*, pp. 31–2.

119 See chapters 4 and 5 for an account of the Romanian "national debate."

120 Such was the case with Italy, Germany, Austria, and for a short period even with France.

121 Many of these essays are collected in two volumes. Cf. Dan Ciachir, *Cronica ortodoxă* (Iași: Editura Timpul, 1994); Dan Ciachir, *Ofensivă Ortodoxă* (București: Editura Anastasia, 2002).

122 Gabriel Andreescu, *Naționaliști, antinaționaliști: O polemică în publicistica românească* (Iași: Editura Polirom, 1996), pp. 36–46.

123 Teodor Baconsky, "Sfada elitelor" in *Dilema*, Nr. 183 (1996), p. 11.

124 R. Preda, *Biserica în stat*, pp. 14–15.

125 Cf. Adrian Marino, *Pentru Europa. Integrarea României: Aspecte ideologice și culturale* (Iași: Editura Polirom, 1995), p. 14.

126 "Soluții și direcții de acțiune necesare pentru însănătoșirea vieții morale și spirituale a societății românești contemporane" *Comunicat Oficial*, Simpozionul Național "Sfântul Andrei-Apostolul Românilor" (24–27 September, 2002). [Online] Available at: http://www.rugulaprins.go.ro/comunicat. htm, accessed March 2005.

127 Mihaela Moraru, "Legea cultelor, fără formula biserica națională" in *Evenimentul Zilei* (12 June 2006).

128 Răzvan Theodorescu, quoted in Corlățan and Voica, "Schimbarea la față a BOR" (28 May 2009).

129 For a discussion of the various debates the cathedral project sparked, see the "The National Salvation Cathedral" section in Stan and Turcescu, *Religion and Politics*, pp. 56–63. See also Lavinia Stan and Lucian Turcescu, "Politics, National Symbols and the Romanian Orthodox Cathedral," in *Europe-Asia Studies*, vol. 58, no. 7 (November 2006), pp. 1119–39.

130 Stan and Turcescu, *Religion and Politics*, p. 58.
131 Gabriel Andreescu, *Extremismul de Dreapta în România* (Cluj-Napoca, 2003), p. 40. See also "Catedrala Neamului a intrat în linie dreaptă" in *Cotidianul* (9 February 2005).
132 According to Andreescu, ASCOR gathers all the fundamentalist and extremist elements of the ROC's ideology, benefiting from its support. See G. Andreescu, *Extremismul de Dreapta*, p. 36.
133 Bartolomeu Anania, "Totul este să începem construcţia" in *Dilema* (24–30 October 1997), quoted in Stan and Turcescu, *Religion and Politics*, p. 58.
134 Dan Pavel, *Cine, Ce şi De ce?: Interviuri despre politică şi alte tabuuri* (Iaşi: Editura Polirom, 1998), 37–48. Cf. also Dan Pavel, *Leviathanul bizantin: Analize, atitudini şi studii politice* (Iaşi: Editura Polirom, 1998), p. 148.
135 The biased attitude of political representatives in drafting the Law on Religious Freedom has raised legitimate questions about the neutrality of the Romanian state in representing the interests of all its citizens. As Daniel Mănăstireanu has stressed, the preoccupation with the ambiguous language of "religious proselytizing" employed by liberal deputy Emil Strunga is reminiscent of the discriminatory Orthodox labeling and should therefore be avoided by the representatives of a state whose constitution clearly warrants freedom of religious belief and association. Daniel Mănăstireanu, "Legea cultelor sau a cultului?" (2005). [Online] Available at: http://www.adoramus.ro/legea Cultelor.htm , accessed January 2006.
136 Ioan Dumitru-Snagov, *Relaţiile Stat-Biserică* (Bucureşti: Editura Gnosis, 1996), p. 180.
137 The most famous of these is the notorious *Ruginoasa* incident (1997), when an Evangelical community attending Sunday church service was met outside and beaten violently by the members of the local Orthodox Church who had been instigated to violence by the parish priest. APADOR-CH Press Release, "On Failure to Recognize Religious Denominations in Romania" (19 May 1997). [Online] Available at: http://www.apador.org/old/rapoarte/anuale/1997e.htm , accessed March 2006.
138 The Bureau of Democracy, Human Rights, and Labor "Country Reports on Human Rights Practices – 2005" (8 March, 2006).
139 Cf. R. Preda, "Lupta pentru Patriarhie continuă," p. 2.
140 Joy Junction, "Romanian Religious Minorities Concerned About New Religion Law," in *The American Daily: Political and Social Commentary* (10 Aug 2005), p. 1. See also Jeremy Reynalds, "Romania's Christian Minorities Protest Proposed New Legislation" in *ASSIST News* (3 October , 2005), p. 1.
141 The 2004 U.S. Report on Human Rights identified the hostility of the Orthodox Church toward other denominations in relation to the draft on Law on Religious Freedom. "Libertatea religioasă în România" in *BBC Romanian* (16 September 2004). [Online] Available at: http://www.bbc.co.uk/romanian/news/story/2004/09/040916_religie_romania.shtml , accessed March 2006. See also a letter of protest signed by various civil organizations from Romania and abroad concerning the discrimination and disregard for human rights that the proposed draft Law on Religious Freedom exhibits. "Letter of Protest," Bucharest, 27 October 2005.[Online] Available at: http://www.areopagus.ro/index.php?option=content&task=view&id=144&Itemid=179, accessed March 2006.

[142] The Commission on Security and Cooperation in Europe, also known as the U.S. Helsinki Commission, monitors progress in the implementation of the provisions of the 1975 Helsinki Accords. It consists of nine members from the U.S. Senate, nine from the House of Representatives, and one member from the departments of State, Defense, and Commerce. Commission on Security and Cooperation in Europe, United States Helsinki Commission, "Religious Freedom Gains in Romania Threatened by Regressive Draft Law" *CSCE News Release* (9 June, 2006). [Online] Available at: http://www.csce.gov/index.cfm?Fuseaction=ContentRecords.ViewDetail&ContentRecord_id=513&ampContentRecordType=P&ContentType=P&CFID=21571097&CFTOKEN=71565957, accessed June 2006.
[143] CSCE, *Religious Freedom*.
[144] CSCE, *Religious Freedom*.
[145] Helsinki commissioner Joseph R. Pitts stressed that it is blatantly discriminatory to force "religious associations" to wait more than a decade before qualifying for the highest "religion" status. CSCE, *Religious Freedom*.
[146] "Legea privind libertatea religioasă stârnește controverse" in *BBC Romanian* (11 Aprilie 2006). [Online] Available at: http://www.bbc.co.uk/romanian/news/story/2006/04/printable/060411_libertate_religioasa.shtml, accessed May 2006.
[147] BBC Romanian, *Legea privind*.
[148] Felix Corley, "Romania: Sudden Secretive Rush to Adopt Controversial Religion Law" in *Forum 18 News Service*, Oslo, Norway (12 December 2006), p. 1. Cf. Felix Corley, "Romania: Controversial Religion Law's Passing Violated Parliamentary Processes" in *Forum 18 News Service*, Oslo, Norway (15 December 2006), p. 1.
[149] Pat Ashworth, "Romania's Tough Law on Religion" in *Church Times*, issue 7504 (5 January 2007), p. 5.
[150] Institute on Religion and Public Policy, "Institute Deeply Disappointed by Promulgation of Contentious Romanian Religion Law; Romania Now Identified with Worst Religion Law in Europe," Washington, D.C. (3 January 2007). [Online] Available at: http://www.religionandpolicy.org/show.php?p= 1.1.1844, accessed January 2007. Cf. Evina Aloys, "Romania President Approves Europe's 'Worst Religion Law'," in *Journal Chretien* (4 January 2007). [Online] Available at: http://www.spcm.org/ Journal/spip.php?article5250, accessed January 2007.
[151] The concerns are that by not defining what those religious symbols are, freedom of expression in art, literature, and in the activities of other religious denominations could be perceived as infringing on Orthodox "religious symbols." Oana Crăciun, "Legea cultelor religioase, mai presus de legile societății" in *Cotidianul* (13 December 2005).

Chapter 2

German Protestantism and Nazism in Third Reich Germany

Introduction

This chapter proposes a comparative approach by contrasting Romanian Orthodoxy with the Protestant Church in Germany. This approach entails revisiting the struggles of the Protestant churches in Third Reich Germany and how they encountered the totalitarian ideology of the National Socialist party. The purpose of this chapter is multilayered, first by showing that the Protestant churches' ideological entrapment by Nazism stemmed from a combination of factors, namely the influence of nineteenth-century German Protestantism and the self-identification of the church in historical continuity with the Protestant Reformation and the German national awakening. Furthermore, this chapter will indicate the problems encountered by German theologians as they attempted to dissociate critically from the discriminatory goals of the Nazi regime, and the difficulty arising from the theologians' alleged fascination with, and theological support of, nationalist, racist and *völkisch* ideologies.

The conditions that led to the formation of the German Christians' movement and the support and loyalty they bestowed on Nazism will be surveyed, pointing to the movement's desire to renew church life by emphasizing German culture and nationalism. The theoretical evidence presented here will suggest that the movement's entrapment with the cultural and nationalist ideology led to the coupling of two utterly irreconcilable belief systems: Christianity and National Socialism. The result was that the German Christians' becoming an instrument for the institutional and ideological support of Nazi policies had devastating implications for the church. Thus described, church–state relations in Germany during National Socialism will represent a useful point of reference for the study of the Orthodox Church in Romania.

The Concept of Totalitarianism in National Socialism and Communism

Is there an inherent similarity between National Socialism and Marxist Communism as totalitarian systems and ultimately as political religions? The task of defining the precise meaning of the term "totalitarianism" is riddled with problems. Using the notion of totalitarianism appears to be outdated, given that over the past 30 years attempts have been made to banish the term from polite academic society.[1] However, for many commentators this still is the best term for describing Nazism and its attempts to pervert the notions of individual freedom and autonomous civil society through the influence of ideology, propaganda, and often even through terror.

The history of the concept of totalitarianism goes back to the times of Fascist Italy and right-wing German intellectual circles where the attempt to reject liberal democracies and negatively defined modern societies led to this theory being formed.[2] While originally referring to an "all-embracing, total state," the notion has been applied in a critical sense to a wide variety of regimes and ruling orders.

Karl Popper developed his famous critique of totalitarianism by contrasting the "open society" of liberal democracy with totalitarianism, and arguing that the latter is grounded in the belief that history moves toward an immutable future, in accord with knowable laws.[3] In defense of the open society and liberal democracy, Popper developed a critique of 'hegelian' historicism. Historicism stresses the progress of history according to knowable general laws and with a determinate end in focus.[4] Popper, in contrast, argued that historicism was founded upon mistaken assumptions regarding the nature of scientific law and prediction and, as such, is the theoretical presupposition to blame for the emergence of most forms of authoritarianism and totalitarianism.[5]

Criticism of totalitarianism as a political theory came from the Marxist theorist Leon Trotsky, who was among the first to distinguish between the notions of "limited absolutist regimes" and modern totalitarianism.[6] Although Trotsky criticized Stalin's totalitarianism for abusing the limits of the state in regard to family control and private morality, he did not see in the arbitrary government exerted by the absolutist regimes a negative implication for the rule of law.[7] Nevertheless, that Trotsky and his followers (Trotskyite sectarians) used the term "totalitarian" negatively, speaking against the deplorable political situation in their own Soviet Union, challenges the perception that such terminology belongs to external critics of Communist regimes, so-called "Cold Warriors."[8] As Michael Burleigh stressed, totalitarianism remains a useful notion in comparing National Socialism with Soviet Communism, as long at it is employed critically and thoroughly so that it moves beyond the superficial.[9]

National Socialism versus Communism

States that have most commonly been described as totalitarian, namely the regimes of Nazi Germany, the Soviet Union, and Fascist Italy, have experienced different forms of totalitarian constraints. For example, while the Soviet Union sought the universal fulfillment of humankind through the establishment of a Communist, classless society, German National Socialism attempted to establish the superiority of the Aryan race.

In her controversial work on the origins of totalitarianism, the Jewish-German philosopher Hannah Arendt postulated a theory of totalitarianism that identified Nazism and Stalinism as similar totalitarian movements.[10] Arendt distinguished between tyranny and dictatorship on one side and totalitarianism on the other side, by emphasizing that none of the forms explicated by the former—violence, force, limitation of free action—is as dangerous as the latter's negation of the very concept of action, of the fundamental condition of human existence: "Everything we know of totalitarianism demonstrates a horrible originality . . . its very actions constitute a break with all our traditions. . . ."[11] Thus, as Margaret Canovan noted, the paradox of this originality of totalitarianism was that it assaulted one's very ability to act and think as a unique individual.[12]

Arendt's portrayal of totalitarianism came under damaging criticism from sociologists of her generation. Many of the limitations of her argument result from the exaggerated distinction she makes between "the social" and "the political," which she elaborated upon in *The Human Condition*.[13] She depicts "the social" as a negative force that represses and distorts what is left of genuine human action and freedom, caused by powerfully effective underground forces.[14] According to Richard Bernstein, the concerns expressed by Arendt defined the world where the author was situated, the disappearance of the public spaces where human beings argue and debate, and where they form, exchange, and define opinions—activities that in essence constitute "the political" life.[15] She was concerned with the lawless no-man's land of occupied Eastern Europe and Russia where civilized beings degenerated into demi-human predators. Arendt was not a prophet of doom, and her primary concern reflected the need for cultivating and institutionalizing public freedom and the creation of public spaces where social and political life can reassume its interrupted course. She rightly pointed to the centrality to free societies of the rule of law.

Criticism concerning her coupling of Nazism and Communism came from quarters that disputed her generalizations and undifferentiated critique of European imperialism, as well as the swiftness with which she moves from one theme to another. Thus, Burleigh noted that the link between themes is not explicitly spelled out when Arendt discusses the grand themes of the Boers of South Africa, then moves to Lawrence of Arabia and through to the British imperial bureaucracy.[16] Raymond Aron, for example, differentiated sharply between Nazism and Communism, arguing that terror and ideology, ostensibly elemental to totalitarianism, are in fact an "amplification of revolutionary phenomena."[17] Based on such an interpretation, stressed Aron, the Bolsheviks were nothing less than "Jacobins who succeeded."[18] Daniel Bell insisted that Arendt's conservative indictment of societal atomization, the mob and the masses are the result of overinterpretation of the idea that terror can have such an exaggerated effect.[19]

Nevertheless, whereas Arendt based her theory of totalitarianism on questionable arguments, her attempt to find common ground between Stalinism and Nazism was not entirely flawed. Aron, although drawing a sharp distinction between Nazism and Communism, did not find it necessary to abandon totalitarianism as a means of describing their similarities in terms of "the extent of ambition, the radicalism of attitude, and the extremism of the methods used."[20] Likewise, Carl Friedrich and Zbigniew Brzezinski argued that Nazi and Communist totalitarian regimes were "basically alike" without being "wholly alike."[21] As stated in the introduction, without forcing a comparison between what are two obviously dissimilar contexts, uncovering the ideology fusing these totalitarian regimes is informative and can help elucidate some questions about the role played by churches in these circumstances.

Totalitarianism in Nazism and Romanian Communism

At a glance, there are some basic aspects that both Third Reich Germany and Communist Romania shared in common, without having a direct bearing on each other. Following the end of World War I, National Socialism managed to mobilize society and to conquer most of Europe in less than 10 years from assuming power. In post-war Romania, the Communist Party assumed total governmental control in 1948 and violently dismantled all political opposition, leading the country back into the Middle Ages, although 10 years previous this party was virtually nonexistent as a player in interwar Romanian politics.

In the case of Germany, the single-party state was completely subjected to a representative of the nation, namely the Nazi Party, through a national community (*Volksgemeinschaft*) that had to gain control of all aspects of German cultural and social life in order to succeed (*Gleichschaltung*).[22] Similarly, in the case of the Romanian Communist regime, the single-party state is subjected to the proletariat, which is represented by the totalitarian Communist Party.

An important aspect of the Nazi regime was its irrational and self-destructive use of power. The precedence that ideology took over rational self-interest was evidenced by the role played by ordinary citizens in helping impose and enforce control in society. In a study of the relations of the Gestapo (*Geheime Staatspolizei*, secret state police) to German society, Robert Gellatery noted how Nazism was assisted not simply by the Gestapo but even by ordinary citizens.[23] To strengthen the Nazi dictatorship, propaganda was used to keep the people involved in the "bread and circuses" of party organizations, parades, and festivals. Such propaganda encouraged citizens to participate in more insidious developments such as the emergence of a secret police that relied heavily on citizens' denunciations.[24]

The realization that, in the long term, Nazism was powerful not just because of the large numbers or efficiency of the Gestapo, but because millions of Germans were prepared to inform on one another and obey orders, strikes a familiar cord with Romanian Communism. Although the Romanian secret state police—the *Securitate*, established in 1948 after the Soviet model of the KGB—was, in proportion to the country's population, the largest secret police force in the Eastern bloc, it could not have functioned so efficiently without the support of the "informants."[25] The Romanian secret police massively increased the number of informants by claiming to "appeal to the people's conscience," and although some were blackmailed into spying on friends and family, there were enough who saw a civic duty in signing contracts promising to "signal threats to the state."[26]

Finally, coercion was an important tool used by German National Socialism in order to consolidate its political power. In the political climate that developed after Hitler's rise to power, an atmosphere of suspicion ensured that perceived political enemies and dissidents were identified and dealt with. Thus, Gellately notes how in the first few months of the Third Reich, mass arrests, sporadic political violence, and killings became part of a chaotic reign of terror.[27] The arbitrariness and brutality of this terror ensured the rapid consolidation of the Nazi regime's power. However, as Charles Maier suggested, it was only during the early months of the Third Reich that such coercive measures were used, and they ceased after the execution of Ernst Röhm and his faction, which led to the consolidation of the Nazi Party.[28] In Communist Romania, the reign of terror continued to be used by the Communist party in order to eliminate opponents.

During Communism in Romania, the terror that ensued after the abusive political takeover of power led to the imprisonment and condemnation of over a hundred thousand dissidents in only a few years.[29] The secret archives of the *Securitate*, which are reluctantly being revealed in twenty-first-century Romania, show the randomness and lack of predictability that characterized the repressive arrests, as well as the brutal methods and cruelty used by the interrogators. From former legionnaires to rival politicians, intellectuals, and clergy, everyone could have become a potential threat to the Communist totalitarian regime. In the chapters to follow, the evidence brought to bear will suggest that, akin to Nazism, Romanian totalitarianism thrived on terror and generated a pervasive culture of fear and suspicion.

National Socialism as Political Religion

The investigation of the extent to which Nazi ideology was grounded the nineteenth-century German intellectualism and emerging German *Volk* nationalism draws attention to the theory of political religions that is used extensively in the contexts of totalitarian regimes.[30] Viewing political movements as pseudo-religions with corresponding liturgies, theologies, and "ethical" codes is based on a legacy that stretches back to Alexis de Tocqueville, the French historian who compared the French Revolution to "a religious revival" that "has overrun the world with its apostles, militants and martyrs."[31] As Burleigh stressed in the introduction to his study of Nazism as a political religion, Italian Fascists, German Nazis, and Stalinists espoused the politics of faith and created idols and symbols that placed them on already-provided nationalistic altars, while their preachers appropriated the language of patriotism.[32]

Of particular interest is looking at National Socialism as a political religion, and many of the proponents of this approach have been keen to show its relationship to theories of totalitarianism.[33] The emphasis of such studies has been on National Socialism's pseudo-liturgical rites or deliberate evocations of the Bible for rhetorical purposes. Part of this effort has been the examination of how various regimes utilize sacred language and rites, even while they aggressively reject religion.

As Karl Barth stressed in 1939:

> National Socialism, according to its own revelation of what it is—a self revelation to which it has devoted all the time and chance till now allowed—is as well without any doubt something quite different from a political experiment. It is, namely, *a religious institution of salvation*.[34]

Therefore, Nazism was not a political party that merely accommodated religious belief, but was in fact a political religion. As will be argued, its combination with certain forms of Christianity, the fruit of nineteenth-century Protestantism, made Nazism comparable with a pseudo-religious ideology that used whatever means necessary to gain political power in interwar Germany. This prompts an examination of the ideological development beginning with the German intellectual context and then consideration of the function played by "Positive Christianity" and the subsequent intoxication with the concept of *Volk*.

National Socialist Gemeinschaft

In the second part of the nineteenth century, German social scientists attacked Classic Liberalism with the distinction between *Gemeinschaft* (community understood as an association governed by common beliefs, or unity of will, about the appropriate behavior and responsibility, in which individuals are oriented to the large association because of their own self-interest) and *Gesellschaft* (society understood as the association in which for the individual, the larger association can never surpass self-interest in importance, and is therefore sustained by individuals acting in their own self-interest and without a unity of will or shared beliefs). In his *Gemeinschaft und Gesellschaft* (1887) sociologist Ferdinand Tönnies developed a theory about the organic and social-contract concepts of society.[35] Although he stressed the interchangeable nature of these terms, community and society—in other words that a society can at times be both *Gemeinschaft* and *Gesellschaft*—his theory was misinterpreted by German romantics, who sought to distinguish between the two in order to ground a utopian return to *Gemeinschaft*.³⁶ *Gemeinschaft* was supposed to be the system in which the only way an individual can live a meaningful existence is through partnership in a group. Unconscious factors shape the cohesion of such a group: deep, vital forces of instinct, growing organically as part of nature and independent of man's free will. As Stephen Berry noted, some Germans identified *Gemeinschaft* as being peculiarly German and deemed it superior to the mechanistic and legal superficiality of *Gesellschaft*.³⁷ In turn, *Gesellschaft* became a characteristic of Western bourgeois society, which emphasized the individual and the individual's rational motivations.

The dispute between *Gemeinschaft* and *Gesellschaft* resurfaced ever more vigorously in relation to the antagonism between German culture (*Kultur*) and Western technological civilization. Heinrich von Treitschke, an important contributor to the concept of German nationalism, contrasted the alleged superiority of German *Gemeinschaft* (community, with its rich culture and achievements), to Western attempts to transform that community into a bourgeoisie, a social class of owners of capital.³⁸ The *Gemeinschaft* concept was taken further by Friedrich Meinecke, chairman of the *Historische Reichskommission* (The Imperial Historical Commission) (1928–35), who wrote, "by cleansing the idea of the nation of everything political and infusing it instead with all the spiritual achievements that have been won, the national idea was raised to the sphere of religion and the eternal."³⁹

The concept of *Gemeinschaft* was applied to historical research and particularly to the concept of *Sonderweg*, or "special path," to explain the continuity of this distinct German self-representation among the other nations in Europe. German historiography has long held an important place in the *Sonderweg* argument. The *Sonderweg* holds that Germany followed a different route to modernization than did other European states.⁴⁰ This alternate route enshrined pre-modern social values in the German society and character that ultimately made Nazi religious nationalism possible. Because of this, various historians portrayed Nazism as the unavoidable outcome of German history, reflecting unique defects in "German national character."⁴¹ Against such linear views, Meinecke and others contended that the Nazi period represented a unique occurrence in German history, and that the totalitarianism of the Nazi movement was at odds with German traditions.⁴²

The controversy between the 'special path' and linear views of German history led in the 1980s to the *Tendenzwende* (Turning Point), a series of professional and public controversies over the history of the Third Reich, which then led to *Historikerstreit* (Historians' Dispute), a broader debate over the social and political meaning of history.⁴³ Of importance for the present study is that the archival research prompted by the controversy provided evidence that suggests the expansionist objectives of 1914 German diplomacy had been extensively supported by the majority of the population.⁴⁴ This means that the Nazis' plans were in continuity with those of earlier generations and as such they neither represented a rupture in German history nor were lacking popular support in Weimar.⁴⁵

It is important to stress that supposed German superiority in its sense of *Kultur*, culture, as opposed to "Western civilization" resonated well at the turn of the century with Romanian traditionalists, who emphasized the autochthonous rural past as the "real" Romanian culture. According to historian Keith Hitchins, what attracted the traditionalist's interests were certain particularities in Tönnies' definition of *Gemeinschaft*. Specifically, Tönnies associated "unity of will" (*Gemeinschaft*) with its foundation on tradition and on natural connections between its members, defined as a primitive, organic form of social life.[46] Moreover, Tönnies' views about the "village" as the quintessential expression of "community" would have been deeply sympathetic to Romanian traditionalists whose ideology retained a similar concept.[47] In fact, as an organic form of social life, the idealized "village" was deeply integrated into the nationalist propaganda of the Orthodoxy-derived Iron Guard legionnaires. Such an understanding of the German superior "community," along with its *Sonderweg* historical path, echoed the ROC's self-perception as a community endowed with special responsibilities toward the state, and as bearer of a long historical path of identification with the state. In both cases, questions of historical accuracy are less important than the fashioning and interpreting of the past in ways that suit the nationalist goals of the people.

"Positive Christianity" and Nazism

In 1920, the *Nationalsozialistiche Deutsche Arbeiter Partei* (NSDAP, the German Workers' Party that came under Hitler's control) launched its 25-point manifesto, which was explicitly anti-Semitic and seemed to threaten religious freedom in Germany.[48] However, the manifesto was not directed against the churches and, in fact, advocated for the institution of Positive Christianity. The manifesto, commonly accredited to Gottfried Feder, identified three important points: a spiritual struggle against the Jews, the promulgation of a social ethic, and a new syncretism that would bridge Germany's confessional divide.[49]

In 1937, German theologian Cajus Fabricius devoted a volume to the subject of Positive Christianity, wherein he explores the main tenets of this concept.[50] The author begins by describing the religious policy of National Socialism (point 24), with the typical totalitarian rejection of liberalism and the perception of Bolshevism as an attack on Christianity. Furthermore, Positive Christianity stands for the recognition of the Christian faith by the Nazi Party. Finally, the author defines the Christian foundations of the party, making reference to the kinship shared by Christians and the German Nazis, who together strive for dominion over the world. The truest sense of this Positive Christianity is then identified in the practical aspects of this faith: loving one's neighbor, doing justice, giving honor. However, such practical Christianity has to focus its efforts on the nation, whose redemption from national corruption is jointly given by God and by the German nation's leader, *Der Führer*.[51]

Positive Christianity owed its influence to nineteenth-century Higher Criticism, which stressed the distinction between the historical Jesus and the divine Christ.⁵² Rooted in the Enlightenment, Higher Criticism was preoccupied with "historical criticism" of the Old and New Testaments as well as with issues of authorship and literary analysis of the texts, using rationalistic and naturalistic approaches.⁵³ Following Friedrich Schleiermacher's groundbreaking New Testament studies, the next generation, which included scholars like David Strauss and Ludwig Feuerbach analyzed the historical records of the Middle East, from Early Church and Old Testament periods, in search of independent confirmation of recorded biblical events. These latter scholars built on the tradition of Enlightenment and Rationalist thinkers such as John Locke, David Hume, Immanuel Kant, Gottlieb Fichte, Georg W.F. Hegel.⁵⁴

Those who held to the Positive Christianity manifesto argued that traditional Christianity had emphasized Christ's life in passive rather than active terms. According to this view, Christ's sacrifice on the cross and other-worldly redemption were lacking a more positive emphasis on the role he played as an active preacher, organizer, and fighter who opposed the institutionalized Judaism of his day.⁵⁵ A more radical version of Positive Christianity was developed by Alfred Rosenberg, the Nazi ideologist and author of *Der Mythus des 20. Jahrhunderts* (The Myth of the Twentieth Century).⁵⁶ Regarded in its time as a blasphemous attack upon Christianity, Rosenberg's volume was treated by Hitler as a private publication for which the author alone was responsible.⁵⁷

Positive Christianity was thus the indirect result of the rising preoccupation with popular and political nationalism in nineteenth-century Germany. As such, National Socialism gained in Positive Christianity the first religious system that attempted a combination of Christianity and nationalist *Volk* ideology. Moreover, it performed a bridging role between nineteenth-century German Protestantism and the emergence of the German Christian movement.

The Deification of Volk

Positive Christianity emerged in a theological context where nineteenth-century Protestantism had encountered a German culture preoccupied with racial and nationalist sentiments. One other use of the *Gemeinschaft* concept was in combination with German racial categories to describe a unique "national community of German people," or *Volksgemeinschaft*. However, this was no longer connected with the organic and social-contract concepts of society because *Volk* became a heavily politicized term. During the Nazi era, the term *Volk* and its adjective *völkisch* were employed with different meanings, depending on the context, to refer to "people," "race," "Germanic," or "European."

According to Garnet Peet, National Socialism perceived *Volk* in its nineteenth-century usage, as a religious ideology that suggests that Christ came to help Germans fulfill their potential as a separate folk and nation, with its own law, that of struggle: "Germans were born for struggle: they would fulfill their folkishness by that means."⁵⁸ For Nazis, then, the *Volksgemeinschaft* represented an earthly version of a heavenly kingdom. All their goals, whether to conquer

Europe or to eliminate "non-Aryan" peoples, were guided by this apocalyptic vision of a thousand-year German Reich (*Das Thousande Jahre Reich*).[59]

It is striking that the euphoric eschatological vision of the "eternal German nationalist ideal" corresponded to the millennialist perspective inherent in the Romanian version of Communism. Historian Lucian Boia stressed that Romanian intellectuals were very much attracted by voices proclaiming the Nazi Reich's thousand-year reign—a generic interval underlining an infinite space.[60] They also saw Communism as the last political system. The mythological return to the mysterious Aryan race was matched by the Orthodox mysticism of the Romanian legionnaires, which was carried over into Communist ideology.[61]

To summarize, the sociological rejection of the liberal-rationalist worldview, the superiority of the *Gemeinschaft* with its elitist German *Kultur* and historicist view of the *Sonderweg*, and the millennialist expectations of the idealized *Volksgemeinschaft* were all trademarks of National Socialist totalitarianism. In the NSDAP manifesto, Nazi ideology gained one last but crucial ingredient, namely Positive Christianity's religious system. This was the edifice on which the Third Reich was built, and from which the German Christians' movement emerged.

The German Christians' Movement

As J. S. Conway stressed, significant studies have emphasized the military and political events of the years of the Nazi tyranny, but the internal developments and the consequences for the established German institutions have largely been overlooked.[62] An important institution that claimed the allegiance of a large number of Germans was represented by the Protestant Church. A religious census taken in 1925 revealed that of an overall German population of 65 million, 40 million belonged to the main Protestant church, the Evangelical Lutherans; 21 million belonged to the Roman Catholic Church, and 620,000 to various smaller, mostly Protestant, denominations.

Hitler's strength relied upon his ability to eliminate any hindrance by uniting all Germans behind the Nazi ideology. The instrument used for achieving this goal was the systematic *Gleichschaltung* (synchronizing) of German society. *Gleichschaltung* was a system of totalitarian control that involved tight coordination of all aspects of society and commerce.[63] The effective restructuring of German society according to the goals set in the *Gleichschaltung* was possible because new structures were initially created parallel to, not in place of, old ones. Thus, Hitler's tactic was to set up organizations that gradually took control over, or absorbed, the existing structures.

This same tactic was used in relation to the churches in the Third Reich. As pointed out earlier, one of Positive Christianity's three points highlighted the development of a new syncretism that would bridge Germany's confessional divide. Set in non-confessional terms, the language of the 1920 manifesto intentionally did not differentiate. Thus, the German Christians' movement became a new parallel structure that Hitler wanted to use in order to appeal to all of Germany's Christians as an effective political strategy.

During 1930s the German Christians emerged as a group of pro-Nazi Protestants in Third Reich Germany. Until recently, few studies in German church historiography would have mentioned the movement other than to dismiss it as a group of extremists, heretics, career opportunists, or political adventurers in clergymen's clothes.[64] By comparison, there have been extensive studies carried out in relation to the small but significant Protestant group that opposed the Nazi tyranny, represented by the Confessing Church (*Bekennende Kirche*). As has been pointed out, much of these efforts were aimed at dissociating the activity and role played by the members of the Confessing Church from the rival movement that openly supported National Socialism, as was the case with the *Deutsche Christen*, and moreover to distinguish themselves from the larger majority of Protestants who remained quiet during the Nazi period, the so-called "bystanders."[65]

Although the German Christians movement was officially born in 1932, formed and led by Lutheran Pastor Ludwig Müller, it was preceded in 1921 by the League for a German Church (*Bund für Deutsche Kirche*), then by the Thüringian German Christians, and finally by the Christian-German Movement (*Christlich-Deutsche Bewegung*).[66] Their public statements were openly anti-Semitic and supportive of the Nazi Party platform for Positive Christianity that does not stress human sinfulness.[67] The German Christians enthusiastically supported Nazi propaganda and expressed their support for a Reich Church that would join all regional churches of the German Protestant Church into a national one. In July 1933, German Christians won a majority in the Protestant Church elections throughout Germany. Hitler decided the movement would help him "coordinate" the Protestant Churches, and he secured the election of *Reichsbischof* (Reich Bishop) Ludwig Müller as the leader of all 28 Protestant Churches in Germany.

Adolf Hitler and Protestantism

Several attempts have been made to describe the beliefs that animated Adolf Hitler, relating to his adherence to atheism, humanism, or some ancient Nordic pagan mythology.[68] Whatever his personal views, Hitler concealed them behind grand speeches about the important place of religion and Christianity in Germany. Even among the leadership of his party, he often distanced himself from the radically anti-religious, as was the case with Alfred Rosenberg. His interest in religion was purely driven by the political agenda of his party, and that became an obvious fact in 1933, when the NSDAP began consolidating its political control over the opposition.

In order to eliminate the Communist Party from active German politics, the Nazi regime justified their violent disbanding by stressing the atheism and materialism of the Communists and the need for Germans to protect their Christian culture from such influences.[69] Hitler was aware that his German electorate was overwhelmingly Catholic and Protestant and he, therefore, kept private his personal beliefs concerning Christianity. Archival work revealed his initial indifference toward the Christian faith, which according to Conway, would turn into total contempt when challenged by the churches' unexpected stubbornness.[70]

Until that time, however, Hitler had to secure a majority of votes in parliament in order to pass an "enabling bill" that would give him control over all legislative powers in the country. The strategy used in order to achieve this goal involved the luring of the Roman Catholic Center Party into voting favorably for the bill. Persuaded by promises of safeguarding of the churches' constitutional status, and by the Vatican's fears that the anti-Communist front would be disrupted by an open breach between the Nazis and the Center Party, Monsignor Kaas, the Center Party's leader signed an agreement with Hitler. In his first statement on government policy delivered in the new *Reichstag* (the German parliament), Hitler hailed the beginning of a fruitful relationship between church and state.[71]

The churches' problem with such speeches was that Hitler's National Socialism was ambiguous when it came to the relationship between ideology and political strategy. As Burleigh stressed, on the one hand such a church–state policy was welcomed by many Protestants who were enthusiastic about the inauguration of a new ethical and spiritual age in Germany, but on the other hand this policy worried those who looked at the anti-Christian propaganda of Nazi Party leaders such as Alfred Rosenberg.[72]

Nonetheless, Hitler continued his strategy toward the Protestant churches, and in July 1933 used the Nazi propaganda apparatus to influence church elections to have his Reich Bishop at the head of the newly founded *Deutsche Christen*. With the support of the Nazi Party and their expressed allegiance to the *Führer*, the German Christians presented a program of revival and renewal within the church that included campaigns against Marxism, racial purity demands and the Positive Christianity manifesto: "The Church must enter completely into the Third Reich, it must be coordinated into the rhythm of the National Revolution, it must be fashioned by the ideas of Nazism, lest it remain a foreign body in the unified German Nazi community."[73]

Hitler's support for the German Christians did not last, as the movement quickly became very radical and controversial. Following their triumphant success in the Protestant church elections in July 1933 and the election of Ludwig Müller as Reich Bishop, the German Christians felt they had reached the zenith of their power over church policy. Seeking to introduce the "Aryan paragraph" into church governance, a radical faction within the newly established German Christians, the self-styled "SA (*Sturmabteilung*, storm troopers) of Jesus Christ" forced ministers of non-Aryan descent to retire and become part of a Jewish Christian church.[74] Reinhold Krause, the leader of this radical group, called for a massive rally of German Christians in the Berlin Sport Palace in November 1933, where they sought to introduce a Positive Christianity approach that spoke against the "Old Testament with its Jewish morality of rewards, and its stories of cattle dealers and panderers," while the New Testament "had to be expurgated of all perverted and superstitious passages, and the whole scapegoat and inferiority complex theology of the Rabbi Paul . . . an exaggerated portrayal of the Crucified had to be guarded against."[75]

The November rally had various consequences: Bishop Müller left the German Christian movement; the movement separated into numerous groups, while dissatisfied Protestants, including Martin and Wilhelm Niemöller and Pastor Jacobi, became leaders of the Pastors' Emergency League. Despite Hitler's attempts to reunite the Protestant groups during a meeting in January the next year, the Emergency League had already been joined by 7,000 of the existing 18,000 Protestant pastors in Germany.

Later on, when it had become clear that German Christians could not be used as a vehicle for assimilating Protestants into the Nazi state, members and pastors of the Confessing Church, which opposed the Reich's Church, began facing persecution. The church struggle caused Hitler a lot of embarrassment, and so a few years later he would put Martin Niemöller under house arrest (1937) and send many members of the Confessing Church to concentration camps.[76] As Burleigh again stressed, Hitler disowned the troublesome priests, leaving other Nazis to attack Christianity itself.[77]

Despite Hitler's unsuccessful plans to use German Christians and the Reich Bishop as a self-coordinating movement for the Protestant state churches, this episode illustrated the extent to which Protestant churches in Germany fell into the nationalist and racial temptation of National Socialism. Even when the interest in the German Christians' movement was lost, many Protestant pastors remained bystanders rather than joining the Confessing Church in its rejection of Nazism as a political religion. As has been pointed out, "Nazi attacks on Christianity hardly encountered a resilient citadel, and were facilitated by Trojan horses constructed, rather than dispatched, within."[78] How it came about that a movement like that of the German Christians gained support among Lutheran and Evangelical pastors, and Protestant theologians of renown aligned behind the efforts to reconcile Nazism with Christianity, is the focus of the following investigation.

German Christian Volk

For Karl Barth, the German Christians' movement was "a small collection of odds and ends from the great theological dustbins of the despised eighteenth and nineteenth centuries."[79] The German Christians merely perpetuated an already present preoccupation of Liberal Protestant theologians with the *Volk*. Under the influence of the Higher Criticism school of thought, Protestantism had been determined to Germanize the Christian Gospel by reconciling it with cultural and philosophical traits of nineteenth-century descent.[80] Descending from such a liberal, nationalistic ancestry, German Christians retained a paradoxical relationship to church doctrine. Doris Bergen stressed that the majority of them remained within the official Protestant Church, held services in church buildings, and used the vocabulary and symbols of Christianity.[81] However, despite these elements of Christian tradition, German Christians theologically denied the universal claims of the Christian faith and attacked the notion of the church itself as independent from the nation.[82] In addition, one of the main characteristics that distinguished the German Christians was the emphasis on a "people's church" as a community of race and blood, which formed the basis for their symbiosis of Protestant tradition and Nazi ideology.

Völkisch terminology adopted crucial religious overtones when it was associated with the notion of a "people's church." As Bergen emphasized, a "people's church" was a tradition of church–state relations dating back to the Reformation, when regional Protestant churches in German territories constituted themselves around a geographic space, a secular ruler, and its own baptized community.[83] Friedrick Schleiermacher came later and used the term *Volkskirche* to describe that form of church–state relationship still in use in the Nazi era.[84] Thus, when Germany was defeated in World War I and the Kaiser abdicated, Protestants feared German democrats would force the "people's church" toward complete church–state separation, just as Bismarck did to the Catholics during the *Kulturkampf* of the nineteenth century.[85] This fear led to a distancing from the democratic state and inevitably to an emphasis on the links between the church and German culture and ethnicity.[86] Such openness to German culture exposed churches to the nationalist and racial categories that defined *Volk*. This is how the German Christians' movement began to emphasize race as the fundamental principle of human life, and to interpret it in religious terms.

According to Karl Barth, the "novel elevation of the concept of *Volk* to the front rank of theological and ethical concepts was one of the most curious and tragic events in the history of Protestant theology."[87] Barth could give no theological explanation for the deification of the nation and *Volk*, which occurred only as a "*factum brutum.*"[88] The religiosity of the German *Volk* was based upon a dubious doctrine of election that envisaged Germany as having been given a divine world mission.[89] The substitution of the nation for Christ as the bearer of election was Protestant theology's most fateful contribution to the nineteenth-century elevation of *Volk* along nationalistic lines. As Barth would stress, modern secular imitations of the doctrine of election conceived the true elected community to be the nation, constituted by race, language, and history.[90]

Not only were the divine attributes of Christ substituted for the nation, but the person of Jesus was Germanized as well. Starting with David Strauss who was advocating that humankind was to be guided by the idea of the race, a new perspective promoting the supersession of Christianity by a German-centered religion was taking shape.[91] Rejecting orthodox Christianity, Strauss adopted a *völkisch* pantheism that perceived Germany's military victory of 1870–71 to be a revelation of religious significance.[92] However, it was in Strauss's *Life of Jesus* (1835) that the Old Testament itself was made irrelevant to German Christianity. Stressing that, as eternal truth, the biblical message is independent of the historical context, Strauss contested that Judaism was essential to the message of Christ.[93] Such anti-Judaist tendencies opened the door to theological arguments that underscored Jesus's Jewish heritage by separating his religious significance from his ethnicity, as R. Kendall Soulen observed.[94]

The contributions of Emile Burnouf, Houston Stewart Chamberlain, Paul de Lagarde and others built further on the view that the German *Volk* was the true revelation of God's Spirit.[95] Their input was to reconstruct a historical Jesus redefined as an "Aryan" hero who fought against Judaism.[96] Chamberlain in particular developed some of the most influential ideas, his volume *The Foundations of the Nineteenth Century* (1899) becoming a standard of the racist and ideological anti-Semitism in Germany of the early twentieth century.[97] Not surprisingly, his ideas would re-emerge in the Positive Christianity concept and become the foundation for Rosenberg's racial theory.

Protestantism's derision of Judaism in the nineteenth century continued with another German theologian, Adolf von Harnack, whose liberal theology led him to a rejection of the Old Testament. With an emphasis on resuscitating the second-century heresy of Marcionism that taught a distinction between the God of love found in the New Testament and the imperfect God of the Old Testament, Harnack wrote:

> [T]he rejection of the Old Testament in the second century was a mistake which the great church rightly avoided; to maintain it in the sixteenth century was a fate from which the Reformation was not yet able to escape; but still to preserve it in Protestantism as a canonical document since the nineteenth century is the consequence of a religious and ecclesiastical crippling.[98]

Thus, although the Aryanization of Jesus would prepare the ground for the physical violence against Jews during the Third Reich, this Aryanization was primarily a theological perversion of the basic Christian doctrine under German nationalist influences. Protestantism continued its entrapment with the German *Volk* through the Positive Christianity phase of the 1920s and flowed directly into the German Christians' movement.

The German Christians and Race

Hannah Arendt stressed that "race-thinking" was not a German invention, although it became state doctrine only in Nazi Germany.

> The historical truth of the matter is that race-thinking, with its roots deep in the eighteenth century, emerged simultaneously in all Western countries

during the nineteenth century. Racism has been the powerful ideology of imperialistic ideologies since the turn of our century.[99]

However, in Nazi Germany racism went beyond ideology and became a religion in itself. What separated the German Christians among other *völkisch* Christian groups in German Protestantism was the importance they ascribed to racial thought. For them, the National Socialist view of race was perceived as the fundamental reality of human existence.[100] As already stated in the discussion on Positive Christianity, the Nazi Party heralded racial thought as a protest against a deformed, passive Christianity and highlighted the uncompromising nature of the unity of race and blood. However, there were groups within Protestantism that entertained *völkisch* ideas and supported Hitler's nationalist ideology but were reluctant to use it as a critique of the doctrines and views of Protestantism.

Thus, in 1932 the League for the Free People's Church (*Bund Freie Volkskirche*) convened to break from the newly formed German Christians' movement because the league felt that such teachings on blood and race ran in opposition to Christianity and to the precepts set by the Sermon on the Mount.[101] Another movement, *Christlich-Deutsche Bewegung* (Christian-German movement), which had among its members the Reich Bishop Müller until he was elected to lead the German Christians in 1933, encountered similar discontent with the issue of race despite being the forerunner movement for the German Christians.[102] It has already been pointed out that the Pastors' Emergency League and later the Confessing Church were constituted after the decisive Berlin rally, where the Aryan race became a condition for service in the German Christian churches.

Not only Protestant groups but pastors and theologians voiced this paradoxical ambivalence between nationalist and *völkisch* support on the one hand, and rejection of the combination of Christianity and racial thought on the other. Among them was the Confessing Church pastor Martin Niemöller, who admitted his personal antipathy toward Jews and his anti-Semitism, but refused to accept the Aryan clause as part of the church's teaching.[103] There were other pastors, such as Theodor Haug and Hans Ehrenberg, who openly rejected the imposition of this racial stand in relation to the teaching and doctrines of the church, but as Dietrich Bonhoeffer has emphasized, it was frustrating that, even within the Confessing Church, few were willing to protest against the German Christians' view of race.[104]

In its inverted form, this ambivalence occurred among Protestant pastors who resolutely opposed racial anti-Semitism, and yet believed there was a common denominator between the Jew and the racist. Observed by Uriel Tal, this tendency seems to have occurred with pastors who identified with the Confessing Church and were staunch opponents of racist anti-Semitism.[105] There can only be one rational explanation for this phenomenon, namely that Protestant pastors holding these views considered that both Jews and Nazis had certain things in common: Both refused to acknowledge Christian dogma, and their self-understanding was in terms of blood-relationship, kinship, and exclusive, superior descent.[106]

Such preoccupation with race affected large numbers of Protestant pastors who could not dissociate from the cultural and ideological influences of Third Reich Germany. For Uriel Tal, these Protestants equated and compared Judaism with the racist and the *völkisch* National Socialists because they made use of two historical traditions: the old Christian antagonism against the Jews and Luther's own combined struggle against Jew and pagan.[107]

Luther and Racism

The German Christians' movement evidenced a form of historical continuity in its identification with racial thought. Thus, from its very inception, the movement's 1932 guiding principles included the statement: "We take our stand upon the ground of Positive Christianity. We profess an affirmative and typical faith in Christ, corresponding to the German spirit of Luther and to a heroic piety."[108] The German Christians identified with the goals of National Socialism not only in the *Volksgemeinschaft*, the earthly apocalyptic vision of the inauguration of the "Third Reich" that was to last for a thousand years, but moreover in the historical continuity of which Nazis perceived themselves to be part. Speaking at the German Christians' first national convention (Berlin, 1933), Wilhelm Kube, leader of the Prussian *Landtag* faction of the Nazi Party, identified his work along party lines as part of "the effort to carry on in the twentieth century the German revolution in the spirit of Martin Luther."[109]

Such self-perception was internalized by the German Christians so that in the speech given at the notorious November 1933 rally at the Berlin Sports Palace, Dr. Reinhold Krause declared that the German Reformation begun by Luther would be completed in the Third Reich by the formation of a new all-embracing German national Church.[110] Martin Luther's racist and anti-Semitic views were well known, expounded in Luther's volume entitled *Against the Jews and their Lies*. That the German Christians self-identified themselves in this historical continuity with National Socialism is not surprising, given their openly declared enthusiasm for, and total support of, Nazi Party policy, of which racial discrimination was a part.

The link between the Protestant Reformation that spawned the Lutheran and Calvinist churches and German nationalism, and the completion of this historical process in the Third Reich, represented National Socialism's point of identification with German popular aspirations. It was this particular religious-nationalist linkage that attracted the German Christians' movement and made Nazism appealing to them. Thus, the claims of the German Christians' movement to becoming the new German national church were based on its identification with Nazism, with an all-encompassing source in the German *Gemeinschaft*, *Kultur*, *Volk*, Positive Christianity, and racism.

German Christian Theologians

During one meeting, a German Christian spokesperson contrasted the "courageous spirit of faith of a Dr. Martin Luther" with the spiritual dryness of "Pharisees and scribes" obsessed with orthodoxy and scriptural texts, namely the theologians.[111] Despite the professed anti-intellectualism of the German Christians, several theologians actually provided support for the movement. Their most cherished voices included those of Paul Althaus, Emmanuel Hirsch, and Gerhard Kittel.[112] However, there were others to whom Barth referred when he wrote:

> Why till now I have not spoken [about German Christians] is simply because what I have to say on this topic was sufficiently obvious: anyone who knows me but slightly could say it just as well himself. But there have been some doubts as to this obviousness. Certain members of the Reformed Church with whom I collaborated during the last few months, and also some who have passed as being pupils of mine, have appeared in the ranks of the "German Christians."
> ... I say, absolutely and without reserve, NO! to both the spirit and the letter of this doctrine.[113]

Barth's uncompromising "No!" to both Hitler and the German Christians, along with the publication of the pamphlet "*Theologische Existenz Heute*" (Theological Existence Today) in 1933, made him unpopular among many Protestant theologians who sympathized with the movement. Although an unlikely collaborator or pupil of Barth, Paul Althaus was certainly a staunch critic of the Swiss theologian. A confessionalist Lutheran, Althaus's constructive theological work emphasized the importance of "community" for an understanding of Christianity, and the centrality of the notion of "peoplehood" for ancient Israel and for the early Christian community.[114]

Althaus was a respected interpreter of Martin Luther via the *Erlangen* theological approach that informed his defense of the "two kingdoms" theory, and as such he viewed church–state and Gospel-law as forming two separate realms.[115] Owing to this theological distinction, Althaus became critical of Barth's support for the Weimar's liberal constitutional state. He ascribed Barth's "misguided" politics to what he deemed was an equally faulty Barthian theology.[116] Nonetheless, Luther's doctrine of "two kingdoms," defended by Althaus, dominated German Protestantism in 1930s and offered a cultural and social understanding of church–state relations that proved to make ineffective any theological opposition of the church to Nazism. Unable to conceptualize such opposition, Althaus welcomed a return to "law and order" and to a new glorious age of German dominion that the Nazis were proclaiming.[117]

In 1933, Althaus applauded Hitler's rise to power in the volume entitled *The German Hour of the Church*: "Our evangelical Churches have welcomed the turning point of 1933 in Germany as a gift and miracle of God."[118] He became a supporter of the German Christians and an outspoken critic of the Confessing Church and the Barmen Declaration (a statement of the Confessing Church opposing the German Christians movement during the Synod of Barmen in 1934), identifying himself with National Socialism's call to "peoplehood" and racial purity. Nonetheless, as James Stayer alluded to, while affirming the revelation of God in the German *Volk*, Althaus remained a moderate supporter of the German Christians' movement.[119]

Emmanuel Hirsch was described by colleagues and students at Göttingen University where he was a professor of theology as brilliant, possessor of unmatched linguistic proficiency and prodigious memory.[120] Hirsch was animated by a nationalist, philosophical theology that attracted him to the German Christians' movement. Hirsch's doctrine of the "two kingdoms" limited the church's sphere of activity to the individual's inner life, while he saw the state to have unlimited authority over the political and social orders.[121]

German Christians recognized the breadth of knowledge Hirsch retained and, as a result, always appealed to him whenever theological justification for their tenets was needed. Hirsch gave uninterrupted support to National Socialism and condemned the Weimar Republic because he regarded the *Volk* to be more important than democracy. He described the Nazi revolution as a "holy storm," a "power full of blessing," in which God's work would be seen, and in whose *Weltanschauung* (comprehensive worldview) "Germans of Evangelical faith should find their sustaining natural historic dwelling place."[122] Eventually, Hirsch radicalized his views, and in *Das Wesen des Christentums* (The Nature of Christianity) argued against the Jewish ancestry of Jesus.[123]

Gerhard Kittel is probably the most famous of the three, not least because of his editorship of the *Theologisches Wörterbuch zum Neuen Testament* (Theological Dictionary of the New Testament).[124] An expert in ancient Judaism, Kittel invested great effort in developing a theological justification for a Christianity that is in sharp contrast to Judaism. To that extent, Harrelson is correct to argue that Kittel cannot be exempt from the charge of having found support in his scholarship for his Nazi position with regard to the Jews.[125] Kittel perceived in National Socialism a "call of God" and expressed gratitude that God had given to the German people in Adolf Hitler a leader and deliverer.[126] In 1939 the German Christians regrouped and drew up a proclamation wherein they pledged to transform the Protestant Church into an instrument of racial policy. Kittel was one the signatories of the Godesberg Declaration, among leaders of at least 11 regional churches, who labeled Christianity "the irreconcilable opposite of Judaism" and announced the establishment of the *Institut zur Erforschung und Beseitigung des jüdischen Einflusses auf das deutsche kirchliche Leben* (The Institute for Research into and Elimination of Jewish Influence in German Church Life).[127]

Kittel insisted that the Nazi phenomenon was "a *völkisch* renewal movement on a Christian, moral foundation" and that he was speaking for other theologians, too, when he maintained that agreement with state and *Führer* was obedience to the law of God.[128] Moreover, he made a number of practical recommendations concerning how Jews should be dealt with by the Nazi state. According to Kittel, the elements of a strong, principled anti-Jewish force included the stripping of Jews' German citizenship in order to deprive them of civil rights, debarring them from the professions, keeping them from marrying Germans, prohibiting them from teaching Germans, in addition to imposing numerous other disadvantages and hardships.[129]

The three theologians sketched here were neither radical extremists nor heretical and isolated theologians but respected and esteemed professors and prolific minds of 1920s and 1930s German Protestantism. As has been pointed out, their assumptions, concerns, and conclusions represented a position that evidently was common to many professors, theologians, and pastors in Germany. The largest moderate group in the churches, Robert Ericksen observes, "probably held views resembling those of Kittel, Althaus, and Hirsch."[130]

In his study, Ericksen concluded that, in a certain sense, these three scholars showed intellectual integrity in the positions they held, a point that seems to raise fundamental questions about Christian theology as such. Thus, how can a person's theology be sound and yet enable one to support the monstrous ideology of Adolf Hitler? Walter Harrelson, who deemed Ericksen's conclusions incomplete, asks a question that reached under the surface of the problem:

> How can one separate theological thought entirely from the political, social, and cultural setting and from the consequences of the thought? Christianity is claimed by Ericksen to contain strains at once anti-Jewish and anti-modern. But some of the German theologians with whom he deals (Barth, Tillich, even Bultmann in most respects) have theological constructions neither anti-Jewish nor anti-modern.[131]

While this is a valid question, the approach proposed here is to ask the question in the opposite sense: What is in the political, social, and cultural background that so blinds the churches and its theologians and binds them to serving the prevailing culture, state, and ideology? The purpose of this chapter has been to illustrate how the Protestant churches' theological and confessional allegiances have been subdued by the dominant ideological power of National Socialism. The evidence presented here suggests the German Christians, along with a majority of the bystanding Protestant churches, were entrapped by the totalitarian demands of the Nazi state as they attempted a complete ideological merging of Christianity and Nazism. As emphasized, such deception gives evidence to the theologians' failure to discern between the Christian message of the Gospel and the *völkisch* cultural and nationalist influences that stem from a *Weltanschauung* based on an idolized concept of *Volk*, race, and history.

Conclusion

By investigating the historical and ideological context in which Nazi totalitarianism emerged, moral judgments have been made concerning the failure of nineteenth-century Protestantism to guard theology from German nationalist and *völkisch* influences. Moreover, it has been argued that National Socialism was more like a political religion than simply a secular party that used religion in the interest of its policies; and evidence was brought suggesting the important role played by Positive Christianity in its ideological development. The historicist self-identification of the German Christians' movement with the *Sonderweg* and its eschatological fulfillment in the thousand-year German Reich was in continuity with the aspirations of earlier German generations, thereby enjoying popular support.

What prompted this investigation is the contention that Nazi totalitarianism is comparable with Marxist-Communist totalitarianism and that they share many common features. Moreover, such a comparison does not limit itself to shared political and ideological strategies but identifies deeper resemblances concerning the role played by the state as a political religion that is seeking to enmesh the whole of human life. As indicated by the analysis of the Third Reich, where it cannot replace religious life, the totalitarian state is eager to control and regulate that life, with dire consequences for the churches. In Nazi Germany, this was the case with the Protestant churches and its pastors, professors, and theologians who either joined the German Christians' movement or adopted a passive "bystander" attitude. Their ideological surrender to, and legitimization of, the goals and methods employed by the state illustrate the pervasiveness of the nationalist and racist ideas aided by the theological structure of nineteenth-century liberal Protestantism.

The discussion has drawn two conclusions regarding the emergence of Nazism and the churches' collaboration with it. First is that the churches fell victim to the state because of the error of identifying with the historical continuity in which Nazism proceeded with its grand ideas for German nationalist renewal. Secondly, the inability of the Protestant Church and its theologians to dissociate critically from the prejudicial goals of the state resulted from their fascination with, and theological support of, nationalist, racist and *völkisch* ideologies. The investigation of the Romanian Orthodox history of church–state relations that occupies the following three chapters will consider these two conclusions as essential.

As the possessor of a historical self-identity that goes back much farther than Luther's Protestant Reformation, the ROC's constant battling with the *caesaropapist* charge will be further analyzed. The investigation of Orthodox thinking on church–state relations will suggest that Romanian Orthodoxy has developed a historicist understanding of its inception, formation, and development, yet one that is closely linked with the emergence of Romanian nationalism and ethnicity. Based on this argument, what generated the ROC's reliance on the state, its negative view of political autonomy, and even enabled the ideological coupling of Orthodox Christianity with Marxist totalitarianism is directly linked to this nationalist entrapment to the state.

Identifying the source, the elements, and the ideological presupposition that shape Romanian church–state relations will help to comprehend the subservient and collaborationist attitude displayed by the church toward Communism. This will then be compared to the German situation wherein the use of Orthodox theology to inform and justify an obedient position of the church toward the atheistic state was similar to the attitude taken toward Nazism by German theologians. This will allow for a comparison between Karl Barth's contribution to the theological refusal of Nazism in the Barmen Confession and the Marxist-Orthodox synthesis during Communism.

Notes

[1] Michael Burleigh, *The Third Reich: A New History* (London: Pan MacMillan, 2001), p. 14.
[2] The term was first employed by the Italian philosopher Giovanni Gentile to describe a society in which the main ideology of the state had influence, if not power, over most of its citizens. Cf. A. James Gregor, *Giovanni Gentile: Philosopher of Fascism* (New Brunswick, NJ, London: Transaction Publishers, 2001), pp. 67–94.
[3] Cf. Karl Popper, *The Open Society and Its Enemies*, 2 vols. (Princeton: Princeton University Press, 1971) and Karl Popper, *The Poverty of Historicism* (London: Routledge & Kegan Paul, 1961).
[4] K. Popper, *Open Society*, vol. 1, pp. 7f. Cf. Bryan Magee, *The Story of Philosophy* (New York: DK Publishing, 2001), p. 221.
[5] K. Popper, *Open Society*.
[6] Leon Trotsky, *Stalin: An Appraisal of the Man and His Influence* (London: Hollis and Carter, 1947), p. 421.
[7] See Burleigh's critique of his stance. M. Burleigh, *Third Reich*, p. 15. See also Leon Trotsky, *The Revolution Betrayed* (London: Faber and Faber, 1937), pp. 250–1.
[8] Cf. H. W. Brands, Jr., *Cold Warriors: Eisenhower's Generation and American Foreign Policy* (New York: Columbia University Press, 1988).
[9] M. Burleigh, *Third Reich*, p. 14.
[10] Hannah Arendt, *The Origins of Totalitarianism* (London: Allen and Unwin, 1967), p. 306.
[11] H. Arendt, *Origins of Totalitarianism*, p. 309.
[12] Margaret Canovan, "Arendt's Theory of Totalitarianism: A Reassessment" in *The Cambridge Companion to Hannah Arendt*, edited by Dana Villa (Cambridge: Cambridge University Press, 2000), p. 27.
[13] Cf. Hannah Arendt, *The Human Condition* (Chicago: University of Chicago Press, 1998).
[14] Richard J. Bernstein, "The Origins of Totalitarianism: Not History but Politics" in *New School of Social Research*, vol. 69, No. 2 (Summer, 2002), p. 1.
[15] R. Bernstein, *The Origins of Totalitarianism*.
[16] M. Burleigh, *Third Reich*, p. 17.

17. Raymond Aron, "The Essence of Totalitarianism According to Hannah Arendt" in *Partisan Review*, vol. 60 (1993), p. 374, and Raymond Aron, "On Totalitarianism" in Raymond Aron, *Democracy and Totalitarianism: A Theory of Political Systems* (New York: Frederick A. Praeger, 1969), pp. 203–4.
18. R. Aron, "Essence," p. 374.
19. Daniel Bell, "America as a Mass Society: A Critique" in Daniel Bell,. *The End of Ideology: On the Exhaustion of Political Ideas in the Fifties* (New York: Free Press, 1962), p. 25–6.
20. R. Aron, "Essence," p. 374.
21. Cf. Carl J. Friedrich and Zbigniew Brezinski, *Totalitarian Dictatorship and Autocracy*, 2nd ed. (Cambridge, MA: Harvard University Press, 1965), pp. 51ff. See also Lucy B. Golsan, et al, *Stalinism and Nazism: History and Memory Compared* (Lincoln, NE: University of Nebraska Press, 2004).
22. *Gleichschaltung* is a Nazi term loosely translated as "synchronization" and refers to the processes by which the Nazi regime controlled the individual, as well as all aspects of society and commerce. Richard J. Evans, *The Coming of the Third Reich* (London: Penguin Books, 2003), pp. 376–7.
23. Robert Gellately, *The Gestapo and German Society: Enforcing Racial Policy, 1933–1945* (Oxford: Clarendon Press, 1991), pp. 72–4.
24. Daniel J. Goldhagen, *Hitler's Willing Executioners: Ordinary Germans and the Holocaust* (New York: Knopf, 1996), pp. 253–5.
25. Cf. Ioan Mihai Pacepa, *Cartea neagră a Securității*, vol. 2, *Viața mea alături de Gheorghiu-Dej* (București: Editura Ziua, 1999).
26. Marius Oprea, "Securitatea și mostenirea sa" in *Comunism și represiune în România: Istoria tematică a unui fratricid național*, edited by Ruxandra Cesereanu (Iași: Editura Polirom, 2006), pp. 23–37.
27. R. Gellatery, *Gestapo and German Society*, p. 40.
28. Ernst Röhm was the *Stabschef* (chief of staff) of the *Sturmabteilung* (Stormtroopers, also known as the SA), a political army that protected the Nazi Party leadership and terrorized Hitler's political opponents in the formative years. Increasingly divergent views about the direction of the party estranged him, and ultimately forced Hitler to execute Röhm and do away with the *Sturmabteilung*. Charles Maier, *The Unmasterable Past: History, Holocaust and German National Identity* (Cambridge, MA: Harvard University Press, 1988), p. 81.
29. M. Oprea, "Securitatea și mostenirea sa," p. 26.
30. An extensive scholarship of exponents of political movements as religions is available. See Waldemar Gurian, *Hitler and the Christians* (New York: Sheed & Ward, 1936); Eric Voegelin, *Die politische Religionen* (Munich: Wilhelm, 1996); R. Aron, *Democracy and Totalitarianism*; Jacob Talmon, *Political Messianism: The Romantic Phase* (London: Secker and Warburg, 1960).
31. Alexis de Tocqueville, *The Old Regime and the French Revolution*, translated by Stuard Gilbert (New York, London: Anchor Books, 1955), p. 13.
32. A. Tocqueville, *The Old Regime*, p. 8.
33. A selective list would include: Norman Cohn, *The Pursuit of the Millennium: Revolutionary Millenarians and Mystical Anarchists of the Middle Ages* (London: Secker and Warburg, 1957), George Mosse, *The Nationalization of the Masses: Political Symbolism and Mass Movements from the Napoleonic Wars through the Third Reich* (New York: Howard Fertig, 1975), James Billington, *Fire in the Minds of Men: Origins of the*

Revolutionary Faith (New York: Basic Books, 1980), James Rhodes, *The Hitler Movement. A Modern Millenarian Revolution* (Stanford: Hoover Institution Press, 1980), Uriel Tal, *Faith, Politics, and Nazism: Selected Essays* (London: Frank Cass, 2003), Klaus Vondung, *Magie und Manipulation: Ideologischer Kult und Politische Religion des Nationalsozialismus* (Göttingen: Vandenhoeck & Ruprecht, 1971).

[34] Karl Barth, *The Church and the Political Problem of our Day* (London: Hodder & Stoughton, 1939), p. 41.

[35] Cf. Ferdinand Tönnies, *Community and Society*, translated and edited by Charles P. Looomis (Michigan State University Press, 1957).

[36] Mathieu Deflem, "Ferdinand Tönnies (1855–1936)" in *The Routledge Encyclopedia of Philosophy*, edited by Edward Craig (London: Routledge, 2001). [Online] Available at: http://www.cas.sc.edu/socy/faculty/deflem/zToennies.html accessed May, 2004.

[37] Stephen Berry, "No Tears for the Führer" in *Libertarian Alliance*, No. 3 (5 April 2001), p. 2.

[38] Heinrich von Treitschke, *Politics*, translated by Blanche Dugdale, vol. 1 (New York: The MacMillan Company, 1916), p. 321.

[39] Friedrich Meinecke, quoted in James J. Sheehan, *German Liberalism in the Nineteenth Century* (London: Methuen, 1982), p. 279.

[40] For an elaborate treatment of *Sonderweg* and its detractors, see David Blackbourn and Geoff Eley, *The Peculiarities of German History: Bourgeois Society and the Politics of Nineteenth-Century Germany* (Oxford: Oxford University Press, 1984).

[41] Supporters of this historicist view after World War II included J.P. Taylor, Sir Lewis Bernstein Namier, as well as journalists like William L. Shirer. Cf. J.P. Taylor, *The Course of German History* (London: H. Hamilton, 1948); Sir Lewis Bernstein Namier, *In the Nazi Era* (London: Macmillan, 1952); William L. Shirer, *The Rise and Fall of the Third Reich: A History of Nazi Germany* (New York: Simon & Schuster, 1960).

[42] Cf. Hans Rothfels, *The German Opposition to Hitler, An Appraisal* (Chicago, Ill.: Henry Regnery Company, 1948) and Gerhard Ritter, *Europa und die Deutsche Frage: Betrachtungen über die geschichtliche Eigenart des Deutschen Staatsdenkens* (München: Münchner Verlag, 1948).

[43] According to Michael Stürmer, Germany's modernization over the last two centuries ended in crisis and catastrophe, culminating in Nazism. Constant structural upheaval supplied both causes and consequences which led to a fractured and incoherent political culture. Since 1945 however, "historical debate had become politicised, partisan and divisive: the technocrats of the political right ignored history, while the left laboured it to death." Michael Stürmer, "Geschichte in Geschichtslosen Land" in *"Historikerstreit": Die Dokumentation der Kontroverse um die Einzigartigkeit der nationalsozialistischen Judenvernichtung* (Munich: Piper Verlag, 1987), p. 36.

[44] See, for example, John A. Moses, *The Politics of Illusion. The Fischer Controversy in German Historiography* (New York: Barnes & Noble Books, 1975).

[45] I am indebted to Nick Baron for this discussion on the *Historikerstreit* controversy. Cf. N. Baron, "History, Politics and Political Culture," p. 1.

[46] Keith Hitchins, *România, 1866–1947* (București: Editura Humanitas, 1994), p. 339.

[47] See the discussion in chapter 5.

[48] Fabricius Cajus, *Positive Christianity in the Third Reich* (Dresden: H. Poeschel, 1937), p. 7.
[49] Richard Steigmann-Gall, *The Holy Reich: Nazi Conceptions of Christianity* (Cambridge: Cambridge University Press, 2003), p. 14.
[50] F. Cajus, *Positive Christianity*.
[51] F. Cajus, *Positive Christianity*, pp. 13–72.
[52] "Positive Christianity" in Louis L. Snyder, *Encyclopedia of the Third Reich* (London: Robert Hale, 1998), p. 271.
[53] Theologians connected with this school analyzed biblical New Testament texts where they often undermined the miraculous aspects of the narratives. See Philip P. Wiener, *Dictionary of the History of Ideas*, vol. 1 (New York: Charles Scribner's Sons, 1973), pp. 421ff.
[54] P. Wiener, *Dictionary*.
[55] F. Cajus, *Positive Christianity*, p. 7.
[56] His volume on racial theory *The Myth of the Twentieth Century* deals with key issues in the national Socialistic ideology such as the Jewish question. It was intended as a sequel to Houston Stewart Chamberlain's *The Foundations of the Nineteenth Century*, one of the key proto-Nazi books of racial theory. Rosenberg's racial interpretation of history concentrates on the supposedly negative influence of the Jewish race in contrast to the Aryan race. He equates the latter with the Nordic peoples of Northern Europe. According to Rosenberg, modern culture has been corrupted by Semitic influences, which has produced degenerate modern art, along with moral and social degeneration. In contrast, Aryan culture is defined by innate moral sensibility and an energetic will to power. See Savitri Devi, *Gold in the Furnace* (Uckfield, England: Historical Review Press, 2005), pp. 211–22.
[57] Arthur Cochrane, *The Church's Confession under Hitler* (Philadelphia: Westminster Press, 1962), p. 80.
[58] Cf. Garnet Peet, "The Protestant Churches in Nazi Germany" in *Clarion* vol. 37, No. 22 – 24 (28 October 1988), pp. 440–2.
[59] Victoria Barnett, *For the Soul of the People: Protestant Protest against Hitler* (New York, Oxford: Oxford University Press, 1998), p. 32.
[60] Lucian Boia, *Mitologia științifică a comunismului* (București: Editura Humanitas, 2005), pp. 85–6.
[61] Cf. Nicholas Goodrick-Clarke, *The Occult Roots of Nazism* (New York: New York University Press, 1985).
[62] J. S. Conway, *The Nazi Persecution of the Churches, 1933–45* (New York: Basic Books, 1968), p. xvi. Cf. Victoria J. Barnett, *Bystanders: Conscience and Complicity during the Holocaust* (Westport, Conn.; London: Praeger Publishers, 1999), p. xiii.
[63] R.. Evans, *Coming of the Third Reich*, p. 377.
[64] J. S. Conway stressed that it was only in 1996 that a first serious scholarly work on the German Christians appeared in English-speaking circles. J. S. Conway, review of *Twisted Cross: The German Christian Movement in the Third Reich*, by Doris Bergen, in *German Studies Review*, vol. 19, no. 3 (October 1996), p. 575.
[65] V. Barnett, *Bystanders*; see especially first chapter, "Who is a Bystander?" and chapter 7, "The Dynamics of Indifference."
[66] The Christian-German Movement was different from the German Faith Movement (*Deutsche Glaubensbewegung*) led by Jakob Wilhelm Hauer (1881–1962) who became incorporated into the German Christians' movement between 1933

and 1935. Cf. Jakob Wilhelm Hauer, *Germany's New Religion: the German Faith Movement* (London: Allen and Unwin, 1937). For a recent examination of Hauer's movement see Karla Poewe, *New Religions and the Nazis* (New York: Routledge, 2006).
67 J. Conway, "Review of *Twisted Cross*," p. 575.
68 Adolf Hitler, *Mein Kampf*, translated by Ralph Manheim (London: Hutchinson Press, 1974). Here are some secondary references: Eberhard Jäckel, *Hitler's Worldview: A Blueprint for Power* (Cambridge, MA: Harvard University Press, 1972); Joachim Fest, Hitler: *Eine Biographie* (Ullstein Tb: Neuausg, 1998); Hermann Rauschning, Hitler Speaks (London: Thorton Butterworth, 1939); Ian Kershaw, *Hitler 1889–1936: Hubris* (London: W. W. Norton & Company, 1998); William Carr, *Hitler: A Study in Personality and Politics* (London: Edward Arnold, 1986).
69 J. Conway, *Nazi Persecution of the Churches*, p. 17.
70 Apparently, Hitler remarked: "The parsons will be made to dig their own graves. They will betray their God to us. They will betray anything for their miserable jobs and incomes." J. Conway, *Nazi Persecution of the Churches*, p. 16.
71 Franz Joseph Hermann Michael Maria von Papen, *Memoirs* (New York: Dutton, 1953), p. 278.
72 M. Burleigh, *Third Reich*, p. 719.
73 J. Conway, *Nazi Persecution of the Churches*, p. 46.
74 A. Cochrane, *Church's Confession under Hitler*, p. 111.
75 A. Cochrane, *Church's Confession under Hitler*, p. 112
76 Frank McDonough, *Hitler and Nazi Germany* (Cambridge: Cambridge University Press, 1999), pp. 57–8.
77 M. Burleigh, *Third Reich*, p. 259. See also a similar view expressed in Geoff Layton, *Germany: The Third Reich 1933–45* (London: Hodder and Stoughton, 2000), pp. 78–81.
78 M. Burleigh, *Third Reich*, p. 258.
79 Karl Barth, *Theological Existence Today: A Plea for Theological Freedom* (London: Hodder & Stoughton, 1933), p. 53.
80 Cf. Will Saunders, "Cross and Swastika: The Nazi Party and the German Churches: To What Extent Did Christians Support Hitler, and for What Reasons?" in *History Review*, No. 46 (2003).
81 D. Bergen, *Twisted Cross*, p. 45.
82 D. Bergen, *Twisted Cross*.
83 D. Bergen, *Twisted Cross*, p. 10.
84 D. Bergen, *Twisted Cross*.
85 *Kulturkampf*, literally "culture struggle" refers to German policies in relation to secularity and the influence of the Roman Catholic Church, enacted from 1871 to 1878 by the Chancellor of the German Empire, Otto von Bismarck.
86 D. Bergen, *Twisted Cross*.
87 Karl Barth, *Church Dogmatics*, vol. III/4 (Edinburgh: T. & T. Clark, 1957), pp. 305–6.
88 K. Barth, *Church Dogmatics*, p. 307.
89 Cf. Helmut Walser Smith, *German Nationalism and Religious Conflict: Culture, Ideology, Politics, 1870–1914* (Princeton, NJ: Princeton University Press, 1995), pp. 50–78.
90 Karl Barth, *Church Dogmatics*, vol. II/2 (Edinburgh: T. & T. Clark, 1957), p. 312.

91 See D.F. Strauss, *Der Alter und der Neue Glaube: Ein Bekenntnis* (Liepzig, 1872).
92 A year after German unification (1872) Strauss wrote another work "The Old Faith and the New" where it is said that he abandoned the dogmatism of the idealism in exchange of that of naturalism and by the idea of race. For a more detailed discussion see Mark Lindsay, *Covenanted Solidarity: The Theological Basis of Karl Barth's Opposition to Nazi Antisemitism and the Holocaust* (New York: Peter Lang, 2001), pp. 65–6.
93 M. Lindsay, *Covenanted Solidarity*, p. 71.
94 R. K. Soulen, *The God of Israel and Christian Theology* (Minneapolis: Fortress Press, 1996), p. 76.
95 Émile-Louis Burnouf (1821–1907) was a leading nineteenth-century Orientalist and racialist whose ideas influenced the development of Aryanism. Paul Anton de Lagarde (1827–91) was a German biblical scholar and orientalist. He was a violent anti-Semite whose work "*Deutsche Schriften*" (1878–81) became a nationalist textbook in Germany.
96 Burnouf, for example, argued that the population of Galilee was racially distinct from that of Judea.
97 "Whoever makes the assertion that Christ was a Jew is either ignorant or insincere . . . the probability that Christ was no Jew . . . is so great that it is almost equivalent to a certainty." H.S. Chamberlain, quoted in M. Lindsay, *Covenanted Solidarity*, p. 73.
98 Adolf von Harnack, *Marcion: The Gospel of the Alien God* (Partial Translation; Durham, NC: Labyrinth, 1990), pp. 134, 138.
99 H. Arendt, *Origins of Totalitarianism*, p. 158.
100 D. Bergen, *Twisted Cross*, p. 34.
101 Wittkopp Lörcher, quoted in D. Bergen, *Twisted Cross*, p. 34.
102 Kyle Jantzen, review of "Die Christlich-Deutsche Bewegung: Eine Studie zum Konservativen Protestantismus in der Weimarer Republik" by Christoph Weiling, in *The Catholic Historical Review*, vol. 88, No. 3 (July 2002), pp. 608–9.
103 Niemöller circulated a letter which stated his stand on the issues (1933): "In making this pledge, I testify that the application of the Aryan paragraph within the Church of Christ has violated the confessional stand." A. Cochrane, *Church's Confession under Hitler*, p. 109.
104 Pastor Theodor Haug would have said: "Can one so simply speak of German blood and the holy Gospels as if the two stood as equal next to each other?" "No." In a similar tone, Bochum Pastor Hans Ehrenberg argued that it was the incorporation of "Jewish Christians" that affirmed a church as an authentic community of spirit. D. Bergen, *Twisted Cross*, p. 35.
105 U. Tal, *Faith, Politics and Nazism*, p. 192
106 U. Tal, *Faith, Politics and Nazism*, p. 197.
107 U. Tal, *Faith, Politics and Nazism*, p. 200.
108 A. Cochrane, *Church's Confession under Hitler*, p. 222.
109 A. Cochrane, *Church's Confession under Hitler*, p. 86.
110 A. Cochrane, *Church's Confession under Hitler*, p. 111. Cf. Andrew L. Drummond, *German Protestantism since Luther* (London: The Epworth Press, 1951).
111 D. Bergen, *Twisted Cross*, p. 173.

112 Cf. Robert P. Ericksen, *Theologians under Hitler: Gerhard Kittel, Paul Althaus, and Emmanuel Hirsch* (New Haven: Yale University Press, 1985). Cf. also Robert P. Ericksen, "The Political Theology of Paul Althaus: Nazi Supporter" in *German Studies Review*, vol. 9, No. 3 (October, 1986), pp. 547–67.
113 K. Barth, *Theological Existence Today*, p. 47.
114 Walter Harrelson, review of *Theologians under Hitler: Gerhard Kittel, Paul Althaus, and Emmanuel Hirsch* by Robert P. Ericksen, in *Theology Today*, vol. 43, no. 1 (April 1986), p. 144.
115 "Erlangen school" is the name given to a group of German theologians who rejected Rationalism, Repristination, and Romanticism and asserted a theology that recognized the relationship of faith to history.
116 As David Haddorff indicated, it should not automatically be assumed that Martin Luther's two kingdom position leads unilaterally to Christian political inactivity or that it can be blamed for the Nazi atrocities. David Haddorff, "Karl Barth's Theological Politics" in *Community, State and Church: Three Essays* (Eugene, Oregon: Wipf and Stock Publishers, 2004), p. lxi, n. 24.
117 D. Haddorff, "Karl Barth's Theological Politics."
118 Paul Althaus, *Die deutsche Stunde der Kirche*, 3rd ed. (Göttingen: Vandenhoeck & Ruprecht 1934), p. 5.
119 James M. Stayer, *Martin Luther, German Saviour: German Evangelical Theological Factions and the Interpretation of Luther, 1917–1933* (Montreal and Kingston: McGill-Queen's University Press, 2000).
120 Jason Byassee, "Theologians and Nazis" in *The Christian Century*, vol. 123, No. 11 (30 May 2006), p. 11.
121 Robert W. Bretall, Charles W. Kegley, eds., *The Theology of Paul Tillich* (New York: Macmillan, 1952), p. 32.
122 Paul Tillich, "Kritisches und Positives Paradox" in *Theologische Blätter*, vol. XIII (1934), p. 313.
123 Cf. Emanuel Hirsch, *Das Wesen des Christentums* (Berlin: Walter De Gruyter & Co., 1939, 1963).
124 Gerhand Kittel, *Theological Dictionary of the New Testament*, translated by Geoffrey W. Bromiley, 10 vols. (Grand Rapids, Michigan: Eerdmans, 1965–76).
125 W. Harrelson, "Review of *Theologians Under Hitler*," pp. 144–5.
126 Kittel's response to Barth, quoted in A. Cochrane, *Church's Confession under Hitler*, p. 184.
127 Apparently, Kittel later denied having signed the declaration, which in three of its points addressed directly the racial question. D. Bergen, *Twisted Cross*, pp. 24.
128 R. Ericksen, *Theologians under Hitler*, epilogue.
129 R. Ericksen, *Theologians under Hitler*. See also Michael Hakeem, "The Protestant Reaction to the Nazi Holocaust" in *Freethought Today* (March, 1993), p. 1.
130 R. Ericksen, *Theologians under Hitler*, epilogue.
131 W. Harrelson, "Review of *Theologians Under Hitler*," p. 145.

Chapter 3

From Caesaropapism to Religious Nationalism

Introduction

Let us turn now to the Orthodox historical record on church–state relations as they have emerged amid the perceived East-West dichotomy that is said to exist between the Eastern Orthodox and the Western churches. The investigation will proceed from the assessment of church–state typological categories, arguing that they are difficult to account for in the complex relationship between the ROC and the state. Attention will further be given to the so-called caesaropapist charge that has generated polemics in Romanian society since the publication and translation into Romanian of the Huntingtonian theses on the clash of civilizations. This debate has reopened questions about the Byzantine legacy of Orthodoxy and its compatibility with a modern democratic society. The caesaropapist allegation generated Orthodox responses that emphasized the so-called "symphony" tradition of collaboration with the ruler or the state. Thus, this chapter will concentrate on the historicist approach that characterizes Orthodox thinking on church–state relations, illustrating how this *Weltanschauung* operates.

The purpose of the exploration in this chapter is twofold. First, it uses the available evidence to suggest that the historicist approach emphasized by Orthodox scholarship, with its peculiar theory of culture, does not account for justified allegations of the political subordination of the church, especially in relation to the Eastern Empire. Attention will be given here to the organic legacy of the historical developments employed in the Orthodox perception of the church–state model. The second goal of this chapter is to stress that as a result of post-Enlightenment nationalism, the relationship between the Orthodox Church and the nation-state has undergone significant changes due to the new role played by religion.

Thus, in the case of Orthodox Russia, the ideological context in which Slavophilism and Bolshevism have led to the emergence of Communism will be investigated. Here, it will be argued that the tradition of caesaropapism has had a negative impact on the form taken by nationalism, which emerged in reaction to this subordination of church to the state. The Bolshevik movement has therefore been detrimental to the Orthodox Church and has generated extreme forms of nationalism that endeavored to emulate religion and become political religions. This examination will enable a better contextualization of the nationalist identification between the ROC and the state. Lastly, the emphasis of this chapter is also on understanding Orthodox self-identity in relation to the broader European struggles that have shaped the relationships of churches to nation-states.

Church–State Typologies

Generically defined as the institutional representation of the interaction between religion and politics, the church–state relationship is often described as the most significant power alliance in history between two of the most powerful and longest lasting of human institutions. Going back many centuries, it is not surprising that for contemporary scholars the subject resonates with memories of a primitive or traditional arrangement long gone. The images associated with church–state discussion include kings and queens, bishops, established churches, and popes enthroning emperors. This may be one of the reasons why some contemporary scholars will react dismissively to any mention of the role of religion in politics, associating it with residual religious fundamentalism that should at best be restricted as a private matter for the individual.

Traditionally, the church has blessed and given legitimization to the state, providing meaning and setting certain morality claims, while the state rewarded such service by protecting the church's rights and interests, recognizing its special position and providing it with material support.[1] Nonetheless, there are others who see more significant contributions that churches and Christian principles have given to society and politics, such as fundamental beliefs and values that are intrinsic and essential to the functioning of state and civil society. Emil Brunner once wrote that this relationship comprises the greatest subject in the history of the West.[2]

Modern attempts at establishing a typology of church–state relations across the cultures have illustrated the difficulty conceptualizing relations between religion and politics in contexts shaped by differing socio-political and cultural circumstances. Nevertheless, these efforts have led to the development of categories such as partial/full establishment (United Kingdom), strict separationism (United States), and pluralism or structural pluralism (Netherlands, Germany).[3] Others have identified theocracy as a model describing primitive societies, Erastianism as a typology for states that control and use religion for their own interests, friendly church–state separation (United States) and finally unfriendly church–state separation (France, Mexico, etc.).[4] Other typologies have suggested four main categories: First, the principle of unity or complementarity, which entail either theocracy (Jewish, Egyptian, Arab), or caesaropapism (Great Britain). The second category entails the principle of separation, and more specifically the complete separation (United States), partial separation (Belgium, etc.) and hostile separation (French Revolution). The third suggested category is the church–state system regulated by a concordat, while the fourth entails autonomy and subsidiarity.[5]

Concerning Western and Eastern European countries specifically, four possible typologies proposed include radical separation (France, Netherlands, and Ireland), complete identification/establishment (United Kingdom, Sweden, Denmark, Norway, and Finland), distinct cooperation/unfinished separation (Germany, Spain, Italy, Belgium, Luxemburg, Austria, and Portugal) and finally the post-Byzantine subsidiarity (Orthodox countries).[6] The post-Byzantine model envisaged by Romanian Orthodox Professor Fr. Radu Preda entails a cultural and spiritual unity in which the "democratic" organization of the Orthodox Church is best encompassed by the model of subsidiarity based on the principle that matters ought to be handled by the smallest (or, the lowest) competent authority.[7] In 1994, the Ecumenical Patriarch Fr. Bartholomew I of Constantinople stressed that the form of organization practiced by the Orthodox churches—which includes administrative autonomy of the bishops and patriarchs and of the autocephalous churches, and an emphasis on the Eucharistic unity of faith—is a prototype that has been recently institutionalized by the European Union as the "principle of subsidiarity."[8] According to Fr. Preda, this model of subsidiarity should not remain restricted to the organization of the church but should be emulated by the secular state as an alternative to democracy.[9]

However, as the investigation of the history of church and state relations in Orthodox countries seems to indicate, there is a great gulf between the ideological conceptualization of the subsidiarity model and the organization of the church hierarchy under the influence of the state. Stan and Turcescu have constructed a typological framework based on the Monsma-Soper church–state categories, which includes four broad models of church–state relations and then, using a thematic and multidimensional approach, highlights how these inform church–state interaction in six areas of public affairs.[10] To illustrate the complexity involved in such an approach, one study has suggested that in Orthodox Russia the Monsma-Soper typological categories cannot be generalized because of the government's inconsistency when it comes to church–state relations.[11] Stan and Turcescu are aware that the categorization of relations (developed by Monsma and Soper) that tie religious groups to established democratic states does not perfectly fit the case of Romania.[12] Hence, their thematic and multidimensional approach envisages the "twin toleration," which entails the ability of Romanian civil society to marginalize nondemocratic church–state models while promoting the more democratic models.[13] Moreover, as indicated in previous chapters, the secular state lacking consistency in its interaction with the church tends to use the church hierarchy whenever and however political circumstances require it.

The East-West Dichotomy

Following the collapse of the Communist regime in Romania and the controversial position of the Orthodox Church in the emerging society, debates over the Byzantine legacy of Orthodoxy regained an impetus comparable only to that of the interwar period. The ease with which the ROC left behind its past of collaboration with the Communist regime, and the close relations it maintained with the totalitarian leadership, generated concerns about the nature of its identity. In a bid to prove that Romanian Orthodoxy represents an impediment to the democratization of society, Olivier Gillet asked:

> To what extent have the traditions of the ROC, inheritor of a Byzantine model saturated in 'caesaropapism' and ignorant of the separation between the temporal and the spiritual powers, influenced the democratic behaviour in a European country like Romania, where this church is dominant?[14]

Gillet's statement sums up a more general opinion that is occupying the minds of journalists, political scientists, theologians, and historians in contemporary Romania. At its heart, Gillet's concern has to do with the perennial question about the Byzantine legacy of Romanian Orthodoxy.

The Caesaropapist Romanian Orthodoxy

In his study, Gillet aimed to demonstrate a prevalent political, cultural, and religious continuity between the Byzantine era, the Ottoman domination in the Balkans, and the Communist regime. His contention is that the Byzantine model of symphony between the Orthodox Church and the emperor during the rule of Byzantium does not do justice to the subordinated status enjoyed by the church during Emperor Justinian's time. If the issue raised may seem perennial, one has only to look at the reaction generated in Romania by the publication and translation of Samuel Huntington's controversial theory about the clash of civilizations.[15]

According to Huntington's thesis, the West is distinguished from Orthodox Christian countries by the experience of the Renaissance, the Reformation, the Enlightenment, overseas colonialism, and the reinfusion of Classical culture through Rome.[16] This is contrasted by the contiguous expansion and colonialism, and the continuous trajectory of the Byzantine Empire. By arguing that Europe ends where Eastern Orthodoxy begins, Huntington followed in the steps of older mentors like Oswald Spengler and Arnold Toynbee. Oswald Spengler's view on the division represented by the Russian Orthodox and the Catholic and Protestant West underlined the idea of a conceived "pseudomorphosis"[17] that Russian culture was forced to achieve with the "alien mould of full Baroque, then of Enlightenment and then of the nineteenth century."[18] Although Arnold Toynbee wrote about a more sympathetically defined difference between Western and Eastern Christianity by referring to them as "sister civilizations," he too stressed that Western culture owed its superiority to Roman Catholic and Protestant Christianity.[19]

Huntington's sweeping generalizations have been refuted by studies that are contrary and disapprove of the assumptions on which his theory is based. Among the most potent studies, it is important to mention Paul Berman's *Terror and Liberalism*, in which Huntington's categories of "civilization" and "cultural boundaries" are questioned.[20] Others have emphasized empirical data that disprove Huntington's theory about an increase in "intercivilizational" conflicts since the end of the Cold War.[21] Still other critics regret the idealized portrayal of Western democracy and values, charging Huntington with failing to take into account the West's own history of despotism and fundamentalism.[22]

In Orthodox circles, Huntington's demarcation of the cultural patterns of Orthodoxy and Catholicism was described as the most comprehensive recent attempt to deal on a worldwide scale with the relationship between cultural history and the international political scene.[23] The result of such religious-philosophical ideas only serves, as pointed out by Nonka Bogomilova, to justify the century-long rivalry between the two parts of the Christian culture: "This type of thinking has the quality of inertia in making of Orthodoxy a distinguishing trait, an emblem of a comparatively homogenous, closed cultural and social system, radically different from the Western Christian one."[24]

In Romania, the volume's translation initiated a debate that brought back into discussion the Orthodox identity and the country's historical Byzantine tradition.[25] The division of religions into the categories of those that are superior (Catholic and Protestant) and those that are inferior (Oriental and Orthodox), which allegedly reinforces an already present perception of Eastern Europe as a deprived version of Western Europe, an underdeveloped space under the influence of equally passive and corrupt Orthodox state churches—has been dismissed as a regrettable stereotype of post-schism medieval Western Europe.[26] Sorin Antohi, stressing the link between the Byzantine heritage and the division implied by Samuel Huntington's thesis, cautioned:

> Let us avoid the Huntingtonian divorce which is used to blame the Orthodox Church and to reduce all these [lack of social presence of the church during Communism] to a problem of political theology, i.e. the persistence of the Byzantine model of *symphony* [author's italics] and other such clichés.[27]

Antohi's observation summarizes well the negative position adopted by a large contingent of Romanian Orthodox intellectuals and laity concerning the continuity between today's Orthodox Church and the Byzantine "symphonic" church–state relation legacy.[28]

Nonetheless, the union between the Orthodox Church and the ruler based on the symphony model was a historical reality. In their volume, *Religion and*

Politics in Post-communist Romania, Stan and Turcescu aptly identified the extent to which the Orthodox churches saw collaboration with the ruler as a form of protection against all forms of danger resulting from territorial and religious expansions into Southeastern Europe.[29] At the other end, the ruler or monarch ensured that collaboration with the Orthodox Church would strengthen control over the uneducated population, maintain order in the community, or develop relations with regional neighbors. Although this reciprocal relationship meant the Orthodox Church continued to maintain a privileged position in the state, it was always a privileged servant of the state. This was more evident during Communism, when the Orthodox Church was reluctant to oppose the dominant atheist state. As noted: "*Symphonia* never entailed a partnership of equals, but the communist regime tipped the balance in its favor, leaving the Orthodox Church little maneuvering room."[30] As described later in this volume, the concept of symphony would justify the silent endorsement of the anti-religious campaigns of the totalitarian state.

After the fall of Communism, the ROC was often associated with this tradition because of the close ties it maintained with the state. As Stan and Turcescu noted, this was not surprising given centuries of collaboration with the state.[31] The same symphony legacy would also explain the perceived gulf between ideological concepts uttered publicly by Orthodox Church officials after the fall of Communism, and the hidden power struggle within the ranks of the church hierarchy.

Byzantium After Byzantium

At the beginning of the twentieth century, a nationalist Romanian historian argued that all democratic institutions that epitomized Western society's influence, that is to say, constitution, parliament, elections, press, university, etc., were simple "forms without substance," "shells devoid of content."[32] Such a view suggests the existence of something deeper that pertains to the Romanian soul, or the "Romanianness." This deeper "truth" about the Romanian society was revealed by Nicolae Iorga, for whom Byzantium did not disappear in the fifteenth century with the fall of Constantinople, but continued to exist in Orthodox Eastern Europe.[33] It did not simply live as an exterior form but in its very "substance," as a complex set of institutions, political systems, religious organization, and a civilization built on a framework consisting of Greek wisdom, Roman law, Orthodox religion and its art.[34] The "Byzantium after Byzantium" then was supposed to represent the real truth or the foundation that from a "form-without-substance" perspective, generates the perceived incompatibility between Romanian society and Western forms and influences (exposed as artificial).

However, this argument was questioned by critics who suggested an alternative way of coming to terms with the Byzantine heritage of contemporary Romanian society. Toward the end of the twentieth century, the historian Valentin Georgescu proposed the interpretation that Byzantium is not perceived to have continued after the fall of Constantinople, but that it subsided merely as a political, institutional, religious, and cultural origin for Orthodox societies from Eastern Europe.[35] Such a view reinterprets negatively Iorga's "Byzantium after Byzantium" by suggesting the idea of non-Byzantium, namely that the nations of Eastern Europe and particularly Romania, have always defined themselves in relation to Byzantium, but often against it, in their quest to fashion their own non-Byzantium.

This ambivalence toward the Byzantine heritage of Romania is evident in other historical-political analyses that tend to underline the positive contribution of the Byzantine tradition to Romania's political and religious life, on the one hand, but to stress that this tradition was reinterpreted and therefore functioned on a different set of principles, making it difficult to define it as a Byzantine heritage per se.[36] The Huntingtonian resuscitation of the caesaropapist Orthodox Church stereotype, and the resurfacing of the perpetual Byzantine indictment that links the ROC with a linear tradition kept alive for centuries, brings us to an investigation of Orthodox identity amid this East-West distinction being made in scholarship.

The Caesaropapist Charge

In modern scholarship, caesaropapism is often mistaken by both Western and Byzantine medievalists for the concept of combining the power of secular government with the spiritual authority of the church, more properly describing a Byzantine symphony.[37] The concept of Byzantine symphony characterizes a political theory in which the power of secular government is combined with the spiritual authority of the church. Together, the emperor's power and the church's authority represent the basis for the universalist vision of Constantinople as the "New Rome." The Byzantine symphonic model of church–state relations defines the interpenetration of the theological authority of the church with the legal and juridical authority of the government.[38] The harmonious collaboration between the two spheres has its roots in the Eastern Orthodox Empire, where legal Byzantine texts speak of interdependence between the imperial and ecclesiastical structures rather than of a unilateral dependence of the latter on the former.[39]

Caesaropapism however is the concept in which the head of state, notably the emperor (Caesar, king) is also the supreme head of the church (pope, archbishop, or another analogous religious leader). The *Oxford Dictionary of the Christian Church* properly defines caesaropapism as: "the system whereby an absolute monarch has supreme control over the church within his dominions and exercises it even in matters normally reserved to ecclesiastical authority (e.g. doctrine)."[40] Such an arrangement implies a monarchical control over ecclesiastical affairs and connotes the intrusion of a civil officer in the sanctuary, the crossing of the line from the imperial to the priestly.

Such an understanding of caesaropapism does take into account occurrences when authoritative Byzantine theologians like John Chrysostom cautioned the church against the state's interference and publicly denied the emperor's meddling in church affairs. Caesaropapism is then a concept that has negative connotations, describing a perversion of the ideal symphony. According to Olivier Gillet, the Eastern Orthodox Empire is the only one eligible for such a distinct qualification, as it evidences a pervasive involvement of the emperor in the churches' affairs and the total dominion of civil power over the religious.[41] The confusion in identifying the symphony with the negatively perceived caesaropapist understanding of church–state relations has led to numerous debates that shall now be examined.[42]

Between Symphony and Harmony

The starting point of the debate concerning the distinction between the Eastern and the Western models of church–state tradition is the Constantinian era of the fourth century A.D. From a Western perspective the "politicization" of the church, that is to say, the use of the church by the imperial or the ruling power, began in the West with Emperor Constantine but afterwards continued only in the Eastern part of the empire, in Constantinople.[43] Thus, for Adrian Hastings, while Emperor Justinian I inaugurated in Constantinople a Christian monism, a church–state led by a single person as both *Imperator* and *Pontifex Maximus*, the Western church maintained a distance from the state, which secured its independence.[44]

The collapse of the West Roman Empire following the fall of Rome in 476 left the church fragmented and in disarray while the church in the Byzantine East enjoyed the continuity and protection of the political authority in Constantinople. However, it was amid the political discontinuity caused by the dismantling of Western imperial authority brought about by the Barbarian invasion of Rome that the Western church experienced a relatively independent position of authority in temporal and eternal matters. In the long run, these historical circumstances were fundamental to the development of a critical relationship between church and state in a way that was not possible in Constantinople.[45]

The Acacian Schism

One of the earliest attempts of the Roman church to distinguish itself from temporal authority took place amid the first serious theological disagreements between Constantinople and Rome, known as the Acacian Schism.[46] It was in this context that Rome's Pope Gelasius I developed the "two swords" doctrine (spiritual and temporal) based on the Augustinian tradition, which offered a comprehensive theological vision in which the purpose and contribution of the church could be understood in relation to the state. Gelasius taught a distinction between the two "powers," which he called the "holy authority of bishops" (*auctoritas sacrata pontificum*) and the "royal power" (*regalis potestas*). These two powers, *auctoritas* lending justification to *potestas*, and *potestas* providing the executive strength for *auctoritas* were to be considered independent in their own spheres of operation, yet were expected to work together in harmony (or symphony, though the Latins did not use this expression).[47] The Gelasian formula stressed that the roles of priest and king were combined uniquely by Christ and that thereafter it is impossible for anyone else to hold both offices. This was based on the Augustinian tradition as laid out in *The City of God*, which prevented the fusion of secular and ecclesiastical power by maintaining the offices of pope and emperor as distinct.[48]

In the thirteenth century, the principle of separation stressed by the Gelasian doctrine was influential enough to find reverberations amid Pope Innocent III's extreme claims, arguing that the state (Holy Roman emperor) was subordinated to the church (pope) because of the relative significance of the different jurisdictions given to the two institutions. Whereas temporal power was concerned with physical bodies, the church (and specifically the pope) was concerned with souls.

> Just as the founder of the universe established two great lights in the firmament of heaven, the greater light to rule the day, and the lesser light to rule the night, so too He set two great dignities in the firmament of the universal church ... the greater one to rule the day, that is, souls, and the lesser to rule the night, that is, bodies. These dignities are the papal authority and the royal power. Now just as the moon derives its light from the sun and is indeed lower than it in quantity and quality, in position and in power, so too the royal power derives the splendour of its dignity from the pontifical authority.[49]

It was Thomas Aquinas who reflected on Aristotle's concept of the mixed constitution—one that combines the best qualities of monarchy, aristocracy, and democracy—for the different layers of religious and secular authority.[50] Having established a biblical authority for Aristotelian political views, Aquinas had established in theory a paradigm for constitutional government in church and state.[51] Such views formed the basis for the high papal assumption that regal authority derives its dignity from the pontifical, an idea reflecting the influence of Aquinas in the thirteenth century.[52]

Despite these high points of claims on behalf of the church, the Western papacy has constantly attempted to gain control over the emperor, much in the same way in which the emperors of the Western Empire have constantly attempted to subordinate the papacy. This concentration on political control rather than spiritual matters led to the church's authority being weakened and discredited. Thus, between 1309 and 1377 the popes were forced to live in Avignon in the south of France under the domination of several French monarchs; this papal exile is sometimes referred to as the "Babylonian Captivity." The return of the papal court to Rome was promptly followed by the so-called "Great

Schism" that lasted from 1378 to 1417. During this period, no fewer than three contenders vied for the title of pope.[53] As Owen Chadwick has noted, when the Council of Constance unified the papacy in 1417 with the election of Pope Martin V, papal political authority outside the church was virtually terminated.[54]

Orthodox Perspectives on the Gelasian "Schism"

Orthodox theology's approach to the origins of the division between church and state has been to employ a Trinitarian argumentation. John Meyendorff argued that the church (*sacerdotium*) and the state (*imperium*) are united in the one Christian commonwealth just as the divine and human natures of Christ are united in the incarnate Son of God.[55] Such a view generalizes the intrinsic differences between the everlasting dynamic of the persons of the Trinity and any horizontal relations that are fluid amid changing social and political circumstances and thus cannot support such a comparison.[56] Nonetheless, the Byzantine symphony model was employed by Emperor Justinian (483–565) to underline the doctrine of church and state.[57] The main tenet of this doctrine was that while clearly distinguished, the religious and the secular realms were not separated but complemented each other in harmony. For Fr. Harakas, the notion of symphony entailed here supported the view that church and state cooperate as part of the organic whole in fulfillment of their purposes, with each supporting and strengthening the other without it causing the subordination of the one to the other.[58]

It was because of this emphasis on the idealized organic and complementing unity stressed between the church and the state, that the Orthodox theologians discussed above juxtaposed the Justinian symphony with the Gelasian distinction between the secular and the spiritual. However, the symphony pattern that emerged out of the historical circumstances of Eastern Christendom was different from the emphasis on the equality between the *auctoritas* and the *potestas*.

The Eastern symphony between the *sacerdotium* and the *imperium* was distinct from the Western separation between *auctoritas* and *potestas* insofar as they stressed different aspects of the relationship. This point was highlighted by Oliver O'Donovan who noted the characteristic of the Gelasian distinction between priestly authority and royal power:

> The distinction lies between the respective spheres of responsibility: "the reception and appropriate administration of the sacraments" on the one hand, "what pertains to order and public discipline" on the other. Balance between the two, rather than differentiation, was Gelasius' primary concern; and in this he drew the implications of a century and more of Roman practice in which the popes had carefully modelled their office upon that of the emperors.[59]

The Gelasian doctrine laid great emphasis on the view that the church and the state were coequal in status and sought to strike a balance between each of their responsibilities. However, the Gelasian distinction had been interpreted outside its intended context, which stressed "responsibilities." Idealized, and used as an aspirational vision, it became a theory about how to prevent the fusion of secular and ecclesiastical "power."[60] Similarly, in the East, as Bishop Kallistos noted, whereas the distinction made by Justinian between the priesthood (*sacerdotium*) and the imperial power (*imperium*) was meant to stress a constructive relationship that did not imply a loss of autonomy for either of the two, the theory came to cement a subordination of the church to the state.[61] Intrinsically, the Justinian theory was in line with the Augustinian notion that preserved the independence of the two powers in their own spheres of operation. The concept of symphony stressed the mutual harmony said to exist between the two realms, with no complete or absolute interference. The emperor would summon councils and put their decrees into effect, but the responsibility for the content and definition of the doctrines would rest with the church's clergy and the bishops.[62] Meyendorff thus referred to such an idealized church–state arrangement when he stressed that the organic unity between church and state envisaged by Justinian coincided with the Gelasian distinction between *potestas* and *auctoritas*.[63]

Nevertheless, the historical and political realities of the Eastern Roman Empire were never ideal, as emperors interfered incessantly with the church's doctrine while patriarchs sought political power with equal vigor. This constant struggle for power led to the relationship between the church and the emperor in Constantinople to be termed negatively as caesaropapism. According to Meyendorff, the meaning of the term caesaropapism, employed by the doctrine, implied that emperor and pope were combined into one person, in other words that they had a positive relationship.[64] Had the Byzantine state recognized ecclesiastical law as an interior guide for its activity, the term caesaropapism would not have done justice to the doctrine developed by Justinian. As Bulgakov stressed, symphony and caesaropapism could not be equated, since the latter is to be perceived as an abuse by the church.[65] Caesaropapism implied a situation where ecclesiastical supremacy belongs to the emperor when the emperor moves beyond the limits of his administration of the state to interfere in the dogmatic deliberations vis-à-vis theological controversies.[66] Although he recognized this important difference, Bulgakov was not readily keen to admit that in Constantinople the emperor had ever attempted to impose on the church certain dogmatic directives.[67] This, nevertheless, was the case during the reign of the Comnenian, Angeli, Lascarids of Nicaea, and Palaeologi emperors for whom the symphony was only theoretical, and all manifestations of religious life in Constantinople had to be controlled by the imperial power.[68] The ambivalent view is best expressed by Bishop Kallistos: "Admittedly, there were many occasions on which the Emperor interfered unwarrantably in ecclesiastical matters; but when a serious question of principle arose the authorities of the Church quickly showed that they had a will of their own."[69]

Orthodox theologians would argue that the symphony model is a misleading mode to characterize the church–state relationship in Eastern Orthodoxy. As Fr. Alexander Schmemman suggested, the very concept of Byzantine symphony relies on ambiguous theological and political concepts inherited from the Constantinian era that might have caused the problems it encountered.[70] As the argument goes, in the West as much as in the East, the very idea of a "Christian Empire," which emerged after the Edict of Milan, was uncritically bestowed upon a virtually pagan political organization characterized by a form of theocratic absolutism of the state resembling that of ancient Rome; faced with the challenge of achieving a Christian state, the church overlooked its temporal character.[71] Fr. Schmemman admits the limitation of the terminology applied to the Eastern Empire but argues for the commonality in the harmony between *potestas* and *auctoritas* and the symphony between *sacerdotium* and *imperium*.

Unlike the romantic approach of Bulgakov, who taught that by embracing the Roman Empire the church has somehow sanctified and anointed the pagan state, Fr. Schmemann insisted that this "unholy union" led to a leveling out of the distinction between the ontological and historical nature of the Christian community and secular society.[72] Byzantine concern with the nature of the symphony between church and state attempted to harmonize a distinctiveness that was already lost. Fr. Schmemann was willing to admit that Emperor Justinian never actually distinguished between Roman state tradition and Christianity and thus considered himself to be both a Roman and Christian emperor, which accounted for his inability to see a place for the church in his theory about the Christian Roman Empire; the emperor's concept of the Christian world envisaged the planting of Christianity in the heart of all official acts of the Roman political organization, but oversaw the place for the church in it.[73]

Despite these admissions, modern Orthodox thinking offers no real basis for the dichotomy between the Gelasian and Justinian concepts of church–state relations. If the Byzantine symphony attempted to harmonize a "lost" distinctiveness, then that was also the case with the Gelasian attempt at a harmony between two "non-harmonizing" entities. John Romannides retaliated, stressing that while the Gelasian distinction was based on the Augustinian formulation of the dichotomy between the visible and invisible cities, the implications for church–state relations in the West were often compromised by the papacy's constant quest for affirmation and superiority above the earthly rulers, a tendency termed *papocaesarism*.[74]

Emperor Justinian's symphony as a theory of the closely interdependent church–state relations encountered difficulties that emerged from trying to bring into harmony two very different entities that by default tended to subordinate each other. The religious absolutism of the Roman state and the emperor's belief that he was the representative of God on earth prevented the church's being independent from political government in the same way in which the papal quest for spiritual supremacy led to the church's compromising its otherworldly character. With this resolute argument, the majority of Orthodox scholars today refuse to admit that the caesaropapist tune plays a false note in the Byzantine symphony they celebrate.

Caesaropapism and European Religious Movements

In his church–state study, Hastings makes an interesting connection between the Protestant Reformation and the caesaropapism characterizing the Eastern Empire. For him, after the Protestant Reformation Justinian's concept of the single empire, spiritual and temporal, ruled by its supreme head, the emperor, was transferred to the national state and later, in due course, was effectively transferred to every German princeling.[75] This unlikely correlation between Eastern symphony and modern Western nation states is intriguing and worth analyzing.

The strongest proponent of an argument aiming in the same direction is Gilbert Dagron who, in an important study on the relationship between church and state in the Eastern and Western Empires, aims "to expose the mechanisms of a historiography that describes a Christian world divided from the beginning into two cultural zones, one western, where the temporal and spiritual powers were differentiated, the other eastern, where they were combined."[76] Dagron admits the caesaropapism that characterized the Eastern Roman Empire since the times of Justinian was a typically Byzantine perversion of the church–state symphony relationship, but argues that this was the product of religious movements in modern Europe.[77] Dagron's challenging views stress that the caesaropapist terminology originated from the German Protestant theologians of the eighteenth and nineteenth centuries, who used the categories of papocaesarism and caesaropapism to denounce and dismiss from a Protestant position both the papacy that ascribed to itself political power and any Justinian-styled princes and sovereigns who sought to manipulate and interfere in religious problems.[78] Dagron argues that the post-Reformation West actually projected upon the writings and historical setting of Pope Gelasius I in an attempt to distance itself from the East.[79] The political Augustinianism that emerged from such a reinterpretation of history was then used to justify a doctrine of the distinction of powers in the context of historical rupture between the two empires and amid the fragmentation of power in the West.[80]

In his rather twisted logic of suspicion, Dagron does contribute an important argument to the discussion. The Protestant Reformation of the sixteenth century reflected the political tensions between emerging national groups and centralized imperial authority, as well as the social and economic transformations caused by the Renaissance in late medieval Europe. In general, Protestant religious groups, particularly the Lutherans and Calvinists, aligned with local and national political authorities (emperors and princes) from Northern Europe who were seeking to break from the Catholic Church's tutelage. Similar issues of balance between power, responsibility, and interference that have characterized Byzantine and Roman church–state struggles were now being transferred to the level of national communities.

Almost prophetic in suggesting a line of thinking that would characterize Western thought on church–state separation, Martin Luther pushed to the point of paradox the distinction between the spiritual and the temporal realms. Based on the Augustinian "two kingdoms" doctrine, he developed his famous two-kingdom doctrine, which argued that a Christian who belonged to both the spiritual and temporal kingdoms is both absolutely free and absolutely enslaved.[81] For Luther, temporal rulers were arrogant in demanding a central role in the church's affairs, much in the same way as the popes who were claiming to be invested with a "power" and not simply a "function."[82] However, Luther was here concerned with something other than proving the lack of doctrinal basis for the separation of the two powers in the Western theological tradition.[83] Like his insistence on religious liberty and spiritual independence of the church, Luther's concern with balancing the "powers" was moderated by a need for state support and personal protection from the Catholic Church's persecution.[84] Thus, in his manifesto wherein the German nobility and princes are urged to reform the church, Luther conveniently stresses that the radical distinction between the temporal and spiritual does not lead to the recognition of two powers, and therefore there is no reason to refuse Christian princes the "titles of priest and bishop."[85] This is how Luther's pragmatic use of the doctrinal separation between the two powers came to be perceived in favor of both the Gelasian tradition of church–state separation and also of modern concepts like individual freedom and religious tolerance.[86]

Nevertheless, as James Wood stressed, religious freedom and church–state separation were not the immediate result of the Reformation, since most Protestant reformers looked backward rather than forward; they were revisers and conservers rather than innovators and rebels.[87] Unlike the patterns of the magisterial Reformation of the so-called "great comfortable sects" of the Roman Catholics, Lutherans, and Zwinglians, each depending upon the power of the sword,[88] the radical Reformation of the Mennonites, Anabaptists, and Spiritualists consisted of grassroots movements whose political thinking and practice enabled them to determine and regulate their social life.[89] It enabled them to criticize the immorality of the clerical elite (Catholic and Orthodox alike) and to reject civil society as Christian in a way that evaded Luther. Soon after the Reformation, as has been pointed out, the Northern European religious establishment changed from Catholicism to a Protestant endorsement of the political authorities that broke with the papacy, while religious freedom remained an ideal.[90]

Luther's paradoxical teaching on powers and use of the two-kingdom distinction had an important contribution to the rediscovery of an old principle brought forward by the Confession of Augsburg (1530), which is the doctrine of *cuius regio, ejus religio*, that each political entity should establish its own religious allegiance.[91] Literally meaning "whose rule, his religion," the principle stressed that the subjects of a prince were obliged forthwith to change their faith, if their sovereign for any reason changed his, or bequeathed, gave, sold, or ceded those subjects to another monarch of a different belief. The speculation that every society must have a religious identity that shapes its social ethos became not only a temporary solution to the religious conflicts of the sixteenth century, but also provided for the later emergence of modern nationalism.

Thus, the Protestant Reformation was not sufficiently capable of breaking with the pattern of church–state caesaropapism or papocaesarism, except in its radical forms inherent in the Reformation "sects," the Puritans and the Spiritualists. Although critical of the papacy and its abuse of power, the Reformed churches soon assumed the role previously played by the Catholic churches in a number of European countries. However, in the *cuius regio, ejus religio* doctrine is found the emergence of a crucial coupling between religious and national identity, which radically shaped the church–state distinction, both in Byzantium and the West, during the eighteenth and nineteenth centuries.

European Nationalism and Religion

The arguments that have been considered so far indicate that a common Orthodox understanding of church–state relations emphasizes the lack of a real difference between the symphonic model of Eastern Christendom and the Western Gelasian distinction model. However, as indicated, there is evidence to suggest an Orthodox admission of the fact that the Eastern symphony did not always follow Emperor Justinian's pattern of distinction and complementarity. Although some historians have attempted to dismiss such views by locating the origins of the caesaropapist charge in eighteenth and nineteenth-century German Protestantism, which projected the existence of such East-West dichotomy, this attempt does not account for the historical relationship of subordination characteristic of the Eastern Orthodox Empire. The goal thus far has been to underline the limitation of the historicist approaches and to argue that, after the dawn of the Enlightenment, church–state relations would take an important turn, with religion playing a new role in the modern nationalist states that began challenging the authority of the church and redefining its role.

The Construction of Nationalist Identities

The traditional general understanding has been that nationalism emerged in the European origins of the nation-state. Thus, the Treaty of Westphalia (1648) created the system of states that recognized each other's sovereignty and territory. Beginning with romantic nationalism and accelerated by the French Revolution, nationalist movements arose throughout Europe. Prior to the nationalist emancipation, these nation-states were thought to have been constituted solely by local, regional, or religious loyalties. Nationalism thus introduced the idea that each nation has a specific territory, and while in principle they would not seek to conquer, they rarely agreed on where the border should be. Moreover, nationalism is said to have introduced the struggle against older autocratic regimes, a struggle often carried by liberal antimonarchical movements.

This standard theory of the nineteenth-century origin of nation-states has been disputed by twentieth-century scholarship that underlined the existence of struggles for independence and national identities that predate most European nationalist movements, since countries such as the Netherlands and England seem to have had a clear national identity well before the nineteenth century.[92]

In his volume *Construction of Nationhood*, Hastings argues that the emergence of nationalism as being theoretically central to Western political thinking in nineteenth-century Europe could not have happened unless it had already existed as a powerful reality long before that.[93] He proceeds from there to an analysis of the formation of nationhood, ethnicity, nations, nation-states, and finally nationalism, arguing the crucial role played by religion in their formation. In distancing himself from the "modernist" view of nationalism represented by Gellner, Breuilly, Anderson, and Hobsbawm, Hastings notes that the categories they developed can be readily applicable to earlier periods of history, such as between the late fifteenth and eighteenth centuries, to describe forms of nationhood, while a sociological emphasis of these studies, such as found with Hutchinson, Greenfeld, and Smith, are much more useful at dismantling the modernists' presuppositions.[94] When using the "modernist" critique to make a point about England presenting the prototype of both a nation and a nation-state—detectable already in Saxon times, by the end of the tenth century—Hastings argues that the English model was the earliest in Europe, America, and elsewhere.[95]

Hastings presents a useful analysis of current theories of nationalism by pointing to a major omission, namely the lack of a stress on the importance played by religion in the formation of European national identities, ethnicities, and nation-states. As an integral element of many cultures, ethnicities, and states, religion has produced the dominant character of some state-shaped nations and nationalisms:

> Biblical Christianity both undergirds the cultural and political world out of which the phenomena of nationhood and nationalism as a whole developed and in a number of important cases provided a crucial ingredient for the particular history of both nations and nationalisms.[96]

Thus, unlike England, where Hastings would argue that a national consciousness had developed long before, the French Revolution brought to the fore that "powerful reality" that had existed with European peoples for many centuries.[97]

Whereas it was generally perceived to have been a movement against the church and religion in general (and in France, in particular), the Revolution served as a transition phase from ethnic religious identities to nationalist religious identities. The outburst of nationalist ideas that characterized this period led to a lasting change of the *status quo* in church–state relations in the whole of Europe.

The French Revolution

During the French Revolution, Europe experienced a transformation that has been compared with the conversion to Christianity, both in the Dark Ages and in the Reformation and Counter-Reformation.[98] The nationalist forces are said to have adapted and used religious symbols that ranged from secular catechisms to images of St. Joan of Arc, seeking to invest events and personalities, such as Giuseppe Garibaldi (1807–88), with vicarious sacredness.[99]

The French Revolution, which started as a reaction to the Catholic Church's abuses, and in search of a basis for public life that was independent of religious loyalty, gave birth to the doctrine of "liberalism."[100] This ideology translated into social and political transformations across Europe that saw the demise of monarchies in favor of democracies, as well as the emergence of religious freedom and tolerance for the Protestants in Catholic countries (France) and for Catholics in Protestant ones (Britain). By disrupting the balance between various European national governments and their religious establishments, the Revolution was continuing what the explosion of denominations and subsequent religious wars of the sixteenth and seventeenth centuries had already put in motion in Europe.

In the France of the Revolution, for the first time in the history of Europe, a state was said to have rejected traditional Christianity openly and actively. The providential state which stressed the divine right of kings offered an alternative culture to that traditionally promoted by the church, and began a process of de-Christianization of France. As Walter Lippmann stressed, the providential state was the result of the union of science and government, possessor of all knowledge and of the power to enforce it; it was the fulfilment of the Platonic vision when reason will be crowned and the sovereign will be rational.[101] According to Hobbes, the main thrust of the secularization process was the state's need for legitimization beyond religious disputes, putting the goals of the state before those of churches and religion.[102] The emancipated political thinking that emerged during the Enlightenment substituted the providential state for God and the church, while politics and economics were substituted for theology. This process of redefinition of modern humanity around the autonomous human being was thought to liberate the individual from the constraints of theology and religion.[103]

The radical stage of the French Revolution was short-lived as the church was allowed gradually to reemerge in society, this time much more under the control of the nationalist state.[104] The revolutionary nationalist and liberal forces undermined the historical roots that existed between the Catholic Church and the monarchy, as well as the close links Catholicism had in French society. Nevertheless, those who supported the Civil Constitution of the Clergy (1790), hoping that, following the modernization of the church the papacy would regain some of its lost privileges, undermined the irreversible change the Revolution brought about to the relationship between religion and politics.[105]

After the radical period of the National Convention (1792–95), the church would gradually re-emerge in France as tolerated during the Directory (1795–99), with the Concordat between Pope Pius VII and Napoleon Bonaparte (1801) finally normalizing the relationship between the papacy and the French state. Nonetheless, the civil constitution of the clergy reduced the status of the priests to simply state employees and, aided by the Declaration of the Rights of Man and Citizen (1789) and the abolition of the monarchy, the Catholic Church lost its status as the state religion, as confirmed by the French Constitution of 1791. The separation between church and state led to the founding of public education, which replaced religion as a subject of study with the 1789 Declaration, Constitution, and republican morality.

Despite the important changes the Revolution brought to French society, and its reverberations in other countries of Europe, the notion that states should have a common and unique religion remained pervasive. Hegel stressed this view when arguing that such a religion "expresses the innermost being of all people, so that all external and diffuse matters aside, they can find a common focus and, despite inequality and transformations in other spheres and conditions, are still able to trust and rely on each other."[106] The modern nationalist state assumed the role previously played by religion. As Burleigh noted, nationalism did not disturb the traditional religious beliefs of many people, because it was replaced by their patriotic faith, and the distinctions between the two could easily be blurred.[107] Nationalism fused with religion because priests and pastors played a vital role in their transmission, offering moral and spiritual connotations that were received well at a time when Christianity seemed under attack by the militant Jacobin godless.[108]

The "powerful reality" that has existed since before the French Revolution found a way eventually to accommodate the new European realities of the day. As Elie Kedourie stressed, nationalisms did not have tidy starting points and, as has been pointed elsewhere, countries like England would have developed national consciousness long before the industrial revolution.[109] Moreover, Ernest Gellner only strengthened this point when he argued that nationalisms were rarely invented out of thin air, but were "constructed" from preexisting components that included institutions, landscapes, language, law, particular religion, and the more rehearsed areas of myth and memory.[110]

As a result, while in a variety of Western European countries the official relationship between churches and nationalist states witnessed a diminishing of the authority of the established churches, many churches maintained their official state endorsements by means of adaptation and compromise with the new nationalist state.[111] Nevertheless, this adaptation process led to an increase in the power of the secular government that, in its extreme forms, gave birth to totalitarian states. As Hasting stressed: "The more the monism of Caesaropapism came to prevail within any ecclesiastical tradition, the more the church has subsequently given almost unlimited support to nationalism as well."[112]

Similar tendencies (*Kulturkampf*) concerning the place of the Catholic Church in public life ensued in parts of Germany with preponderantly Protestant majorities. In fact, in the nineteenth century this conflict was transferred to most of the Catholic and Orthodox countries in Europe where the alternatives swayed between the liberal anticlerical forces, the aim of which was to minimize the church's caesaropapist role, and the conservatives who supported the decision making role of the church in aspects like education and public policy. Until then, clubs and societies became centers of national consciousness, providing the institutional focus that Christianity derived from churches, although churches themselves were used as vehicles for propagating nationalist doctrines.[113]

With the propagation of the nationalist awakening across Europe, the countries from the Orthodox East experienced changes in church–state relations. Ethnicity and Orthodox religious identity merged with nationalist sentiment, giving birth to a nationalist-grounded religious identity. This coincided in many cases with the birth of the nation-states, which had the effect of sealing the caesaropapist relationship between the Orthodox Church and the state. As Hastings observed earlier, the closer the monism, the stronger was the tendency of the churches to support the nationalist state. Moreover, the more influential religion was to the ethnic constitution of a people, the more it was likely also to influence every expression of nationalism.[114] In the East, Hastings observed, a new nationalist religious identity was constructed from a combination of Orthodox faith, language, law and a caesaropapist view of church–state relations.

> The classical Eastern Orthodox form stressing the power of the emperor was in principle universalist enough in its vision of Constantinople as the 'New Rome', but in practice Byzantium became a rather narrowly Greek empire, alienating non-Greeks in Egypt, Syria or the west. This combined with its considerable degree of Caesaropapism led to the generation of a type of church–state relationship characteristic of Eastern autocephalous churches of a highly nationalist type.[115]

It is this highly nationalist type of church–state relations that will now be addressed, seeking to better understand the context in which Romanian Orthodoxy would fashion its nationalist religious self-identity later on.

Eastern Orthodox Nationalism

In the Orthodox East, important transformations took place beginning with the fifteenth century, after the final collapse of the Eastern Roman Empire

(1453) and the transfer of the Orthodox see to Moscow. The Russian Orthodoxy of the fifteenth century adopted a millennialist eschatological understanding, based upon which Moscow became the Christian Empire's Third Rome, capital of Holy Russia. According to Florovsky, under Russian influence Orthodoxy would soon take the form of a state religion that did away with the Justinian symphony model for triumphalist exaltation, harboring a populist self-perception of a Russian Christianity, sentimentalist and pietistic in character, whose Orthodoxy was to be found in the ritual and in the Russian soul rather than in church tradition.[116]

The social and political transformations emerging across Western Europe were gradually being experienced in the Orthodox East as well. The nationalist awakening of Western Europe reverberated into the Orthodox countries, especially after 1856, concomitant with the receding of Russian influence following the end of the Crimean War and the signing of the Treaty of Paris. The new social-political milieu was characterized in the East by a form of political religion in which, as Burleigh stressed, "sacred violence" was intrinsic to individuals who considered themselves to be "just" murderers on the grounds that their terror only affected the oppressors.[117] This political religion merged with totalitarianism during the Russian Revolution of 1917, giving birth to the Bolshevik and, subsequently, the Communist totalitarian regimes.

Religion was a powerful factor in the formation of nations and national identities. The Orthodox Church remained an important and influencing factor in this region of Europe, although in the case of Russia its influence in politics was very limited. The national awakening thus integrated the formation of the Eastern European states and the role played by the Orthodox churches, leading to a religious nationalist identity and identification of the church with the goals of the state.

Third Rome's Pseudomorphosis

In Russia, the effects of iconoclastic disputes had disturbed the balance between powers, particularly after the 1054 schism.[118] The theological crisis and the mystical Christianity that began to characterize Russian Orthodoxy reached a climax in the two emerging currents of nationalism and hesychasm.[119] Victoria Clark was right to observe that between 1054 and the twentieth century nationalism and hesychasm became the two main Orthodox modes of expression; the first was the external, social reaction to societal and political transformation, while the second was the internal, individual response when confronted with change.[120] Clumsy attempts by the Russian Patriarchate to rejuvenate a Justinian form of symphony notwithstanding, the Orthodox Church continued struggling to redefine its identity in a changing society that was preparing the way for centuries of revolutions.[121]

In an attempt at a Russian-style Protestant Reformation, Tsar Peter the Great (1682–1725) dispersed the Russian Patriarchate (1721), replacing it with the "Rule of Faith," which promoted the tsar as the indirect head of the Russian

Orthodox Church, with the church implicitly becoming an institution of the state.[122] During his reign, the Orthodox hierarchy was replaced by a Presbyterian type of leadership inspired by the Lutheran churches of Western Europe. However, this arrangement proved unsuccessful and led to the subordination of the church to the state. The eighteenth century theological reforms of the tsar's ecclesiastical adviser, Theophanes Prokopovich, amounted to what Florovsky called "Lutheranized Orthodoxy," unsuccessful attempts to achieve a pseudomorphosis between Western and Eastern Orthodox religions.[123]

With the signing of peace treaties between the Turks and Russians in 1829, Orthodox countries were beginning to experience "The Spring of Revolutions." The revolutionary ideas fuelling the liberal forces were sending reverberations across Europe, and concepts of national identity were penetrating Eastern European nations as well. In Russia, waves of modernity and secularization began shaping the nationalist state into an absolute monarchy, a nationalist providence-state after the French model. The political theology that resonated mostly with the Orthodox tsarist Russia included such ingredients as autocracy, rural populism (nationalism), and hesychasm.[124] According to Ioan Ică, Jr, these elements melted together into an ideological "systematization" to give birth to a conservative utopia that would be responsible for Slavophilism and later for Communism.[125]

Although the Russian Patriarchate in Moscow remained an important, though symbolic, influence in the Southern and Eastern part of Europe, its popularity was now much decreased. The decentralized nature of Orthodoxy accounted for the establishment of over 15 autocephalous national Orthodox churches in the eighteenth and nineteenth centuries.[126] This characteristic made it possible for Orthodox countries like Romania to separate from Russian Orthodox influence and become national entities.

Thus, despite the challenges facing Russian Orthodoxy under the tsar, other Orthodox churches in Eastern Europe could enjoy a somewhat uncharacteristic level of cooperation or symphony with the ruling princes. In places like the Romanian principalities strong control by the state had not ensued until the late eighteenth century. As Andrei Pippidi stressed, however formal the relationship, the patriarch gained authority over the ruler's obedience to the Orthodox ancient past, in exchange for the ruler's responsibility to decide who would be the next elected patriarch.[127] In addition, Orthodox churches maintained their own judicial courts as well as seats and influence alongside *boyars* (Romanian land-owners with a patent of nobility) on the highest tribunals of the land.[128]

Slavophilism

Toward the end of the nineteenth century the Russian Orthodox Church evidenced a lack of social and political engagement, the direct result of its caesaropapist submission to the ruler. The Russian intelligentsia had remained committed to the development of ideas derived from the perceived "true doctrines" of Russian Orthodoxy. At the center of this interest was the concept of *sobornost*, understood to define "community" as "individual diversity in free unity," meant as a Russian Orthodox alternative to inappropriate social models derived from Western Enlightenment individualism.[129]

Slavophilism developed as a movement advocating the uniqueness and superiority of Slavic culture in opposition to other, especially Western, forms of culture. Emerging in the nineteenth century, this intellectual movement was actually constituted from smaller movements or branches with similar slavophilist interests. The political options of the slavophils were not coherent; some moved left and advocated a progressive form of democracy (medieval Novgorod) while others pointed to the tsarist autocracy as representative of the Russian tradition.

Initiated by the Kireyevsky brothers, Ivan (1806–56) and Petr (1808–56), the movement would attract among its members Russian intellectuals such as the Aksakov brothers, Konstantin (1816–60) and Ivan (1823–86), Aleksei Khomyakov (1804–60), and others. The movement materialized in attempts to counter scholastic rationalism and German idealism with an interpretation of Russian Orthodox theology and practice.[130] Slavophilism was supposed to represent the break from the pseudomorphosis of the Russian soul with Western ideas, which would later give birth to the "neo-patristic synthesis" of George Florovsky, Vladimir Lossky, Dumitru Stăniloae, and others.[131] Lacking any form of social implication besides the praising of the Russian soul, Slavophilism became a conservative reaction to rationalism in the name of sentiment, against law and instituted rights in the name of love, and against capitalism and liberalism in the name of rural and traditional society.[132]

After 1825 the pseudomorphosis program had not caused the desired introduction of liberal Western-inspired reforms in Russia.[133] Therefore, the imperial government adopted a program that was somewhat similar to the Slavophile movement but was aimed at consolidating tsarist autocracy. It was summarized in 1832 by Count Uvarov as "Orthodoxy, autocracy and nationality," and guided the policies of the last two Russian tsars and of Konstantin Pobedonostsev (1827–1907), Procurator of the Holy Synod from 1880 to 1905 and a dedicated conservative.[134]

The Bolshevik Revolution

The political tensions characterizing Russian society were not isolated, but an indirect consequence of the Enlightenment, the influence of which would give birth to the Russian Revolution (1917) and subsequently to Communism. In the last decade of the nineteenth century, Russians began to polarize politically as increasingly extremist programs were adopted by the revolutionaries, and particularly with Marxism and materialism taking central stage in these programs. By the beginning of the century, the quest to bring Orthodox values to bear on pressing cultural, social, and even political questions took on a new urgency, which led to a reform of Orthodoxy.[135] Although some members of the hitherto positivist intelligentsia began to voice deep concern about the implications of such programs for human freedom, the Bolshevik movement had been set in place and there was no easy way of stopping it.

Jacob Talmon looked at the turn taken by the Russian Revolution and compared it with the Jacobin phase of the French Revolution[136] defining it as a form of "totalitarian democracy," opposed to liberal pragmatism.[137] Applying a psychoanalytical method to the revolutionary-Salvationist mentality he thought underpinned several radical causes, Talmon described the frame of mind of the Russian revolutionaries to have been one of an imposition of an ought-to-be world on reality. To paraphrase Talmon, clairvoyant revolutionary elite discerned the general will and the direction of history "guillotining into existence" their universal view of happiness until it consumed them.[138] Concerning the Bolshevik prototype, Russian philosopher Semyon Frank wrote: "This feeling of hatred for the enemies forms the concrete and active psychological foundation of his life. Thus the great love of mankind of the future gives birth to a great hatred for people; the passion for organizing an earthly paradise becomes a passion for destruction."[139] He mocked them as "military monks of the nihilistic religion of earthly contentment," and described them as "shunning reality, avoiding the world and living outside genuine historical everyday life in a world of phantoms, daydreams and pious faith."[140]

The early forms of Bolshevism could be seen in the more advanced sections of the intelligentsia, often describing themselves as "new men," a term that suggested baptism into a new moral mode of being whose corollary was sometimes the rejection of moral discernment in general.[141] Emerging in the context of the intergenerational struggle waged within the Russian post-slavophilist intelligentsia in the 1860s, the "new man" was often an activist, a totally politicized type of moral personality, the forerunner of Bolshevism's "leather men in leather jackets." They included Nikolai Chernyshevsky (1828–89), Nikolai Dobrolyubov (1836–61), and Ivan Turgenev (1818–83).

Chernyshevsky's novel, *What is to be Done?* (1863), had a significant impact on Vladimir I. Lenin (1870–1924), founder of the Marxist Russian Social-Democratic Labor Party (RSDLP), which split from the Menshevik faction at the Second Party Congress in 1903, and ultimately became the Communist Party of the Soviet Union.[142] The Bolsheviks were thus an organization of professional revolutionaries possessing a strict internal hierarchy governed by the principle of democratic centralism and quasi-military discipline. They considered themselves a vanguard of the revolutionary proletariat, and were led into the October Revolution by Lenin. The Bolsheviks militated for a strongly centralized hierarchy and sought to overthrow the tsar and achieve power. A rigid adherence to the leadership of the central committee, based on the notion of democratic centralism, was their party's main characteristic. While the Menshevik faction favored open party membership and desire for cooperation with other (non-) socialist groups in Russia, the Bolsheviks generally refused to cooperate with liberal or radical parties (which they labeled "bourgeois") or even, eventually, with other socialist organizations.

The Communist Party of the Soviet Union, known later simply as the Communist Party, became the model for most other socialist parties in Europe that converted to Communism. Following on the Marxist orientation of the Bolsheviks, Communism advocated for a process of class conflict and revolutionary struggle that would result in victory for the proletariat and the establishment of a Communist society in which private ownership is abolished over time and the means of production and subsistence are transferred to the community.[143] Like Nazism in Germany, Communism combined religious ideas with scientifically proven concepts and aimed at subversively replacing traditional Christian theological virtues that have been the source for modern liberal and democratic ideas.[144] It was the result of the ideological "innocence," as used by Stephen Koch to refer to the new socialist and revolutionary humanism that was exploiting the defeat of the ideas of divine and natural law (theodicy) at the hands of Empiricism, Positivism, Marxism, Relativism, Nihilism, etc.[145]

The illusion of the twentieth century was that politics had taken the central stage of moral life, thus giving birth to the "political theodicy," understood as the transferring of the debates of rational theology unto the pragmatic field of politics. According to Dan Pavel, "political theodicy" defined the efforts of the Bolshevik political engineers to substitute God by converting theological discourse into political discourse without leaving the sphere of religion.[146] Thus, the party and the leader were described as possessing the infallibility and divine perfection once ascribed to God.[147]

The paradox was that while the Russian Orthodox Church was integral to tsarism, the Bolsheviks were militant atheists, although not without a surrogate religiosity of their own. As philosopher Nikolai Berdyaev wrote: "Just as pious mystics once strove to make themselves into an image of God, and finally to become absorbed in Him, so now the modern ecstatics of rationalism labour to become like the machine and finally to be absorbed into bliss in a structure of driving belts, pistons, valves and fly-wheels."[148]

The Bolshevik Revolution, combining political theodicy with unresolved yet violently repressed social tensions amid a latent, politically subservient, and socially irrelevant Orthodox Church, led to the victory of Communist forces in Russia and to the emergence of almost a century of horror, evil, and violence across Europe.

Communism as Political Religion

The problem with Marxist Communism was that it completely dismissed the traditional sources of Western and Eastern European identity. As a form of totalitarian "political religion" its ideology replaced and homogenized the separated domains and values that have emerged out of the two parts of Europe.

As British philosopher Bertrand Russell sarcastically noted upon his travels to post–World War I Russia:

> The hopes which inspire Communism are, in the main, as admirable as those instilled by the Sermon on the Mount, but they are held as fanatically, and are likely to do as much harm. . . . The war has left throughout Europe a mood of disillusionment and despair which calls aloud for a new religion, as the only force capable of giving men the energy to live vigorously. Bolshevism has supplied the new religion. It promises glorious things.[149]

According to Ioan Ică, Jr, Western liberalism, capitalism, and democracy that had given birth to a society separating the religious and the political were being perverted by an illegitimate mixing between religion and politics into a mold of secularized religion and sanctified politics.[150] Although a process similar to German Nazism, Communism and its Marxist extreme ideology developed amid a context characterized by the Russian Orthodox "symbiosis" between religion and politics. Combined, the Jacobin and Bolshevik ideologies used the medieval type of clericalism to motivate their political cynicism with the thesis of the nationalist state as a "system," and the church as a "subsystem," dispensable, and controlled by strict laws.[151] This combination led to Communism emerging as a perversion of Christianity just like Nazism; the deified nation and the total state were being molded into secular divinities placed at the center of lay theocracies that cancelled individual liberty.[152]

The fate of the Orthodox countries of the Europe of the nineteenth and twentieth centuries, prisoners to extremist ideologies sweeping across cultures, was to encounter a form of nationalist state where control of the churches was maintained for political ends. As Wogaman pointed out, Joseph Stalin's (1878–1953) sudden accommodation of the Russian Orthodox Church after the German invasion in 1941 had less to do with a softening of the generally hostile attitude of the state toward religion and more with a need for national unity in time of crisis.[153] Similar attempts to rally religion behind war efforts in various European countries during World War I showed the politicians' predisposition to use and exploit the presence of the church in society for political legitimization or other pragmatic ends.

The problem with this nationalist form of church submission was that, by absolutizing the political ends, it involved a rejection of the transcendence of God. When the state itself is regarded to be the highest good, two major changes take place: The state becomes God, and the integrity of the church along with other religious institutions is undermined.[154] However, this realization only serves to underline that the integrity of the church must always be a matter of theological struggle. As it will be argued in the following chapters, the loss of church integrity during Communism was generated by this combination of nationalism and caesaropapism that would gain prominence in Marxist-Communist countries like Romania.

Conclusion

The investigation of the history and tradition surrounding the emergence of the caesaropapist thesis has revealed two focal points in the conceptualization and development of both Eastern Orthodox and Western Catholic and Protestant European church–state relations. This chapter has shown that the caesaropapist charge has generated polemics in Romanian society along the line of the Huntingtonian thesis, and has reopened questions about the caesaropapist Byzantine heritage of Romanian Orthodoxy. The investigation went on to describe the Orthodox response to the caesaropapist challenge, noting the logic of their historicist approach. The first important aspect of this analysis has been to point out the limitation of the historicist approach in providing a defense against charges of political subordination of the church, especially in the Eastern Empire. By stressing the significant changes that occurred with the emergence of post-Enlightenment nationalism, the analysis shows how they transformed irreversibly the relations between the traditional role of authority, played by the church, and the place of religion. Having shown that the new political milieu characterized by the transcendent nationalist state led to tensions between religion and politics all across Europe, this analysis was then applied to the history of this relationship as it unfolded in Eastern Orthodox Russia. Here were indicated the close ties maintained by the Orthodox Church with Tsarist Russia as evidenced by Tsar Peter's failed attempts to achieve a cultural and political pseudomorphosis. Furthermore, this exploration provided a sketch of the ideological context in which Slavophilism and Bolshevism would lead to the emergence of Communism as a political religion.

The second goal of this investigation has been to underline the crucial role played, after the French Revolution, by religion in relation to nationalism. Thus, it was shown that in the case of Tsarist and Bolshevik Russia, the tradition of caesaropapism has had a negative impact on the particular form of nationalism that it fashioned, and which has emerged as a reaction against it. The Bolshevik movement has, therefore, been detrimental to the Orthodox Church and has generated extreme nationalistic ideologies that attempted to replace religion and, thus, became political religions. This analysis will be continued in the next chapter, in which it will emphasize the particular case of Romania and how the ideological coupling of religion and nationalism concretized in the eighteenth- and nineteenth-century efforts characterizing the emergence of Romanian nationalist self-identity as a nation and state. The key aspects emphasized in the analysis of the formation of the caesaropapist Romanian Orthodoxy will be the shift of perception and the mythologizing of its own past in order to secure the church's identification with the modern state. This will elucidate further how the collaboration of the church with the Communist regime and the theological symbiosis of Orthodoxy and Marxism was achieved. The "Romanian solution" will thus reveal a certain continuity with the peculiar homogeneity of Orthodoxy, Romanianness, and law, culminating in the unprecedented social apostolate developed under the nationalist pressure of the Marxist regime.

Notes

1. Tom Inglis, "Understanding Religion and Politics" in Tom Inglis, et al., eds., *Religion and Politics: East-West Contrasts from Contemporary Europe* (Dublin: University College Dublin Press, 2000), p. 1.
2. Emil Brunner, *The Divine Imperative* (Philadelphia: Westminster Press, 1947), p. 552.
3. Cf. Stephen V. Monsma, J. Christopher Soper, *The Challenge of Pluralism: Church and State in Five Democracies* (Lanham: Rowman & Littlefield, 1997).
4. J. Philip Wogaman, *Christian Perspectives on Politics* (Louisville: Westminster John Knox Press, 2000), pp. 249–74.
5. I. Dumitru-Snagov, *Relațiile Stat- Biserică*, pp. 48–50.
6. R. Preda, *Biserica în Stat*, pp. 102–26.
7. R. Preda, *Biserica în Stat*, p. 43. The *Oxford English Dictionary* defines subsidiarity as the idea that a central authority should have a subsidiary function, performing only those tasks that cannot be performed effectively at a more immediate or local level.
8. Ecumenical Patriarch Bartholomew I, "L'apport de L'eglise Orthodoxe a la Construction de L'europe," in *Service Orthodoxe de Presse*, 190 (July–Aug 1994), pp. 24–5.
9. R. Preda, *Biserica în Stat*, p. 43.
10. Stan and Turcescu, *Religion and Politics*, p. 10.
11. Glanzer and Petrenko have pointed out that the Russian government treats state-sponsored education following the model of strict separation but when it comes to religious education it employs a form of managed historical pluralism. Perry L. Glanzer and Konstantin Petrenko, "Religion and Education in Post-Communist Russia: Making Sense of Russia's New Church–State Paradigm," paper presented at the International Symposium "Church and State in Eastern Europe," Iași, Romania, September 2005.
12. Stan and Turcescu, *Religion and Politics*, p. 12.
13. Stan and Turcescu, *Religion and Politics*, pp. 36–9.
14. O. Gillet, *Religie și Naționalism*, p. 17.
15. Cf. Samuel P. Huntington, *The Clash of Civilizations and the Remaking of World Order* (New York: Simon & Schuster, 1997).
16. S. Huntington, *Clash of Civilizations*, pp. 70ff, 163–8.
17. The concept of "pseudomorphosis" is introduced by Spengler as a way of explaining what are in his view half-developed or only partially manifested cultures. Applied to Russia, Spengler thought Peter the Great's reforms forced Russia into an artificial history before its culture was ready, or capable of understanding its burden, hence "pseudomorphosis" or pseudo-transformation. Cf. Oswald Spengler, *The Decline of the West* (London: Allen and Unwin, 1961).
18. O. Spengler, *Decline of the West*, pp. 265ff.
19. Arnold Toynbee, *Studiu asupra istoriei*, Sinteză de D.C. Somervell, vol. 2 (București: Editura Humanitas, 1997), pp. 109–67.

20 Berman questions whether there are clearly defined cultural boundaries today and argues that conflict arises based on philosophical beliefs between groups, regardless of cultural or religious identity. Likewise in the case of "Islamic civilization" or "Western civilization" and the civilizations that clash with them, Berman is suggesting a consideration of the relationships between the United States and Saudi Arabia as a disclaimer to the theory. Paul Berman, *Terror and Liberalism* (London: W. W. Norton & Company, Ltd., 2003), pp. 78ff.

21 Andrej Tusicisny, "Civilizational Conflicts: More Frequent, Longer, and Bloodier?" in *Journal of Peace Research*, vol. 41 No. 4 (2004), pp. 485–98.

22 Edward Said argued against Huntington's categorization because it omits the dynamic interdependency and interaction of culture. According to Said, this creates an "imagined geography," where certain politics are legitimated through a certain type of presentation of the world. Cf. Edward Said, "The Clash of Ignorance" in *The Nation* (22 October, 2001). Bruce Russett stressed that values are more easily transmitted and altered than Huntington proposes. Also, by looking at the examples of India and Japan, which have become successful democracies, Huntington's theses are disproved as generating self-fulfilling prophecies and reasserting civilizational differences. Bruce Russett, et al., "Clash of Civilizations, or Realism and Liberalism Déjà Vu? Some Evidence," in *Journal of Peace Research* vol. 37, No. 5 (2000), pp. 583–608.

23 Bishop Basil Osborne, "Orthodoxy in a United Europe: The Future of Our Past" in *Orthodox Christianity and Contemporary Europe* by Jonathan Sutton, Wil van den Bercken, eds. (Leuven: Uitgeverij Peeters, 2003), p. 3.

24 Nonka Bogomilova, "Eastern Orthodoxy: The New Age and the Old Myths" in *Orthodox Christianity and Contemporary Europe*, p. 23.

25 The translation of Huntington's "Clash of Civilizations" generated a lot of debate in the press and among academics. An abundance of studies and critical evaluations addressing the implication of the author's theses for Romania emerged in a short time. Cf. Samuel P. Huntington, *Ciocnirea civilizațiilor și refacerea ordinii mondiale* (Oradea: Editura Antet, 1998) which includes additional responses by Radu Carp, Iulia Moțoc, et al.

26 D. Năstase, "Secularizare și Religie în Integrarea Europeană," p. 240. Other commentators who make this distinction include Stjepan G. Mestrovic, *Habits of the Balkan Heart: Social Character and the Fall of Communism* (College Station: Texas A& M University Press, 1993); A. Georgiev, E. Tzenkov, "The Troubled Balkans" in *Redefining Europe New Patterns of Conflict and Co-operation*, Hugh Miall, ed. (London: Royal Institute of International Affairs, 1994). A typical approach to the use of Huntington's theses to explain Orthodoxy's cultural inferiority is Dragoș Petrescu, "Biserica Ortodoxa Română sub regimul comunist" in *Teologie și Politică: De la Sfinții Părinți la Europa Unită*, by Miruna Tătaru-Cazaban, ed. (București: Editura Anastasia, 2004), pp. 194–208.

27 Alexandru Zub, Sorin Antohi, *Oglinzi Retrovizoare: Istorie, memorie și morală în România* (Iași: Editura Polirom, 2002), p. 84. A similar point has been made by Sandu Frunză, who adds that Huntington's demarcation line following the Carpathian curve is also misleading, as Transylvania has a large Orthodox presence as well, which is difficult to be accounted for in the American sociologist's speculative theory. Sandu Frunză, "Statul național și politicile multiculturale" in *JSRI*, No.5 (Summer 2003), p. 55.

28 Nonetheless, since the publication of his defense against Orthodoxy's "detractors" Antohi, a formerly renowned historian, essayist, and journalist, has been shockingly revealed to have been a secret police informant and subsequently discredited. Cf. Cristian Pătrășconiu, "Sorin Antohi: Am turnat la Securitate" in *Cotidianul* (5 September 2006).
29 Stan and Turcescu, *Religion and Politics*, p. 7.
30 Stan and Turcescu, *Religion and Politics*, p. 7.
31 Stan and Turcescu, *Religion and Politics*, p. 7.
32 Titu Maiorescu, *Critice*, vol. I (București, 1967), p. 147.
33 Cf. Nicolae Iorga, *Bizanț după Bizanț* (București: Editura Gramar, 2005), p. 6.
34 N. Iorga, *Bizanț după Bizanț*, pp. 6–9.
35 Valentin Al. Georgescu, *Bizanțul și Instituțiile Românești până la mijlocul sec. al XVIII-lea* (București, 1980), p. 289.
36 Andrei Pippidi, *Tradiția politică bizantină în Țările Române în sec. XVI-XVIII* (București: Editura Corint, 2001), p. 215.
37 Deno Geanakoplos, "Church and State in the Byzantine East: A Reconsideration of the Problem of Caesaropapism" in *Church History*, vol. 34, No. 4 (December, 1965), p. 381.
38 In Encyclopaedia Britannica, such a definition is mistakenly ascribed to "caesaropapism." "Caesaropapism" in *Encyclopædia Britannica* (2007). [Online] Available at: http://www.britannica.com /eb/article-9018527 , accessed March 2004.
39 Philip Wogaman noted that the Eastern Orthodox Empire was never characterized by a mere subordination of the church to the state. Cf. Philip Wogaman, "The Changing Role of Government and the Myth of Separation" in *Journal of Church and State*, vol. 5 No. 1 (May 1963), p. 251.
40 "Caesaropapism" in *Oxford Dictionary of the Christian Church*, edited by F.L. Cross and E.A. Livingstone, 2nd ed. (Oxford: Oxford University Press, 1983), p. 218.
41 O. Gillet, *Religie și Naționalism*, pp. 17–18.
42 Concerning Romania, such views make the subject of historical studies such as: Keith Hitchins, *The Romanians, 1774–1866* (Oxford: Clarendon Press, 1996); Andrei Banțaș, *The Romanian Orthodox Church Yesterday and Today* (București, 1979); A. Pippidi, *Tradiția Politică Bizantină*, p. 215.
43 Adrian Hastings, *Church and State: The English Experience* (Exeter: University of Exeter Press, 1991), p. 8.
44 A. Hastings, *Church and State*, p. 8.
45 The conquest of the West Roman Empire by the Alaric invasion (410) signified not only a changing political circumstance but an economic one, especially for the church. Thus, the indirect result of this economic collapse was that the church could be independent from the state in a way that would not be possible in the Eastern Roman Empire.
46 Acacius, Patriarch of Constantinople, compiled an edict known as the Henotikon (482), which was supposed to clarify the Christological controversy of Nestorianism. However, because the papacy in Rome was not consulted, Acacius and the Eastern patriarch were excommunicated by Rome, giving way to the first schism between east and west, which lasted for 34 years. The schism brought forward the issue of jurisdiction over the church, with Acacius claiming to have it with regard to the Greek churches and Pope Gelasius I (492–6) countering the Byzantine conciliar ecclesiology with the apostolic succession of St. Peter in Rome.

Henry Chadwick, *East and West: The Making of a Rift in the Church: From Apostolic Times until the Council of Florence* (Oxford: Oxford University Press, 2003), pp. 50–1

47 "There are two things, august emperor, by which this world is principally ruled: the sacred authority of the pontiffs and the royal power (*auctoritas sacrata pontificum et regalis postestas*)." Pope Gelasius I, in a letter to Emperor Anastasios, in "Epistle 12," edited by Andreas Thiel, *Epistolae Romanorum pontificum genuinae*, vol. 1 (Brunsbergae, 1868), pp. 350–2.

48 Cf. Saint Augustine, Bishop of Hippo, "The City of God," in *Nicene and Post-Nicene Fathers*, Alexander Roberts and James Donaldson, eds., revised edition, vol. II (Peabody, MA: Hendrickson, 1994), pp. 1–511.

49 Pope Innocent III, "Letter to the prefect Acerbius and the nobles of Tuscany" (1198). [Online] Available at: http://www.fordham.edu/halsall/source/innIII-policies.html, accessed April 2006.

50 Bert Roest, "Franciscan Views on Papal and Royal Sovereignty: A case for a contextual approach" in *Franciscan Authors, seventeenth to eighteenth Century: A Catalogue in Progress* (2006) [Online] Available at http://users.bart.nl/~roestb/franciscan/GILLEEDS.html , accessed August 2006.

51 The consequences of this were drawn by the Dominican John of Paris, who in his work *De Potestate Regia et Papali* (ca. 1301), gave religious and secular authority different tasks and different spheres, and placed the origin of secular authority in natural law, making it, in principle, independent from the church, except for matters of faith and doctrine. B. Roest, "Franciscan Views."

52 According to Fergusson, the organic unity of church and political society is settled and affirmed in Thomas Aquinas's writings, where we find a consonance of interest and a coordination of temporal and spiritual functions as each serves the divine law. In this respect, for Aquinas the temporal must serve the spiritual just as the body serves the soul, while kings in Christendom must remain subject to the Pope as to Christ himself. David Fergusson, *Church, State and Civil Society* (Cambridge: Cambridge University Press, 2004), p. 33.

53 The three popes mentioned here are John XXIII, Gregory XII, and Benedict XIII. Cf. Serge Berstein, Pierre Milza, *Istoria Europei*, vol.3 (Iași: Institutul European, 1998), pp. 38–42

54 Owen Chadwick, *A History of Christianity* (New York: St. Martin's Press, 1995), pp. 288–90.

55 John Meyendorff, *Byzantine Theology* (New York: Fordham University Press, 1974), p. 193.

56 Karl Barth stressed this important theological concept in the Barmen Declaration. See the discussion in chapter 6.

57 Runciman notes that the very name of "Byzantium" encompassed the idea of an empire in which church and state were completely merged. Steven Runciman, *The Orthodox Churches and the Secular State* (Auckland: Auckland Univ. Press, 1971), p. 13.

58 Stanley S. Harakas, "Orthodox Church–State Theory and American Democracy" in *Greek Orthodox Theological Review*, vol. XXI, no. 4 (Winter 1976), p. 399.

59 Oliver O'Donovan, *The Desire of the Nations: Rediscovering the Roots of Political Theology* (Cambridge: Cambridge University Press, 1996), p. 167. Cf. also O. O'Donovan, Joan L. O'Donovan, eds., *From Irenaeus to Grotius: A Sourcebook of Christian Political Thought 100–1625* (Grand Rapids, Cambridge: Eerdmans, 1999).

60 O. O'Donovan, *Desire of the Nations*.
61 Bishop Kallistos Timothy Ware, *The Orthodox Church* (Harmondsworth: Penguin, 1963), p. 49.
62 T. Ware, *Orthodox Church*.
63 John Meyendorff, *The Byzantine Legacy in the Orthodox Church* (New York: St. Vladimir Seminary Press, 2001), p. 50.
64 J. Meyendorff, Byzantine Legacy.
65 Sergius Bulgakov, *The Orthodox Church* (New York: St. Vladimir's Seminary Press, 1988), p. 157.
66 S. Bulgakov, *Orthodox Church*.
67 Bulgakov did eventually admit that in the centuries following Justinian, the symphony was often disrupted by false tunes emperors sang in the Byzantine history. S. Bulgakov, *Orthodox Church*, pp. 157–59.
68 Deno Geanakoplos, "Church and State in the Byzantine East," p. 390.
69 T. Ware, *Orthodox Church*, p. 49.
70 Alexander Schmemann, *The Historical Road of Eastern Orthodoxy* (London: Harvill Press, 1963), p. 69.
71 A. Schmemann, *Historical Road*.
72 A. Schmemann, *Historical Road*, p. 145. See also S. Bulgakov, *Orthodox Church*, p. 156.
73 A. Schmemann, *Historical Road*, p. 146.
74 Papocaesarism is the opposite of caesaropapism, that is, the subjection of the state to the church. For an elaborate discussion on the distinction between caesaropapism and papocaesarism, see John S. Romannides, "The Orthodox Churches on Church–State Relations and Religious Liberty" in *Readings on Church and State*, edited by James E. Wood, Jr. (Waco: J.M.D. Institute of Church–State Studies, 1989), pp. 255–64.
75 A. Hastings, *Church and State*, p. 21.
76 Gilbert Dagron, *Emperor and Priest. The Imperial Office in Byzantium*, translated by Jean Birrell (Cambridge: Cambridge University Press, 2003), p. 8.
77 G. Dagron, *Emperor and Priest*.
78 Reference is here made to Halle University professor Iustus Henning Bohmer (1674–1749) who devoted a passage in his Protestant ecclesiastical law textbook to the principles of "Papo-caesaria" and "Caesaro-Papia." G. Dagron, *Emperor and Priest*. p. 283.
79 G. Dagron, *Emperor and Priest*.
80 G. Dagron, *Emperor and Priest*, p. 9.
81 Cf. Martin Luther, "Of the Liberty of a Christian Man" (1520); "Of Temporal Authority" (1523). [Online] Available at: http://www.fordham.edu/halsall/mod/luther-freedomchristian.html , accessed May 2004.
82 Cf. Martin Luther, "To the Christian Nobility of the German Nation" (1520). [Online] Available at: http://www.iclnet.org/pub/resources/text/wittenberg/luther/ web/nblty-01.html , accessed May, 2004.
83 Gilbert Dagron argued misleadingly on this point that Luther's manifesto to the German princes concludes that the separation of the two powers had no basis. He is nevertheless right to point that Lutheranism often evolved into caesaropapism. G. Dagron, *Emperor and Priest*, p. 284.

84 Luther needed the civil protection of the German princes because of his precarious relationship with the Catholic Church, which reached a climax in 1521 when he was excommunicated.
85 Martin Luther, "To the Christian Nobility of the German Nation," p. 1.
86 Fergusson makes a case for Luther's political theology seen as transitional between the medieval and the modern period. However, he seems to underestimate Luther's complete dependence on and thus servitude to the German princes, as well as overstates Luther's goals as seeking to "reform the Christendom, the whole of the civilized Christian world." D. Fergusson, *Church, State and Civil Society*, pp. 36–45.
87 James Wood, et al., *Church and State in Scripture, History, and Constitutional Law* (Waco: Baylor University Press, 1958), p. 67.
88 Menno Simons, quoted in Timothy George, *The Theology of the Reformers* (Nashville: Broadman Press, 1988), p. 285.
89 For more on the political thought of the radical Reformers see Michael G. Baylor, ed., *The Radical Reformation* (Cambridge: Cambridge University Press, 1991).
90 The support of the Reformation by the Scandinavian princes led to Protestant churches now inheriting the legal protection Catholic churches once enjoyed. Catholic Church properties were confiscated by the monarch, while the new established religion was kept under strong governmental control. Derek Davis, "An Historical Overview of Church–State Relations in Northern Europe" in *Religious Liberty in Northern Europe in the Twenty-First Century*, Derek H. Davis, ed. (Waco: Baylor University, 2000), p. 5.
91 This doctrine was reasserted a century later during the Treaty of Westphalia (1648) which became the general rule for most of Western Europe into the eighteenth century. D. Davis, "Historical Overview," p. 4.
92 Cf. Benedict Anderson, *Imagined Communities*, 2nd ed. (London: Verso, 1991). Anderson argues that nations are imagined political communities, and are imagined to be limited and sovereign. Their development is related to the decline of other types of imagined community, especially in the face of capitalist production of print media. John Breuilly, *Nationalism and the State*, 2nd ed. (Manchester: Manchester University Press, 1992). This approach focuses on the politics of nationalism, in particular on nationalism as a response to the imperatives of the modern state. It employs the mode of comparative history to study numerous cases of nationalism. Ernest Gellner, *Nations and Nationalism* (Oxford: Blackwell, 1983). This work links nationalism to the homogenizing imperatives of industrial society and the reactions of minority cultures to those imperatives. Liah Greenfeld, *Nationalism: Five Roads to Modernity* (Cambridge, MA: Harvard University Press, 1992). Greenfeld argues that nationalism existed at an earlier age than previously thought: as early as the sixteenth century in the case of England. Eric Hobsbawm, and Terence Ranger, eds., *The Invention of Tradition* (Cambridge: Cambridge University Press, 1983). This collection of essays, especially Hobsbawm's introduction and chapter on turn-of-the-century Europe, argues that the nation is a prominent type of invented tradition. Elie Kedourie, ed. *Nationalism in Asia and Africa* (London: Weidenfeld and Nicolson, 1971). Kedourie's introduction to this volume of nationalist texts extends his analysis in his earlier work to the efforts of intellectuals in colonial states. Anthony D. Smith, *The Ethnic Origins of*

Nations (Oxford: Blackwell, 1986). Smith traces modern nations and nationalism to pre-modern ethnic sources, arguing for the existence of an "ethnic core" in modern nations.

[93] Adrian Hastings, *The Construction of Nationhood: Ethnicity, Religion, Nationalism* (Cambridge: Cambridge University Press, 1997), p. 4.

[94] A. Hastings, *Construction of Nationhood*, p. 8. Cf. John Hutchinson, *Modern Nationalism* (London: Fontana, 1994).

[95] A. Hastings, *Construction of Nationhood*, pp. 9–10.

[96] A. Hastings, *Construction of Nationhood*, p. 4.

[97] In his study of English nationhood, Hastings makes a case for the presence of a form of national consciousness in the England of the tenth century.

[98] Michael Burleigh, *Earthly Powers: Religion and Politics in Europe from the Enlightenment to the Great War* (London: Harper Perennial, 2006), p. 145.

[99] M. Burleigh, *Earthly Powers*.

[100] The liberal doctrine rested on the distinction between civil society and the state, which according to Rousseau was only possible because of a third term, "society," in which civil society and state have their source and foundation. Pierre Manent, *An Intellectual History of Liberalism* (Princeton: Princeton University Press, 1994), pp. 80–3.

[101] See Walter Lippmann, *The Good Society* (New Jersey: Transaction Publishers, 2005), p. 22.

[102] The citizens' fear of being killed is what motivates them to support a social contract in which the right to kill is transferred to the state. The state thus becomes an earthly god whose authority discourages violence among citizens, by channelling their urge for religious polemics toward a competitive behaviour in the capitalist economy. Hobbes wrote: "[N]o one can lay down the right of defending himself against the threat of death, wounds, imprisonment—the natural right to all things is laid down for the sake of avoiding them." Cf. Thomas Hobbes, *The Leviathan*, Oxford World's Classics (Oxford: Oxford University Press, 1996), p. 90 (par. 14.28)

[103] In his study on *Christianity and Liberal Society*, Robert Song summarizes well the influence that philosophical thought of Hobbes, Machiavelli, Rousseau, Montesquieu, Kant and Hegel as well as Marx and Nietzsche to the relationship between Christian religion and politics. Cf. Robert Song, *Christianity and Liberal Society* (Oxford: Clarendon Press, 1997).

[104] Ulrich Ruh stressed that the radical Revolution was short-lived and in the long run the Catholic Church was helped in the transition from feudal system of organization to a structure adapted to the modern state. It is unclear, in my view, to what extent the Catholic Church did eventually adapt, given its antimodern reactions in the nineteenth and twentieth centuries. One can hardly talk about a "modern" Catholic Church before the Second Vatican Council. Cf. Ulrich Ruh, "Europa și Secularizarea: Trăsăturile Principale ale Unui Proces cu Multe Fațete" in *Un Suflet pentru Europa*, Radu Carp, ed. (București: Editura Anastasia, 2005), p. 3. Cf. Sheridan Gilley, "The Papacy" in Ulrich Ruh and Brian Stanley, eds., *World Christianities, c. 1815–c. 1914* (Cambridge: Cambridge University Press, 2006), pp. 1–29.

[105] As Gianpaolo Romanato stressed, both traditions that met in the French Revolution suffered from abstraction and idealism. The revolutionary, anti-religious,

and secularizing forces could not realize that it was impossible to achieve a completely separatist state without giving birth to a totalitarian state. On the other hand, the adjudicators of a national church could not understand that an arrangement such as altar-throne was no longer possible in a disestablished France. Gianpaolo Romanato, "Biserica şi Statul Laic" in Ioan P. Culianu, et al., *Religie şi Putere* (Bucureşti: Editura Nemira, 1996), pp. 14–5. Cf. also P. Wogaman, "Changing Role of Government."

106 Georg W. F. Hegel, "Die Verfassung Deutschland" in G. Hegel, *Politische Schriften*, edited by Hans Blumenberg (Frankfurt am Main: Suhrkamp, 1966), p. 37.

107 M. Burleigh, *Earthly Powers*, p. 145.

108 M. Burleigh, *Earthly Powers*, p. 153.

109 E. Kedourie, *Nationalism in Asia and Africa*, p. 1.

110 Ernest Gellner, *Chosen Peoples: Sacred Sources of National Identity* (Oxford: Oxford University Press, 2003), pp. 115ff.

111 This was the case with the Lutheran Church in Scandinavia, the Calvinist in Scotland, the Anglican in Britain, while in Holland, Switzerland, and Austria the predominant religion held positions of distinction, though not officially established. D. Davis, "A Historical Overview," p. 5.

112 A. Hastings, *Construction of Nationhood*, p. 204.

113 M. Burleigh, *Earthly Powers*, p. 161.

114 A. Hastings, *Construction of Nationhood*, p. 187.

115 *Construction of Nationhood*, p. 202.

116 Cf. George Florovski, *Christianity and Culture*, vol. 2 (Belmont: Nordland Publishing Co., 1974), p. 187.

117 M. Burleigh, *Earthly Powers*, p. 276.

118 The unsteady balance between the church and the state after the symphonic model was disturbed by the iconoclastic controversy. In this context, at least two emperors, Leo III (717–41) and Constantine V (741–75), claimed total supremacy over both the spiritual and the temporal powers in an attempt to establish imperial control over all the manifestations of religious life in Byzantium.

119 Hesychasm is a spiritual tradition associated with Mt. Athos, emphasizing inner stillness through the practice of the prayer of the heart. Its theological connotations consist of a distinction between God's "essence" and his "uncreated" energies. Regarding the crisis, the main actors of this theological controversy were Patriarch Joseph of Volokolamsk (1439–1515) and Nil of Sorsk (1433–1508). Whereas Patriarch Joseph and his supporters employed the state to fight heresy in the church, Patriarch Nil showed a tolerant attitude toward heretics and tried to contain the problem within the church. Nevertheless, the latter was unable to impose its approach and the practice employed by Patriarch Joseph became the norm of church–state cooperation for centuries to come. Cf. Georgii Petrovich Fedotov, *A Treasury of Russian Spirituality: Reflections from the Revolutions* (London: Sheed and Ward, 1950), p. 164.

120 V. Clark, *Why Angels Fall: A Journey through Orthodox Europe from Byzantium to Kosovo* (London: Picador, 2001), pp. 414–5.

121 Patriarch Nikon (AD 1652–67) attempted to achieve a form of Byzantine symphony between the Orthodox Church and the Russian state by ordering to have installed in the Kremlin's Cathedral in Moscow two thrones, one for the emperor and the other for the patriarch. Fortunately, the attempt was unsuccessful.

Cf. Ovidiu Bozgan, *Studii de Istoria Bisericii* (București: Universitatea din București, 2002), p. 5. Ioan Rămureanu, *Istoria Bisericească Universală*, vol. 2 (București, 1993), pp. 283–290.

[122] Having succeeded the Byzantine emperor, the Russian tsar saw himself as the direct successor of the Orthodox Empire. John Meyendorff, *The Orthodox Church: Its Past and Its Role in the World Today*, fourth edition (Crestwood: St Vladimir's Seminary Press, 1996), pp. 109–11. Cf. S. Bulgakov, *Orthodox Church*, p. 158.

[123] G. Florovski, *Christianity and Culture*, pp. 187–97.

[124] Ioan Ică Jr., "Biserică, societate, gândire în răsărit, în occident și în Europa de azi" in *Gândirea socială a bisericii*, edited by Ioan Ică Jr., Germano Marani (Sibiu: Editura Deisis, 2002), p. 38.

[125] I. Ică, Biserică, "Biserică, Societate."

[126] Nicolai N. Petro, "The EU: The Orthodox are Coming" in *Transitions Online* (25 March 2005), p. 1.

[127] A. Pippidi, *Tradiția Politică Bizantină*, pp. 185–6.

[128] *Boyar* is the Romanian name for a class of landowners or freemen with a patent of nobility who represented the remnant of the medieval Romanian nobility in Transylvania. Concerning the judicial courts, cf. Alexandru Constantinescu, "Contribuții ale Bisericii în Justiția Țării Românești sub Alexandru Ipsilanti," in *Biserica Ortodoxă Română*, vol. 97, no. 1–2 (1979), pp. 165–78.

[129] Philip Walters, "Eastern Europe since the fifteenth century" in *History of English Christianity 1920–1985*, edited by Adrian Hastings (London: SCM Press, 1991), p. 301.

[130] Cf. Aleksei Stepanovich Khomyakov, Ivan Vasilevich Kireevskii, *On Spiritual Unity: A Slavophile Reader* (Hudson, NY: Lindisfarne Books, 1998). Also Abbott Gleason, *European and Muscovite: Ivan Kireevsky and the Origins of Slavophilism* (Cambridge, MA: Harvard University Press, 1972).

[131] B. Osborne, "Orthodoxy in a united Europe," p. 5.

[132] Dualist in construction, Slavophilism opposed enlightened modernizing Westernism, replacing historical, political, social, and religious reality with a mental fiction that was supposed to reconcile the tension that existed between them. I. Ică, "Biserică, Societate, Gândire," p. 40.

[133] Another Peter I-like attempt to pseudomorphosis was initiated by Tsar Alexander I (1801–25) who was attracted to German Pietism and mysticism; as part of the liberating tendencies, a Russian Bible Society was organized after the Protestant model.

[134] P. Walters, "Eastern Europe Since the Fifteenth Century," p. 301.

[135] P. Walters, pp. 309–10.

[136] Occurring between 1793 and 1794, when the Jacobin faction that most closely identified with the people of Paris and with democracy was supreme. Characterized by the effective removal of their political opposition and proclamation of "republic one and indivisible," in which legislative power would be predominant. But, by the summer of 1793, when the Jacobins had reorganized the Committee and effectively controlled the government, the revolutionaries were exhibiting a political ruthlessness unlike any seen before. As they set out to eliminate their enemies, they seemed to follow the cynical imperative coined at the time: "Be my friend, or I will kill you." Cf. Raymond F. Betts, *Europe in*

Retrospect: A Brief History of the Past Two Hundred Years (D C Heath & Co, 1979), p. 24.
137 Yehoshua Arieli, "Jacob Talmon—An Intellectual Portrait," in *Totalitarian Democracy and After: International Colloquium in Memory of Jacob L. Talmon*, by The Israel Academy of Sciences and Humanities, eds. (Jerusalem: Magnes Press, Hebrew University, 1984), pp. 1–34.
138 Y. Arieli, "Jacob Talmon."
139 Philip Boobbyer, *S. L. Frank. The Life and Work of a Russian Philosopher 1877–1950* (Athens, OH: Ohio University Press, 1995), pp. 65–7. Cf. Michael Burleigh, *Sacred Causes: Religion and Politics from the European Dictators to Al-Qaeda* (London, Harper Press, 2006), p. 39.
140 M. Burleigh, *Sacred Causes*.
141 M. Burleigh, *Earthly Powers*, pp. 277–8.
142 Irina Paperno, *Chernyshevsky and the Age of Realism: A Study in the Semiotics of Behavior* (Stanford: Stanford University Press, 1988), p. xiii. Cf. Stephane Courtois, Mark Kramer, *The Black Book of Communism: Crimes, Terror, Repression* (Cambridge, MA, London: Harvard University Press, 1999), pp. 39–52. Cf. Nikolai Chernyshevsky, *What is to be Done?* (Cornell: Cornell University Press, 1863, 1989); Nikolai Dobrolyubov, *Selected Philosophical Essays*, translated by J. Fineberg (Moscow: Foreign Language Publishing House, 1956).
143 This view has been presented in a number of studies. Cf. "Communism" in *Dictionary of the Social Sciences* edited by Craig Calhoun (Oxford: Oxford University Press, 2002).
144 Dan Pavel argues that this was the case with the values of the Christian culture that were converted into values of classical philosophy and were at the heart of modern liberal and democratic ideas. Pavel refers to these Christian values as virtual "systems of protection" that have been constantly undermined by German thinking in the eighteenth and nineteenth centuries. Paradoxically enough, it was the rational inquiry about the existence and nature of God that offered the best tools for thinkers who negated the existence of God. D. Pavel, *Leviathanul Bizantin*, pp. 16–17, n.14.
145 Cf. Stephen Koch, *Sfârşitul Inocenţei: Intelectualii din Occident şi tentaţia Stalinistă; 30 de ani de război secret* (Bucureşti: Editura Albatros, 1997). For an elaborate discussion of the relationship between theodicy and the political transformations during the last three centuries, see Dan Pavel, *Etica lui Adam: Sau de ce rescriem istoria* (Bucureşti: Editura Du Style, 1995), also D. Pavel, *Leviathanul Bizantin*, pp. 5–33.
146 D. Pavel, *Leviathanul Bizantin*, p. 19.
147 This faith actually concretized into what was called the "God-building" ideology associated with Alexander Bogdanov, Leonid Krasin, and above all Anatoly Lunacharsky, who in 1909 founded a "God-building" summer school. It was Marxist-inspired anthropocentric religion striving toward the moral unity of mankind. Cf. Arthur Jay Klinghoffer, *Red Apocalypse: The Religious Evolution of Soviet Communism* (Lanham: University Press of America, 1996), pp. 49–51.
148 Nicolas Berdyaev, *The Russian Revolution* (Ann Arbor: University of Michigan Press, 1966), p. 58.
149 Bertrand Russell, *The Practice and Theory of Bolshevism* (New York: Harcourt, Brace and Howe, 1920), p. 17.

[150] Ioan Ică Jr., "Europa Politicului, Europa Spiritului" in Radu Carp, *Un Suflet pentru Europa*, p. 25.
[151] I. Dumitru-Snagov, *Relațiile Stat-Biserică*, p. 9.
[152] Cf. Alain Besancon, *Nenorocirea Secolului. Despre Comunism, Nazism și Unicitatea Șoah-ului* (București: Editura Nemira, 1999), pp. 75–92.
[153] P. Wogaman, "Changing Role of Government," p. 251.
[154] P. Wogaman, "Changing Role of Government," p. 255.

Chapter 4

Nationalist Orthodoxy and the Romanian State

Introduction

The investigation of the relationship between Romanian Orthodoxy and the nationalist state will begin by concentrating on the role nationalism played in influencing the church in the Eastern Orthodox context. Instead of using a chronological approach to the history of church–state relations in this field, a number of topics have been selected in order to help us understand the circumstances that led to the confluence of religion and nationalism. The structure of the categories used here was suggested by Adrian Hastings in his study of the relationship between religion and nationhood, to whom the author of this volume is indebted for such a creative approach.

The categories examined here will address those aspects that have contributed to a paradoxical unity between religion and nationalism in Romania, such as the adoption of religious national heroes, the mythologizing of threats to national identity, and the social role the clergy have played in the nation's past. Each of these will be related to the history of the Orthodox Church in Romania, which culminates with the emergence of the Orthodox autocephaly, when religious nationalism has, in the fullest sense, identified with the Romanian national formation.

A necessary consideration of the development of relations between Orthodox clergy and rulers will be in order—first in Wallachia and Moldavia, the southern territories of today's Romania, and then in Transylvania, the northwestern territory added to Romania proper in the twentieth century. This analysis will ensure a better understanding of the effects that Orthodox nationalism has had in interwar Romania, when that nationalism became incorporated into the extremist ideology of the Iron Guard and gave birth to an Orthodox legionnaire, ethnocratic, and nationalist ideology, which advocated that collective mysticism, homogeneity, fusion, and totalitarian integration, are elements making up the substance of the Orthodox faith.

Sanctification of Origins

As underlined in the previous chapters, the more influential religion was in the construction of nationhood, the more likely it was to influence every expression of nationalism. Hastings' categories aptly describe how the mix between Orthodoxy and nationalism resulted in a political religion being created.[1] First, Christianity has shaped national formation by sanctifying the starting point of a nation. Examples that support this argument can be found in France's origin as a Catholic nation as early as the fifth century, Christianity and the origins of England back in the eleventh century, and in the history of other nations like Ireland, Serbia, or Russia.[2] Applying this category to the relationship between Orthodoxy and Romania, there is evidence to suggest an attempt by Orthodox historiography to emphasize the important role played by the Orthodox Church in the shaping of the origins of Romanians.

At its core, this is a question about the church's own identity addressed through a historical reading that attempts to identify a close connection between the formation of the nation and the church's contribution to that process. Fred Halliday, talking about the different characteristics nationalism embraces, described this tendency as the "vocabulary of anthropomorphic denomination."[3] It represents the attempt to claim the origins of a nation by making reference to anthropomorphic elements like soil, hills, or rivers and ascribing them certain sacred or ancestral meanings, which could then be used to justify one nation's claim of belonging.

For the Orthodox Church in Romania, this process of the "sanctification" of origins concretized in the claims that: "the Romanian people were born Christian." The so-called theory of "Daco-Roman Romanian continuity" on which this argument was based in Orthodox historiography of the nineteenth century suggests the Romanians are the result of a mixture of Christianized Roman soldiers, colonists, and the indigenous Dacians whom they defeated in the two wars of 102–3 and 105–6.[4] As Gillet noted here, this theory represents a fundamental truth for Orthodox historians and any questioning of its historical validity is therefore regarded as a direct threat to the political and religious identity of the country.[5]

Romanian historiography developed these theories in the nineteenth century, amid a larger movement of the Eastern European countries that resulted in freedom from the Ottoman Empire's oppression. In the context of this sudden liberation, the national identity needed to be consolidated through a national history that would quickly establish the right of the Romanian nation to exist in that given geographical area. The solution came from Transylvania, the territory north of the Carpathian Mountains, inhabited by a large Romanian majority but under Hungarian or, at times, Austro-Hungarian jurisdiction.

Transylvania is a prominent territory in terms of the important role it plays in the national identity of both Romanians and Hungarians. The debate emerges around the Romanians' claims (based on dubious historical evidence) that they can prove Transylvania was first settled by the Romanians. Hungarians, however, have their own historical evidence that support their claims of primacy of settlement in ancient Transylvania.[6] Both Romanians and Hungarians thus perceive Transylvania to be the core of their land and "the cradle of their civilization."[7]

Owing to the Romanian-Hungarian debate on the origins of Transylvania and on the primacy of inhabitancy of this region, there was a growing conviction as early as the eighteenth century that Transylvania existed as a "naturally given land."[8] Tom Gallagher has identified two different stances in the historical narrative of Transylvania.[9] One was represented by Romanian intellectuals who, after 1918 (when Transylvania became part of Greater Romania), began to stress the importance of Transylvania to the national consciousness, describing it as "the very core of Romanian nationhood during the long stretches of history when Romanians had been unable to control their own collective fate."[10] The other stance was taken by nationalist Hungarians who attempted to show how Transylvania had been crucial for the preservation of the Hungarian national ideal in an interwar Hungary where doctrinaire nationalism shaped its politics.[11]

Thus, Romanian historiography began using the argumentation that was employed a century earlier by the so-called "Transylvanian School" to generate a national, not simply a Transylvanian, identity. Adolf Armbruster attributed the development of the theory of "Daco-Roman Romanian" continuity to the seventeenth-century Baroque movement, which was a reaction to Enlightenment and humanist historical scholarship trends.[12] The result of this historicist awakening gave Romanians the *National Chronicle*, a first attempt at a history and drafted from research attributed to foreign historiography interested in discovering the origins of the Romanians.[13] However, as Constantin Schifirneț indicated, it was during the eighteenth century that the debate about the origin of the Romanians left the academic world and acquired a nationalist nuance in Transylvania.[14]

The first evidence of a national awakening of the Romanians concretized in the demands of Inocențiu Micu-Klein, the bishop of the Greek Catholic Church in Transylvania (1729–51).[15] The bishop had initially intended to conduct a census of all the Romanians from Transylvania (1733).[16] However, he soon became the spokesperson of the Romanian population in Transylvania, signaling to the political authorities of the country that they now represented a significant percentage of the population in the region and, as such, demanded recognition for Romanians as the fourth nation in Transylvania.[17] Concerned about the low status of the Romanians in Transylvania, Bishop Inocențiu unsuccessfully presented his plea for Romanians' rights to Queen Maria Theresa (1740–80).[18] Nevertheless, by 1754, the Greek Catholic Church had established a primary school, high school, and a theological seminary in the town of Blaj, Transylvania, which was transformed into a center of "Romanian self-consciousness and organization," later called *Şcoala Ardeleană* (the Transylvanian School).[19] Following in the steps of Bishop Inocenţiu, the members of the Transylvanian School, all Greek Catholic clergy,[20] made the first efforts to write a history of the Romanians based on the theory about their ancient Daco-Roman roots, which would be used in their nationalist claims.[21]

In light of the situation of the Romanian population in Transylvania, the memorandum entitled *Supplex Libellus Valachorum* that was presented by the Transylvanian School to Emperor Leopold II (1790–92) in 1791, and later to the Transylvanian Diet, was drastically rejected.[22] The memorandum, regarded by Romanian historians as "the birth certificate of the Romanian nation,"[23] requested among other things, equal status for Romanians with the three recognized groups and political representation in the diet.[24] In this document, the members of the Transylvanian School supported their claims by referring to Bishop Inocenţiu's demands, to the myth of "Daco-Roman Romanian" continuity, and to the Emperor Joseph II's (1780–90) "Co-civilly Edict" that gave equal rights, at least in theory, to all the groups in Transylvania, including the *Vlachs*.[25]

The interesting aspect is that prior to the eighteenth century, the theory had actually been affirmed and supported persuasively, first by Hungarian chroniclers and other foreigners, and only later by Romanian historians.[26] However, when the Transylvanian School borrowed it from the academic context and used it as a nationalist argument, the theory began to be rejected by Hungarian historiography.

As noted earlier, such ideas became evident in Bishop Inocenţiu's claims to the Habsburg diplomacy in the middle of the eighteenth century. However, as soon as this myth became the motivating factor for the Romanians' demands for equal rights in Transylvania, not only the political leaders, but also Saxon and Hungarian scholarship, relentlessly attempted to counter their requests and dismantle their theory through historical and polemical works, especially through the "Immigration Theory" that would become an alternative to the Romanians' use of the "historical right" to demand acceptance as a political entity in Transylvania.[27]

This Transylvanian struggle for nationalist self-consciousness became the argument of Romanian historiography in Moldavia and Wallachia in the nineteenth century, especially after their union (1878). The ROC adopted the Daco-Roman Romanian theory and added their own interpretation, stressing, as already mentioned, the Christian heritage of the first Romans who conquered the Dacians. As Gillet remarked, the Orthodox Church saw in the Daco-Roman origins of nationalist Romania the beginning of the church's struggle for the establishment of a national autocephalous Orthodox Church.[28] Thus, one can see how Romanian Orthodoxy has used and interpreted history, without much credible evidence to support it, to identify itself with the origins of the Romanian nation.

Religious National Heroes

The sanctifying of the origin of a nation and the mythologization and commemoration of threats to national identity are often interrelated with religious personalities who become dominant figures in the formation of national consciousness. Hastings stressed that for Ireland and Serbia such a function is performed by saintly personalities like St. Patrick and St. Sava. As he noted:

> Sava was a far more political figure than Patrick, one very easily appropriated by nationalists whereas Patrick's greatness lies in setting so powerful a mark on a country's identity while appearing as unpolitical as Christ. Celebrating St. Patrick's Day is, doubtless, often a highly nationalist affair, but the connection has not the near inescapability there is in celebrating St. Sava's.[29]

St. Sava of Serbia (1175–1236), originally the prince Rastko Nemanjic, was the son of Serbian ruler and founder of the Serbian medieval state, Stefan Nemanja. The first Archbishop of Serbia (1219–33), St. Sava is the archetype of the combination between nationalism and Orthodoxy; together with the Kosovo martyrs and St. Tsar Lazar, they represent the earliest defining marks of a Serb national identity.[30] As Hayes stressed, the growth of a new Serb nationalism in the 1980s provided the Serbian Orthodox Church with an opportunity to revive nationalism by stimulating a new interest in the religious figure of St. Sava.[31]

The Orthodox Church in Romania has its own sacred religious personalities who have become instrumental in the church's identification with nationalism. Of them, the two most important figures are the Greek Catholic Bishop Inocențiu Micu Klein and the Orthodox Metropolitan Andrei Șaguna, both originating from Transylvania.

Bishop Inocențiu Micu Klein

In her challenging study, Katherine Verdery sets out to investigate how historical, and particularly religious, personalities have been used in religious discourses to justify or glorify national identities or historical pasts.[32] This approach allowed her to devote an entire chapter to the use of Bishop Inocențiu Micu Klein as a religious role model by both the Orthodox and the Greek Catholics in Romania. As she has pointed out, the problem with Bishop Inocențiu is that both churches, Orthodox and Greek Catholic, regard him as their national hero.[33]

The interpretation of the historical person of Bishop Inocențiu proposed a substantial revision of Romanians' national genealogy and added new values for the temporal landmarks of Romanian history. It underscored a clash between two competing alternatives on how to sanctify political authority: by making one particular church (Romanian Orthodox) an official "monopoly" church of the state, or by insisting on plural faiths, each with its own civil guarantees, all sanctifying authority jointly through an emphasis on faith as central to Romanian identity.[34]

What was the social status of the Romanian population in Transylvania, and what role did Bishop Inocenţiu play in their rights' struggle? Schaser's study of the events surrounding the "Josephine Reforms" (1780–90) in Transylvania highlights the low political and social status of the Romanians in the eighteenth century.[35] Schaser emphasized that although the Romanians were more than a half of the population in Transylvania,[36] they enjoyed few rights and were not allowed to have properties or citizenship, a situation that did not change much even in 1820s.[37] Romanians retained the status of "tolerated," most of them forming the lower strata of society, as shepherds, serfs, or soldiers. Roman and Hofbauer suggested there was only a handful of Romanian boyars,[38] who had been completely *Magyarized* and were part of the Transylvanian Diet on the side of the Hungarians.[39]

Bishop Inocenţiu was born in 1692 of an Orthodox family, and attended a Jesuit school, being later accepted into the Basilian monastic order. In 1729 he was appointed Greek Catholic Bishop of Transylvania, gaining the title of baron and a place in Transylvania's diet. Having already begun to insist that the Austro-Hungarian court in Vienna should fulfill its promise that Orthodox conversion to Greek Catholicism would bring an end to their serf status, Bishop Inocenţiu extended this plea to the whole Romanian population of Transylvania. Most of his views were compiled in the *Supplex Libellus Valachorum* petition of the "Transylvania School" that explicated the theoretical arguments for defense of the Romanians' political rights.[40] His insistence eventually drew the anger of Empress Maria Theresa and that of the diet, and led to his exile in Italy (1751), where he died (Rome, 1768). Nevertheless, Bishop Inocenţiu strengthened the Greek Catholics for over 40 years, in which time he hoped to use the church to gain recognition of the Romanian serfs as a nation in Transylvania.[41]

The problem with Bishop Inocenţiu is that both the Greek Catholics and the Romanian Orthodox came to regard him as their national hero. He was indeed a remarkable character, having reworked the feudal idiom of *natio* in service of Romanian ethnic nationalism.[42] David Prodan had no doubt when he stressed that Bishop Inocenţiu "unquestionably stands out in Romanian history as the most powerful political personality of the Romanian people in eighteenth-century Transylvania."[43] Based on this historical legacy and personal characteristics, the Orthodox Church has created icons with the portrait of Bishop Inocenţiu, in which he is labeled an "Orthodox bishop."[44] However, Orthodox historiography refuses to grant any appreciation to the other Greek Catholics of Transylvania apart from the bishop. Accordingly, they are not pioneers of Romanian nationalism but mere opportunists who betrayed the ancestral faith and sabotaged the struggle by dividing the Romanian nation between two faiths, one pure and ancestral and the other a distortion from the West.[45] Thus, by regarding Bishop Inocențiu as a virtual Orthodox bishop forced to become a Greek Catholic, the Orthodox Church can continue to demonize the catholicized Orthodoxy of Transylvania. To strengthen this association, the exiling of the bishop to Rome is interpreted by the Orthodox to be the result of his threat to the Habsburgs that unless they kept their promise, he would revert to Orthodoxy. As expressed by a Romanian Orthodox priest: "Inocențiu was a fighter for Romanian rights. He was not in the Greek Catholic Church for reasons of faith but was permanently tied to our traditional [Orthodox] beliefs."[46]

There is another layer to the hagiographical interpretation of this personality. An Orthodox current in the Romanian historiography at the beginning of the twentieth century maintained that the demands of Bishop Inocențiu were not limited to the clergy or the Romanian population in Transylvania but were made in the name of all Romanians.[47] This interpretation tends to "forget" that the Transylvanian School identified with the Romanian nationalist intelligentsia from Transylvania, who were keenly opposed to the idea of union with the "Orthodox" Romanians in Wallachia and Moldavia. As Prodan has pointed out, there were two different views circulating at the time: the first, which appears in the "Leopoldine Diploma" of 1699 (following upon the Act of Union of 1698), stated clearly that the Greek Catholic clergy would be freed of feudal obligations; the second, in the "Leopoldine Diploma" of 1701, made this same promise to all Romanians who would join the Greek Catholic Church.[48] Thus, at first the Transylvanian School was only interested in the integration of the upper-class Romanian clergy into political membership in the Transylvanian Diet.[49] Later, however, Bishop Inocențiu extended this demand to the recognition of the whole Romanian population in Transylvania, which can be seen in the difference between the Habsburgs' edicts of 1699 and 1701.[50]

Nevertheless, historical accuracy aside, both Greek Catholics and Orthodox identify in Bishop Inocențiu a national hero worth celebrating. In the case of the former, they use him to consolidate social and political capital as the source of Romanian national consciousness and emancipation and the moral claims to compensation for their sufferings under Communism.[51] By making a claim in Bishop Inocențiu's struggle for national emancipation, the Greek Catholics hope to increase their visibility in Romanian post-1989 society. In the case of the latter, the ROC wants to consolidate its link with Romanian nationalism and its demands for special status among the churches by identifying with Bishop Inocențiu's fight for national emancipation.

Bishop Inocențiu plays an important part in Romanian national identity. Regarded as a national hero, he is adopted by the ROC as a contributor to a reshaping of Romanian identity as bound up with the Orthodox religion, reinforcing a historical perspective that links Orthodoxy with the origin and development of Romanian national consciousness. The sanctification of the origins and the celebration of an "Orthodox" national hero strengthen the "sacred" character of Romanianness. Romanian self-identity can no longer be perceived as separated from religion, while its land cannot be seen as "godless." The nation and the land take on eschatological significance by fusing the patriotic with the sacred; as Bishop Inocențiu himself observed concerning the Last Judgment: "Only from the soil of your homeland can you rise from the dead."[52] Romanian territory becomes a sacred space where Orthodoxy has always represented the essence of the Romanian self-identity and nationalism.

Metropolitan Andrei Șaguna

Verdery's emphasis on the important role played by Bishop Inocențiu as a national hero would have been strengthened by a comparison with the Metropolitan Andrei Șaguna of Sibiu (1808–73), another notable Transylvanian personality to have an important contribution to the national emancipation of the Romanians. Although accurately stressing that Bishop Inocențiu's efforts for the emancipation were directed to the Romanian population in Transylvania alone, Verdery's account of the way in which Orthodox historiography mythologized Bishop Inocențiu's demands to the Romanian population in Wallachia and Moldavia would have benefited from an investigation of nineteenth-century Transylvania.

The main characteristic of Șaguna's thinking was the carrying forward of the ecclesiastical leadership of the Orthodox Church in Transylvania, while at the same time upholding the primacy of religion in the life of the Romanian population. Șaguna's main approach concerning church–state relations included the necessity of distinguishing between the two entities in such a way so as to ensure the church would enjoy a level of autonomy from the state.[53] He considered this to be the solution to the problems that affected the Orthodox Church under the Habsburg Empire's hegemony and which prevented the church from carrying out its social mission. Equally important, he thought, was the organization of the internal life of the church in accordance with the Eastern tradition of Byzantine Orthodoxy, which he believed would help establish a beneficial working relationship with the state.[54]

Thus, although interested in cultivating a relationship with the state that resembled the Byzantine symphony, Șaguna's concept of such a relationship differed significantly from Emperor Justinian's harmony between *sacerdotium* and *imperium*. Șaguna thought the Austrian Empire and the Orthodox Church could never be one entity because the origins and nature of each were different.[55] Whereas the church was founded by Christ and its purpose was to prepare the faithful for eternal salvation, the state was created by worldly leaders—in Transylvania's case, by a union of families under an accepted leader.[56] Here Șaguna employed a moderate form of mystical nationalism that asserted Romanian Orthodoxy was the religious expression of the "Romanian soul" and, hence, the source of national progress.[57]

However, although Șaguna recognized the idea of nationality as the dominant motivation in contemporary European social and political life, he always equated the goals and achievements of those secular ideas in relation to what he called "eternal values" of the church's teaching.[58] Șaguna was thus convinced the development of the Romanian nation in Transylvania depended in the first instance on the well-being of the Orthodox Church and loyalty to the Austrian Empire. To that extent, Șaguna never challenged the emperor or criticized the ruling class but rather distinguished between the Habsburg dynasty and the Austrian bureaucracy, attacking the latter.[59] For Șaguna, the role of the Orthodox Church was to give moral support to the nationalist state regardless of whether it was absolutist, republican, or constitutional.[60]

The idea of a church–state separation was not relished by Șaguna, at least not in the ordinary sense of this separation; he saw nothing unusual in seeking state subsidies for the priests' salaries or for religious education in state schools.[61] The state had a moral duty and practical interest in supporting the work of the church in exchange for the spiritual development of law-abiding citizenry, the foundation of a prosperous society. Nonetheless, this mutual embrace would not interfere with the full autonomy of the church from the state.[62] Șaguna wanted to make sure the church would be free from dependence on the nationalist state, dissociating the church from any particular political system that could cause the church to be sidetracked by letting itself be manipulated by the state.

Șaguna took practical steps toward the achievement of this autonomy by campaigning for the restoration of the Orthodox metropolitanate in the town of Alba Iulia, as well as bringing about a total reorganization of church government.[63] In the meantime, however, taking advantage of the weakening Austrian Empire, then at war with Italy and France, the Hungarians crowned Francis Joseph as their king and initiated the inclusion of the autonomous territory of Transylvania under the Hungarian kingdom.[64] Șaguna's response to Hungarian nationalism, which he perceived as threatening all legislation concerning non-Hungarian nationalities, came in the form of a church constitution that he submitted to the Austrian emperor for consideration.[65] In Șaguna's opinion, the passing of this constitution was making the autonomy of the Orthodox Church a reality in Transylvania, and that was indirectly giving the Romanian population its only chance to obtain political rights and economic prosperity. Called Organic Statutes, the constitution demanded broad representation accorded to laymen in managing the church's financial and educational affairs, as well as an increase of independence for the clergy, who were indirectly loosening the emperor's supervisory power over the church.[66]

The passing of the Organic Statutes was met with fervent criticism by Romanian nationalist intellectuals who did not wish to entertain the idea of allowing the ecclesiastical leadership to meddle in the political affairs of the nation.[67] Thus, it was evident that Șaguna's concept of the nature of the church and its role in society was quite different from that of the post-1848 intellectuals. Moreover, during the tensions between Șaguna and the nationalists, the Greek Catholic Church's intellectuals joined the debate on the side of the nationalists, supporting the official document known as the *Pronunciament* (1868), which reiterated the Romanian intellectuals' desire for recognition of Transylvania's autonomy and political representation as well as calling for a limitation of the church's role in political affairs.

However, Şaguna's notion and support of the idea of national emancipation for Romanians in Transylvania were not very different from those shared by enlightened intellectuals like Ioan Raţiu and George Bariţiu. What unsettled them was not Şaguna's rationalist and liberal thinking but rather his insistence on church autonomy from the state. He believed the clergy should be leaders of the church's organs, while certain questions such as those of a dogmatic or ritualistic nature, as well as ecclesiastical justice, should concern solely the clergy. Moreover, Şaguna lobbied in the Organic Statutes for the bishops' power to ordain and appoint priests and for metropolitans to preside over their synods without state interference.[68] The elements of church hierarchy that Şaguna proposed in the Statutes were augmented by his understanding of the social role of the church. Thus, although he reserved legislative and judicial power primarily for the church hierarchy, he envisioned a role for laymen in various branches of church administration, such as education and finance.

Eventually, the Committee of the Twenty-Seven, who led the congress that studied the Organic Statutes proposed as the new church constitution, modified its stipulation so as to allow for a more extensive role for the laity (more state control). Furthermore, it divided the Episcopal Synod into three separate committees: an ecclesiastical committee to deal with matters such as dogma, ritual, and clergy discipline; an educational committee, and an administrative committee, both consisting of a majority of laymen. The Organic Statutes were approved in this revised format in 1868 and a year later they received the emperor's sanction.

Şaguna's contribution to the reaffirmation of the role of the Orthodox Church in the Romanian state could not be overstated. Though he did not achieve all he intended, his influence reasserted in a practical way the church in the new national movement that developed in Transylvania at the end of the nineteenth century. Unlike the role played in Wallachia and Moldavia, the Orthodox Church in Transylvania broadened its horizons by attempting to harmonize Western traditions with Eastern Orthodoxy. Whereas, in the two Romanian principalities, Orthodoxy maintained its subordinate position out of conformity, offering moral and ethical support for the nation as an Orthodox *lex*, the Orthodoxy in Transylvania represented a different model of church–state relations. This model was based less upon the role played by religion as an ethical and moral form of conduct for the people, and more on a combination of rationalist and liberal elements and on the pursuit of nationalist goals.

Despite his inclusion among Orthodox national heroes, Bishop Inocenţiu remains a symbol of national emancipation. The real contribution to the identification between Romanian nationalism and Orthodoxy was made by Şaguna. As already indicated, the Greek Catholic Transylvanian School identified with the Romanian nationalist intelligentsia and formed a common front that opposed Șaguna's unifying attempts. His political thinking about the role of the Orthodox Church offered a programmatic approach to church–state relations that was designed to unite all the Orthodox Romanian population. Based on these eminently nationalist efforts, Șaguna represents the archetypal Orthodox national hero. Moreover, his Organic Statutes would grow in importance following the union of Transylvania with Romania proper as they became the basis for the transformation undertaken by the autocephalous ROC.

Mythologizing Threats to National Identity

The perception of Bishop Inocențiu as an "Orthodox" national hero represents an important argument in the rivalry between Romanian Orthodoxy and Greek Catholicism around the question of the contribution to national consciousness. This links well with another category suggested by Hastings, namely the ways in which religion mythologizes and commemorates threats to national identity.[69] For this English historian, occurrences like the Gunpowder Plot, the siege of Derry, the Battle of Kosovo, or the career of Joan of Arc represent episodes in which the concept of national salvation sharpens the sense of "us" and "them."[70] While these episodes differ in context and content, and in the specific role played by religion, they share a common characteristic in the way in which they are reinterpreted in order to reinforce a special national identity. Thus, although inherently secular events, they become ritualized and are ascribed quasi-religious meaning that serves to draw a distinction between "us" and "them," and reinforcing this distinction in order to maintain and promote nationhood.[71]

In the case of Romanian Orthodoxy, the episode concerning the efforts of the Transylvanian School to generate a Romanian national identity becomes one such mythologized event. Whereas Romanian historians have claimed that Bishop Inocențiu's *Supplex Libellus Valachorum* inaugurated the emancipation of Romanians from Transylvania, at best, or only of the upper class Romanians, at worst,[72] it was during Communism that the ROC challenged this interpretation by making its own claim to prominence in the national consciousness.[73] In this context, the ROC stressed that nationalist Orthodox resilience has enabled the Romanian population to survive centuries of foreign rule as a single unified nation, despite their separation across the three spheres of Habsburg (Transylvania), Russian (Moldavia), and Ottoman influence (Wallachia).

The interpretation by ROC historiography of Transylvania as inherently an ancient Orthodox territory was meant to strengthen its identification with Romanian nationalism, questioned at times by the Greek Catholic Church. To sharpen the distinction between "us" versus "them," the Orthodox Church pointed to the relations between Greek Catholics and the pope in Rome, blaming them as non-Romanian "agents" of the West, foreigners guilty of anti-Romanian invasion of liberalism that would undermine nationalist values.⁷⁴ In extreme forms, this xenophobia went as far as identifying the Greek Catholics as Hungarian, using the simplistic logic that Transylvanian Romanians are Orthodox while Hungarians are Catholic, and therefore Greek Catholics are Hungarians.⁷⁵ This identification was meant to reduce the Greek Catholics' chances to any claim of contribution to Romanian national consciousness because of the dual place, stressed earlier, Transylvania plays in the origins of both Hungarian and Romanian nationalism.

In response, the Greek Catholics represented the Orthodox Church as having collaborated with the Soviet Communists who after World War II took power in Romania, and especially with the "foreign" Russian Patriarchate that was under the tutelage of Stalin.⁷⁶ Therefore, each side suspected the other of "internationalism" and employed history to prevent the other from being perceived as a faithful defender of Romanian nationalism. Both churches have in common an emphasis on the place of religious belief in the Romanian national identity, and both are willing to make Bishop Inocențiu central in their versions of national genealogy. Of the two churches, it becomes obvious that the ROC has gone to extra lengths to stigmatize the other churches as "non-Romanian" in order to strengthen its association with the Romanian state. In their most extreme forms, these monopolist designs rest on fully identifying the ROC not just with the state but with the very survival of the Romanian nation, and the other churches with "foreign invasion."⁷⁷

The Social Role of the Clergy

The clergy is thought to have fulfilled an indirect role in the affirmation of nationalism and in the developing of early forms of national consciousness. According to Hastings, in many parts of Europe during the medieval and modern periods, societies were composed of two distinct categories: elite and masses; literate and illiterate.⁷⁸ Admittedly, in early medieval societies the priesthood would have been illiterate, but literate priests from the late medieval and early modern periods would have arbitrated between rulers and ruled; Hastings argues that it was these literate priests who played a social role, shaping the mutual identification of religion and the nationalist identity of a state.⁷⁹

The argument concerning the social role of the clergy in the affirmation of national consciousness has been questioned by Hobsbawm, who skeptically argued that: "it is clearly illegitimate to extrapolate from the elite to the masses, the literate to the illiterate, even though the two worlds are not entirely separable."⁸⁰ This is a justifiable criticism, as it underlines the gap that existed between lords and peasants, based on which it is superfluous to assume that powerless peasants would have been interested in identifying with a national consciousness enforced by the powerful elite.⁸¹ However, this argument fails to take into account a third social class that composed these societies, namely the clergy. The lower clergy, who lived in parishes throughout Europe, were relatively poor, literate, and had been educated in cathedral schools that fostered a sense of shared local, regional, or national identity.[82] In regular contact with both the elite and peasantry while fulfilling the requirements of their work and of the church, the clergy had to think in local, vernacular, and, increasingly, in national terms.[83]

> Linking the classes as the clergy did (and they were often very numerous), they had an inevitable role, through their shared existence as well as through their ministry, in ensuring something of a collective consciousness between rich and poor, literate and illiterate, nobles and peasants. They were not in a narrow way simply teachers of religion, but also of history and much else.[84]

By simply carrying out their vocational activities, the clergy enhanced national consciousness in a process that, in the course of the nineteenth century, would be transferred to the nationalist struggles for emancipation characterizing the Spring of Nations.

In the Romanian territories, the Orthodox clergy has indeed played a similar social role, although it started later than in Western Europe. During the middle ages the influence of the Orthodox priesthood has been felt mainly among the Romanian peasants, who represented the ruled social class, a class of uneducated and politically voiceless people. Unlike the Catholic Church, which was influential among the political leadership and helped develop a professional internal bureaucracy and a practical form of monasticism, the Orthodox faith of the Romanians retained an archaic religious idealism, oriented toward the otherworldly, and therefore difficult to relate to social and political concerns of the day.[85] Some have suggested that the Orthodox clergy's lack of social relevance in the first part of the middle ages was linked with the delay in political organization and the rural circumstances of Romanian peasantry.[86]

However, the clergy's lack of a social role was apparent only if one takes into account that Romanian Orthodoxy offered peasants not simply a religion but an alternative communal life with its own rules. For example, the old religious vocabulary of the early Romanian churches includes a consistent number of Latin words with a judicial function. Along these lines, Vasile Pârvan, a historian at the beginning of the twentieth century, argued that Romanians understood Orthodox Christianity more in terms of laws and regulations (*lex*) than in terms of faith (*fides*) and, therefore, looked to the church for "a form of conduct, a moral and political law for organizing life in this world."[87]

Not only the vocabulary but the role played by the clergy fulfilled a social and political function that predated the political organization of the Romanian territories. Thus, in 1391, a Romanian landowner from Maramureş went to Constantinople to ask Patriarch Antonie to bestow the title of *stauropegion* (religious site under direct and exclusive supervision of the patriarchate) to his monastery in Romanian territory.[88] As part of the title, the landowner received authority to "lead the people according to laws and canons," which gave the church political and judicial authority over local rulers. The "nomocanonic" law of the ecumenical patriarchate was thus transferred to, and generated a rule of law with the potential of becoming a common law for, that territory. While questionable whether such instances represented the norm rather than the exception, it emphasizes the social role clergy sometimes fulfilled.

Romanian Orthodox thinkers point to this specific understanding of Orthodoxy as law in their argument about the close relationship between Orthodoxy and "Romanianness." For example, Nichifor Crainic, the mind behind the dreaded Iron Guard, stressed that *lex* means Romanianness and Christianity; it combines the national with the spiritual, and has a dogmatic sense because it refers to the Orthodox faith, an ethnic sense because the Romanian identifies with the same faith, and finally a moral sense because it represents the traditional discipline of Romanians' lives.[89] Other interwar Orthodox thinkers extended the social role played by the clergy by stressing that the special bond between Orthodoxy and the Romanian peasantry was the main ingredient of "Romanianness." These views were brought forward by personalities such as Fr. Dumitru Stăniloae, Petre Țuțea, Mircea Eliade, and Nicolae Iorga, all of whom represent the most distinguished voices of Romanian society, and whose ideas have shaped Romanian nationalist thinking.[90]

Romanian Orthodox Autocephaly and Nationalism

The development of autocephalous state churches, characteristic of the Orthodox countries of Eastern Europe, was the most crucial and lasting contribution to the strengthening of the bond between religion and nationalism. As Hastings noted on this point: "The total ecclesiastical autonomy of a national church is one of the strongest and most enduring factors in the encouragement of nationalism. . . ."[91] The autocephaly (literally "self-headed") is the status of a church, in an Orthodox country, whose primatial bishop does not report to any higher-ranking bishop. When an ecumenical council or a high-ranking bishop, such as a patriarch or other primate, releases an ecclesiastical province from the authority of that bishop, while the newly independent church remains in full communion with the hierarchy to which it then ceases to belong, the patriarch or primate is granting autocephaly.

The development of the Romanian autocephaly has its roots in the constant interplay between church and clergy, on the one hand, and the rulers and political leadership, on the other hand. The creation of the national and autocephalous Orthodox Church of Romania was achieved in 1865 against the wishes of the ecumenical patriarchate in Constantinople, which eventually recognized the autocephaly in 1885. In the first part of the twentieth century, following the annexation of Transylvania, the Romanian patriarchate added the Orthodox Church in Transylvania to the Romanian Orthodox autocephaly. The stages in the development of the autocephaly were thus influenced by the growth of Romanian nationalism that was developing in parallel, and as such it is worth investigating their interaction.

Early Developments in Wallachia and Moldavia

In 1381, the Orthodox churches of the southern Romanian territories, Wallachia and Moldavia, officially adopted the Byzantine Orthodox tradition, events that coincided with the first political organization of the two principalities.[92] The political structures and religious hierarchy of the first Romanian principalities followed loosely those in Constantinople as well as those of the neighboring Bulgarians and Serbians. As a form of political organization, Wallachia and Moldavia had all the characteristics of an absolute monarchy. Although the princes were not invested by Constantinople or Rome, they were viewed as having absolute power via their divine ordination and, accordingly, received the church's blessing as "God's chosen one."[93] This situation was observed in 1534 by an emissary of the Ecumenical Patriarchate in Constantinople, who noted that in Wallachia the form of government was best described as "paranomy," that is, the church and the ruler lived outside Byzantine laws.[94]

The Wallachian and Moldavian metropolitanates were officially recognized by the ecumenical patriarchate in the fourteenth century.[95] Earlier, in the tenth century, the territories occupied by the Romanian population had adopted a Byzantine form of Orthodox Christianity from south of the Danube River, where recent wars had led to Byzantine jurisdiction over the Bulgarian territories and to the expansion of the church in the region.[96] However, in comparison to other predominantly Catholic territories, the political organization of the Romanian territories was delayed.[97] The Orthodox faith of the Romanian peasantry remained rural and popular until the political organization of Wallachia and Moldavia.[98]

Romanian rulers maintained this form of hierarchy until the seventeenth century, when the aristocracy was successful in imposing what was called a "*boyar* state." Throughout this period, and especially following the fall of Eastern Christendom in 1453, the aristocratic leadership subscribed to a "paranomic" type of symphony between the political power and the church. At times, the Orthodox patriarch was granted formal authority over the ruler's deference to Orthodox ancient traditions, in exchange for the ruler's responsibility in deciding who would be the next elected patriarch.[99]

However, such an "ideal" relationship between the church and the ruler was rarely the norm in the Romanian context. In accordance with the caesaropapist tradition of Emperor Justinian, the Romanian rulers subordinated the church and patriarch, irrespective of any other form of ecclesiastical constriction.[100] This tendency took the form of unceasing meddling of the Romanian princes in church affairs, electing and discharging patriarchs and clergy, consistent with the commonly held view of the divine rendering of the ruler's absolute power. In exchange for the full support and submission of the clergy, the princes acclaimed themselves as the "defenders of the Orthodox faith," granting protection, building monasteries and places of worship.[101]

Orthodoxy and the Phanariot Period

The eighteenth century provided the Orthodox priesthood with an opportunity to contribute more substantially as a factor of social and political change in Wallachia and Moldavia, as the two principalities came under the jurisdiction of the Phanariot princes, bringing changes for the church.[102] Although it could be described as a period of religious conservatism, anti-Western traditionalism, and political subordination to the Ottoman Empire in Constantinople, the eighteenth century suited the church hierarchy owing to the peculiar nature of Phanariot influence. Phanariotism was not necessarily bound by ethnicity, so that various Phanariot princes who ruled Romanian lands were often Albanian or Bulgarian as well as Romanian. What distinguished the Phanariot princes from other past rulers was that the increasing oppression imposed through them by the Ottoman regime was especially felt by the *boyars* (who continued to represent the ruling class), and to a lesser extent by the clergy.[103]

This new condition allowed the Orthodox priesthood to play a more active role in society, becoming the sole provider of health, education, poor relief, and a variety of other services for which the political leadership no longer took responsibility.[104] The clergy was involved in public administration and sat alongside the *boyars* in the highest state councils, dispensing justice in both ecclesiastical and civil matters.[105] Nevertheless, the links between the Orthodox hierarchy and the rulers in the two principalities were strengthened. An already established tradition ensured the Romanian metropolitans would be elected by the patriarch in Constantinople, who was granted the authority to provide the canonical links and final authority on doctrinal and ritual questions.[106] These special links with the patriarchate in Constantinople ensured the Orthodox monasteries, sources of income and retainers of large estates and lands, could not be touched by the Phanariot princes or the *boyars*. The relationship between the Orthodox clergy and the Phanariot rulers was thus a matter of constant negotiation between them.

The presence in councils of clergy on an equal level with local *boyars* was regarded by the Orthodox Church of the eighteenth century as a great achievement, an ideal form of Byzantine "symphony." The Orthodox clergy saw as its mission providing the rulers with moral and spiritual support that was rewarded with material aid and respect for religious autonomy allowed by the princes.[107] As a result, the church hierarchy was pleased with the privileges granted by the political authority, enjoying not only the official recognition of the princes, but the ability to supersede them altogether at times.[108]

By the time of the nationalist revolutions in Europe, Romanian Orthodoxy had its own judicial courts as well as a place alongside *boyars* on the highest tribunals of the land.[109] Cases of marriage, divorce, and inheritance were not outside the jurisdiction of the church's judicial courts, a position the clergy retained until the fundamental structural changes that took place in the nineteenth century. Although the secularization of judicial institutions and their court procedures had been attempted since the middle of the eighteenth century, the clergy of the Orthodox Church made itself indispensable to the judicial system for another hundred years. This church–state arrangement was firmly based upon the understanding of Orthodoxy as *lex* and was naturalized in such a way that the transformations caused by the Spring of Revolutions were incapable of rooting it out completely.

The nationalist Orthodoxy continued to cooperate with rulers throughout the social and political transformations of the eighteenth century. At times, the cooperation was not between equals but rather between rivals, especially when princes took upon themselves the power to elect the highest clergy and taxed the churches whenever it suited their own purposes.[110] Sometimes, though rarely, rulers felt it was their caesaropapist responsibility to impose on the clergy instructions on religious and theological matters.[111] Nevertheless, the Orthodox Church found the resilience to withstand these interferences, refusing to question the political leadership's right to rule, and thereby avoided creating institutional boundaries to the rulers' power of interference. The Orthodox clergy became the inextricable bond between the peasantry and the political leadership, ensuring the perpetuation of the church's nationalist influence in Wallachia and Moldavia.

The Nineteenth Century and Autocephaly

By the nineteenth century, political and social changes began to take place in the Romanian principalities, which in turn affected the relationship between the Orthodox Church and the political authorities. First, circumstances had turned Wallachia and Moldavia into battlegrounds for the surrounding Austrian, Russian, or Ottoman powers. In addition, in 1821 Wallachia experienced an internal revolution that sought to exclude both the *boyar* and the Phanariot autocratic supremacy and replace it with a revolutionary government. Led by Tudor Vladimirescu, the peasants' uprising turned into a revolution that encompassed all parts of Wallachia but, left without the support of the Russian tsar, it failed to make a lasting change.[112] The outcome of the unrest saw the drafting by the *boyars* of a 75-point memorandum, mainly projects for reform, which were forwarded to Russia, Turkey, and Austria.[113] Following the 1829 peace treaty between the Turks and Russians, the Romanian principalities were able to draft their first constitution, called the Organic Statutes.[114] The statutes introduced to Wallachia and Moldavia a constitutional monarchy in which the princes' authority was counterbalanced by a general assembly with broad legislative powers and control.[115]

Despite the fact that the assemblies were not representative, but composed almost exclusively from *boyars* who were also exempted from paying taxes, the statutes formed a basic set of constitutional changes unfamiliar to the neighboring autocratic empires and to the Orthodox Church. Later, when the Russians ended the Ottoman supremacy (1853–56), the grounds were prepared for the union of the two Romanian principalities into one state, achieved formally in 1859.[116]

During this tumultuous period, the Orthodox clergy remained the sole rallying focus for the Romanian peasantry as well as the administrator of various administrative functions.[117] However, the Orthodox Church was gradually beginning to lose the privileges it had enjoyed during the reign of the Phanariot princes. The constitution placed the church, together with all its adjacent institutions, under direct state control, which meant the election of the clergy, the ecclesiastical administration, religious education, and the judicial cases among the clergy were all subordinated to, and controlled by, the state.[118] Furthermore, one demand of this constitutional reform was for metropolitans to be elected by the "Extraordinary General Assembly" formed by the majority of the *boyars* and eventually confirmed by the ruler.[119] The statutes also gave the state the right to interfere in ecclesiastical matters, prescribing the standards for the selection of priests and abbots, which increased and formalized the prince's meddling in church affairs.[120]

The activity of the judicial and administrative powers, as well as the control and management of the Orthodox dioceses (along with their properties and income), were now the responsibility of the assemblies and of committees made up of both clergy and laymen who communicated with the new secretary for religious affairs.[121] All these reforms were encouraged by the Russian occupiers, who took an active interest in the implementation of the statutes, as it secured their control of the Romanian princes.[122] In some cases, metropolitans who were rejecting the reforms were exiled by the Russian tsar and later replaced with more cooperative ones.[123] Thus, it became apparent that the new constitutional government was progressively more detrimental to the Orthodox Church. Nevertheless, the church maintained some of its former privileges, a situation that was about to change toward the middle of the nineteenth century.

Little could have prepared the Orthodox clergy for what followed during and after the revolution in 1848, when the Romanian principalities experienced a national, cultural, and political renaissance. Amid emerging nationalist ideas about a united Romanian state, which were beginning to crystallize, enlightened intellectuals sought to explain why Romanians were culturally lagging behind other countries in Europe.[124] The result was an unfavorable view of Byzantine and Slavic influences that were closely linked with the Orthodox tradition. However, the ensuing anti-Slavic movement did not gain prominence owing to the peculiar link that developed between Greek and Latin thought in the Romanian lands.

From the start, the impact of Enlightenment ideas on the Slavic Orthodox influence in Wallachia and Moldavia should not be overstated. Perceived as a special cultural merit, Greek culture and tradition maintained its relevance even as the interest in the Latin roots of the Romanian culture came to the fore in historical and linguistic studies.¹²⁵ On the basis of these studies, it has been argued that the Enlightenment and its ideas have had a reduced impact in Southeastern Europe particularly because of the influence of Orthodoxy in the region.¹²⁶ For the Romanian people, noted Rădulescu-Motru, the Orthodox faith did not manage a replacement of ethnic identity, but vitalized whatever cultural tradition it possessed, allowing that tradition to develop in parallel with national identity.¹²⁷ According to this view, the Orthodox Church has created a space that made it possible for intellectuals to be simultaneously part of the Christian (Greek, Orthodox) and of the cultural secular (Latin, Western) communities, without radically separating them.¹²⁸

Moreover, the relevance of the Orthodox Church during this period was maintained owing to the involvement of Orthodox clergy in promoting the ideas of the Enlightenment. In the enthusiasm generated by these reforming ideas in the Romanian principalities, several enlightened and patriotic members of the Orthodox clergy became leading voices for national modernization, unity, and Europeanization.¹²⁹ Nevertheless, their patriotic zeal was often moderated by the majority of the church's hierarchy, which defended an understanding of Orthodoxy as *lex*.¹³⁰ The prevailing view stressed that Enlightenment ideas represented a dangerous foreign influence designed to secularize the society and reduce the church's nationalist identification with the state. Faithful to a tradition that surpasses a mere church–state "symphony," the Orthodox Church maintained its hope for a place in Romanian society following the union between Wallachia and Moldavia, be it symbolical and subordinated.

In the spring of 1848, Wallachia and Moldavia erupted in revolts demanding a new political system and economic and social reforms. Instigated and led by Romanian intellectuals known as *pașoptiști* ("forty-eighters"), the revolutionaries found—in the Western European states generally, and in the liberal and laissez-faire doctrines of the day in particular—a political and cultural model.¹³¹ However, despite their admiration for the West, the *pașoptiști* were unable to replicate the democratic changes for at least two reasons. First, the forty-eighters urged for drastic changes to the existing social and economic systems, but acknowledged that carrying out such a fundamental task would be infeasible. For example, to grant the peasantry full ownership of the land would have required huge sums of money that were simply impossible to provide.¹³² Secondly, based on the Byzantine Orthodox cultural tradition permeating Wallachia and Moldavia, the Western liberal ideas had little connection with the Romanians' historical legacy and therefore were rejected by the peasantry that formed the majority population. Not surprisingly, the experiment of independence lasted only several months and was ended by the insurrection of the Russian armies in Moldavia followed by the Turkish armies in Wallachia a few months later, after failed negotiations between the revolutionary government and the Ottoman Empire.

During the period that followed the Spring of Nations, the Romanian principalities took advantage of conflicting ambitions among the great imperial powers, and after the Treaty of Paris (1856) the political setting was prepared for the union of the two territories into the "United Principalities of Moldavia and Wallachia." Democratic elections in the two principalities ensued, with a majority of votes for the union of the lands under one constitutional monarchy led by King Alexander Cuza (1859–66) and, next by the German prince who would become King Carol I von Hohenzollern (1866–1914).[133] Due to the fact that the United Principalities were still under Russian and Ottoman dominance, the Romanian armies agreed to participate alongside the Russians in the final military defeat of Turkish dominance in the Balkans. This enabled Romanians finally to become an independent nation in 1877.

These major political, social, and cultural transformations were perceived negatively by the Orthodox Church hierarchy, whose former privileges had been greatly reduced. Already, during the middle of the nineteenth century, the clergy was being pushed out of political meddling as princes, *boyars*, and intellectuals requested a limitation of the rights of the metropolitans and bishops in the general assemblies.[134] Also, the competence of the Orthodox clergy to administer church properties through the Ministry of Religion came under criticism. As a result, King Cuza promulgated a set of reforming church laws during the 1860s that ensured the redistribution of the land and properties of the church and monasteries.[135] Thus, in typical despotic fashion, the new government virtually confiscated the land and properties inherited by the Orthodox Church from previous rulers.

In 1857, the Moldavian assembly passed a resolution that decreed a clearer delimitation of the roles and responsibilities of the Orthodox Church and the state by proposing the election of church hierarchy by the assembly and the entrance of clergy on the state's payroll.[136] The impact of King Cuza's church laws meant the Orthodox Church now enjoyed the protection and support of the state. Only some clergy decried half-heartedly the political subjection of the church to the state and the confiscation of the church property. Otherwise, the Orthodox Church embarked on a journey of rediscovery of its newly acquired identity as champion of the Romanian peasantry's struggle during centuries of occupation, and embraced the national and ethnic constitution of the Romanian state.[137] The Orthodox Church began supporting the union and the reforms that ensued despite the fact that these political transformations were essentially liberal in character and, naturally, were regarded by the church as foreign in character. As Ioan Ică, Jr, stressed, the secularization shock was not capable of demoralizing the Orthodox clergy and its cooperation with the government, especially as the Romanian population maintained their trust in the church.[138]

The union of the two Romanian principalities and the perceived threat to the identification of Orthodoxy with Romanian nationalism prompted the church to devise new ways of expressing its allegiance to an alienated, constitutional, and pluralist state. The solution came in the form of the union of the Moldavian and Wallachian Orthodox churches into one national and autocephalous Orthodox Church (1865).[139] King Cuza himself officially declared the united Orthodox Church as "autocephalous," and provisions were made for the metropolitans of Moldavia and Wallachia to maintain their local synods as long as they recognized the supremacy of the Central Synod.

The ecumenical patriarchate refused to recognize the autocephaly of the ROC until after the official political formation of the Romanian state in 1877. In the meantime, the new Romanian autocephaly needed a document that would offer the constitutional basis for the newly formed Holy Synod. The solution came from the Organic Statutes, adopted in 1872 from the Orthodox Church in Transylvania. Eight years later, Ecumenical Patriarch Joachim IV of Constantinople finally agreed to bestow the *tomos,* the official document recognizing the Romanian autocephaly under the metropolitan of Bucharest (1885). The ecclesiastical independence from the ecumenical patriarchate gained by the Orthodox Church bolstered the church's identification with Romanian nationalism. Released from its ties with the ecumenical patriarchate, the Orthodox Church of Romania would soon be found guilty of the sin of "phyletism." Phyletism had been defined during the synod in Constantinople convened by the Ecumenical Patriarch Anthimus VI (1872) as the national or ethnic principle in church organization.[140] As the Romanian autocephaly was becoming the national church of the newly formed state, it was gradually developing precisely this phyletist form of identification with nationalism.[141]

Transylvanian Nationalism

In contrast with Moldavia and Wallachia, where the Orthodox clergy had played a gradual social role that led to a phyletist identification with Romanian national consciousness, for the Romanians in Transylvania the Orthodox Church was bound up more intimately with the struggle for national emancipation. This was so because the Orthodox and Greek Catholic clergy organized the nationalist movement in Transylvania. Political and social aspects caused the Orthodox Church to have an influence in Transylvania that was almost opposite to that in Wallachia and Moldavia. As pointed out earlier in this chapter, the Romanian political representation in Transylvania was rejected by the diet as early as the seventeenth the eighteenth centuries. Thus, "recognition" became the common goal animating both the Romanian population and the clergy. For the Romanian people it was recognition of their political right to be an equal nation with the other three politically represented ethnic groups sharing the country. For the Orthodox and Greek Catholic churches, it was recognition as official religions among the others in Transylvania. Almost paradoxically, this struggle for recognition generated the first signs of national consciousness described earlier (Greek Catholics) and helped the church become more efficient and practical in its approach to the state (Orthodox). Thus, the result of this attempt toward political emancipation gave a first Romanian Orthodox political theology and an Orthodox constitution that would be adopted by the head of the Romanian autocephaly, the Holy Synod.

The majority of the Romanian population in Transylvania was peasantry, either day-laborers or dependent on a landlord, and therefore it played no significant role in the aristocratic political structures of the day.[142] By comparison, there were fewer Romanian *boyars* and landowners in Transylvania than in Wallachia and Moldavia. The political history of the Romanian peasants in Transylvania was linked with a number of events that in many ways determined their condition in relation to the other inhabitant nations. Thus, during the ninth century the Magyars conquered the *voivodates* of the local Romanian rulers of Transylvania, Menumorut, Glad, and Gelu and organized the region, replacing the upper classes of society with Magyar leadership. During the eleventh century, Transylvania was reconquered by Hungarian king, Stephen. In 1365, King Louis I issued a decree that required all noble ranks to have royal confirmation and affirmed Catholicism as the main qualification for holding titles or land properties, denying at the same time any rights and privileges to members of the Orthodox Church.[143]

During the fourteenth century, the Orthodox Church in Transylvania was organized around the life of the village, without a developed structure or links to any particular episcopate.[144] According to historian Radu Popa, the Orthodox Church consisted of parochial centers and monasteries that were the property of various local *boyars*.[145] The local leaders of the famous Bobâlna Uprising (1437), a spontaneous revolt of Romanian peasants against the increasing pressure exercised by the Catholic Szekler nobility, called for some form of political representation, such as the formation of a kind of peasant order or estate in which Romanians would be included. After the revolt was quenched, their request was met with the formation of a "brotherly union" (*Unio Trium Nationum*) that granted political representation to the Hungarian, Saxon, and Szekler nobility, but denied Romanian representation in the political life of Transylvania.[146] As only a merely tolerated faith, Orthodoxy continued to represent the religion of the Romanians in Transylvania, although it could not offer the institutional framework in which Orthodoxy in Wallachia and Moldavia became the politically recognized religion of the Romanian population.

Throughout the seventeenth century, the Orthodox clergy in Transylvania was under constant domination, either by Calvinist superintendents appointed by the empire or by the Catholic Church during the Counter-Reformation.[147] Confronted with a context dominated by the nobility of the Roman Catholic and Protestant churches, the Orthodox Church lacked the material resources and the political power that would have enabled it to have political relevance.[148] This was seen as an opportunity by the Protestant missions to convert Romanians from Orthodoxy; thus they printed the first Romanian-language Bibles and other religious books. A century and a half later the Habsburg Counter-Reformation began, which would alter the religious composition of the Romanian peasantry in a significant way.

In the last decade of the seventeenth century, Transylvania became a province of the Habsburg Empire and, under the rule of Emperor Leopold I, the Romanians were offered the chance to gain favor among the other political groups by joining the Catholic Church. This method had been used before by the Jesuits, who transferred Polish and Ukrainian Orthodox to Greek Catholicism, which used a combination between the Orthodox liturgy and ritual and the Glagolitic alphabet, but whose doctrines followed Roman Catholicism in recognizing the supremacy of the pope, plus several other major differences.[149] In addition to these religious aspects, the Habsburgs promised to the Greek Catholic clergy the same rights and privileges enjoyed by the Catholic clergy, a tempting proposition for the Orthodox priests, who were treated as serfs by the Transylvanian nobility and were subjected to heavy dues in labor and money.[150] However, the privileges promised by the Habsburgs did not materialize, because the other Transylvanian nations realized the threat to the establishment posed by the Romanian population. The Transylvanian nobility objected strenuously to the attempts at emancipation of not just the clergy, but also of any serf who would become Greek Catholic.[151] At most, the nobles granted Greek Catholic clergy a few minor privileges, such as free salt.

Thirty years later, there were six times as many Greek Catholic clergy as Orthodox in Transylvania, and the Romanian-speaking population was divided into two confessions—the Orthodox who accepted catholicization and those who refused and chose persecution.[152] Eventually, the outcome of the move to Catholicism was unprofitable for the Romanian population in Transylvania who saw little improvement in their disadvantaged status. However, as noted earlier in the chapter, the Greek Catholics became instrumental for the development of Romanian nationalist sentiment in Transylvania. The contribution of the Transylvanian School and notably Bishop Inocenţiu Micu offered a first attempt at nationalist emancipation.

Şaguna changed the fate of the relationship between the Orthodox Church and the ruling nations in Transylvania, and his efforts impacted the Orthodox autocephaly in a lasting way. In Şaguna's thinking and work, the Romanians gained their first Orthodox political intellectual one who would nonetheless give new direction to the historical link between the caesaropapist Romanian Orthodoxy and the nationalist Romanian state. The Organic Statutes, which he developed, would have an important role in the consolidation of Romanian autocephaly and, by implication, in the nationalist identification of Romanian Orthodoxy with the modern state.

Romanian Autocephaly in Modern Romania

At the beginning of the twentieth century, a tumultuous political and social situation was shaping church–state relations across the whole of Europe. The nationalist emancipation, the formation of Greater Romania (1918), with its inherent independence from imperial interference and the tendency toward secularization characteristic of the enlightened European societies, formed the new background for debates about the position and role of Romanian Orthodoxy in the newly formed, modern Romanian state. Amid a growing number of political parties, the Orthodox Church was struggling in its own process of unification and homogenization among the Moldavian, Wallachian, Bessarabian, Bucovinean, and Transylvanian churches, which had been brought together with the formation of Greater Romania. Significant differences of perception, especially in regard to politics, made the union between the synods of each mentioned region problematic. Whereas, the Orthodox Church in Old Romania (Wallachia and Moldavia) had been characterized by total submission to the state and hierarchical absolutism, the church in Transylvania developed a tradition of autonomy from the state and was composed by independent synods.[153] Although the Holy Synod of the united Moldavian-Wallachian Orthodox Church had adopted Șaguna's Organic Statutes in 1872, the Statutes had been virtually neglected ever since. Moreover, none of these models was present in the Orthodox Church of Bessarabia, where the tsar was the absolute ruler, or in Bucovina, where the church was highly hierarchical and subordinated to the Habsburg emperor.[154]

The Orthodox clergy in Transylvania demanded the other synods to accept the Organic Statutes of Șaguna as the basis for the constitution of a united Orthodox Church of the Romanians.[155] The Organic Statutes were supposed to answer the need for autonomy of the church from the state, while the independence (that the synods stressed) would protect the church against hierarchical absolutism. After lengthy debates and fierce disagreements, all Orthodox churches finally accepted the Organic Statutes of the Orthodox Church in Transylvania as the new Orthodox Constitution (1919) that would give guidance to the later-inaugurated Romanian Patriarchate (1925).[156] The "Law and Statute of Organization" of the new patriarchate, which identified legislative, administrative, and judicial organisms, and whose members were to be elected every six years, was passed and approved by the Romanian senate.[157] Thus it came that the Romanian Constitution of 1923 declared in article 22 that the Orthodox Church was the "dominant religion" and as such was represented in the senate by the patriarch, who became a *de jure* member.[158] The Byzantine legacy linking Romanian Orthodoxy and the rulers enabled the church to maintain and provide reciprocal support with the state, preserving a privileged relationship with the interwar governments.

The initial commitment to the principle of church–state autonomy, which was a main attribute of the political thinking behind Șaguna's Organic Statutes, was quickly discarded by the increasingly nationalist Orthodoxy at the beginning of the twentieth century. A telling example of this refers to the appointment of lay politicians among the members of the National Church Congress, which amounted to a politicization of the church.[159] Although, according to the church's constitution as elaborated by the Organic Statutes, the autocephalous Orthodox Church was now characterized by a democratic mode of organization, the Holy Synod was unable to devoid itself of political involvement and the hierarchical absolutism that had characterized its dealings with the rulers for centuries in Wallachia and Moldavia.[160] In effect, the Romanian autocephaly was becoming a political agency in service of the state.

Interwar Romanian governments were keen to maintain good relations with the Orthodox Church, despite their pro-liberal affinities. Orthodox clergy salaries and religious education continued to be funded by the state. The government not only guaranteed the financial dependence of the clergy but also managed the church's budget through the administrative functions of the General Fund of the Church.[161] The privileged position enjoyed by the Orthodox Church among the other denominations reached a climax in 1943 when Marshall Antonescu promulgated a law prohibiting the religious activity of all Neo-Protestant churches in the country.[162] In return for its services, the autocephaly would allow state representatives to be elected in the synod and thus have access to financial decisions, replace hierarchy, and reorganize religious education.[163] This subordination and reliance on the state's good will and support was dissonant with the model suggested by the Organic Statutes in Transylvania half a century before.

The church–state autonomy model initiated by the Transylvanian Organic Statutes attempted to achieve fruitful interaction between church and state, by outlining an ontological distinction between the two institutions. The most important aspect of this distinction was the emphasis on the precedence of the church in relation to the nationalist state.[164] However, the Romanian Patriarchate, dominated by a caesaropapist tradition that had characterized much of its interaction with the Wallachian and Moldavian rulers, was not attracted by a form of autonomy from the state that could question its national church status.

The Iron Guard and the Orthodox Church

What was the result of this nationalist Orthodoxy that emerged in the twentieth century organized around the autocephalous church and the Organic Statutes of the Holy Synod? In addition to the political-religious dynamics already described, further ideological challenges characterizing the interwar milieu led to new and extreme forms of Orthodox nationalism. Interwar Romania was the stage for an unconstructive struggle between traditionalist partisans with nationalist inclinations against liberal intellectuals with democratic ideals. The crisis that ensued was referred to as the national debate. An important aspect contributing to this struggle was represented by the European nationalist ideas penetrating the immature political class of Romania.

Although it had emerged after the union of Transylvania with Romania, this debate intensified throughout the entire interwar period. Various liberal reforms during the beginning of the twentieth century brought significant changes to the political and social structure of the country, which included new agrarian laws as well as an electoral system based on universal male suffrage.¹⁶⁵ This ensured the defeat of the Conservative Party and consistent victory for the liberal parties. Furthermore, the liberal and democratic constitution adopted in 1923 following the formation of Greater Romania brought economic reconstruction and social stability.¹⁶⁶

These factors contributed to a political polarization between the liberal tendencies of supporters of Europeanization and modernization (of Romanian democratization after the Western model with leftist political inclinations), on the one hand, and the supporters of an Orthodox traditionalist political agenda with strong autochthonous, collectivist, and authoritarian corporatist tendencies with political right affinities, on the other hand.¹⁶⁷ The influence of Nazi, Fascist, and Communist ideas were impacting Orthodox nationalist thinkers, who would soon develop a synthesis between totalitarian ideologies and personalized versions of Orthodox nationalism, with emphasis on the rural character of the Romanian tradition. The struggle of traditionalist partisans with Orthodox nationalist inclinations against liberal intellectuals with democratic ideals led to the establishment of radical versions of mystical religious nationalism that often took the form of xenophobia, and particularly anti-Semitism.

Unlike other Eastern European countries that faced political extremism under left-wing socialist and Communist parties during this period, the extreme nationalist parties were marginal to Romanian politics.¹⁶⁸ Right-wing extremism gained impetus only nearer to the beginning of World War II in the context of economic repression, growth of international anti-Semitism, and political corruption. The infamous extremist legionnaire movement called the "*Legiunea Arhanghelului Mihail*" (St. Michael's Legionnaire Movement) was founded in 1927. Constituted around its chief ideologist, Corneliu Zelea Codreanu, the movement became the Iron Guard Party (1930) and gained increasing influence throughout the 1930s. The Iron Guard was an extremist group that based most of its political doctrine on the manipulation of Orthodoxy's teachings, and as such, it attracted a large number of clerics.¹⁶⁹ Claiming the superiority of Orthodox nations in Europe, and animated by an intrinsic relationship between the Orthodox faithful and the Romanian nation, the Iron Guard became the only European Fascist movement with religion at its core:

> Few European Fascist movements went so far as to proclaim that 'God is a Fascist!' or that 'the ultimate goal of the Nation must be resurrection in Christ!' Romania was the exception. Romanian Fascists wanted 'a Romania in delirium' and they largely got one.... The goal of a 'new moral man' may have been a totalitarian commonplace, but the 'resurrection of the [Romanian] people in front of God's throne' was not routine in such circles.¹⁷⁰

The legionnaires believed Orthodoxy was the major condition of being a Romanian, while citizens belonging to religious minorities were excluded and considered potential enemies of the country.¹⁷¹ Orthodox Church clergy, theologians, and lay intellectuals who joined the Iron Guard thus manifested a "right-wing spirit" ideology coupled with national mysticism and anti-Semitism that radicalized the young Romanian intelligentsia. Their proposals included, without exception, the creation of an ethnocratic corporatist Romanian state.[172]

The most illustrious of the Iron Guard's luminaries was Nichifor Crainic (1889–1972), a professor at the Faculty of Theology, University of Bucharest, which became a hotbed of anti-Semitism among university students.[173] Just like the German Christian theologians in the Third Reich, Crainic applied his theological and rhetorical skills to severing the relationship between Judaism and Christianity by arguing that the Old Testament was not Jewish, that Jesus had not been Jewish, and that the Talmud, which he saw as the incarnation of modern Judaism, was, first and foremost, a weapon to combat the Christian Gospel and to destroy Christians.[174] Along these lines, Crainic employed other sensitive aspects like the mysticism and nationalism of Romanian Orthodoxy, which formed the basis of his *Gândirism* ideology. The *Gândirism* ideology, also called *autochthonism*, borrowed ideas from Oswald Spengler's *Lebensphilosophie*, which declared the inevitable collapse of Western civilization and the superiority of Byzantine culture. Crainic argued that the traditionalism of Romanian culture together with the Orthodox spirituality and mysticism form a superior Romanian culture.[175]

The fact that such ideas resonated with many Orthodox clergy indicate the Orthodox Church's ideological leanings. Although not directly involved in Jewish repression during the war, the ROC did not act against Jewish deportations and religious discrimination. Characterized by strong anti-Semitism, both its senior hierarchy and local clergy were outspoken in blaming the Jews for Romania's misfortunes, whenever they struck. Thus, when Romania lost its northeastern territories of Bukovina and Bessarabia to a deal between the Soviet Union and Hitler (1940), the population blamed the Jews, routinely alleging that they were spies or Communists. Patriarch Nicodim joined them:

> God had shown to the leader of our country the path toward a sacred and redeeming alliance with the German nation and sent the united armies to the Divine Crusade against the destructive Bolshevism . . . which has found here villainous souls ready to serve him. These companions of Satan have been found mostly among the nation that had brought damnation upon itself and its sons, since it had crucified the Son of God.[176]

Patriarch Nicodim followed in the steps of the previous patriarch, another renowned anti-Semite, who had close affiliation with the Iron Guard. In newspapers Patriarch Miron Cristea denounced the Jewish for exploiting the "poor Romanian people," whose wealth they acquired through their "ethnic and Talmudic sophistication."[177] Such evidence makes imperative the issue of the Orthodox Church's responsibility for the Holocaust in Romania. The common anti-Jewish front made by Romanian Orthodoxy and the Iron Guard, although mysteriously forgotten after the fall of Communism, remains largely unexplored.[178]

The task of implementing the Iron Guard's vision as a political program in interwar Romania was presented to Codreanu, leader of the "Iron Guard." Codreanu's legionnaire association became a religious-political movement, whose doctrinal essence was its Orthodox fundamentalism and nationalism rather than other, typically Fascist, traits. Its followers cultivated pro-German affinities and militated for the transformation of Romania into a legionnaire national state, ethnically purified, and Orthodox fundamentalist.[179] Codreanu's Iron Guard made use of all the traditional themes concerning the Jews, blaming them for having invaded en masse from the East and overpopulated Romania's cities, for exploitation of the peasantry through commerce, for controlling the press and threatening Romanian culture as enemies and representatives of foreign interests.[180]

The Iron Guard's ideology was defined by the party's program: "An organization based on order and discipline, guided by a pure nationalism, protecting the altars of the church, which its enemies wish to dismantle."[181] Thus, the political doctrine of the party had as its main goal the assimilation of the ROC as the most important element defining Romanian nationalism. The form taken by this party was described as "ethnocracy."[182]

Almost the entire generation of Orthodox clergy and theologians that emerged during the interwar period was fascinated by the "ethnocratic" pattern of Christian thinking.[183] The basis of ethnocratic ideology was the common identity inherent in the threefold structure represented by the Orthodox Church, the nation, and the state. Ethnocratic Orthodoxy was supposed to offer the reconciling element between a corporatist society and a totalitarian political leadership.[184] Thus, it was thought that a nationalist and corporatist Orthodoxy would offer the theological-political solution to the interwar social dilemma between liberal capitalist individualism and Communist collectivism.

Ethnocracy was a defensive reaction of conservative Orthodox Church ranks to the challenge secularism and modernity posed to transforming Romania into a pluralist society, which threatened the church's privileged position. The recurrent feature of this Orthodox ethnocracy was a polemical and highly critical attitude toward the West, toward modernity, democracy, and liberalism. All the intellectual and cultural values that were connected with the Western civilization, such as rationalism, individualism, and universality, were discredited as forms of atheism. On the contrary, aspects like collective mysticism, homogeneity, fusion, and totalitarian integration were adopted as elements bearing the substance of Orthodox nationalism.

In response to the legionnaire threat to political stability, Romanian King Carol II dissolved the parliament and all existing parties and instituted a period of soft royal dictatorship by setting up the National Renewal Front (1937).[185] Although one-party politics did not last more than two years, being replaced by the Iron Guard (1940–41), the consequence to Orthodox nationalism of this tumultuous political period was crucial. In 1938, King Carol II liquidated the democratic regime and imprisoned and executed Codreanu. Although the Iron Guard had been the king's greatest enemy, many of the ideological positions, especially the Orthodox religious one, held by the legionnaire movement were adopted by the king's National Renewal Front.[186] Thus, it came as no shock when Orthodox Patriarch Miron Cristea was elected to be the prime minister of the Front. The patriarch was outspoken in his denunciation of political pluralism, a position made clear during the inaugural speech in which he reiterated contempt for the 29 political parties who were supposedly to blame for the country's lack of clarity of vision.[187]

Given the condition of church–state relations described, it was not surprising that Orthodox resistance to the nationalist euphoria generated by the seduction of extreme ideologies in Romania was scarce. The only notable movement among the Orthodox clergy was the *Oastea Domnului* (Lord's Army) concretized in Fr. Iosif Trifa's attempts at renewal initiated in Sibiu, Transylvania (1923).[188] Inspired by the goals of the Oxford Moral Rearmament Movement, Fr. Trifa's concern with the moral depravity of the Orthodox priesthood grew into a movement advocating spiritual renewal and baptism as additional conditions for participation in the church's sacraments.[189] Though initially a lay movement, it attracted many Orthodox clergy and soon came to be regarded as a bridge between Romanian Orthodoxy and Neo-Protestant denominations.[190] Disavowed by the Orthodox Church, the movement was dissolved in 1947 and its leaders imprisoned as a result of the Communist regime's "regularization" of religious life.

Attempts at inner spiritual resistance and formal denunciations of xenophobic and anti-Semitic political activities came only later, when the Romanian Orthodox autocephaly began its cooperation with the Communist regime. Nonetheless, by the time the Communists seized complete control of Romania in December 1947, the terms "Orthodox" and "Romanian" were virtually interchangeable, proving that the continuity between the caesaropapist Orthodoxy and the nationalist state remained unbroken.

Conclusion

The investigation of the history of Orthodox church–state relations has shown that Romanian Orthodox ranks have constantly identified with nationalism. Particularly in Wallachia and Moldavia, the Orthodox faith has had the dimension of *lex*, a law that enabled the clergy to identify with the purposes of the ruler's aspirations and goals. This made it possible for clergy to take on administrative and judicial roles and to lead the Romanian peasantry to a paradoxical conjunction between Orthodoxy and Romanian nationalism. Although the situation was different in Transylvania because of the lack of political representation of the Romanian population in the land, there too religion became a rallying voice in the struggle for ethnic and national "recognition." In the efforts of Bishop Inocenţiu on the side of the Greek Catholic Church, and despite Şaguna's positive efforts to ensure Orthodox Church autonomy from the state, the Organic Statutes were only formally observed into the Holy Synod and the patriarchate of the united Orthodox Church of Romania.

Despite the Orthodox Church's Constitution of 1919, which committed itself to autonomy from the state according to the example of the Transylvanian Organic Statutes, the Romanian Patriarchate achieved the exact opposite, an uncritical and complete identification with the ethnic and nationalist state. Such symbiosis was possible through the assistance offered by the Orthodox nationalist and partisan clergy and theologians of interwar Romania, who raised the Byzantine Orthodoxy's antipluralist and corporatist affinities to a new level. The "real" truth and essence that nationalist Orthodoxy helped retain against the attempts of liberal forces to transform Romania into a "form without substance" consisted of a type of Orthodox legionnaire and nationalist ideology, which advocated an ethnocracy characterized by mysticism, homogeneity, and totalitarian integration. Loyal to its historical tradition, the Orthodox Church in Romania remained a religious community defined as a *lex* rather than as a community of faith and morals. This tradition was consistent with the caesaropapist Byzantine legacy discussed in the previous chapter. The investigation of the role religion plays in strengthening nationalism has showed that Romanian Orthodoxy emerged parallel with the formation of the Romanian state, and developed a religious nationalism that would account for the ROC's peculiar subjugation to the state and for the development of a theology of identification with the atheist and Marxist Communist state.

Notes

[1] Hastings suggested a set of categories that could be used when describing how Christianity shapes national formation. These categories include the role played by religion in sanctifying the origins of the nation, mythologizing and commemorating threats to national identity, emphasizing the social role of the clergy, stressing the crucial role played by the vernacular literature it has produced, providing a biblical model for the nation, underlining its autocephalous character and, finally, regarding itself as the creator of a unique national identity. A. Hastings, *Construction of Nationhood*, pp. 187–8.

[2] A. Hastings, *Construction of Nationhood*, pp. 188–9.

[3] Fred Halliday, "The Perils of Community: Reason and Unreason in Nationalist Ideology" in *Nations and Nationalism*, vol. 6 (February, 2000), p. 168.

[4] Katherine Verdely, *Political Lives of Dead Bodies: Reburial and Postsocialist Change* (New York: Columbia University Press, 1999), p. 74.

[5] O. Gillet, *Religie şi Naţionalism*, p. 137.

6. Constantin Iordachi, *The Anatomy of a Historical Conflict: Romanian-Hungarian Diplomatic Conflict in the 1980's* (MA Thesis, Central European University, 1996), especially chapter 3b.
7. C. Iordachi, *Anatomy of a Historical Conflict.*
8. Eniko Magyari-Vincze, "Politics of Multiculturalism and the Construction of Border Identities" (Research in progress, Center for Comparative Social Analysis, May 1999), p. 9.
9. Tom Gallagher, *Romania after Ceaușescu: The Politics of Intolerance* (Edinburgh: Edinburgh University Press, 1995), p. 33.
10. T. Gallagher, *Romania after Ceaușescu.*
11. T. Gallagher, *Romania after Ceaușescu.*
12. Armbruster argued that during this period the Romanians developed a national consciousness and expressed it in writing. Adolf Armbruster, *Romanitatea românilor: Istoria unei idei* (București: Editura Enciclopedică, 1993), p. 160.
13. Armbruster supported his argument by making references to several foreign and Romanian historians from the seventeenth century who have tried to discover the Daco-Roman roots of the Wallachians. A. Armbruster, *Romanitatea românilor,* pp. 160–1.
14. Constantin Schifirneț, "Studiu Introductiv" in *Teoria lui Rösler: Studii asupra stăruinței românilor în Dacia Traiană,* by A.D. Xenopol (București: Editura Albatros, 1998), pp. v–vi.
15. Florin Constantiniu, *O istorie sinceră a poporului român* (București: Univers Enciclopedic, 1999), p. 178.
16. David Prodan, *Transylvania and Again Transylvania* (Cluj Napoca: Romanian Cultural Foundation, 1992), p. 55.
17. John Cadzow, et al, eds. *Transylvania: The Roots of Ethnic Conflict* (Kent: The Kent State University Press, 1983), p. 18.
18. Viorel Roman, Hannes Hofbauer, *Transilvania: Românii la încrucișarea intereselor imperiale* (București: Editura Europa Nova, 1998), p. 82.
19. J. Cadzow, *Transylvania,* p. 18.
20. The Greek Catholic group that formed the "Transylvanian School" included Samuil Micu, Ioan Molnar, Iosif Mehesi, Ignație Dărăbanț, Ioan Pară, Petru Maior and Gheorghe Șincai. J. Cadzow, *Transylvania.*
21. J. Cadzow, *Transylvania,* p. 19.
22. Angelika Schaser, *Reformele iosefine în Transilvania și urmările lor în viața socială,* translated by Monica Vlaicu (Sibiu: Editura Hora, 2000), p. 215.
23. A. Schaser, *Reformele Iosefine,* p. 214.
24. F. Constantiniu, *O Istorie Sinceră,* p. 180; A. Schaser, *Reformele Iosefine,* p. 215.
25. F. Constantiniu, *O Istorie Sinceră.* Schaser pointed out that the "Co-Civilly Edict" suffered from Emperor Joseph II's lack of knowledge of the actual political and economic situation in Transylvania. By giving equal rights to the Romanians, the emperor underestimated the resentment that the Saxons had towards the Romanians and overestimated the economic possibilities of the latter. For this reason, she contends, the Romanians never really enjoyed their "equality." A. Schaser, *Reformele Iosefine,* p. 215.
26. Schifirneț underlined that before the eighteenth century, the most persuasive arguments about the theory of the Romanian origin and continuity with the

Daco-Romans came in fact from the Hungarian chroniclers. C. Schifirneț, "Studiu Introductiv," p. v.

[27] At the political level, the successors of Joseph II, particularly the emperors Francis I (1792–1835) and Ferdinand I (1835–48) did not recognize Romanians in Transylvania as a political nation. Keith Hitchins, *Orthodoxy and Nationality: Andreiu Șaguna and the Romanians of Transylvania, 1846–1873* (Cambridge, MA: Harvard University Press, 1977), pp. 6–7. In scholarship, Schifirneț notes that the Saxon and Hungarian historians developed the *Immigration theory*, a response to the *Daco-Roman-Romanian* theory. C. Schifirneț, "Studiu Introductiv," p. vi.

[28] O. Gillet, *Religie și Naționalism*, p. 143.

[29] A. Hastings, *Construction of Nationhood*, pp. 189–90

[30] Stephen Hayes, "Nationalism, Violence and Reconciliation" in *Missionalia*, vol. 27, No.2 (August 1999), p. 195.

[31] S. Hayes, "Nationalism," p. 196.

[32] Cf. K. Verdery, *Political Lives of Dead Bodies*, p. 8.

[33] K. Verdery, *Political Lives of Dead Bodies*, p. 63.

[34] K. Verdery, *Political Lives of Dead Bodies*, p. 56.

[35] A. Schaser, *Reformele Iosefine*, pp. 17–20.

[36] 61.8 percent of a total population of 1.38 million according to the census from 1784 in Transylvania. A. Schaser, *Reformele Iosefine*, pp. 21–22.

[37] With the exception of a period of less than 10 years (1781–90), when the Habsburg Emperor Joseph II's "Co-civilly Edict" gave equal rights to all groups in Transylvania, including the *Vlachs* (old name for Romanians), the Romanian population did not enjoy many rights, while their complaints were overlooked. A. Schaser, *Reformele Iosefine*, pp. 66–212.

[38] K. Hitchins, *Orthodoxy*, p. 4.

[39] V. Roman, H. Hofbauer, *Transylvania*, p. 81.

[40] In this document, the members of the Transylvanian School supported their claims by making reference to Bishop Klein's demands, to the myth of *Daco-Roman-Romanian* continuity and to the Emperor Joseph II's (1780–90) "Co-civilly Edict" which gave equal rights, at least in theory, to all the groups in Transylvania, including the Romanians. The *Supplex* was drastically rejected by Emperor Leopold II (1790–92) in 1791. The "Co-Civilly Edict" was the result of Emperor Joseph II's lack of knowledge of the actual political and economic situation in Transylvania. By giving equal rights to the Romanians, the emperor underestimated the resentment the Saxons and Hungarians nurtured towards the Romanians and overestimated the economic possibilities of the latter. Cf. Prodan extensive study on this topic. David Prodan, *Supplex Libellus Valachorum* (București: Editura Academiei, 1971).

[41] Corneliu Albu, *Pe urmele lui Ion-Inocențiu Micu-Klein* (București: Editura Sport-Turism, 1983), pp. 112, 132.

[42] As Prodan stressed, the three groups in Transylvania made up the *populus*, or privileged feudal estates (called *nationes*, or "nations"—though not yet in the ethnic sense). These were known as *nobles*, Szeklers, and Saxons; the first two spoke forms of the Hungarian language, and the third, a form of German. Among the privileged *nationes* were almost no native speakers of Romanian, who formed the bulk of the serf population, or *plebs*. Each of the *nationes* was associated with a territory, whereas (Romanian-speaking) serfs lived interspersed on the territories

of the other three. There were also some free peasants, largely Romanian-speakers and located mostly on the Saxon territories. Bishop Inocențiu stressed that Romanians too were a *natio* based on the common language they shared. Cf. D. Prodan, *Supplex*, pp. 186–7.

43 D. Prodan, *Supplex*, p. 187.
44 K. Verdery, *Political Lives of Dead Bodies*, p. 63.
45 K. Verdery, *Political Lives of Dead Bodies*.
46 Anonymous source, quoted in K. Verdery, *Political Lives of Dead Bodies*, p. 63.
47 Iorga saw in Bishop Inocențiu's requests the demand for a constitutional Romanian nation. Nicolae Iorga, *În Lupta cu Absurdul Revisionism Maghiar* (București: Editura Globus, 1991).
48 D. Prodan, *Supplex*, p. 127.
49 A. Schaser, *Reformele Iosefine*, pp. 214–5.
50 F. Constantiniu, *O Istorie Sinceră*, p. 178.
51 See the discussion about the Stalinist-led persecution of the Greek Catholics in the next chapter.
52 Bishop Inocențiu, quoted in K. Verdery, *Political Lives of Dead Bodies*, p. 91. Verdery quoted here from Bishop Inocențiu's correspondence in exile, from a speech given on the occasion of his final return to Blaj on 3 August 1997. Cf. *Viața Creștină*, vol. 8, no. 16 (August 1997), p. 4.
53 P. Negruț, *Biserica și Statul*, p. 61. See also K. Hitchins, *Orthodoxy*, p. 224.
54 Mircea Păcurariu, *Istoria Bisericii Ortodoxe Române*, vol. 3 (București: Editura Institutului Biblic și de Misiune Ortodoxă, 1981), p. 95.
55 Arhiva Bisericii Mitropoliei, Sibiu, *Colecția Șaguna*, no. 1447.
56 K. Hitchins, *Orthodoxy*, p. 226.
57 A. Webster, *Price of Prophecy*, p. 84.
58 Ion Lupas, *Mitropolitul Andrei Șaguna, Monografie* (Sibiu: Editura Consistorului Mitropolitan, 1909), pp. 215–6.
59 Two important principles animated Șaguna: reliance on the crown as the final source of law, and respect for the dynasty as a guarantor of legal continuity and social stability. K. Hitchins, *Orthodoxy*, p. 226. Cf. M. Păcurariu, *Istoria Bisericii Ortodoxe Române*, vol. 3, pp. 95–6
60 The moral support of the church was regarded to be crucial for the state to achieve its political and economic goals. Without it, Șaguna believed, the state would retain some "system of abstract morality" which would not fulfil the citizens' spiritual needs, jeopardizing the whole reason for being a state. M. Păcurariu, *Istoria Bisericii Ortodoxe Române*, vol. 3, pp. 108–9. Cf. K. Hitchins, *Orthodoxy*, p. 227.
61 M. Păcurariu, *Istoria Bisericii*, p. 228
62 M. Păcurariu, *Istoria Bisericii*.
63 Cf. Keith Hitchins, *Conștiință națională și acțiune politică la românii din Transilvania*, vol 1. *1700–1868* (Cluj: Editura Dacia, 1987), pp. 207–49.
64 Constantin Giurescu, *Istoria Românilor: Din cele mai vechi timpuri până la moartea regelui Ferdinand* (București: Editura Humanitas, 2000), pp. 280–1.
65 C. Giurescu, *Istoria Românilor*, p. 281.
66 The Organic Statutes contained 371 articles in the Wallachian version and 425 in the Moldavian, and included general principles for societal organization as well as articles on numerous administrative and organizational details. K. Hitchins, *Romanians: 1774–1866*, pp. 162–3.

67 Political leaders (George Barițiu, Ioan Rațiu, etc.) realized that Șaguna received a lot of support from the clergy and also was in good relations with the Habsburg monarchy. Although they did not enjoy his ideals about the independence and autonomy of the Orthodox Church in Transylvania, Romanian politicians had to seek the metropolitan's support for raising the question of Romanian independence at the Habsburg courts. However, a year later when the Organic Statutes were being passed, they attempted to boycott Șaguna. K. Hitchins, *Conștiința Națională*, pp. 227–42.

68 K. Hitchins, *Orthodoxy*, p. 245.

69 A. Hastings, *Construction of Nationhood*, pp. 190–1.

70 For Hastings, these episodes sharpen the absolute duty of loyalty to the horizontal fellowship of "us," and the moral gap separating us from the other, from the threat to our "freedom, religion and laws" that they constitute. A. Hastings, *Construction of Nationhood*.

71 Hastings gives the example of Nelson Mandela describing in his autobiography the electrifying effect of the recital of a praise poem to Shaka on detainees in South Africa's first Treason Trial: "Suddenly there were no Xhosas or Zulus, no Indians or Africans, no rightists or leftists, no political or religious leaders; we were all nationalists . . . In that moment we felt the hand of the great past . . . and the power of the great cause that linked us all together." A. Hastings, *Construction of Nationhood*, p. 191.

72 As noted earlier, Romanian historians from the interwar period onward maintained that the demands of Bishop Inocențiu Micu-Klein were made in the name of all Romanians (Iorga), while others argued that the Transylvanian School were only interested in the integration of some upper-class Romanians into the political membership of the Transylvanian Diet (Schaser).

73 According to Oțetea, the Communists rejected the identification of Romanian nationalism with the contribution of Bishop Inocențiu during the period between 1950 and 1965, which coincided with the persecution of the Greek Catholic Church. Cf. Andrei Oțetea, ed., *The History of the Romanian People* (New York: Twayne, 1970), p. 275.

74 Ioan Moisin, "Situația Bisericii Române Unite în primele opt luni din actuala guvernare" in *Viața Creștină*, vol. 8 no. 16 (August 1997), p. 3.

75 Andrei Mureșanu, "Cât de catolici au fost corifeii "Școlii Ardelene'?" in *Vatra*, vol.1 (1998), pp. 81–3.

76 As Verdery stressed, the Greek Catholics view the ROC as too close to Russia. The ROC's fundamentalist current is firmly pro-Moscow, and the Romanian Patriarch Teoctist has sided with Russian Patriarch Alexei on important matters. K. Verdery, *Political Lives of Dead Bodies*, p. 75.

77 Ilie Cleopa (Arhimandrite), "În dreapta credință a neamului românesc" in *Scara* vol. 1, no. 2 (1997), pp. 87–8.

78 A. Hastings, *Construction of Nationhood*, p. 192.

79 A. Hastings, *Construction of Nationhood*.

80 E. J. Hobsbawm, *Nations and Nationalism since 1780* (Cambridge: Cambridge University Press, 1990), p. 48.

81 E. Hobsbawm, *Nations and Nationalism*, pp. 74–6.

82 A. Hastings, *Construction of Nationhood*, p. 192.

83 A. Hastings, *Construction of Nationhood*, p. 192.

84 Hastings noted an example of such social role fulfilled by clergy in the case of Layamon, an obscure priest in a Worcestershire village of the late twelfth century, who composed the poem "Brut," the first history of England in English to include Arthur, Lear, and Cymbeline. A. Hastings, *Construction of Nationhood*, p. 192.
85 Cf. Simion Mehedinți-Soveja, *Creștinismul românesc: Adaos la caracterizarea etnografică a poporului român* (București: Editura Anastasia, 1995), pp. 100–4.
86 Cf. Șerban Papacostea, *Geneza statului în Evul Mediu românesc* (București: Editura Corint, 1998), p. 120.
87 Vasile Pârvan, *Contribuții epigrafice la istoria creștinismului Daco-Roman* (București: Socec and Company, 1911), pp. 238–9.
88 Cf. D. Barbu, *Bizanț contra Bizanț*, p. 27.
89 Nichifor Crainic, "Transfigurarea românismului" in *Ortodoxia II* (București: 1943), p.182.
90 I. Ică, "Dilema Socială a Bisericii," p. 531.
91 A. Hastings, *Construction of Nationhood*, p. 196.
92 Vlad Georgescu, *The Romanians: A History* (London: I.B. Tauris & Co., 1991), p. 33. See also I. Ică, "Dilema Socială a Bisericii," p. 538.
93 This situation was maintained for five centuries, such absolutism being reaffirmed from Basarab I, prince of Wallachia (1310–52) through to Constantin Brâncoveanu, prince of Wallachia (1688–1714) and Dimitrie Cantemir, prince of Moldavia (1710–11). V. Georgescu, *The Romanians*, p. 34.
94 Tudor Teoteoi, "O misiune a patriarhiei ecumenice la București în vremea lui Vlad Vintilă de la Slatina" in *Revista Istorică* V/1–2 (1994), pp. 30–8.
95 Cf. Andrei Bantaș, *The Romanian Orthodox Church Yesterday and Today* (București, 1979), pp. 11–17; Adolf Armbruster, *Romanitatea Românilor: Istoria Unei Idei* (București: Editura Enciclopedică, 1993); Andrei Timotin, "Paleocreștinismul carpato-danubian" in *Archaeus* vol. II, no. 2 (1998), pp. 43–175.
96 After several failed attempts by the Bulgarian armies to defeat Constantinople, Bulgarians were reorganized under a Byzantine ruler. At the initiative of Emperor Basil II, the Bulgarian Church was reorganized after the symphonic model. Cf. Aurelian Sacerdoțeanu, "Organizarea Bisericii Ortodoxe Române în Secolele al IX-lea – al XIII-lea" in *Studii Teologice*, vol. 20, No. 3–4 (March–April, 1968), pp. 242–57.
97 A. Bantaș, *The Romanian Orthodox Church Yesterday and Today*, pp. 10–11; V. Georgescu, *The Romanians*, pp. 32–33. Cf. Mircea Eliade, *Istoria Credințelor și Ideilor Religioase*, vol. II (București, Editura Științifică, 1978), esp. chapter 2.
98 A. Sacerdoțeanu, *Organizarea Bisericii Ortodoxe*, pp. 250–1.
99 A. Pippidi, *Tradiția Politică Bizantină*, pp. 185–6.
100 P. Negruț, *Biserica și Statul*, p. 161.
101 A. Mungiu-Pippidi, "Ruler and the Patriarch," p. 1.
102 The name Phanariot comes from the princes who came from Phanar, the Greek quarter of Constantinople, who were appointed by the Ottoman Empire to rule Moldavia and Wallachia (1711–70). C. Giurescu, *Istoria Românilor*, p. 218.
103 The Romanian *boyars* complained that the Phanariot princes weakened the principalities by dismantling the Romanian armies, which was threatening the relative political autonomy from the Ottoman Empire. V. Georgescu, *Romanians*, p. 75.

104 Keith Hitchins, *Romanians 1774–1866* (Oxford: Clarendon Press, 1996), p. 36.
105 C. Giurescu, *Istoria Românilor*, pp. 218–31.
106 The influence of the Romanian Orthodox churches was so widespread in terms of direct links with other Eastern patriarchates and financial support for the sustenance of other Orthodox churches in the Ottoman Empire, that they enjoyed a privileged place during the meetings of the ecumenical synod. K. Hitchins, *Romanians: 1774–1866*, pp. 36–7.
107 K. Hitchins, *Romanians: 1774–1866*, p. 41.
108 The activity of the higher clergy in the *divan* and other public bodies enabled them to have precedence over the *boyars*. The metropolitan occupied the place next to the prince and in exceptional cases when the throne was vacant, assumed political leadership of the country. When the metropolitan himself presided over a case, he presented a report and recommended a solution to the prince. Though the prince had the final decision, such decisions were rarely against the metropolitan's recommendations. K. Hitchins, *Romanians: 1774–1866*, pp. 41–42.
109 Cf. Alexandru Constantinescu, "Contribuții ale bisericii în justiția Țării Românești sub Alexandru Ipsilanti" in *Biserica Ortodoxă Română*, vol. 97, No. 1–2 (1979), pp. 165–78.
110 A. Constantinescu, "Contribuții," p. 170.
111 One such case occurred with a decree concerning infant baptism, issued in 1785 by Prince Mihai Șutu. K. Hitchins, *Romanians: 1774–1866*, p. 43.
112 V. Georgescu, *Romanians*, p. 104.
113 The document demanded the recognition of many national rights, including the right to have Romanian rulers again. The results were successful and in 1822 the Ottoman Empire appointed a native prince for each of the two principalities: Grigorie IV in Wallachia and Ioan Sandu Sturdza in Moldavia. V. Georgescu, *Romanians*, p. 104.
114 Not to be confused with Șaguna's Organic Statutes discussed earlier.
115 V. Georgescu, *Romanians*, p. 105.
116 In 1859 the two Romanian principalities were united under the Romanian King Alexandru I. Cuza (1820–73) though still under Ottoman suzerainty. Following the Russian-Ottoman-Romanian war of 1877, Romania would finally gain independence, which was internationally recognized during the 1878 Peace Treaty of Berlin.
117 Ioan Rămureanu, *Istoria Ortodoxă Universală* (București: Editura Institutului Biblic și de Misiune Ortodoxă, 1988), p. 548.
118 In chapter IX, article 411, the Organic Statutes stipulated that the metropolitans and the higher clergy were to be elected with the recognition of the ecumenical patriarchate and acceptance of the prince. Furthermore, the foundation of theological seminaries came under the strict jurisdiction of the state. Claudiu Cotan, *Ortodoxia și mișcările de emancipare națională din sud-estul Europei în secolul al XIX-lea* (București: Editura Bizantină, 2004), pp. 233–4; Cf. V. Georgescu, *Romanians*, pp. 107–8.
119 The Extraordinary General Assembly was formed mainly of *boyars*. The Ordinary General Assembly had the legislative authority and functioned like an early form of parliament, while the metropolitan was president of the Assembly. Finally, there was an Extraordinary Administrative Council whose competence extended

over the whole country. M. Păcurariu, *Istoria Bisericii Ortodoxe Române*, vol. 3, pp. 27–29.

[120] Gheorghe I. Brătianu, *Sfatul Domnesc și Adunarea Stărilor în Principatele Române* (Paris: Evry, 1977), p. 414.

[121] The secretary for religious affairs had to make sure that clergy was not interfering in public administration. K. Hitchins, *Romanians 1774–1866*, p. 166.

[122] M. Păcurariu, *Istoria Bisericii Ortodoxe Române*, vol. 3, pp. 49–53.

[123] In Wallachia, Metropolitan Gregory Dascălu was exiled by the tsar in 1829 under the accusation that he opposed the reforms. The new metropolitan elected was in favor not only of the Organic Statutes but also of the amendments that were made to them in 1840, 1842 and 1847. M. Păcurariu, *Istoria Bisericii Ortodoxe Române*, p. 53.

[124] V. Georgescu, *Romanians*, p. 119.

[125] C. Coțan, *Ortodoxia și mișcările de emancipare națională*, p. 38.

[126] Cf. Constantin Rădulescu-Motru, *Etnicul Românesc. Naționalismul* (București: Editura Albatros, 1990), p. 18; C. Cotan, *Ortodoxia și mișcările de emancipare națională*, p. 38.

[127] C. Rădulescu-Motru, *Etnicul Românesc*, pp.18–22.

[128] C. Rădulescu-Motru, *Etnicul Românesc*.

[129] Among them, most significant were Gregory Râmniceanu, Eufrosin Poteca and Gheorghe Lazăr. Cf. I. Ică, "Dilema Socială a Bisericii," p. 534.

[130] Cf. Alexandru Duțu, *Coordonate ale culturii românești în secolul XVIII* (București: Editura pentru Literatură, 1968), pp. 120–2.

[131] K. Hitchins, *Romanians: 1774–1866*, p. 232.

[132] K. Hitchins, *Romanians: 1774–1866*, p. 233.

[133] V. Georgescu, *Romanians*, pp. 273–317.

[134] Mihail Kogălniceanu, *Discursuri Parlamentare din Epoca Unirii* (București: Editura Științifică, 1959), pp. 66–78; Cf. V. Georgescu, *Romanians*, p. 180.

[135] In 1859 in Moldavia and one year later in Wallachia, the Cuza regime confiscated the printing press, workshops and the properties of a number of monasteries. C. Giurescu, *Istoria Românilor*, pp. 149–64; Cf. K. Hitchins, *Romanians*, pp. 312–3.

[136] M. Păcurariu, *Istoria Bisericii Ortodoxe Române*, vol. 3, pp. 113–27; V. Georgescu, *Romanians*, p. 180.

[137] Archimandrites N. Scriban and Melchisedec, from among the Orthodox clergy in Moldavia, were alone to demand autonomy for the church as a national institution and part of the nationalist revival. Other forms of protest included the metropolitans' refusal to consecrate vicars elected by the state. One of the strategies of the Cuza regime was to delay the election of metropolitans and bishops in order to limit any form of church opposition to the laws implemented. When such vacancies appeared, the regime would appoint vicars rather than metropolitans or bishops, and in such situations the existing metropolitans refused to consecrate them for service. M. Păcurariu, *Istoria Bisericii Ortodoxe Române*, vol. 3, pp. 113–4. Cf. Dimitrie A. Sturza, *Acte și Documente Relative la Istoria Renașcerii Române*, vol. 6 (București: Academia Română, 1909), pp. 102–7 and pp. 435–42.

[138] I. Ică, "Dilema Socială a Bisericii," p. 535.

[139] M. Păcurariu, *Istoria Bisericii Ortodoxe Române*, vol. 3, p. 122.

[140] The synod condemned and excommunicated the Bulgarians, who were certainly not alone guilty of "phyletism." T. Ware, *Orthodox Church*, pp. 12–16.

141 Horia-Roman Patapievici, "Biserica Ortodoxă și Modernitatea I," *Dilema*, Nr. 331 (11–17 June 1999), p. 1.
142 According to Hitchins, between the last part of the eighteenth century and the beginning of the nineteenth the Romanians represented over 50 percent of the population in Transylvania. Of them, over 90 percent were peasants. K. Hitchins, *Romanians*, pp. 198–99.
143 Nicolae Stoicescu, *Continuitatea Românilor: Privire Istoriografică* (București: Editura Științifică și Enciclopedică, 1980), p. 62.
144 Radu Popa, *Țara Maramureșului în secolul al XIV-lea* (București: Editura Enciclopedică, 1997), p. 204.
145 R. Popa, *Țara Maramureșului*, pp. 204–5.
146 The peasants have initially called for the recognition of what they called "the Commune of Hungarians and Romanians in this part of Transylvania." V. Georgescu, *Romanians*, p. 41.
147 Historians point to this humiliating condition of the Orthodox Church in Transylvania in the seventeenth century, which was in fact illustrative of the condition of the general Romanian population. M. Păcurariu, *Istoria Bisericii Ortodoxe Române*, vol. 3, p. 94.
148 K. Hitchins, *Orthodoxy*, p. 2.
149 These included the use of unleavened bread, the addition of Purgatory to Heaven and Hell as after death destinations and the "filioque" (the acknowledgment in the Creed that the Holy Spirit of the Trinity proceeds from both the Father and the Son). The combination church that resulted from this union could thus be widely adopted with minimal disruption, for very few village priests comprehended the finer points of doctrine, and to their followers the changes were virtually unobservable. Cf. K. Verdery, *Political Lives of Dead Bodies*, p. 61, n. 10.
150 V. Georgescu, *Romanians*, p. 42.
151 As noted earlier in the chapter, this reaction was prompted by the difference between the 1699 and the 1701 requirements of the Leopoldine Diplomas. D. Prodan, *Supplex*, p. 127.
152 The count, carried out by Bishop Inocențiu shortly after taking office as bishop, yielded 2,742 Greek Catholics in over 85,000 families, and only 458 Orthodox priests. C. Albu, *Pe urmele lui Ion-Inocențiu Micu-Klein*, p. 119.
153 M. Păcurariu, *Istoria Bisericii Ortodoxe Române*, vol. 3, pp. 490–1.
154 M. Păcurariu, *Istoria Bisericii Ortodoxe Române*, p. 491.
155 M. Păcurariu, *Istoria Bisericii Ortodoxe Române*, p. 490.
156 The first Romanian Orthodox Patriarch was appointed in the person of Metropolitan Miron Cristea, who became the driving force for ecclesiastical reforms. He later became Prime Minister of Romania during a political crisis. Cf. G. Sereda, "De la Biserica Autocefală la Patriarhia Română" in *Ortodoxia*, vol. 2, no. 2 (1950), pp. 325–36.
157 M. Păcurariu, *Istoria Bisericii Ortodoxe Române*, vol. 3, pp. 394–5
158 *Constituția României din 1923*. [Online] Available at: http://www.cdep.ro/pls/ legis/ legis_pck.htp_act_text?idt=1517, accessed January 2004. Cf. Hubert Jedin, ed., *The History of the Church*, vol. 10, *The History of the Church in Modernity* (London: Burns and Oates, 1981), p. 487.
159 Metropolitan Nicolae Bălan of Transylvania complained on a few occasions about the politicizing of the church's body through the election of secular politicians, to no avail. M. Păcurariu, *Istoria Bisericii Ortodoxe Române*, vol. 3, p. 397.

160 Cătălin Bogdan notes that such cohabitation between a democratic type of organization and the more autocratic Holy Synod, typical of the Wallachian and Moldavian churches, had the effect of the later cancelling the decisions of the former. Cătălin Bogdan, "Insidioasa Intoleranță" in *ID*, II (15) (December 2005).

161 P. Negruț, *Biserica și Statul*, p. 78.

162 O. Gillet, *Religie și Naționalism*, p. 26.

163 O. Gillet, *Religie și Naționalism*, p. 79.

164 The Orthodox Church, which adopted the Organic Statutes in 1919, failed to grasp that while Șaguna envisaged equal validity and authority in the church canons as in the secular legislation, the church laws would have precedence when a conflict between the two emerged. K. Hitchins, *Orthodoxy*, p. 227.

165 This liberal program had been considered as early as 1913 but was only implemented in 1917, during the war, by King Ferdinand. V. Georgescu, *Romanians*, p. 191.

166 "Greater Romania" included not just the two old Romanian principalities and Transylvania, but also other territories like Banat, Bessarabia, the Northern part of Bucovina, and Dobrudja. This annexation of territories after World War I resulted in an influx of a large number of inhabitants of other nationalities, which generated a defensive reaction concretized in an increased Romanian nationalist propaganda. V. Georgescu, *Romanians*, pp. 189–192.

167 Cf. Zigu Ornea, *Anii Treizeci: Extrema Dreaptă Românească* (București: Editura Fundației Culturale Române, 1995), especially the first two chapters: Democracy and Rationalism under Accusation; Romanianness and Autochthonism.

168 Although by 1921 the political spectrum in Romania was broadened by new parties on the extreme left and right, they only played a limited role in politics. The opposition party throughout the liberal governing period was the National Peasant Party, while others like the National Democrat, National Christian, and People's parties had shorter periods in government power. Z. Ornea, *Anii Treizeci*, pp. 192–3.

169 Lucian N. Leuștean, "Ethno-Symbolic Nationalism, Orthodoxy and the Installation of Communism in Romania: 23 August 1944 to 30 December 1947" in *Nationalities Papers*, vol. 33, No. 4 (December 2005), p. 440.

170 M. Burleigh, *Sacred Causes*, p. 270.

171 Cf. Radu Ioanid, *The Sword of the Archangel: Fascist Ideology in Romania* (Boulder, CO: Columbia University Press, 1990).

172 Cf. Nichifor Crainic, *Ortodoxie și Etnocrație* (București: Editura Albatros, 1997), p. 25.

173 Cf. *Final Report of the International Commission on the Holocaust in Romania*. București, Romania, 11 November 2004. [Online] Available at: http://www.ushmm.org/research/center/presentations/features/details/2005-03-10/#toc, accessed August 2005.

174 Crainic developed these ideas in various writings having been intensely preoccupied by them. See Nichifor Crainic, "Problema biblică" in *Icoanele vremii* (București, 1919), pp. 203–207; *Punctele cardinale în haos* (București, 1936); *Ortodoxie și Etnocrație* (București: Cugetarea, 1937).

175 The Orthodox component of this alternative culture was discussed in some of his articles, like "Isus în Țara lui" (1923), "Parsifal" (1924) or "Sensul tradiției" (1929), all published in the official newspaper *Gândirea*.

[176] Nicodim, Patriarh al României, *Cuvântul Patriarhului pentru Post, pentru Oștire, pentru Ogor* (București, 1942), pp. 5, 11–13.

[177] Patriarh Miron Cristea, quoted in *Curentul* (19 August, 1937). Cf. Leon Volovici, *Nationalist Ideology and Antisemitism: The Case of Romanian Intellectuals in the 1930s* (Oxford: Pergamon, 1991), p. 55.

[178] As Georgetta Pană noted, the Orthodox Church avoids any reference to the consequences of religious anti-Semitism. Cf. Georgetta Pană, "Religious Anti-Semitism in Romanian Fascist Propaganda" in *Religion in Eastern Europe*, vol. XXVI, No. 2 (May 2006), p. 9.

[179] Z. Ornea, *Anii Treizeci*, pp. 240–71.

[180] Corneliu Z. Codreanu, *Pentru Legionari* (București: Totul pentru Țară, 1937), pp. 103, 222–4.

[181] R. Ioanid, *The Sword of the Archangel*, p. 85.

[182] Ethnocracy is a political regime which, in contrast to democracy, is instituted on the basis of qualified rights to citizenship, and with ethnic affiliation (defined in terms of race, descent, religion, or language) as the distinguishing principle.

[183] Cf. Dumitru Stăniloae, *Ortodoxie și Românism* (București: Editura Albatros, 1998). D. Stăniloae, *Națiune și Creștinism* (București: Editura Elion, 2004).

[184] N. Crainic, *Ortodoxie și Etnocrație*, p. 25.

[185] King Carol II reacted in this manner in response to the threat posed by the Iron Guard. Following the dissolution of the parties and the setting up of royal dictatorship, a system of one-party politics was set in place. The National Renewal Front was based on the principle of bureaucratic centralism and its propaganda emphasized general notions such as social harmony and national solidarity. K. Hitchins, *România, 1866–1947*, pp. 421–5.

[186] As Tom Gallagher noted, there are other examples in modern Romanian history when the victorious party makes use of some of the aspects of the defeated party's agenda, if that were to secure national unity. T. Gallagher, *Democrație si Naționalism*, p. 50.

[187] Z. Ornea, *Anii Treizeci*, p. 314.

[188] For an in-depth analysis of this movement, see Alan Scarfe, "The Evangelical Wing of the Orthodox Church in Romania" in *Religion in Communist Lands*, vol. 3, No. 6 (November–December, 1975), pp. 15ff.; A. Scarfe, "The Lord's Army Movement in the Romanian Orthodox Church," in *Religion in Communist Lands* vol. 8, No. 4 (1980), pp. 316ff.

[189] See H. W. Austin, *Moral Re-Armament: The Battle for Peace* (London: William Heinemann, 1938).

[190] Alan Scarfe, "The Romanian Orthodox Church" in *Eastern Christianity and Politics in the Twentieth Century*, vol. 1, by Pedro Ramet, ed. (Durham, NC: Duke University Press, 1988), pp. 217–8.

Chapter 5

The Marxist-Orthodox Symbiosis

Introduction

This chapter will investigate the most important period in the development of the relationship between the nationalist Orthodox Church and the modern Romanian state. During 1944 and 1989 Romania was ruled by a Communist dictatorship inspired by Stalin's Soviet Union. Although the signs were already present during the interwar period, when extreme ideological ideas began gaining impetus, nothing could have prepared Romanian society for what followed when the Communist Party seized political control after the war.

Communism in Romania can be divided into three periods that differ in terms of political direction and with regard to the role played by the Orthodox Church with respect to the state. During the first period (1944–55) Romania was characterized by strong Stalinist domination, whereas during the second period (1956–74) Stalinist influences were diminished by the cultural regeneration of the country. Finally, during the last phase (1975–89) the Communist leadership was animated by the neo-Stalinist reform led by the Ceaușescu family. There is no clear demarcation between these stages. Arbitrary and otherwise chaotic in organization, Romanian Communism excelled in three aspects, namely "systematization," "modernization" and "civilization." The only other systemic structure of Romanian totalitarianism was its organized terror and violence coupled with the cruel "reeducation" programs of the prison persecutions.

In approaching these periods, the focus will be on the condition of the Orthodox Church in the early part of Communist rule, which saw all churches, including the Orthodox, persecuted and their clergy imprisoned or murdered as the regime attempted to eliminate all possible competition. This will enable an investigation of the second phase of the Romanian Communist dictatorship, when the ROC began to experience renewal and cooperation with the regime, particularly due to the efforts of Patriarch Justinian Marina (1901–1977). The climax of this cooperation was reached during the latter part of the totalitarian dictatorship, when Ceaușescu's party increased its pressure toward the Orthodox Church and intensified the nationalist propaganda, to which Orthodox theologians and clergy became active contributors.

The collaborative relationship during this period, and the particular role played by Orthodox theologians in crafting a Marxist-Orthodox theological construct for the nationalist aspirations of the Communist regime, will constitute the elements of the dilemma that will be addressed in the following chapter, where the Orthodox symbiosis with the Communists is compared to the nationalism of German Protestantism under Nazism and the role of Barmen Declaration.

Romanian Churches under Stalinist Persecution

The notable fact about the victory of the Allies over the Nazis in World War II was that within a couple of years half of Europe returned to the single-party totalitarian rule of the cold war. The defeated Nazi totalitarianism was merely replaced by victorious Stalinist totalitarianism. This situation led to the emergence of Marxist political religions all across Central and Eastern Europe. Communism took full advantage of the contribution of the Red Army to the defeat of National Socialism. As Burleigh noted, the postwar situation presented the Communists with a political milieu characterized by democracies that had failed to halt Nazism, by ruined aristocracies, by an industrialist class guilty of collaboration under Nazi occupation, by the memory of the interwar capitalist failure most evidenced by the Great Depression of the 1930s, and by the radical extremism that characterized democratic parties during the interwar period.[1] Thus, it came about that within a few years after the war the minority Communist Party of Romania, which numbered fewer than a thousand members, achieved dominance with a totalitarian regime.[2]

The Soviet takeover of Romania in 1944 inaugurated the transition from military dictatorship to totalitarian Communism, officially completed three years later. This was accomplished by the left-wing political coalition dominated by the Communist Party, which suppressed the legionnaire government and forced Romanian King Michael into exile (1947). In every country where the Red Army and the NKVD (People's Commissariat for Internal Affairs) had established a presence, the accession of Communist parties to governmental structures was rapidly achieved. The methods used by the Communists were a repertoire of limited but effective techniques that included systematized political intimidation, institutionalized violence, and blackmail, all carried by the NKVD's secret police and under the protection of Soviet troops.[3] The Communists began "sovietizing" the country by introducing versions of the Russian Marxist-Leninist model into Romania: reform of the educational system, nationalization of all forms of property, and collectivization of agriculture.

Even before the Romanian monarchy had been completely subdued by Communist pressure, the Soviet leadership had already established a conciliatory approach to Eastern European Orthodoxy. The Soviets' main advocate was

Stalin's tool, the Moscow Patriarchate.[4] In an apparent effort to affirm the church's social and religious activity, the Communists spoke about a Soviet-style church–state "autonomy," which in reality amounted to virtual eradication of the church as a social presence.[5] This period was difficult for all religious denominations in Romania, which faced varying levels of persecution from a Communist Party determined to extinguish any form of political opposition. All church properties, parishes, monasteries, and dioceses went into state administration.[6] The government seized Christian youth organizations, while Orthodox welfare societies were strictly controlled by lay committees informing the regime on their activity.

Greek Catholic Dissolution

As a result of the diminishing influence of opposition parties, the churches were brought back into focus as the last potential source of opposition to the Communists. As limited manifestations of civil society and surviving repositories of a sense of national independence, the churches represented a constituency that was outside the totalitarian state whose atheist desire was to eradicate religion. The first churches that came to the Communist authorities' attention after the war were the Roman and the Greek Catholics. The assault by the authorities on the Greek Catholic Church was part of Stalin's Europe-wide attack on its seven million members living in countries like Ukraine, Czechoslovakia, Bulgaria, Hungary, and Romania. The Greek Catholics' obedience to the pope made them an alternative center of spiritual gravity that was intolerable to the Soviets, who had begun pressing for the unity of all Orthodox churches in Eastern Europe, making them easier to control by the Russian Patriarchate in Moscow, and removing anything that reduced Soviet influence. Stalin's attempt at the dissolution of the Greek Catholics was carried with the support of Russian Patriarch Aleksei I "Simanski" (1877–1970), who regarded this church as schismatic and urged them to revert to their "ancient attachment" because, "Now Divine Providence has restored Russia to her ancient frontiers and you are henceforth with us for ever."[7]

In October 1948, the ROC organized with the assistance of the Communist authorities a synod requesting Greek Catholics to "return" to the Orthodox faith. Presided over by the newly appointed patriarch, Justinian Marina (1948–77), the chairman's speech (said to have been written by the government) was read in the presence of police forces attending the "readmission synod."[8] The synod's decision, legalized in governmental Decree 358 (December 1, 1948), pronounced the Greek Catholic Church as illegal, and in consequence demanded all their institutions, schools, monasteries, congregations, and associations cease their activity.[9] After 250 years of active presence in Romania's political and spiritual life, the Greek Catholic Church was banned, its properties confiscated, and its membership forcibly merged with the Orthodox Church.[10]

The secret police began an operation code named "132," which involved drastic measures intended to respond to Vatican pressures on the Communist regime.[11] As a result of this action, Greek Catholic clergy were interrogated and imprisoned without exception, including all six bishops and their successors, as they all refused cooperation with the Orthodox Church and the Communist Party.[12] Most died in prison, while the congregations went either to the Roman Catholics or the Romanian Orthodox, and a limited number continued to meet in hiding, as Greek Catholics. One estimation calculated that between 1948 and 1964, when the Communist dictator Gheorghe Gheorghiu-Dej (1948–65) announced the first general amnesty, more than a million Romanians had suffered in Communist prisons, of whom 200,000 were murdered or died as a result of exile or torture; among them, there were 33 Orthodox bishops and priests recognizable by name, 12 Greek Catholic clergy, and 17 Roman Catholic clergy.[13]

The Persecution of Orthodox Clergy

Having dealt with the Greek Catholic Church, the Communist Party turned its attention to the Orthodox. It soon became apparent that the newly established totalitarian state would not be shy of using coercion as it began subduing all potential political and cultural opposition, which included the Orthodox autocephaly as one of the targets. The Communists adopted a different strategy whereby they aimed to control and subversively eliminate the Orthodox Church, which was regarded as a threat to the atheist state. For the Communists to gain popular support, they had to allow, at least officially, a place for the Orthodox Church in their party agenda. Nevertheless, due to the close links that had existed among Orthodoxy, the monarchy, and nationalist legionnaires in interwar Romania, the Orthodox clergy would face persecution.[14]

As part of an international program for the development of an "Orthodox front" (the Vyshinsky Plan) the Orthodox Church in Romania was encouraged to strengthen its ties with the Moscow Patriarchate while reaffirming its neutrality in the political decisions of the Communist Party.[15] The Vyshinsky Plan declared by the Soviet High Command of the Southeast European Front called for the "liquidation of undesirable clergy and replacing them with Soviet-trained or sympathetic clergy;" and demanded "forming an alliance with Orthodox Churches under the leadership of the Moscow Patriarchate."[16] Thus, based on the new Education Reform Act and the General Regime of Religion of 1948, the presence of the Orthodox Church in public life—in schools, hospitals, charitable trusts, army, and prisons—was greatly reduced as the country entered a process of nationalization. All religious and private schools were replaced by schools "organized exclusively by the state ... based on democratic, popular and realist scientific principles."[17]

This process of political subjugation was imposed upon any clergy who had voiced political opposition to the Communist regime. Based on suggestions made by the "Vyshinsky Plan," all resistant clergy, whether Orthodox, Greek Catholic, or Protestant, were removed from office and imprisoned, to be later replaced by "collaborating" clergy. As was expected, the close interwar connection between the Orthodox clergy and the legionnaire movement meant many priests from the Orthodox ranks were interrogated or imprisoned. However, as has been revealed by the opening of secret police archives after the fall of Communism in Romania, accusations of a link with the legionnaire movement was often a disguised pretext for removing political opponents or for settling old resentments.[18]

The post-Communist investigation of archival material has revealed that testimonies concerning the persecution of Orthodox clergy after the war have been undermined by inconsistencies regarding the number of persecuted priests, as they attempted to either minimize or exaggerate the distance between collaboration and persecution.[19] While sporadic persecution of the Orthodox clergy due to its links with the legionnaire movement is indisputable, such persecution should be neither exaggerated nor treated separately from the general state of persecution that animated the Soviet-run Communist regime from 1946 onwards, and whose effects were felt by all religious denominations.[20] As described by the experience of an eyewitness to the dreaded Gherla prison:

> [A]t Gherla prison, the number of inmates was not constant—it was increasing and diminishing all the time. Some prisoners were liberated, some were transferred to other prisons, some went to their trials or to those of other prisoners in order to testify. Sometimes, new inmates were added to our cells. At one point there were about 15,000 prisoners in Gherla alone. . . . I found there were priests from different religions in Gherla: Orthodox, Catholic, Unitarian [Greek Catholic], Lutheran, Calvinist. They were all kept in a separate cell. This was because the security police wanted to prevent the priests from preaching in the cells, celebrating mass or converting other inmates.[21]

The climate during this period was one of fear, with clergy and lay dissidents, together with other religious believers, randomly arrested, imprisoned, or banned from the country.[22]

Nevertheless, as Trond Gilberg stressed, Romania was the only Communist country in the Eastern European block where Orthodoxy avoided systematic persecution and instead benefited from collaboration with the regime.[23] The ROC soon learned to make the most of its links with the state, thanks to the efforts of Patriarch Justinian Marina. Although the persecutions were a bad start, the unique religious-political symbiosis that characterized Romanian church–state relations for centuries would facilitate the relatively harmonious cooperation between the Orthodox Church and the Communist state. To substitute a Communist leader for a king or a ruler was a simple process, as long as the leader was Romanian. Under the leadership of Justinian, the ROC strengthened its ties with the Communist regime to the point that it achieved a symbiosis between Orthodoxy and Marxist ideology. The contribution of Justinian to the continuation of the historical pattern of Orthodox identification with the nationalist state ensured a collaborationist positioning that gave legitimacy to the Marxist political religion.

Cultural Regeneration and Orthodox Renewal

The second period of Communist leadership in Romania (1956–74) was characterized by a relative relaxation of Soviet political and cultural pressure, which inaugurated the political process of Romanian de-Russification. The death of Stalin (1953) brought a period of political uncertainty in the Soviet Union, which together with Khrushchev's plans for de-Stalinization allowed the Communist Party in Romania to distance itself from Soviet influence and develop friendly relations with other countries. This period was characterized by a shifting of emphasis from international (Soviet) Communism toward a Romanian form of nationalist Communism that would concretize in Nicolae Ceaușescu's "new man" ideology.

Orthodox Church Renewal

The new Romanian Constitution (1952) did not stipulate any major change in relation to the Orthodox Church, although it further reduced the already limited religious freedom that other denominations might have been permitted.[24] The church–state relationship during this period revolved around the notion of "obedience"—total and unreserved obedience of the church and its clergy to the Communist Party.

The Communists used the church in order to develop contact with other countries that might embrace Communism, and to influence their political leaders' perception of it. As Leuștean noted, as early as 1953 the Romanian Patriarchate headquarters were being visited by delegates from various Latin American countries, as undisputed evidence that Romania enjoyed religious freedom.[25] Obedience became the condition for an undisturbed relationship between the church and the state, and was moreover emphasized by the third Communist Constitution (1965) wherein it was stressed that the state's laws regulate religious life, while education is completely separated from the church.[26] The policy of obedience explains the virtual lack of revolt of the Orthodox hierarchy when scores of historical church buildings were demolished, especially in the capital city, Bucharest, in order to make space for grand (and hideous) architectural projects.[27]

Bishop Kallistos noted the ambiguous character of the church–state relationship in Romania, stressing that although it was one of the churches most subservient to a Communist regime in Eastern Europe, it was also one of the most vigorous spiritually and theologically.[28] Despite the persecution of all churches in the first phase, the Orthodox clergy was soon given the chance to collaborate with the secret police, and many resumed their religious activities.[29] The Orthodox Church alone was allowed to support a mission abroad (Jerusalem) and to have students sent to the Mount Athos monastery. Priests were given permission, and sent to serve to several Romanian emigrant communities in Western Europe and the United States.[30] Orthodox monasteries were allowed to function, and their seminaries did not have to restrict the number of students admitted. To seal this unique relationship with the atheist state, a large number of church buildings and properties that had been confiscated from the Greek Catholics were transferred to the Orthodox, under state directive.

Patriarch Justinian and Marxist-Leninism

Despite what could be regarded as an era of church reform, Justinian's contribution (through skilful diplomacy with the Communist regime) raised questions about his collaborationist attitude. In fact, considering that the Communist regime had been so intrusive with its demands and so brutally oppressive toward the church, it was quite a feat for the Bucharest Patriarchate to achieve such compliance. Known as "the red patriarch" or "sovrom-patriarch,"[31] Justinian enjoyed a special relationship with the Communist leadership, and particularly with the dictator, Gheorghiu-Dej.[32] The history of this special friendship goes back to Marshall Antonescu's regime during the war, when Gheorghiu-Dej, having escaped from prison was hidden by Justinian.[33] Justinian was a simple parish priest from Râmnicu-Vâlcea, who, already in the 1930s, had gained a reputation for being a good organizer, an administrator of finances, and passionate about culture and education.[34] Justinian's influential essay, "*Cooperație și Creștinism*" ("Cooperation and Christianity") showed first signs of Marxist interests, as he drew upon the moral witness of the Gospels and the Church Fathers to justify the clergy's efforts to improve the material status of the people.[35] Having displayed these leftist leanings, and due to his Communist friendships, Justinian was promoted to bishop in the Metropolitanate of Moldavia and Suceava on Communist instructions.[36] His meteoric ascension to the Patriarchate of Romania in 1948 enabled him to engage, just in time, with the canonically questionable act of abolishing the Greek Catholic Church.

Justinian's sympathies enabled the church to survive through the 1950s relatively well. Regarded by his admirers as a major reformer, he encouraged the clergy to become interested in social issues, which was quite a departure from the contemplative Orthodox tradition. He improved theological training and initiated projects that compiled manuals to be used in theological seminaries throughout the country. Some of the most promising clergy were sent abroad after 1964 to study in renowned universities of Europe.[37] The most successful reforms took place in monastery life. The monastics were required to learn a trade, which led several monasteries to register as cooperatives and set up workshops for weaving and other rural handicrafts, the proceeds of which generated a useful income. Other monasteries specialized in farming cooperatives that made them an integral part of village life to the point that the local peasantry was employed for labor. This development of monastery life increased the number of monastics, with 7,000 in 1956, spread throughout approximately 200 monasteries.[38] "Under the new Socialist Orthodoxy," stressed Webster, "monasticism became a matter of proletarians at prayer."[39]

However, Justinian remains famous not only for the pastoral and social creativity he displayed but, moreover, because of the unique ideological synthesis he forged between Marxist-Leninism and the Orthodox faith. Already in 1953, Justinian sent pastoral letters that combined religious teachings with practical advice on collecting the harvest.[40] In the same year, he led a Romanian delegation abroad to attend the enthronement of the Bulgarian Patriarch Kiril in order to prove to the Orthodox commonwealth that the church's position in society had not been threatened by the Communist regime. Upon his return, Justinian stressed before the Holy Synod the propagandistic need to support the defense of peace movements.

After the fall of Communism, there were different views regarding the support offered to the regime by the Orthodox Church. Some thought endorsement of the Communist Party's Marxist-Leninist ideology was too costly a price for the rejuvenation of Romanian Orthodoxy after the war.[41] They suggested that the church survived by employing a form of "Sergianism," by establishing an ideological pact with the Communists similar to the pact between the Soviet Comintern and the Moscow Patriarchate. Others, and here are included most contemporary Orthodox voices, continue to support Justinian's beliefs and actions, stressing he was justified in collaborating with the atheist regime in order to keep the church "alive."[42] The accommodation reached by the Orthodox Church is regarded by this group as a form of resistance, a view that absolves the church from any responsibility for collaborating with the regime. As the argument goes, Justinian did not obey the regime "completely" and did all he could to oppose Communism. However, the situation was far too complicated to fit an either/or approach. The third perspective, Leuștean rightly suggested, is to see that the Communist regimes used religion as a form of ideological propaganda.[43] As political religions, Communism as well as Nazism identified in the nationalist inclinations of the churches a useful instrument that needed to be used rather than persecuted. The churches, in turn, found resources within their own history and tradition to adapt to political conditions. Romanian Orthodoxy made use of its historical identification with the state, employing a nationalist discourse that had been developed in the interwar period to include theological justifications. The doctrine of social apostolate, inspired by Justinian and promoted by the church, represented the confluence of Romanian nationalism and its historical "symphony" model of church–state relations as applied to the current political circumstances of Communist totalitarianism.

The Social Apostolate

The social apostolate is the term for Justinian's theological vision, collected in "Apostolat Social" a 12 volume work written between 1948 and 1977. The starting point envisioned by Justinian is the future renewal of Orthodoxy and the challenges that are bound to threaten its status as the depository of eternal truth.[44] This initial concern of the social apostolate resonated with the theme of renewal that characterized almost all interwar theological thinking. As seen in the previous chapter, the Orthodox clergy was drawn to the Iron Guard's ideologies because of the combination of nationalism and Orthodoxy. Common themes that preoccupied interwar theologians and intellectuals—such as the renewal of the church, service to one's neighbor, the increased social role of the church, and deep spirituality—were reiterated in Justinian's social apostolate texts. In fact, the first volume of the social apostolate works include a number of articles he had published in the interwar period, up until 1940.[45]

Justinian's approach is indicative of radical social reform based on classic Marxist social analysis but assisted by traditional biblical appeals to justice for the poor and oppressed. In those respects, some have referred to it as an early version of "liberation theology" that would later become popular in Latin America, Western Europe, and North America.[46] He identified biblical texts in the Old and New Testaments to justify the transforming power of work, which gives dignity and respect to people.[47] The equation drawn by the social apostolate between the Pauline "new creation" in 2 Cor. 5.17 and the Communist "new man" became Czeslaw Milosz's archetype of what he described to be "the captive mind."[48]

The eternal truth, for which the Orthodox Church is the principal depository, stressed Justinian, was a Jesus Christ interested more in one's deeds than in faith:

> Our church has the responsibility to preach only the truth. Its future depends on how the church defends this truth. The path of the church is Jesus who guides the church's life. The servant of Christ has to walk all his life on the path of Christ's truth through *concrete deeds* [author's italics] for the path of truth is the way of life.[49]

For Justinian, Christ's incarnation had as its purpose the creation of a new humanity and a new ideal model of man and, thus, the goal and mission of the church is the man who is the foundation of nation and society.[50] The problem with the vision of society as painted by the patriarch is that at times the church lives in a society that does not follow Christian principles. He refuses to acknowledge this reality; instead stating, "The church's mission is to confer a divine sense to all earthly interests harmonizing the man with himself and his neighbor" so that he can be used in the service of the nation and society.[51] The focal point of the social apostolate was, thus, service: "The church must cease being preoccupied with itself, its status, its rights, and go out to serve mankind in the name of Christ the Servant."[52] Justinian continually adhered, and encouraged the church to do the same, to the social apostolate, even in times of persecution that struck the church and the monasteries (1958–63). He felt that outright resistance to the Communist regime would have led to greater losses than gains.[53]

The theological vision professed by Justinian attempted to combine Orthodox spirituality and social concerns with contemporary scientific advancement and modern industrial society as viewed through Marxist-Leninist spectacles. Based on his concept of the relationship between faith and science, the Christian faith and the church are thought to be fully compatible with social progress and scientific advancement, as there are no differences between what the Bible and scientific research teach; when religion and science are separated, the harmony is disturbed, and instincts such as pride and ambition take central stage.[54]

The adaptation between the Orthodox Church and the Communist state was not novel, as it had already been tried at the beginning of the century in Russia, through the efforts of Patriarch Sergius, a faithful collaborator with the Communist regime and author of an encyclical wherein he announced that: "Henceforward the joys of the Soviet Communist homeland would be the joys of the church and the sorrows of the Soviet Communist homeland would he the sorrows of the church."[55] Olivier Gillet draws a parallel between Russian "Sergianism" and Justinian's Marxist-Leninist ideology.[56] However, Enache argued that the two ideologies are not identical in that "Sergianism" has had a strictly technical connotation, coming to mean the acceptance and justification by the Russian Orthodox Church of its cohabitation with the Communist state.[57]

Enache thus insisted that the social apostolate should be more properly called "Justinianism," suggesting that Justinian's vision was not a doctrine limited to the adaptation of the church to the current Communist regime, but was a *cosmocratic* vision of the Orthodoxy's role in the world.[58] The social apostolate was thought to be a universal, and more generally conceived, theological vision concerning the social role of the Orthodox Church and how this affects the general principles of the church's social mission in the world.[59] Although one would agree that Justinian surpassed his Russian counterparts by developing a synthetic response to the social, political, and moral challenges posed by the "new" order, it is doubtful that such a Marxist-Orthodox synthesis was anything more than the response of a genuinely socialist patriarch, willing to accommodate Communist social policy and promote the social apostolate. As Webster emphasized concerning this new ethic:

> It purported to represent a necessary updating of the Orthodox theological perspective, a seminal change in the Orthodox world view. In their most

grandiose hopes, Justinian and the other hierarchs may have likened their achievement to St. Augustine's baptism of Plato or Aquinas's christening of Aristotle. The architects of the "social apostolate" rendered the same retroactive service to Karl Marx and Vladimir Ilych Lenin.[60]

The dogmatic justification for Justinian's view concerning the active relationship of the church with the state is summarized in the first volume describing social apostolate doctrine (1948). In interwar Romania "the homeland and the people" expressed an important and all-embracing principle, and the Orthodox Church could not absent itself from that concern.[61] Thus, for Justinian, the church had a responsibility to be engaged in society because the homeland was a supreme source of legitimacy; the church was there to serve the people, an idea that would be carried further by Fr. Antonie Plămădeală in his *servant church* theology.[62] This profound link between church and nation requires the church's support of all transformations taking place in society, as long as they bring happiness, because "divine happiness is conditioned by human fulfillment on earth."[63] Here, the Byzantine symphony is employed: "Both the church and the state serve the same interests, those of the homeland, whose expressions they both are"; for the patriarch, the Byzantine tradition of integrating the church within the state's broader circle of interest is acceptable to the church as long as autonomy is respected.[64]

There is a noticeable chronological change of emphasis in the patriarch's discourse concerning the relationship between the church and state. Whereas, during the late forties and fifties the emphasis of the social apostolate is on the "homeland" and on its people's contribution to social betterment, in the sixties, when the country's policy became more nationalistic, the emphasis changed: "The ROC has always been bound to the needs of the nation, having been a National Church".[65] Using forms of expression reminiscent of the Communist regime, Justinian underlined the important role played by the Orthodox Church throughout history by stressing that "the church has constantly contributed to the forging of national unity and kept alive the national self-consciousness of the nation's political unity."[66] In this context, the Orthodox autocephaly resurfaces in the Orthodox Patriarchy's discourse, understood in an ethnic sense as an expression of independence and autonomy from any foreign authority.[67]

Probably the most damaging contribution made by Justinian to the image of Romanian Orthodoxy during Communism was the ideological support he granted to the state. Ultimately, it was the most important thing the Marxist state wanted from the Orthodox Church. The Communist authorities used the social influence of the church in order to legitimize their political presence in a mainly Orthodox country, while the church, in order to survive, accepted compromising with the atheist government. His mixture of Orthodox theology and Marxist ideology led the patriarch to maintain that the socialist policies of the Communist Party were fulfilling exactly that social apostolate task.[68] Through discourses and sermons, Justinian remained resolute on this perspective throughout his life; he gave his church's blessing to the abdication of monarchy, affirmed the new constitution, and encouraged agricultural collectivization, advising the clergy and the congregations to accept and, moreover, help carry out these undertakings.[69] In relation to the Constitution of 1948, the patriarch stated:

> The ROC noticed that the new Constitution warrants our freedom of religious practice. Thus, the principle that all state power comes from the people and belongs to the people is in accord with the Gospels' principles. . . . Other principles concern the material world . . . the respect and protection of private property, . . . Everyone has to work. . . . The state minds for the health system, according to the spirit of Christian philanthropy. . . . Vote for the Popular Democracy Front.[70]

In 1962, Justinian congratulated the clergy for their work toward the collectivization of agriculture, stressing that the teaching of the Holy Scriptures and the traditions of the church are fully compatible with this endeavor.[71] After offering a biblical exhortation in support of this doctrine, the patriarch announced: "Only that which is intimate to man is individual property, the rest is common good. What is being achieved in this country is what Christians have struggled to achieve in the past 2,000 years. . . ."[72] It did not seem to concern the patriarch that what he implied was that the Communist society was the ideal society.

Finally, Justinian's Marxist social-political analysis extended to what he called "the devil of the century," namely social injustice and inequality. In his view, these bore the mark of imperialism and as such there could be no peace until they were resolved. Evidently, truth and freedom were to be found in socialist society, from which perspective the patriarch addressed issues such as decolonization, atomic experiments, the Greek Communists' struggle, the Vietnam War, and disarmament issues.[73] With every change of political direction, the patriarch modified his views on these topics to fit Communist, Soviet, or nationalist Communist views.

As Webster underlined, the social apostolate entailed the same socialist view of religious freedom and human rights that prevailed with the Moscow Patriarchate, but with a twist: "In Ceaușescu's Romania, the bishops also brazenly maintained to the bitter end the fiction of complete religious freedom and denied all charges of religious persecution."[74] This has been confirmed by Peter Lakatos, who has knowledge of the fact that many of Justinian's contemporaries thought he led the Orthodox Church into fatal subservience to the state and betrayed hundreds of thousands of fellow Christians, while always denying any constriction of religious freedom in Romania.[75] Others, like Enache, tried to excuse Justinian, arguing that he intentionally adopted a paradoxical attitude of manifesting a visible and loud attachment to the regime and its values so the Communists would think the church was well managed.[76]

Thus, the social apostolate attempted to gather, under its umbrella, cosmocracy as a formal principle (structure) and socialism as the material principle (content), which together formed the Romanian religio-political symbiosis. Justinian envisaged a "close natural relation" between the Orthodox Church and the Communist state—one that was reminiscent of the Byzantine symphony relationship between church and empire. As stated, he equated socialist society with the Christian ideal and, therefore, identified faith with citizenship, which meant that "collaboration" was natural.

> The ROC lives within the state and recognizes its authority. Our church is present and active within the state, not only because the members of the church are also members of the state, but also because a close natural relation was set up in the common interest of the members of the church and the citizens of the state: that of the state and the church.[77]

That Justinian's special relationship did not always bring benefits to the church illustrates the government's expectation of full obedience from the church.[78] Ultimately, the patriarch's views were in continuity with the caesaropapist relations that have characterized the Romanian Orthodox legacy, whereby the state was entitled to rule while the church was obliged to collaborate. Because of this, the Orthodox symphony was rather a caesaropapist cosmocracy. As Stan and Turcescu stressed, the social apostolate was a form of accommodation with a hostile atheistic state, a Romanian version of *symphonia* that "entailed theoretical ingenuity and considerable compromises on the part of the Orthodox Church."[79]

Alas, Justinian was not an isolated voice advocating a Marxist-Orthodox synthesis during the era of Communism. As an original apostle of the social apostolate, his pragmatic ideology generated its own disciples. Following his death in 1977, at least three other leading members of the Orthodox hierarchy would use the social apostolate concept to justify their adulation of "the most beloved son of the Romanian people," namely Communist dictator Nicolae Ceaușescu, who ruled from 1965 to 1989.

Neo-Stalinist Reform and the Subservient Orthodoxy

Nicolae Ceaușescu came to power in 1965 and ensured Romania would become a counterproductive society characterized by cultural barbarism, political tyranny, and economic primitivism. In more than two decades of rule he succeeded in compromising the very name of Marxist political and social doctrine. In true Stalinist style, the so-called "Genius of the Carpathians" envisioned himself to be an oracle of revolutionary theory, a new "Coryphaeus of science" and he surrounded himself with people willing to join in this ludicrous fable. In true Napoleonic style, Ceaușescu brought his family into the inner circles of power, with his illiterate wife presiding over the development of science and technology, as second in command, and his hedonist son as secretary of the Youth Communist Union.

The neo-Stalinist reforms initiated by Ceaușescu were reminiscent of the Chinese "Cultural Revolution," stressing a centralized form of economy that emphasized the important place ideology held in this project.[80] The regime engineered by Ceaușescu soon took the form of a political and ideological tyranny that stressed the ideology of the "new man" and a Communist society perfectly homogenized. Unlike the Soviet reforms of *glasnost*, *perestroika*, and *demokratizatsija* ushered in by Mikhail Gorbachev, Ceaușescu's reform included "systematization," "modernization," and "civilization," a scheme that forced Romania into a redundant, inefficient economic and politically suffocating straitjacket.[81] The Romanian Communist vision sought by the ambitious dictator led to forced urbanization and industrialization, systematization of entire cities, and the destruction of some 8,000 villages with the populations moved into proletarian blocks of flats. In the center of Bucharest, he bulldozed priceless historical sites and churches in order to make space for a new and hideous civic center for himself and his clique. The modernization plans were meant to create a new Romania, with a classless society and with no urban and rural categories of population. The Communists constructed large numbers of industrial sites throughout the country, again destroying in the process countless cultural treasures and religious sites.

This was the content of Ceaușescu's vision for a new Romanian civilization, and many of its policies were carried out with the help of a well-organized secret police that insured any skepticism or public criticism would be silenced. Ceaușescu's Romania developed one of the most effective thought-control networks ever imagined on such a large scale. The testimony of Ioan Pacepa (born 1928), the secret police general who deserted Ceaușescu and asked for political asylum in the United States, was almost unbelievable to Westerners who had assumed Romania enjoyed a relatively free society. In his testimony, since confirmed by the opening of the secret police archives, Pacepa reveals the pervasiveness and effectiveness of the ruthless Securitate, whose intelligence-gathering and spying was exhaustive and virtually flawless.[82] Some suggest that about one in three citizens was an informant of the secret police.

Such was the "reform" of a Romanian Communist Party that championed a conservative, Honecker-style approach that attempted to regenerate or revise the revolutionary theory. In 1974, Ceaușescu began to consolidate more strongly his particular totalitarian ideology—an all-encompassing hybrid of Marxism-Leninism, traditional Romanian nationalism, and narcissistic self-centeredness. However, as Tismăneanu noted, the forthright support offered by Ceaușescu to the reemergence of ethnocentric groups and formations made a mockery of their own passionate plea for the preservation of the "sacred values" of historical materialism and internationalism.[83]

The Praise of the Subservient Church

An intrinsic part of this ideology was Ceaușescu's moderate mystical nationalism, based on an interpretation of history that portrayed the courage of the ancient Dacian kings, Decebal and Burebista, in opposing the Roman legions; the mythologized figure of Stephen the Great, defender against the Ottomans, or Michael the Brave, the king who for a short time united Wallachia, Moldavia, and Transylvania into a single unit.[84] As Gilberg noted, Ceaușescu's love affair with Romanian history extended to "claims about the superiority of Romanian culture and its extensive contributions to world civilization."[85] This linked well with the role envisaged by Ceaușescu for the Orthodox Church in legitimizing his mystical nationalism driven by a desire to exploit mythologies about the past for present-day purposes. In 1968, in an attempt to consolidate his power, Ceaușescu received the Orthodox Church leadership in an official visit, in order to acknowledge the positive historical role played by the church in the strengthening of nationalist Romania. In response, Justinian uttered:

> The understanding and cooperation established between the cults in this country, the religious freedom we enjoy, the good will and extensive material and moral support given to the religious cults by the State leadership, the religious faith in itself, as well as the atmosphere and feelings of lofty patriotism prevailing in all sons of our homeland, are inspiring us.[86]

Nearly 30 years after the Communist takeover, the same formulae were still being strictly observed by the Orthodox hierarchy. In 1974, Justinian was praising the "uninterrupted progress of all aspects of life in present day Romania, wisely guided by her best sons under your [Ceaușescu] leadership."[87] During these official speeches, he took the opportunity to assure the Communist leader that the church "enjoyed complete religious freedom, enshrined in the Constitution and guaranteed by the state."[88] Dominated and collaborative, the Orthodox Church became the propagandistic tool for a dehumanized political regime.

Patriarch Justin Moisescu

The attempt to adapt the "social apostolate" doctrine to the new social and political realities prevailed as an official policy of the Orthodox Church. After Justinian's death, the Communist regime's policy toward the church changed from accommodation to infiltration. The ROC was being controlled in its activities by the Ministry of Religion, which regulated all administrative and religious functions of the church.[89] The Orthodox Church's hierarchy and clergy were strictly monitored while arrests and persecutions were carried out against nonconformists. As Ică noted, the regime began using collaborating clergy to spread the Marxist-Leninist ideology regarding collectivization or the strengthening of the campaigns against private property, or at international church congresses.[90] During Ceauşescu's dictatorship the Orthodox clergy grew more silent and more subservient, as the Communists were growing bolder in their "modernization" projects. This could be seen in the lack of protest from the Orthodox Church when scores of churches in downtown Bucharest were torn down, or surrounded and masked by blocks of flats, while other church buildings were literally towed to new locations away from the main boulevards.[91]

In 1977, Patriarch Justin Moisescu (1977–86) stepped onto the throne of the Orthodox Patriarchate to enjoy a relatively short reign and continue the social apostolate inherited from his predecessor and mentor. Born in a Wallachian village and theologically trained abroad (Athens and Strasbourg), Justin had occupied the metropolitan see in Sibiu, Transylvania, in 1956 and in Moldavia and Suceava since 1957. A frequent attendant of the World Council of Churches' meetings, where he was leading the Romanian delegations, Justin became the international promoter of the social apostolate.[92] He was renowned for dedication to theological study, especially New Testament and patristic studies that he combined with the Marxist concerns of the social apostolate. Even before becoming a patriarch, he spoke eloquently about socialism, observing that from the beginning of the Communist regime, the church in Romania "has supported the great reforms and contributed with patriotic élan to the building of Socialism in our country"; this, however, was more than accommodation of the church to reality, because Justin saw in the church's striving for socialism an ideal: "Our whole sacro-human work in the social field, is carried out to a certain purpose, i.e. in serving our socialist country; it is carried out here in the land of our forefathers even more in the stage of building up Socialism."[93]

Justin believed Marxist-Leninism served an important purpose, and that the Orthodox Church should support the state's initiative in carrying this purpose. His cosmocratic understanding concerning church–state relations prompted him to declare, "We have been charged by the Lord to serve with unswerving loyalty our homeland, Romania."[94] As pointed out by a close observer, when Justin traveled to the World Council of Churches' meeting in New Delhi (1961), the Romanian delegation's message was:

> The pastoral programme of the "social apostolate" initiated in 1948 by Justinian has blessed the fraternity that exists between believers of all faiths in Romania. This fraternity is the outcome of an ecumenical theology and of our social work activity.[95]

In 1983 Justin pledged the "unbounded patriotic love" of the Romanian Orthodox people for "the most beloved son of the Romanian people," and later, when Ceauşescu was reconfirmed as president of the Socialist Republic of Romania, Justin expressed the joy of the church to the nation's "hard working and tireless leader."⁹⁶ Only two years later, when Ceaușescu's grand plans for Bucharest led to the demolition of more churches, Justin declared that only a few small churches had actually been destroyed by the authorities.⁹⁷

Finally, Justin appeared as a remote man, lacking the popular appeal of his predecessor. Known abroad mostly for his activity with the church's foreign relations department, the patriarch initiated a number of publishing projects and oversaw the erection of a new ecumenical center on the outskirts of Bucharest.⁹⁸ Despite his propagation of the social apostolate abroad, he merely continued the tradition of subservience to the Communist dictatorship. An attempt to develop this doctrine ideologically would concretize in another Orthodox high clergyman and Communist propagandist.

Metropolitan Antonie Plămădeală and the Servant Church

Metropolitan Antonie Plămădeală of Transylvania (1982–2005) was known for his loyalty to the state and so, upon the death of Justin, he was considered for the available post. However, pending several months of deliberations, the Holy Synod opted for Metropolitan Teoctist Arăpașu of Moldavia. Antonie had distinguished himself in ecumenical and international "peace" circles as an astute theologian, having completed his doctoral work at the Roman Catholic Heythrop College, Oxford (1972). His dissertation investigated the theme that was fundamental throughout his life, that of the servant church.⁹⁹ As an assistant bishop to the patriarch since 1970 he was in charge of the Orthodox Church's foreign relations department, which enabled him to develop friendships among a vast array of churches and organizations worldwide. Like all Orthodox clergy during Communism, the metropolitan was expected to represent the nation's interests abroad; hence, in August 1988, when the central committee of the World Council of Churches took up the subject of human rights violations in Romania, Antonie successfully persuaded the commission to avoid the subject.¹⁰⁰

Views entertained by Antonie—such as that in Romania religious freedom was unscathed by the overriding demands of the Communist "state sovereignty,"—placed him firmly among the collaborationist clergymen of the Communist period.¹⁰¹ His views on church–state relations made it clear that he followed the social apostolate legacy of his predecessors; he saw no strict separation between the Orthodox Church and the totalitarian state.¹⁰² This is confirmed by his insistence on the Romanian religio-political symbiosis whereby the church "has always stood side by side with the Romanian people, with the nation, in its struggle for national freedom and political unity."¹⁰³ As such, the people's church has to continue to "adapt itself in accordance with the times to the new social, political, economic, cultural, and spiritual realities . . . avoiding any interference with the secular field of the state."¹⁰⁴

Antonie's vision for the social apostolate took the form of an *ecclesiology*, wherein he described the biblical and patristic basis for the servant church.¹⁰⁵

Nevertheless, this ecclesiology is not concerned with what the church is—its role in salvation, its origin, or relationship to the historical Christ—but mainly with a church serving mankind. In this attempt, one could see how Antonie has undertaken to counter the charge, often expressed in the West, concerning the otherworldly character of Orthodox Christianity. Similar to its predecessor's blueprint, the servant church conceptualized a combination between the ROC's spirituality and the Marxist-Leninist social practice of the party.[106] Despite the fact that a thorough theological engagement with the servant church has yet to be accomplished, an examination of the suggested goals and methods of argumentation employed makes inescapable the charge of Orthodox Marxist synthesis denoted in metropolitan's endeavor. Described as the theological and ideological structure for the compromise of the ROC with the totalitarian regime during Ceaușescu's dictatorship, the vision of the servant church dominated Romanian Orthodox theology and represented the image of the Romanian church to the outside.[107] Like its archetypal social apostolate, Antonie's vision for a church serving the Marxist-Socialist project had anticipated, in a conformist rather than reformist sense, the liberation theologies of Latin America.

Patriarch Teoctist Arăpașu

When Patriarch Teoctist Arăpașu (b. 1915) was installed to the Patriarchate in 1986, the official statement of the Orthodox Church read: "The hierarchs, the clergy, and the believers, like all the sons of the homeland, are highly appreciative of President Nicolae Ceaușescu's creative capacity, activity [as] genuine builder of a new life in Romania, and daring thought put in the service of Romania's continuous progress, of the entire people's happiness."[108] The patriarch also expressed thanks and deep gratitude for "the conditions of full religious freedom in which the ROC and the other denominations in Romania carry out their activity."[109] Following the usual path of most other Orthodox clergy, he had become a monk, then studied theology in seminary, and held various teaching positions and Episcopal sees. When Metropolitan Justin was appointed patriarch in 1977, Teoctist became Metropolitan of Moldavia and Suceava, a traditional waiting position for most Romanian patriarchs-to-be. His career within the Orthodox Church was more visibly that of a political activist, having served as a deputy in the Grand National Assembly and participant in the congresses of the Socialist Unity Front.[110]

Like Justinian and Justin, Teoctist manifested great support of the social apostolate, which he propagated with astute oratory skills in official government circles. Most of his published work revolved around themes like freedom (as quoted), peace, and security. These latter themes have become official ROC propaganda abroad since the 1970s, when the Soviet Union joined the Non-Proliferation Treaty and began its nuclear disarmament discourse, supported by the Russian Orthodox Church.[111]

As late as 1988, when serious economic deficits and political redundancy were beginning to loosen the grip of the totalitarian regime on Romanian society, Teoctist was assuring Ceaușescu on the president's seventieth birthday that the church was "thinking of you with great appreciation, deep gratitude, and unlimited love."[112] As stated in chapter 1, the controversial role played after the fall of Communism in Romania, and his lack of remorse for many years thereafter, bear witness to Teoctist's consistency with the social apostolate. Nonetheless, his inexcusable contribution to the Marxist-Orthodox symbiosis was detrimental to the prophetic witness of the church, which remained consistently subservient to the Communist regime.

Orthodox Resistance to Official Church Ideology

The Orthodox Church's combination of a Marxist-Socialist utopian society and Christian ideas, its support offered to the atheist state in suppressing the Greek Catholic Church, and its collaboration with the official government whose discriminatory policies it had campaigned for locally among the congregations, nationally and internationally, have been met with little resistance from within the church. Private denunciations of Orthodox identification with the Marxist state reverberated in remote monasteries, prisons, or among groups of friends that met in secret.

Marginalized clergy, theologians, and intellectuals have attempted a form of inner spiritual resistance; two such efforts, known as "Desperate Activism" and "Resigned Historicism," were developed by Mircea Vulcănescu (1904–1952) and Nicolae Steinhardt (1912–1989). Most attempts were thwarted by a brutal secret police that exposed their opposition and imprisoned them.[113] A renowned Christian philosopher and disciple of interwar Nae Ionescu (1890–1940), Vulcănescu rejected the social apostolate synthesis, instead stressing that love, and not class struggle, was the church's goal and life's dynamic force; he died in 1952 from maltreatment in Aiud jail.[114]

Petre Țuțea (1902–1991) was a Christian dissident who spent most of his life in Communist prisons or under house arrest. In his many philosophical essays he offered a spiritual vision grounded in the personal experience of the Romanian Gulag, describing some of the horrors of torture that were involved in the "reeducation" programs of the Communist prison camps.[115] In his work *Christian Anthropology*, Țuțea offered a different perspective on what the church should be, namely an alternative human community whose indestructible strength rests upon the fact that it works with the Creator's purpose for humanity.[116]

The dissident priest and theology professor Fr. Gheorghe Calciu-Dumitreasa (1925–2006) is another case in point. Admired by students, Fr. Calciu began a series of sermons against the atheist government, describing its ideology as a "philosophy of despair." In his sermons, he denounced particular actions of the government, such as the demolition of churches in Bucharest and Focșani, and typified them as indicative of the incompatibility between Orthodoxy and the atheist regime.[117] Such public criticism of the government's actions brought about his imprisonment, although not immediately, since his case was already being publicized in Western media. The regime proceeded to denigrate him and used the Orthodox Church to spread rumors concerning his "neo-Fascist activity," and eventually defrocked him in 1984.[118]

Fr. Nicolae Steinhardt took the vow to become an Orthodox monk after spending four years in prison. There he discovered that "totalitarianism is not the conclusion of an economic or biological theory, but a kind of attraction of death," and as such refused all his life collaboration with the Communist regime. His famous essay, the *Happiness Dairy*, which was confiscated by the secret police in 1972 but later reedited, was a vigorous criticism against Communism in its Romanian utopian version.[119] Other protests against the cohabitation of Orthodoxy and the atheist state were uttered by Orthodox clergy, such as Fr. Cleopa Ilie (1912–1998), who found refuge in the mountains, or Fr. Benedict Ghiuş (1904–1990), Fr. Gherontie Guţu (1887–1937), and Fr. Sofian Boghiu (1912–2002), all of whom were imprisoned and persecuted for their dissidence.[120] Among them should be mentioned Fr. Dumitru Stăniloae, dubbed as one of the most influential Orthodox theologians of the twentieth century, who spent five years in Communist prisons for participating in an Orthodox renewal movement. The case of Fr. Stăniloae will be addressed in the next chapter, as his complex theology and ambivalent relationship to the Communist regime deserves closer investigation.

These individual testimonies underline the fact that "the price of prophecy," as Webster termed it, against the Communist dictatorship in Romania was indeed very high and assumed self-sacrificially. The religio-political symbiosis contributed to transforming Romanian totalitarianism into a political religion in which dissenters against the state automatically became dissenters against the church. As was the case with Fr. Calciu, most of the resisting clergy mentioned above were consequently defrocked by the church. This brings us to the only two organized attempts at Orthodox renewal and anti-Communist resistance ever to have taken place during Communism in Romania.

Rugul Aprins (The Burning Bush)

Having started with Lord's Army (1947) and the Greek Catholic Church (1948), a new wave of religious persecutions began in 1958, when several Orthodox clergy were imprisoned owing to their connection with the so-called *Rugul Aprins* (The Burning Bush) movement. The movement developed around the personality of Sandu Tudor (1896–1962),[121] interwar writer and editor of the daily *Credinţa* (*The Faith*) and of the weekly *Floarea de Foc* (*Fire Flower*). Astute critic of the European leftist and right extremism, Tudor denounced the falsity and antihuman character of the totalitarian ideologies of the day. Some of his most pungent articles, written between 1933 and 1938, such as "Modern Bestiality,"

"Between Sobor and Soviet," and "The Century of the God-killers," underline with remarkable intuition the nature of Communism as being essentially a political religion. In the last of these three articles, Tudor makes reference to the anti-religious character of Leninist Communism in 1930s Russia, underlining the political religion character of Communism that ultimately seeks to destroy the church.[122]

The first phase of the *Rugul Aprins* movement occurred between 1944 and 1948, with the formation of the so-called "Antim Group" around Tudor, Fr. Benedict Ghiuș, and Fr. Ivan Kulâghin, a Russian monk and former member of the Optina Pustnija, the hesychastic[123] community mentioned by Dostoevsky in *The Brothers Karamazov*.[124] This group, which gathered around professors and students, monks and laymen, was composed of men and women who tried to maintain an intellectual life free from the pressure of materialist and atheist theories of the day. Theologians such as Fr. Dumitru Stăniloae, writer Vasile Voiculescu (1884–1963), philosopher Anton Dumitriu (1905–1992), physician Alexandru Mironescu (1903–1973), critic Alice Voinescu (1885–1961), and many others, met at the Antim Monastery in Bucharest for liturgy, meditation, prayer, and intellectual presentations and debates.

The combination of this group and the cohesion it generated was truly astonishing; it brought together lay intellectuals with theologians and clergy in the presence of the hesychastic spiritual tradition represented by Fr. Ivan. As described by André Scrima (1925–2000), one of its adherents, the *Rugul Aprins* enabled free association and equal voice, as no rules or hierarchies were observed, and provided the space for lively expositions. Finally, it attempted to convert all those experiences into an intellectual discourse.[125] Although it was intently apolitical and lacked any external manifestation or instigation to revolt, the movement encountered the persecution of a totalitarian government that could not tolerate dissenters from the Socialist-Marxist ideology. In 1948, the group was disbanded and its members arrested on unsustained charges of legionnairy activity against the "democrat-popular" regime.[126]

After Tudor Sandu's release from prison (1952), the group resumed its activity, this time meeting in private homes and other monasteries as well as Antim, and following a strategy that involved the training of a young elite of priests that would spread the modus vivendi prescribed by the *Rugul Aprins*. Premonitions confirmed about the brutality of the totalitarian system's popular democracy, Tudor Sandu was even more determined to counter the Socialist-Marxist ideology spreading in church and society with an emphasis on Christ as the only way of life. The group continued to grow and develop until 1958 when the secret police arrested 15 of the group's most engaged members and imprisoned them on fictitious charges of legionnairy activism.

Though active for a relatively short period, the movement's contribution was important, as it attempted to train the younger generation an alternative way of allowing the Christian faith to shape the new character and personality, free from Communist ideology. In a period when people were indoctrinated by the party's propaganda, congregations were "renewed" by their clergy's social apostolate, and dissidents were "reeducated" by torture in prison camps, the *Rugul Aprins* was a source of decency, morality, and consciousness. Nonetheless, after the fall of Communism, Orthodox voices pointed to the movement as an indication of the Orthodox Church's resistance against Communism. In his extensive study of the role played by the Romanian Orthodox Church in relation to the Communist Romanian state, Enache uses the *Rugul Aprins* movement as an example of the Orthodox Church's resistance, and refutes arguments stressing the church's collaborative activity.[127] Consistent with this approach, contemporary author Alexandru Duțu's defensive statements sum up well this Orthodox refusal to come to terms with the collaboration of the church, despite the evidence described in this chapter that bears witness to the ideological subjugation of the hierarchy throughout Communism:

> Thus, the Orthodox Church offered an alternative to people who felt permanently the compulsion of propaganda and the secret police. If it is true that nationalism put its imprint on 'Socialist' Romania, this does not mean that the whole cultural discourse was nationalistic. . . . [T]he alternative was sought in veiled statements that contradicted the official doctrine.[128]

At other times, the argument of the ROC has been that its clergy managed to preserve the faith in times of atheistic propaganda, creating a "parallel Christian Romania" to the Communist one.[129] Attention will next be focused on the other notable organized resistance groups, this time in the latter part of the Communist era and encompassing members of other denominations as well.

The ALRC

In 1978, the second attempt to dissent from the official policy of Ceaușescu's regime materialized in the initiative known as the ALRC—*Asociația pentru Libertatea Religioasă Creștină* (Christian Committee for the Defense of Religious Freedom). Emerging through the joint efforts of Orthodox, Baptists, and Pentecostals, the movement became the Romanian branch of the Swiss organization Christian Solidarity International. It demanded, in the program entitled "Stop the Persecution," that the Communist government observe the stipulations of the Universal Declaration of Human Rights and of the International Helsinki Federation of Human Rights concerning religious freedom.[130] The group sent a six-point declaration to the Romanian government, the Communist Party, the Securitate, and the leaders of religious denominations, demanding the cessation of religious persecution.[131] Although the group's majority was made up of Baptist believers, the *ALRC* focused on the situation of the churches in general.[132]

The enthusiasm, warmth, and practical generosity of its members—even outside their own denomination—and the challenge of their demands on personal behavior, acted as a magnet in a society suppressed in every aspect of consciousness and life. The ALRC group drafted several documents about religious human rights in Romania, which called into question Ceaușescu's "liberal" reputation, demanding the reopening of the Greek Catholic Church, the official recognition of the persecuted *Oastea Domnului* underground movement, the reformation of church–state relations so that persecution and arbitrariness would be exchanged for mutual respect, loyalty to the Constitution and the observance of international agreements on human rights and peace. The final program underlined 24 aspects that went beyond denominational boundaries, criticizing the appalling social morality and the declining standards in every sphere of life.[133] It called into question the regime's disregard for international agreements ratified by the Communist state, and contested the ideological monopoly of the Communist Party. The program concluded: "We are not Marxists, we are Christians . . . [and] our Christian ideal is a free church in a free state."[134]

The reprisal of the Communists was swift. Under state pressure, ALRC members were expelled from the Baptist Union and the movement was declared "illegal" and deemed an attack on the interests of both the state and of the denominations.[135] As in the case of other denominations, the authorities successfully corrupted many of the church's leaders and used them to control the leadership committees, as it also did with the local Baptist communities. The Orthodox Church criticized and distanced itself from any of its clergy who had joined the ALRC, despite the fact that ALRC had constantly protested the persecution and imprisonment of Orthodox priests like Fr. Calciu-Dumitreasa. Finally, after intimidation and harassment, the authorities began suppressing the movement by imprisoning its leaders. Afraid of losing the privileges that came with state collaboration, the Orthodox Church excommunicated all their dissenters.

Conclusion

In a prison letter dated February 21, 1944, Dietrich Bonhoeffer (1906–1945) wrote:

> The boundaries between resistance and submission cannot therefore in principle be defined. But both must exist and both must be grasped with determination. Faith demands this elasticity of behaviour. It is only in this way that we can sustain the present situation and make it fruitful.[136]

One is left wondering where the Orthodox Church should have drawn a line at its submission to the Communist ideology of the totalitarian state, just as Bonhoeffer wondered in his prison cell as to where the line should be drawn between necessary resistance to "fate," and equally necessary submission.

The historical and political aspects presented in this chapter point to the failure of the Orthodox Church to preserve its critical and prophetic witness amid an atheist political religion that used the church for its own legitimization, and its theology as a tool for the indoctrination and submission of society to Marxist-Socialist ideology. Owing to its fascination with the extreme nationalist ideologies of the nineteenth and twentieth centuries, the church became involved in attempts to combine Orthodox religion and nationalism in the particular form presented by the Iron Guard Fascist movement and then by Marxist-Leninist ideology.

The theologians' contribution to combining Orthodoxy with the ethnocratic ideology resulted in a weakened critical rebuttal of Communism. During the Communist era ensuing after the war, this weakness became obvious, when the ideological doctrine of the social apostolate was readily accepted and, moreover, promoted by the best Orthodox theological minds. A consequence of the centuries-long submission of the Orthodox Church to the ruler, church–state relations in Romania were characterized by the recurrent caesaropapist pattern of state control over every church activity. In embarking on the journey of the Orthodox social apostolate and of the servant church during Communism, one begins to see how theology was used to strengthen the centuries-old link between the Orthodox Church and the state. That such a Marxist-Orthodox synthesis was not only propagated by the patriarchs and metropolitans discussed but was, moreover, internalized by Romania's foremost Orthodox theologian, raises questions that demand an answer.

The focus of the next chapter will be on the theological and political activity of Fr. Dumitru Stăniloae, participant in the *Rugul Aprins* movement, and later prison camp detainee, in an attempt to investigate how the social apostolate and his nationalist inclinations effectively influenced his theology. This will enable the narrative's return to the Nazi German context and compare the role played by Karl Barth in the theological rejection of Nazism during the Barmen Confession.

Notes

[1] M. Burleigh, *Sacred Causes*, pp. 322–4.
[2] Lucian Boia described the Communist Party as a totalitarian dictatorship dressed as a democracy. From less than 1,000 members during the interwar period, the Communist Party multiplied to 710,000 in 1947, an increase of 700 per cent. Lucian Boia, *România: Ţară de frontieră a Europei* (Bucureşti: Editura Humanitas, 2002), p. 101.
[3] The first secret police organized by the Communist Party was composed of soviet spies, terrorists and agents of the Comintern (Third International), and Soviet GPU (State Political Directorate) who had been captured and imprisoned during the 1930s in Romania. Some key names included Pantiusa Bodnarenko, Sergei Nikonov, Petea Goncearuk, Serghei Babenko, and Alexandru Nicolski. Cf. Stelian

Tănase, *Clienții lu' Tanti Varvara: Istorii clandestine* (București: Editura Humanitas, 2005), p. 436.

[4] Apparently in favor of religion, the Soviets released a decree requiring the Orthodox churches to continue their religious activity and social work as long as they did not criticize the Communist regime. Robert Tobias, *Communist-Christian Encounter in Eastern Europe* (Indianapolis: School of Religious Press, 1956), p. 321.

[5] As Burleigh noted, the Communists had never been satisfied with a Western-style separation of church and state, but sought total submission of the former to the latter, in line with the totalitarian goals they pursued toward society as a whole. M. Burleigh, *Sacred Causes*, p. 340.

[6] V. Georgescu, *Romanians*, p. 234.

[7] Patriarch Alexei, quoted in M. Burleigh, *Sacred Causes*, p. 327. Cf. Nathaniel Davis, *A Long Walk to Church* (Boulder, CO: Westview Press, 1995), pp. 16–25.

[8] M. Burleigh, *Sacred Causes*, p. 327.

[9] "Decree No. 358" in *Official Monitor*, Year CXVI, Part I-A, No. 281 (2 December 1948), p. 9563.

[10] There are numerous studies and testimonies about the Greek Catholic persecution in Romania. See Cristian Vasile, *Istoria Bisericii Greco-Catolice sub regimul comunist 1945–1989* (Iași: Editura Polirom, 2003); Cristian Vasile, *Între Vatican și Kremlin: Biserica Greco-Catolică în timpul regimului Communist* (Editura Curtea Veche, 2003); Sergiu Grossu, *Calvarul României creștine* (Iași: Editura Polirom, 1992); Alexandru Rațiu, *Persecuția Bisericii Române Unite* (Oradea: Editura Imprimaria de Vest, 1994); Letiția Gavrilă, et al., *Credința noastră este viața noastră: Memoriile Cardinalului Iuliu Hossu* (Cluj: Casa de Editură Viața Creștină, 2003).

[11] Marius Oprea, "Problema 132: Biserica Română Unită în Atenția Securității" in C. Vasile, *Istoria Bisericii Greco-Catolice*, p. 5.

[12] A. Mungiu-Pippidi, "Ruler and the Patriarch," p. 1. The Greek Catholic Church was the only church to be openly and systematically persecuted by the Communist regime in Romania based on Decree No. 358 from December 1, 1948. More than 600 of their clergy were imprisoned, some of them more than once or twice in this period, often times maltreated and forced to revert to Orthodoxy. Cf. C. Vasile, *Istoria Bisericii Greco-Catolice*, p. 179.

[13] Roman Blaga and Gheorghe Calciu-Dumitreasa, "The Church in Romania under Communist Rule" in *Solia*, vol. LI, no. 2 (February, 1986), pp. 7–9.

[14] As we have seen in interwar Romania, both the king and the legionnaires emphasized the important place that Orthodoxy has in relation to Romanian nationalism.

[15] R. Tobias, *Communist-Christian Encounter*, p. 323.

[16] Paul Mojzes, *Religion Liberty in Eastern Europe and the USSR Before and After the Great Transformation* (Boulder, CO, New York: Columbia University Press, 1992), p. 317.

[17] Cf. Cristian Vasile, "Comunismul și Biserica: Represiune, compromitere și instrumentalizare" in *Comunism și Represiune în România: Istoria Tematică a unui Fratricid Național*, edited by Ruxandra Cesereanu (Iași: Editura Polirom, 2006), p. 187. Cf. P. Negruț, *Biserica și Statul*, p. 114.

[18] Cf. Dorin Dobrincu, ed., *Proba Infernului: Personalul de Cult în Sistemul Carceral din România Potrivit Documentelor Securității, 1959–1962* (București: Editura Scriptorium, 2004), p. xxx.

[19] Eager to counter the "collaborationist" charge, Orthodox historians have suggested exaggerated numbers of clergy who would have suffered imprisonment during Communism, without supportive evidence. Thus, Lidia Stăniloae spoke about more than 10,000 persecuted Orthodox clergy, while more recent archival material suggests the number to be around 2,000 imprisoned Orthodox clergymen. Cf. Lidia I. Stăniloae, *Lumina Faptei din Lumina Cuvântului. Împreună cu Tatăl Meu, Dumitru Stăniloae* (București: Editura Humanitas, 2000), p. 222. Cf. also Dorin Dobrincu, *Proba Infernului*, p. xxi.

[20] Cristian Vasile indicated to some Romanian Orthodox historians who used appalling methods to avoid writing about the persecution of the Greek Catholic clergy in the 1948–50 and 1955–70 periods. C. Vasile, "Comunismul și Biserica," p. 180.

[21] Vasile Vasilachi, *Another World: Memories from Communist Prisons* (New York, 1987). Cf. Alexandru Duțu, "Traditional Toleration and Modern Pluralism: The Case of Orthodox Europe" in *East European Quarterly*, vol. 29 (1995), p. 145.

[22] See also testimonies gathered in the volumes based on secret police's archives: Stelian Tănase, *Anatomia Mistificării* (București: Editura Humanitas, 2003); S. Tănase, *Clienții lu' Tanti Varvara*, p. 496.

[23] Trond Gilberg, "Religion and Nationalism in Romania" in *Religion and Nationalism in Soviet and East European Politics*, edited by Sabrina P. Ramet (Durham, NC: Duke Press Policy Studies, 1989), p. 170.

[24] The limited freedom of consciousness and freedom of religious cults that the 1948 constitution allowed were significantly reduced, while freedom of worship was totally abandoned, affecting mostly all non-Orthodox Churches. By 1955, other officially "tolerated" denominations were required to reduce the number of religious services and the number of priests while most of their activities came under police surveillance. P. Negruț, *Biserica și Statul*, pp. 126–7.

[25] L. Leuștean, *Orthodoxy and the Cold War*, p. 123.

[26] Philip Booth, "Romanian State Fears Too Much Believers' Independence" *Religion in Communist Lands*, vol. 12, no. 2 (1984), pp. 204–5.

[27] Cf. Lidia Anania, et al, *Bisericile Osândite de Ceaușescu: București 1977–1989* (București: Editura Anastasia, 1995).

[28] T. Ware, *Orthodox Church*, pp. 175–6.

[29] Concerning the role played by Orthodox clergy as secret police informants, agents and spies, see D. Pavel, *Leviathanul Bizantin*, pp. 26, 44, n. 27.

[30] Nonetheless, the activity of the Romanian Orthodox missions in the Diaspora was closely watched by the Securitate.

[31] Czeslaw Milosz, *Gândirea Captivă* (București: Editura Humanitas, 1999), p. 203. Reuben Markham, a US reporter who traveled to Romania in 1949 refered to him as "an agent of the Kremlin." Reuben H. Markham, *România sub jugul sovietic* (București: Editura Fundația Academia Civică, 1996), pp. 347–52. Cf. Miranda Villers, "The Romanian Orthodox Church Today" *Religion in Communist Lands*, vol. 1, no. 3 (May–June 1973), p. 4.

[32] G. Enache, *Ortodoxie și Putere Politică*, p. 90.

[33] Sabrina P. Ramet, *Nihil Obstat: Religion, Politics, and Social Change in East-Central Europe and Russia* (Durham, NC: Duke University Press, 1998), p. 191.

[34] G. Enache, *Ortodoxie și Putere Politică*, p. 36, n. 44.

[35] The focus of the essay was on questioning the concentration of wealth in a small social elite at the disadvantage of the peasantry and the proletarians. Keith Hitchins,

"The Romanian Orthodox Church and the State," in *Religion and Atheism in the USSR and Eastern Europe* by Bohdan R. Bociurkiw and John W. Strong, eds. (London: Macmillan Press, 1975), p. 320.

36 Some scholars suggested he was helped by Ana Pauker, the secretary in charge of recruitment for the Communist Party, or by Gheorghiu-Dej, already a leading Communist at that time. See R. Markham, *România sub jugul societic*, pp. 475–6; G. Enache, *Ortodoxie și Putere Politică*, p. 90, n. 162. Justinian had an unusual progress; in normal circumstances, in order to be appointed bishop a person has to live a long period of his life as a monk. However, Justinian was made a monk on August 11, 1945 and a bishop on the following day. Cf. L. Leuștean, "Ethnosymbolic nationalism," p. 444.

37 In 1973, there were 8,185 parishes and 11,722 places of worship served by 8,564 priests and 78 deacons. In Bucharest alone, there were almost 250 churches and 400 priests. The church possessed two theological institutes of university standing, in Bucharest and Sibiu, with respectively 496 and 780 students in 1972–3. The majority of the clergy was trained in the seven cantors' schools and seminaries where 1,597 students were in residence over the same period. T. Beeson, *Discretion and Valour: Religious Conditions in Russia and Eastern Europe* (London: Fontana, 1974), p. 303. Cf. Dennis Deletant, *Ceaușescu and the Securitate: Coercion and Dissent in Romania, 1965–1989* (Armonk, New York: M. E. Sharpe, 1996), pp. 213ff.

38 T. Beeson, *Discretion and Valour*, p. 304.

39 A. Webster, *Price of Prophecy*, p. 111.

40 L. Leuștean, *Orthodoxy and the Cold War*, p. 123.

41 O. Gillet, *Religie și Naționalism*. Cf. Peter Lakatos, "Denominational and Cultural Models and a Possible Ecumenical Strategy from a Romanian Context" *Religion in Eastern Europe*, vol. XVIII, no. 5 (October, 1998), p. 8.

42 Such views were expressed in post-1989 Romania in the speeches of main Orthodox clergy, including Archbishop Bartolomeu, Metropolitan Daniel, Patriarch Teoctist, and others.

43 L. Leuștean, *Orthodoxy and the Cold War*, pp. 190ff.

44 Patriarh Justinian Marina, *Apostolat Social*, vol. I (București: Editura Institutului Biblic, 1948), p. 80.

45 The entire multi-volume "social apostolate" is really a compilation of the patriarch's letters, speeches, sermons, official statements, some already published articles, etc. It does not have a coherent argument running through it, other than the commitment to an Orthodox-Marxist synthesis, lived out every day.

46 A. Webster, *Price of Prophecy*, p. 99.

47 P. Justinian, *Apostolat Social*, vol. I., p. 14.

48 C. Milosz, *Gândirea Captivă*, p. 203.

49 P. Justinian, *Apostolat Social*, vol. I, p. 137.

50 P. Justinian, *Apostolat Social*, vol. I, p. 81.

51 P. Justinian, *Apostolat Social*, vol. I, p. 89.

52 P. Justinian, *Apostolat Social*, vol. I.

53 "If some say that the church finds herself at a turning point in her history, then it is the clergy's duty to pay full attention to how she turns that corner, by obeying the voice of God and not heeding the rumours of Satan." This is part of a speech Justinian gave during his time as Administrative Vicar of the Diocese of Moldova and Suceava. A. Scarfe, "Romanian Orthodox Church," p. 165.

54 P. Justinian, *Apostolat Social*, vol. I., p. 87.
55 Bishop Tikhon (Fitzgerald), "About Sergianism" in *The Orthodox West* (Summer 1992), p. 11.
56 O. Gillet, *Religie și Naționalism*, p. 37. "Sergianism" comes from Metropolitan Sergius (Stragorodsky, 1887–1944), who issued in 1927 a declaration accepting Soviet authority over the church as legitimate, pledging the church's cooperation with the government, and condemning political dissent within the church. It led to a split with the Russian Orthodox Church outside of Russia abroad and the Russian True Orthodox Church (Russian Catacomb Church) within the Soviet Union, as they remained faithful to the Canons of the Apostles. The part of the church led by Metropolitan Sergius schism was since identified with the term sergianism. Cf. Vladimir Moss, "Sergianism as an Ecclesiological Heresy," in *Monastery Press* (February–March, 1999). [Online] Available at: http://www.monasterypress.com/sergianism.html, accessed December 2005.
57 G. Enache, *Ortodoxie și Putere Politică*, pp. 41–2.
58 Cosmocracy is government of whole world, world domination. Webster too suggested Justinian's "social apostolate" claims aimed at a Socialist-Orthodox cosmocracy. A. Webster, *Price of Prophecy*, pp. 109ff.
59 G. Enache, *Ortodoxie și Putere*, p. 42.
60 A. Webster, *Price of Prophecy*, p. 128.
61 Alan Scarfe, "Justinian of Romania: His Early Social Thought," *Religion in Communist Lands*, vol. 5, no. 3 (Autumn, 1977), p. 164.
62 A. Scarfe, "Justinian of Romania." See Antonie Plămădeală, "Biserica Slujitoare în Sfânta Scriptură, Sfânta Tradiție și în Teologia Contemporană" in *Studii Teologice*, vol. 24 No. 5–8 (București, 1972).
63 Patriarh Justinian Marina, *Apostolat Social*, vol. VIII (București: Editura Institutului Biblic, 1966), p. 182.
64 Patriarh Justinian Marina, *Apostolat Social*, vol. X (București: Editura Institutului Biblic, 1971), p. 41.
65 I. Marina, *Apostolat Social*, vol. X, p. 196.
66 "Biserica a contribuit în mod constant la făurirea unității și a ținut mereu vie conștiința de sine a poporului nostru de unitate politică." I. Marina, *Apostolat Social*, vol. X, p. 129.
67 I. Marina, *Apostolat Social*, vol. X, p. 99.
68 P. Lakatos, "Denominational and cultural models," p. 167.
69 Cf. G. Enache, *Ortodoxie și Putere Politică*, pp. 59–60.
70 I. Marina, *Apostolat Social*, vol. I, pp. 96–7.
71 I. Marina, *Apostolat Social*, vol. VIII, p. 61.
72 I. Marina, *Apostolat Social*, vol. VIII, p. 62.
73 On decolonization see Patriarh Justinian Marina, *Apostolat Social*, vol. VII (București: Editura Institutului Biblic, 1962), p. 51; on atomic experiments see *Apostolat Social*, vol. V (București: Editura Institutului Biblic, 1955), p. 75; on Greek Communists see *Apostolat Social*, vol. I., p. 66; on the Vietnam War see *Apostolat Social*, vol. VIII, p. 83; on disarmament see *Apostolat Social*, vol. V, p. 40.
74 A. Webster, *Price of Prophecy*, p. 129.
75 Cf. P. Lakatos, "Denominational and cultural models," p. 9.
76 G. Enache, *Ortodoxie și Putere Politică*, p. 90.

77 Patriarh Justinian, quoted in Bishop Antonie Plămădeală, "Church and State in Romania" in *Church and State: Opening a New Ecumenical Discussion, Faith and Order Paper*, No. 85 (Geneva: World Council of Churches, 1978), p. 104.
78 In 1956 the government drew up a decree for Justinian to sign, mandating a reduction in the number of nuns and monks. Justinian hesitated, and the government put him in prison briefly, just long enough to persuade him of the disadvantages of disobedience. Cf. A. Scarfe, *Romanian Orthodox Church*, p. 222.
79 Stan and Turcesc, *Religion and Politics*, p. 7.
80 V. Georgescu, *Romanians*, p. 255.
81 Mark Almond, *Decline without Fall: Romania Under Ceaușescu* (London: Institute for European Defence and Strategic Studies, 1988), p. 9.
82 Cf. I. Pacepa, *Orizonturi Roșii; Cartea Neagră a Securitătii*.
83 Vladimir Tismăneanu, "From Arrogance to Irrelevance: Avatars of Marxism in Romania" in *The Road to Disillusion: From Critical Marxism to Post-Communism in Eastern Europe*, by Raymond Taras, ed. (Armonk, NY: M. E. Sharpe, 1992), p. 135.
84 Vladimir Tismăneanu, "Byzantine Rites, Stalinist Follies: The Twilight of Dynastic Socialism in Romania" in *Orbis*, vol. 30, No. 1 (Spring 1986), p. 83. For a critical analysis of the Communist mythologizing of these historical characters see Lucian Boia, *Istorie și Mit în Conștiința Românească* (București; Editura Humanitas, 2002); see also Walter Kolarz, *Mituri și Realități în Europa de Est* (Iași: Editura Polirom, 2003), esp. chapter 9 "Imperiul Daco-Român."
85 T. Gilberg, "Religion and Nationalism in Romania", p. 341.
86 Patriarch Justinian, quoted in Sabrina P. Ramet, *Nihil Obstat*, p. 193.
87 *Romanian Orthodox Church News*, vol. IV, No. 3 (July–September, 1974), p. 4.
88 *Romanian Orthodox Church News*.
89 P. Negruț, *Biserica și Statul*, p. 134.
90 I. Ică, "Dilema socială a bisericii," p. 538.
91 When, in 1976 Ceaușescu decided to build a large palace for himself, he pulled Romania out of a UNESCO agreement on the preservation of architectural heritage and proceeded with the wholesale demolition of much of downtown Bucharest, destroying some 30 churches and monasteries. M. Almond, *Decline without Fall*, pp. 188–9. Cf. Constantin Galeriu, "Biserici demolate, bisericii omorâte, biserici deplasate, biserici deportate din sânul odrăslirii sacre" in *Biserici Osândite de Ceaușescu: București, 1977–1989* by Lidia Anania, et al. (București: Editura Anastasia, 1995), pp. 7–9.
92 O. Gillet, *Religie și Naționalism*, p. 211.
93 *Romanian Orthodox Church News*, vol. IV, Nos. 1–2 (January–June, 1974), p. 6–8.
94 *Romanian Orthodox Church News*, vol. XV, No. 1 (January–March, 1985), p. 14.
95 *Romanian Orthodox Church News*, vol. XVII, No. 5 (September, 1987), p. 60.
96 *Romanian Orthodox Church News*, vol. XIII, no. 1 (January–March, 1983), p. 7.
97 Patriarch Justin, quoted in Dinu C. Giurescu, *Distrugerea Trecutului României* (București: Editura Museion, 1994), p. 87.
98 As Alan Scarfe stressed, this may have been an attempt by the government to remove the physical presence of the church from the center of Bucharest in accord with the new city planners' design for a socialist capital city. A. Scarfe, "The Romanian Orthodox Church," pp. 224–5.

99. Metropolitan Antonie Plămădeală, "Biserica slujitoare în Sfânta Scriptură Sfânta Tradiţie şi în teologia contemporană" in *Studii Teologice*, vol. XXIV, No. 5–8 (1972), pp. 325–625.
100. He actually threatened to leave the meeting unless the subject was dropped. S. Ramet, *Nihil Obstat*, p. 193.
101. A. Webster, *Price of Prophecy*, p. 129.
102. Bishop Antonie Plămădeală, "Church and State in Romania," in *Church and State: Opening a New Ecumenical Discussion*, Faith and Order Paper, no. 85 (Geneva: World Council of Churches, 1978), pp. 94–7.
103. A. Plămădeală, "Church and State in Romania," p. 101.
104. A. Plămădeală, "Church and State in Romania," p. 103.
105. A. Plămădeală, "Church and State in Romania," pp. 95ff.
106. A. Plămădeală, "Church and State in Romania."
107. I. Ică, "Dilema socială a bisericii," p. 534.
108. Patriarh Teoctist, quoted in Sabrina P. Ramet, *Nihil Obstat*, p. 193.
109. Patriarh Teoctist.
110. Cf. *Journal of the Moscow Patriarchate*, No. 4 (1987), p. 39.
111. As Ramet stressed, the Russian Orthodox Church had been an instrument in Moscow's peace propaganda against the West and has lent its support to Soviet foreign policy in diverse ways. See Pedro Ramet, "Autocephaly and National Identity in Church–state Relations in Eastern Christianity: An Introduction" in *Eastern Christianity and Politics in the Twentieth Century*, pp. 12ff.
112. Patriarh Teoctist, quoted in S. Ramet, *Nihil Obstat*, p. 193.
113. Others, like Dinu Pillat and Valeriu Strainu, were imprisoned because they attended the church. See A. Duţu, "Traditional Toleration," p. 146.
114. See Mircea Vulcănescu, *Către Fiinţa Spiritualităţii Româneşti:* vol. 3, *Dimensiunea Românească a Existenţei* (Bucureşti: Editura Eminescu, 1996); *Bunul Dumnezeu Cotidian: Studii despre Religie* (Bucureşti: Editura Humanitas, 2004).
115. A good account, though maybe one-sided, can be found in Alexandru Popescu, *Petre Ţuţea: Between Sacrifice and Suicide* (Oxford: Ashgate, 2004).
116. Petre Ţuţea, *Omul: Tratat de Antropologie Creştină* (Iaşi: Editura Timpul, 1992).
117. A. Scarfe, *Romanian Orthodox Church*, p. 228.
118. In an English-language letter sent to Keston College, Oxford, a committee of five Romanian Orthodox priests from the Orthodox Theological Institute in Bucharest, led by Fr. Dumitru Popescu and claiming to represent "all the priests of our country," denounced Fr. Calciu as a member of the Fascist "Iron Guard" describing him as "an unbalanced man and a megalomaniac" who attempted "to poison the souls of the seminarians with fascist ideas." Fr. Dumitru Popescu, quoted in A. Webster, *Price of Prophecy*, p. 125.
119. See Nicolae Steinhardt, *Jurnalul Fericirii* (Cluj: Editura Dacia, 1991).
120. See the volume of "Spiritual Dialogues" which gathers testimonies that shed light on the hidden life of the Christian Church under the Communists. Ierom. Ioanichie Bălan, *Convorbiri Duhovniceşti*, 2 vols. (Episcopia Romanului, 1984).
121. Sandu Tudor was an acronym for his real name Alexandru Teodorescu.
122. In "The Century of God-killers" Sandu Tudor makes reference to the anti-religious character of the Leninist Communism in 1930s Russia, underlining the political religion character of Communism that ultimately seeks to destroy the church. See "Veacul Ucigătorilor de Dumnezeu" quoted in "Rugul Aprins:

de la Mănăstirea Antim la Aiud," in *Detenția*. [Online] Available at: http://www. literaturasidetentie.ro/detentia/carte_3.php , accessed May 2006.
[123] T. Ware, *Orthodox Church*, pp. 72–80.
[124] Horia-Roman Patapievici, "Rugul Aprins" in *ID*, vol. II, No. 12 (2006), p. 1.
[125] André Scrima, *Timpul Rugului Aprins* (București: Editura Humanitas, 2000), p. 157.
[126] George Enache, "Din Arhiva Rugului Aprins: Daniil Sandu Tudor, un sfânt în gulagul românesc" in *Clouds Magazine*, vol. 11 (Fall, 2002).
[127] In his essay "Religious Repression in Communist Romania. Case Study: Rugul Aprins" Enache takes note of Dennis Deletant and Olivier Gillet's charges of collaborationism and contests their validity based on a complex analysis. To summarize it, Enache would argue that the *Rugul Aprins* movement was protected by Justinian hence his reforms of monasticism during the 1950s. Moreover, based on this view, the arrest of the Antim group in 1958 resulted from the Communist regime's attempt to attack the patriarch. There are two problems with such argumentation: If the regime wanted Justinian removed, they could have imprisoned him any day, as they did in 1956. Also, this interpretation does not correspond to the removal by the patriarch of four notable clergy of the movement who were sent to a seminary at the Neamț Monastery, between 1950 and 1953, in an attempt to disband the group. For the details of this removal, see H.-R. Patapievici, "Rugul Aprins," p. 1. For Enache's argument, see G. Enache, "Represiunea Religioasă în România comunistă. Studiu de Caz: Rugul Aprins" in *Ortodoxie și Putere Politică în România Contemporană*, pp. 381–400.
[128] A. Duțu, "Traditional Toleration," p. 219.
[129] Liviu Vânău, "The Easter Ball: Interaction between Secularism and Religion in Romania" in *Religion in Eastern Europe*, vol. XVI, no. 6 (December 1996), 9.
[130] Dorin Dobrincu, "Libertate religioasă și contestare în România lui Nicolae Ceaușescu: Comitetul Creștin Român pentru Apărarea Libertății Religioase și de Conștiință (ALRC)" in *Analele Sighet* vol. 10 (2003), pp. 203–27.
[131] The six main points of the group's program included the affirmation of moral and spiritual values of the Christian faith; the protection of freedom of conscience and religious freedom; the support and protection of those persecuted for religious convictions; the promotion of interdenominational dialogue between Romanian and other foreign religious denominations; freedom of the press so that citizens would be informed about the religious persecutions taking place in Romania; and an evaluation of the role of religion in the socialist context. "*ALRC* Declaration."
[132] The final program edited by the *ALRC*, which drew up 24 points, was signed by one Orthodox priest, one Pentecostal, and 25 Baptists. See Comisia Prezitențială pentru Analiza Dictaturii Comuniste din România, *Raport Final* (București, 2006). [Online] Available at http://www.gardianul.ro/documente/ capitolul2.pdf, accessed December 2006.
[133] Janice Broun, Grazyna Sikorska, *Conscience and Captivity: Religion in Eastern Europe* (Washington: Ethics and Public Policy Center, 1988), pp. 227–8.
[134] D. Dobrincu, "Libertate religioasă și contestare," p. 210.
[135] J. Broun, G. Sikorska, *Conscience and Captivity*, pp. 211–14.
[136] Dietrich Bonhoeffer, *Letters and Papers from Prison* (Macmillan, 1971), p. 217.

Chapter 6

The Theological Error of Nationalism: Barth and Stăniloae

Introduction

The Orthodox Church's collaboration with the atheist regime, and the theological subservience described in the previous chapter, raise fundamental moral and theological questions. How was it possible for a whole generation of patriarchs, theologians, and the rest of the clergy to offer their support of such an abominable regime and its atheist ideology? This same question was raised in postwar Germany with reference to the German Christians' movement, which encompassed numerous pastors and theologians who pledged their allegiance to National Socialism all through the Nazi regime. The survey of the historical and political conditions that have led to the nationalist identification of the church with the totalitarian state has indicated that the churches' subservience to caesaropapist nationalism in the Orthodox context, and *völkisch* nationalism in the case of the German Christians, generated the conditions for the emergence of what Burleigh called political religions.[1]

What remains to be investigated is the role played by theology in relation to nationalism. Theology can function in numerous ways: It can be undertaken to help the theologian understand his or her own religious tradition; it can make comparisons between religious traditions in order to defend or generate reform of a particular tradition, or it can assist by propagating a particular religious tradition to address a certain situation. Thus, in most situations, exposure to a different religious tradition can have a positive effect. The dialogue between two utterly different religious traditions such as the Reformed and the Orthodox will focus on how deeply held theological convictions can inform the political thinking and practice of a theologian operating within a particular tradition.

This chapter will explore the role Karl Barth played in relation to German nationalism and the theological contribution he offered to the rejection of Nazism, most explicitly in the pamphlet "Theological Existence Today," and a year later during the Synod of Barmen. Here, attention will be given to the development of Barth's rejection of *völkisch* nationalism through a critique of natural theology. In the second part of this chapter, attention will be drawn to the personality of Fr. Dumitru Stăniloae, tracing the development of his theology along issues pertaining to the church's life in the *polis*, and especially in relation to nationalism. This investigation is, then, related to the issue of theological resistance and collaboration in order to evaluate how nationalism has influenced his theology and views of church–state relations.

Karl Barth's Rejection of Nationalism

Voicing his "*Nein!*" to both the spirit and the letter of the German Christians' movement in his 1933 manifesto *Theologische Existenz Heute*, Barth took a stand against many of his colleagues who had become involved with the movement and with supporting German nationalism.[2] However, Barth based his rejection of National Socialism on a theological construct that informed his opposition to the fascination with *Volk* that emerged in early twentieth-century German Protestantism.

The ideological context encountered by Barth in interwar Germany was characterized by a dichotomized approach to spiritual and secular responsibilities. As Mark Lindsay noted, nineteenth-century German Protestantism functioned as a civil community on the basis of its willing and voluntary participation at the institutional level.[3] The support German Christians offered to Hitler's nationalist cause was the domino effect of liberal Protestantism's failure to sustain an effective theological critique of this voluntary association between the church and the political regime. The general rise of nationalism and the drive for political unification after the chaos and political strife of the Weimar Republic found, in the Protestant churches, a willing partner, especially because of the latter's desire to unite.[4] Thus, although the Germany of the nineteenth century had been infused by liberalism on the one hand and nationalism on the other, it was the latter that gained the largest influence among the churches. As Bethge stressed on this point, "[W]hen the once strong liberalism was shoved behind in favor of national unification, Protestant Christians hailed the move."[5]

Nevertheless, Barth's theological opposition to German nationalism had less to do with the political struggles of the Weimar or the churches' desire for unification. He was concerned with the nineteenth-century liberal theology that he saw as responsible for the cultural and nationalist tendencies of the German churches. As Villa-Vicencio noted on this point:

> Karl Barth's critique of liberal theology as a legitimization of the dominant cultural trends of the nineteenth century is well established. As theology drifted deeper and deeper into synthesis with the dominant ideological trends of the period so it became increasingly willing to leave ever larger sections of society to the specialized control of others.[6]

As Barth noted in 1933, "The teaching and attitudes of the *Deutsche Christen* is nothing else than a particularly powerful consequence of the whole neo-Protestant development since 1700."[7] The deeper problem of the institutional condition of the church was the theological justification for nationalism inherent in the natural theology of the German liberal tradition in theology. German nationalism, with its *Volksgemeinschaft* that combined *Volk* and race, had gained a religious component based on the dubious doctrine of election that envisaged Germany as having been given a divine world mission. This ideological conviction reemerged forcefully in Hitler's Reich and in National Socialism's adoption of Positive Christianity and enabled German theologians like Emmanuel Hirsch, Paul Althaus, and Werner Elert to construct theologies that incorporate or attempt to explicate German nationalism.

Theological Liberalism, Socialism, and Dialectics

Born in Basel, Switzerland, in 1886, Barth studied theology in Bern, Tübingen, and eventually in Marburg, where he came under the theological and neo-Kantian influence of Wilhelm Herrmann.[8] In 1909 he moved to Geneva to become an assistant pastor in a German-speaking Reformed Church. A dedicated and convinced theological liberal, Barth had become increasingly dissatisfied with the Ritschlian and Troeltschian theological liberalism.[9] In 1914 he was shocked to learn that a group of 93 German intellectuals led by Adolf Harnack had signed a proclamation supporting Wilhelm II's war policy, and to find among them many of his theological teachers; by his own admission, "I suddenly realized that I could not any longer follow either their ethics or dogmatics or their understanding of the Bible and of history. For me, at least, 19th century theology no longer held any future."[10]

Barth's disappointment with liberal theology led him to Religious Socialism, which he had already encountered due to the impact in Switzerland of the ideas promoted by Leonard Ragaz (1868–1945), Hermann Kutter (1863–1931), and Christoph Blumhardt (1842–1919). Barth spent 10 years as a pastor in Safenwil, a small industrial Swiss village where he developed a theological understanding based on the relationship between Gospel and socialism.[11] However, the split in the Religious Socialism and its inability to challenge the political aims of the Kaiser led Barth toward theological objectivism and critical realism: "To take moral action seriously, we must first take God seriously."[12] Rejecting Ragaz's moralizing, Barth embraced Kutter's emphasis on experiencing God and, with insights from Christoph Blumhardt's strictly eschatological and God-centered understanding of God's actions, he discovered a "strange new world within the Bible."[13] Barth's rediscovery of God as the "wholly other" in relation to humanity is explored in the first edition of his commentary on the Epistle to the Romans (*Der Römerbrief*, 1918).[14] Here he speaks about the fundamental *diastasis* that exists between God and humanity, Christ and culture:

a theology of crisis in which he challenges liberal anthropocentrism, Pietism, Religious Socialism, idealistic ethics, and all established religion.[15]

As a member to the Swiss Social Democratic Party (SDP), Barth came to reject Bolshevism as well as the moderate capitalism of the Weimar. By the time he published the second edition of the *Römerbrief* (1922), the failure of the SDP revolution in Switzerland and the brutal success of the Bolshevik Revolution had convinced him that revolution is an idealistic hope for a new regime, so he emphasized a positive political ethic founded on the Christian ethic based on love.[16] While he continued to reject Religious Socialism, he drew on the Tambach lecture (1919), where he developed the "dialectical" concept of Christ, who is both the "Yes!" and the "No!" of the social order.[17] The "No!" of God's judgment to all human endeavor is answered dialectically with the "Yes!" of God's movement of grace that leads to the positive ethics of political responsibility. Finally, in the 1922 *Römerbrief* he employs the "dialectical" approach to reject the historicism and the Biblicism of the liberals.[18]

To summarize, Barth's disillusionment with the failed Swiss revolution, his movement from Ragaz to Kutter and encounter with Blumhardt, as well as the discovery of the "strange new world within the Bible" and his disillusionment with the Russian Revolution of 1917 all led to Barth's pronunciation of divine diastasis over the nature of the claims of Religious Socialism as much as over theological liberalism, and idealism, religion, and culture. All identifications between the Kingdom of God and human accomplishments are to be regarded as idolatrous, convictions that provide the theological backdrop for Barth's critique of Nazism, which in its turn fuelled the passions of his rejection of the implicit natural theology he would later detect in Brunner.[19]

Barth's Rejection of Natural Theology

Barth's theological dialogue with natural theology informed his opposition to the German Christians and ultimately to Hitler. Already during his early years as a professor of theology in Göttingen, he engaged with this aspect: "The Triune God, the God of real revelation, is not the object of this natural or rational religion, but the one God, the Creator of heaven and earth."[20] For him, even as a "Christian" natural theology, it still remained a suspicious pointer to God, referring to the "proofs" of the existence of God suggested by Thomas Aquinas. Barth contends they have often been misunderstood as attempts to find an intellectual basis for belief in revelation.[21] Barth stressed that for Aquinas, the existence of God did not represent a "problem" and therefore he did not have to devise "proofs" because these would only submit God to human hands and therefore make him less than God.[22]

However, Barth's denial of natural theology did not eliminate the possibility that God could be revealed in nature or creation. As Hunsinger stressed, the rejection of natural theology played an epistemological role; it did not imply that nothing good, beautiful, true, or worth noticing existed outside Scripture or the church.[23] For Barth, all of creation, not only humans, testifies in gratitude to the grace of the Creator. The only thing that distinguishes humans from the rest of the creation is God's revelation in Christ. As he would stress later in his *Church Dogmatics*, "God may speak to us through Russian Communism or a flute concerto, a blossoming shrub or a dead dog. We shall do well to listen to him if he really does so."[24] The crucial distinction from natural theology is that none of these objects can ever be allowed to become a source of authority for the church's preaching because nothing in the created world can have revelatory or epistemological status.

This is where Barth's rejection gains force in confrontation with German nationalism and with Hitler. He believed that Christians' political outlook is dictated by their loyalty to Jesus Christ. Since the Christ of natural theology often becomes the relativized Christ of culture, this trajectory leads to Christ being not supreme, not sufficient, and ultimately not necessary.[25] Natural theology as the knowledge of God revealed in nature and culture, leads to a culture-religion wherein Jesus Christ "no longer speaks the first and the last word, but only at best an additional word," something Barth would later call an "assimilated and domesticated theology."[26] The relativization generated by this assimilated theology was problematic because it weakened any defense against culture-religion. Inherent in German liberal theology, natural theology came to play an important role in the ideological constitution of the German Christians along the lines of race and nationality, which were central to Positive Christianity.

Theological Existence Today

Barth's resistance to nationalism was thus informed by his refusal to accept natural theology. That is not to say Barth did not hold to a moderate form of nationalism. In his lectures in Münster (1928–29) and Bonn (1930–31), he stressed the distinction he saw between "people" and "state." Barth argued that modern Europe was no longer constituted by states or nations in the political sense—who are also people in the sense of common descent and blood—but only more or less strong and pure majorities of such people.[27] As such, the greatest danger to a state was "the stirring up [of] one of the people united within it against the other or others. . . ."[28] Barth was thus rejecting the claims of German nationalism, or *Volkstum*, which constituted a claim of primacy over another nationality or race (i.e., Jewish or non-Aryan). For him, nationalism was valid only as loyalty to the way of his people, not because they are better (superior beings) but solely because they are "his" people.[29] He thus refused to give supremacy to the concept of *Volk* and to National Socialism by pointing to God's command of life that was for the whole of humanity without privileging one nation or race above the other. In astonishing opposition to the general tendency in the theological circles of his day, Barth spoke about "the remarkable apostasy of the church to nationalism."³⁰

Barth's rejection of German nationalism during the Münster and Bonn period was revisited in 1933, when the rise of the German Christians' movement prompted him to publish the "Theologische Existenz Heute." This pamphlet illustrates poignantly Barth's belief that, precisely as a theologian, he was making a contribution to the struggle against Hitler. The message of the manifesto called the church to be faithful to its witness in a context where Hitler's police were engaging in daily violence and where many intellectuals had already been imprisoned. More importantly, the manifesto voiced Barth's clear and uncompromising "No!" both to the German Christians and to Hitler, their "leader":

> The German Evangelical Church, through her responsible representatives, had not comported herself as the church which *possesses* her Leader [Hitler], during these recent months. And yet *He* [Christ] possesses *her*: as surely as we have to hear His Law and His Gospel ever again from Him. When it is recognized that *He* and *He alone* is the Leader, there is the possibility of theological existence.³¹

The position taken here by Barth in refusing to recognize the absolute, totalitarian leadership of the *Führer* was courageous given that a copy of the pamphlet was sent to Hitler.³² A few years later (1938) Barth observed that what he wrote in this pamphlet was what he was always trying to say, but pressed by the political situation it came out as "a summons, a challenge, a battle cry, a confession."³³

Barth detailed his opposition to the German Christians in eight specific points, where the political principles that animated his manifesto emerge clearly. Thus, Barth stresses that the church's function is not to help the German people recognize and fulfill any vocation different from the calling of Christ; that the church believes in the divine institution of the state and the guardian and administrator of public law and order, but that the church does not believe in any state, not in the German one, thus not even in the National Socialist state; the church preaches the Gospel throughout the world and therefore also in the Third Reich, but not "under" it and not in "its spirit."³⁴ Finally, Barth joined in with those who that year would become part of the Confessing Church to reject the "Aryan clause": "The fellowship of those belonging to the church is not determined by blood, therefore not by race, but by the Holy Spirit and Baptism."³⁵

Moreover, in the manifesto Barth aims at the natural theology of the German Christians and the theologians supporting the movement:

> While the apparently successful case of a victory for the 'German Christians' appears at present to us a sort of 'Age of Terror' seen from the theological

viewpoint . . . it would only result in a new, perpetual adjustment and compromise (Creation *and* Redemption, Nature *and* Grace, Nationalism *and* Gospel) which of yore has ever been more congenial to the 'natural' man. . . .[36]

The opposition to such specific political aspects was dictated by the nature of the German Christians' movement, which as described in chapter 2, was theologically anthropocentric and immanentist while ideologically it supported the National Socialist Party. Such a public and clear "No!" uttered by Barth to the German Christians brought him admiration but also criticism. He made it clear in the conclusion of the pamphlet that the Protestant churches had to resist to Hitler's totalitarian ideology and the *Gleichschaltung* (assimilation) initiated by the Nazis, not only toward German society but moreover toward the church, not least through the appointment of the Reich's bishop. Because of the church's existence under the Word "No moratorium and no *Gleichschaltung* can befall them. . . . They are the natural frontiers of everything, even of the Totalitarian State. . . . They are this for the salvation of the people: *that* salvation which neither the State nor the church can create, but which the church is called upon to proclaim."[37]

Although the pamphlet was well received in Germany, the problems generated by the German Christians within the larger Protestant body of the churches persisted, a situation that would lead to the constitution of the Pastors' Emergency League.[38] Nevertheless, the crisis Hitler generated among the churches enabled Barth to come to a clear political judgment against Nazism. Barth would have the chance to express it theologically once more in the Barmen Declaration.

The Barmen Declaration

Organized around a council led by Martin Niemöller, the Confessing Church comprised of Lutheran, Reformed, and Union church pastors and lay people, some of whom had been part of the Pastors' Emergency League.[39] Although some of its members engaged in various forms of resistance, ranging from hiding Jews to training pastors in an illegal seminary, or secretly plotting the assassination of Hitler, the Confessing Church was by no means a uniform group or movement and as such their resistance to Nazism is a matter of debate. It would be an inaccuracy to equate, as many indeed have, the Confessing Church with Protestant resistance to Nazism.[40] A simplistic polarization of resistance versus collaboration omits the fact that for most Germans national loyalty dictated their political outlook, even in the Confessing Church.[41] Organized under the slogan "Church must remain church," the Confessing Church never actually broke completely with the established Protestant Church.[42]

Nevertheless, with the German Christians gaining control over a number of regional churches in an effort to assimilate (*gleichschalten*) them to the Nazi order, the Confessing Church and its constituting Synod of Barmen was an attempt to mount a resistance. German Christians were openly in support of Hitler, whom they exalted for bringing salvation to Germany. The Confessing Church asked Barth in 1934 to draft the Barmen Theological Declaration. Barth was convinced that one's political outlook ought to be dictated by one's loyalty to Jesus Christ. Though the declaration was not a political manifesto that opposed Hitler explicitly or advocated for liberal democracy, for political pluralism, or for the Jews' human rights, Barth was convinced that it contained enough force to dispel from the church all political views based on national loyalties. His early experiences in Safenwil and disappointment with revolutions had taught him that only in calling the church to be faithful to the Word of God could a contribution be made to politics. In drafting the Barmen declaration, Barth wanted it to resemble a "confession" to God's faithfulness, out of which the prophetic witness of the church would rise against the heresies of the German Christians. As such, the declaration was an attempt to voice a coherent theological opposition to National Socialism and could only take the form of a confession that stressed the churches' theological commitment to the true Lord, who could be confused with neither Hitler nor the *Volk*.

The declaration consisted of six succinct paragraphs that begin with a clear indication about the function of this confession:

> In view of the errors of the 'German Christians' and of the present Reich Church Administration, which are ravaging the church and at the same time also shattering the unity of the German Evangelical Church, we confess the following evangelical truths. . . . Jesus Christ, as he is attested to us in Holy Scripture, is the one Word of God which we have to hear, and which we have to trust and obey in life and in death. We reject the false doctrine that the church could and should recognize as a source of its proclamation, beyond and besides this one Word of God, yet other events, powers, historic figures and truths as God's revelation.[43]

The first thesis contains an affirmation and a rejection. It affirms the necessity and sufficiency of Jesus Christ as the only voice that carries authority and gives identity to the church. This is the basis on which Barth launched his famous rejection of natural theology. No other voice apart from, or alongside, the scriptural voice of Jesus Christ may become a source of authority. Against the attempts of natural theology to assimilate and domesticate the supremacy of Christ, Barth stressed the falseness of any theology that looks for an alternative or secondary authority that may be found in nature, events, powers, historic figures, or cognitive constructs.

Paul Althaus, the respected theologian who sympathized with the German Christians and defended the totalitarian state, the *Führer* principle, and *völkisch* ideals, took issue with Barth's rejection of natural theology. Barth's Christology, clearly stated in this first Barmen thesis, posits that revelation comes only through Christ as revealed in the Bible, a conviction that goes back to his *Römerbrief*.

Althaus, however, is impatient with such a narrow Christological understanding, primarily because it rules out history as the medium of a secondary revelation of God.[44] Althaus' own position distinguished between primary revelation in Christ and the *Uroffenbarung*, a basic or original revelation of God in nature and history, which is meant to deepen one's understanding of God as revealed in Christ. While this addition may seem harmless, for Althaus it was crucial because he used history to interpret God for modern Germans. Thus, he recognized in the "orders of creation" (*Ordnungen*) God's ideal plan for modern society; the Law of God . . .

> . . . binds each in the position to which he has been called by God and commits us to the natural orders under which we are subjugated, such as family, *Volk*, race (i.e. blood relationship). . . . In that the will of God also meets us continually in our here and now, it binds us also to a specific historical moment of family, *Volk* and race, i.e., to a specific moment of their history.[45]

This is why Althaus finds threatening Barth's insistence on Christ's Lordship against inroads of cultural self-assertions in the church. The *Ordnungen* theology enables the concept of *Volk* to become part of Althaus' theology. Whereas Luther's Catechism stated, "I believe that God created me," Althaus' version adds, "The belief that God created me includes also my *Volk*."[46]

It was exactly this type of error that Barth feared when he cautioned about the danger that culture-religion poses to relativizing Christ so that He no longer speaks the first and the last word. For this reason, the first thesis of the Barmen Declaration represents the basis on which the other theses are built. The second thesis states that no area of life can be regarded as outside the Lordship of Jesus Christ, which implies that Christocentric theology cannot be severed from political judgments in the church.[47] The third thesis claims that the church as Jesus Christ's exclusive possession cannot be subordinated to prevailing social ideologies or political convictions.[48] As Hunsinger noted here, whereas the second thesis implied that theology and politics may not be separated or divided, the third thesis stresses that theology and politics may not be confused or mixed.[49] In the fourth thesis, Barth argues that the church does have a proper form of government, but he rejects the idea that the *Führer* might be invested with any special privileges or permission to interfere over, or within, the church.[50]

The Two Kingdoms

The fifth Barmen thesis that deals most specifically with the relationship between church and state is worth examining in more detail.

> Scripture tells us that by divine appointment the state, in this still unredeemed world in which also the church is situated, has the task of maintaining justice and peace, so far as human discernment and human ability make this

possible, by means of the threat and use of force. The church acknowledges with gratitude and reverence toward God the benefit of this, his appointment. It draws attention to God's Kingdom (Reich), God's commandment and justice, and with these the responsibility of those who rule and those who are ruled. It trusts and obeys the power of the Word, by which God upholds all things. We reject the false doctrine that beyond its special commission the state should and could become the sole and total order of human life and so fulfil the vocation of the church as well. We reject the false doctrine that beyond its special commission the church should and could take on the nature, tasks and dignity which belong to the state and thus become itself an organ of the state.[51]

Building on the previous four, and particularly on the Christological foundation of the first thesis, this fifth paragraph has the most critical potential for political opposition to Hitler's National Socialism. In the history of the church, the views on the authority of the state have been divided: On the one hand the Protestant tradition, associated with Luther and Augustine, believed Scripture taught that, being instituted by God, the state could command unconditional loyalty in its sphere of competence and was to be resisted only if it attempted to interfere in the church's affairs. The other view, associated with Calvin and Aquinas, agreed with the first except for one important distinction, namely that Scripture did not teach unconditional compliance to any state so long as it merely respected the boundaries of the church. According to the second view, Scripture teaches that the state, having been instituted by God, has obligations to fulfill, such as dispensing justice and protecting the peace; failing to fulfill its tasks (as with Hitler's policies of war and injustice) the state loses its divine legitimacy and may be opposed by the church.

These two views differ in that the first holds that to obey the state, even the unjust state, is to offer obedience to God (i.e., social apostolate or servant church); the second holds that in certain situations obedience to God requires political disobedience and resistance to the state. At heart, this latter thesis challenged the traditional Protestant Two Kingdoms doctrine (*Zweireichlehre*) by refusing to separate the state, as an order of creation (*Ordnungnen*), from the church as an order of redemption. By viewing both the church and the state as part of the "still unredeemed world," Barth rejects the ideology of noninterference of the church in state affairs, a theory that grossly exaggerated became an apologetic doctrine for the German Christians' support of the Nazi regime.

Having refused this separation, the fifth thesis does stress that the church is distinct from the state; the church must not seek to undermine the state's legitimate task, but it must remind the state that God's Kingdom is above both church and state. Finally, through its witness, the church reminds the state to be a responsible dispenser of justice and an agent for peace. Once this positive relationship is explained, the document rejects the "totalitarian" state, which must resist the temptation of interfering beyond its confines, and it rejects the church's theocratic temptation to control society by using the state's strategies and thus becoming an "organ of the state."[52] On the basis of the Christological framework set out in the first thesis, Barth places both church and state under the "one Word of God."

A few weeks after the Synod of Barmen, a meeting of the "Ansbach Counsel" was held, gathering theologians of the Erlangen school, such as Althaus, Hirsch, and Werner Elert, who joined in rejecting the Barmen Theological Declaration.[53] These German Christian theologians were concerned that by placing both the church and the state under the Word of God, Barth implied that Gospel would come before the Law.[54] Although the Barmen Declaration did not address the Law-Gospel relationship, Elert—a professor of systematic theology and history of dogma at Erlangen—and Althaus were concerned because they held that church–state and law-Gospel form two separate realms, which affirms the theological legitimacy of the state and the orders of society. However, as shown concerning the theological difference between Althaus and Barth, the latter realized that, just like the traditional Lutheran doctrine of the Two Kingdoms, the Law-Gospel pattern that identified divine Law with human laws in society was ineffective in securing the church from the nationalist ideology of the German Christians. Althaus, though, called for a return to "law and order" and saw this to be possible only in the Nazi regime; henceforth, he would become a theological supporter of the German Christians' movement.[55]

Barth's Theological Resistance to Nationalism

In the Barmen Declaration Barth spoke for the church in general (and for the Confessing Church in particular), concerned to save it from the seduction of political religion that German Christians and Nazism represented. His rejection of natural theology, of the Two Kingdoms doctrine and the Christological basis that included the state under the Word of God, was a prophetic statement on the cultural and political entanglement of the church and the ideological fixation with race, *Volk*, and the *Führer*. The reaction against the declaration witnesses to the validity of this claim.

Not only the Erlangen school, but the German Christians from the Reformed congregation in Siegen (Westphalia), produced in 1934 a lengthy denunciation of Barthian theology, labeling it "demonic magic" that ensnared professors, pastors, congregations, and young theologians.[56] Alfred Rosenberg, the Nazi ideologist, published in 1935 his counterattack on Protestantism, called *Protestant Pilgrims to Rome: The Treason against Luther and the Myth of the Twentieth Century*, wherein he accuses the Confessing Church of treachery for becoming "Jewish prophets," and labeled Barth as a "Calvinist pseudo-pope" who worked for the destruction of German Protestantism.[57]

In the same year, 1935, Barth had to return to the Law-Gospel theme, prompted by Emil Brunner, also a Swiss theologian who, having misinterpreted Barth's rejection of natural theology, insisted the Law served as a "point of contact" in preparing the way for the Gospel by revealing both an incipient knowledge of sin and of God's righteousness.[58] Barth reacted swiftly and vehemently to this attack, in his famous reply, "*Nein!*" stressing that such a "point of contact" led to an assimilated and domesticated theology because it removed the priority of the Gospel's uniqueness in unveiling Christ.[59] For Barth, this error was at the heart of theological liberalism and, thus, of the German Christians' *Zweireichlehre*. Barth's reaction was, moreover, prompted because Hirsch, Althaus, and Elert congratulated Brunner for the essay, although Brunner was a staunch critic of the German Christians.[60]

Not all Protestant theologians caught in the Nazis' doomed Third Reich were as outspoken and as resolute in rejecting German nationalism as Barth. As has been pointed out, the majority of German pastors, theologians, and congregations remained silent and neutral, taking sides with neither the German Christians nor the Confessing Church.[61] Some were apolitical, while most supported National Socialism but remained aloof from any resistance to or defense against religious nationalism. After the war, many repented for not having rejected Nazi totalitarianism (The Stuttgart Confession of Guilt).[62] In fact, Barth too was confronted with a similar accusation, issued by none other than his Swiss friend, Emil Brunner (1889–1966). In the 1933 introduction to his *Theologische Existenz Heute*, Barth stressed he would continue to teach theology "as if nothing has happened."[63] In a letter after the war, Emil Brunner used this phrase to condemn Barth for what he perceived was a political evasion.[64]

However, not for the first time, Brunner misunderstood Barth's insistence that only by being a theologian had he something distinctive and useful to offer in politics, even though that should not become the primary reason for involvement in theology. Barth said: "The essential service of the church to the state simply consists in maintaining and occupying its own realm as church."[65] His contribution to the Barmen Declaration, his theological rejection of German Christians' natural theology, and rejection of Hitler's political religion was a distinct contribution to politics, although it was ultimately a theological contribution. It was this significant effort and his radical rejection of National Socialism that led to his split from the Confessing Church and eventually to his removal from his teaching position and expulsion from Germany.[66]

To conclude, the argument developed thus far is that Karl Barth's resistance was against a German nationalism whose particular dangerous combination of *Volk*, race, and natural theology effectively turned it into a political religion. Given the character of this nationalism and the fascination of the Reformed Church with Hitler, Barth responded, not by taking a political stance but by theologically rejecting not only Hitler's depiction as the savior of Germany, but also his totalitarian claims. In both his 1933 pamphlet and in the Barmen Declaration, Barth did just that by speaking to the church in its confrontation with the German Christians. Since theology is true only as obedience to the Word of God, Barth's freedom from nationalist temptations enabled him to expose the theological error of the German Christians.

In the next section, attention will be on another theologian of great potential who was confronted with a totalitarian regime, the ultimate claims of which transformed it into a political religion, a godless, atheist regime that demanded full allegiance and sanctioned violently any form of resistance or opposition.

Dumitru Stăniloae and Resistance Through the Dogmatic

The French Orthodox theologian and writer Olivier Clément (1921–2009) has been traditionally identified as the person who introduced Fr. Dumitru Stăniloae to the Western world. In the preface to the French translation of some of Stăniloae's essays (1981), Clément noted:

> Father Dumitru Stăniloae is certainly the greatest Orthodox theologian of today. And with time, as his work will be translated into Western languages, it will be clear that this is one of the greatest creations of Christian thought in the second half of our century.[67]

John Meyendorff, another "great" theologian, continues in the antinomian tone,[68] regarding Stăniloae to be the most influential and creative Romanian theologian of our time.[69] Such embellished eulogies could only be meant as an encouragement of the outside world to discover and engage further with a virtually unknown, and only partially translated, theologian—encouragement for the Orthodox world in general and for the West in particular.[70]

There is a popular tendency in Romania, as well as in foreign theological circles, to picture Stăniloae as "the" theologian of the Orthodox Church, or even as "a prophet of Romania."[71] Such admiration is dangerous because it is not based on real engagement with his theological contributions and efforts, especially since his work has lacked a serious critical analysis and evaluation within the broader Orthodox theological spectrum.[72] It is almost bewildering, as pointed out by Bielawski that, considering Stăniloae's profuse and impressive theological creativity and the eulogies and praise they generate, so little study has been dedicated to his work.[73] In this process of mythologizing, Stăniloae's staunch Romanian nationalism, his open relations with the collaborating Orthodox hierarchy, as well as his dependence upon the Communist government, are conveniently overlooked.

The task of reinventing Stăniloae as a theological champion of the Orthodox Church could not be difficult; he remained an active and creative theologian and writer throughout his life and up until his death. His publishing activity spans 60 years, during which he worked on an impressive number of books, translations, and articles.[74] In other respects, Stăniloae has maintained good links with the Orthodox Church's hierarchy; his studies and travels abroad during the interwar period and under Communism have often been supported by Metropolitan Bălan of Sibiu (1882–1955) and even Patriarch Justinian had some good things to say about Stăniloae. The only evidence suggesting a different view is hinted at by Fr. Bria (1929–2002), who notes that: "[Members of the] Faculty of Theology in Bucharest seem to be willing to take advantage of the fall of Communism in order to minimize any reference to Fr. Stăniloae's *Dogmatic* and to denigrate the theologians in his school."[75]

Probably a more thorny area encountered in this process of "canonization" is represented by the Communist period and the role played by Stăniloae in relation to the Communist regime. At first glance, the fact that he suffered imprisonment because of his involvement with the *Rugul Aprins* (Burning Bush) could be used as a proof of his resistance to the totalitarian and brutal Romanian regime. Although Stăniloae refused to talk about his imprisonment throughout his life, and was equally mysterious about his conformism in relation to the secret police or the regime-controlled Ministry of Religion, there is a current in contemporary Romanian circles that suggests his resistance to the totalitarian regime concretized in the focused theological activity to which he devoted all his energies in an effort to generate the spiritual renewal of the country.[76] In investigating this claim, the focus will be on how his theological thinking engaged the dominant doctrine of the social apostolate and how it related to pervasive Romanian Orthodox nationalism.

Life and Theological Work

Stăniloae's life spanned each of the three major periods of Eastern European twentieth-century history; he was privileged to express his creativity in the interwar nationalist-Fascist era, the Communist, and for a short though active period, in post-1989 Romania. He was born in a village in Transylvania and, after completing his theological training, traveled to Athens, Munich, Berlin, and Paris to further his research.[77] In 1929, he began teaching theology, dogmatics, apologetics, and pastoral theology at the Orthodox Theology Faculty in Bucharest, where he was also involved in translation work, editing, and publishing. His first major volume, *The Life and Teaching of St. Gregory Palamas* (1938), was regarded as a pioneering work offering an alternative view of *Palamitism* to the negative picture drawn by Roman Catholic scholarship.[78] In Stăniloae's understanding, *Palamitism* is a relevant doctrine because it views God as being personal and acting in the history and hearts of people.[79] By emphasizing *Palamitist* theology, Stăniloae joined neo-Patristic theologians like Vladimir Lossky (1903–1958), Georges Florovsky (1893–1979), John Meyendorff (1926–1992) and others who sought to transform and revitalize Orthodoxy by rediscovering the theology of the Greek Fathers.[80]

Nevertheless, especially in the early part of his life, Stăniloae evidenced openness to modern Western approaches to philosophy and theology that he employed in a self-professed attempt to protect Orthodox theology from Lucian Blaga's (1895–1961) pantheistic influences that he deemed compromising for the church.[81] Although in the first part of the nineteenth century Romanian society had undergone the transition from an Orthodox culture with an ecclesiastical character to a didactic Orthodoxy, Stăniloae remained critical about the conceived compromise between Orthodox theology and currents like rationalism, theosophy, positivism, and scholasticism that were influencing theological colleges. Thus, Stăniloae combined in his theological method the modern approach to philosophical and dogmatic studies, gained through his exposure to Western scholarship with neo-Patristic sources.

This style became ever more evident in his Christology, the second major volume published by Stăniloae during the war, entitled *Jesus Christ, or the Restoration of Man* (1943).[82] In this work, a first Romanian Orthodox engagement with the ontological aspect of redemption, Stăniloae employed a novel approach to Orthodox theology, combining references to Greek Church Fathers (including Gregory of Nyssa (335–394), Athanasius (293–373), Cyril of Alexandria (412–444), and especially Maximus the Confessor (580–662)), with insights from contemporary Western theologians and philosophers, among which references to Barth and dialectical theology were numerous. The Greek Church fathers who were central to Stăniloae's thinking were also essential to the neo-Patristic synthesis that is associated in the West with the names of Lossky and Florovsky, which placed him among the Orthodox theologians whose names are most familiar to Westerners. The theme of the study is Christ as the key to our human personhood; "Only in the light of incarnation can we discover our own authentic humanity."[83] Stăniloae wanted to extend the Greek Fathers' understanding of incarnation in order to reflect on humanity in a new way.[84] According to Andrew Louth, Stăniloae's intense use of the Greek Fathers and the issues he tackled made him not simply marginal, or even a bridge, between Eastern and Western theology, but placed him at the center of the liveliest and most original movement in modern Orthodox thought.[85]

Stăniloae's *Orthodox Dogmatic Theology*, his magnum opus, is a three-volume work completed and published in 1978 at the age of 75.[86] The fruit of a lifetime's encounter with the Greek Fathers, the work deals, in the first part, with "Revelation as the source of the Christian faith and the church as the organ and the medium of realizing the truth of revelation and letting us bear fruit."[87] The second part addresses the Creation, described as "the world as the work of God's love, brought into being to be deified," and has a section that includes the doctrine of fall and providence.[88] The second volume continues into part three, discussing "Jesus Christ as person and work of salvation he accomplished through his assumption of human nature"; while the fourth part, which completes the second volume, concerns "the fulfillment of Christ's work of redemption."[89] The last volume includes in the fifth part "the Holy Sacraments," and the work finishes with the sixth part on "eschatology or the doctrine of the future life."[90] This synthesis of modern Orthodox theology thus starts from the mystery of God as Trinity and revelation, and almost following the order of the creed, proceeds through creation to Christology, ecclesiology, and eschatology.

In 1981, Stăniloae completed a manual of Orthodox moral theology entitled *Orthodox Spirituality*, which is organized following the classical Orthodox structure of three degrees: purification, illumination, and union with God.⁹¹ This was followed by a further theological work, *Spirituality and Communion in Orthodox Liturgy* (1986), comprising a commentary on Byzantine liturgy and the spirituality that emerged from it, its place, time, elements and objects (icons); and the Byzantine liturgy of Eucharist, with emphasis on the mystery of sacrifice.⁹²

Finally, it is worth mentioning Stăniloae's secondary activity with the translation and editing of the Romanian version of the Greek *Philokalia*, which occupied most of his life during the Communist period. Based on the "Philokalia of the Holy Ascetics" (Venice, 1782), a collection of texts compiled by St. Nikodimos of the Holy Mountain and St. Makarios of Corinth, the Romanian version translated by Stăniloae differs from the Greek version in that he supplemented the original texts with his own commentaries as introductions for the modern reader. He commenced his work on *Philokalia* in 1947 and published the 12th and last volume in 1991. Even some of his most sympathetic commentators admit that "the image of him [Stăniloae] sitting at his desk, trying to understand and translate the *Philokalia* while Communist terror continued to grow and increase not only in his country but in a large part of Europe is somewhat ironic and grand."⁹³

Social Apostolate and Double Polarity

Having been introduced to what is an intimidating biography, one can understand why even some of the most renowned Orthodox theologians of today eulogize Stăniloae's theological productivity. The next step is to investigate the claim that, in the midst of the prevailing Marxist ideology of the surrounding society, Stăniloae managed to oppose the Communist regime through his theological activity. Fr. Bria, a passionate supporter and friend of Stăniloae, depicts accurately the context in which Stăniloae lived and worked:

> A dominant trend marking Romanian theology for an extended period (1950–1975) was discussion of the *Social Apostolate*, redefined later by the notion of *The Church in Service – Biserica Slujitoare*. Of course, this trend went together with a certain political conformism and with exaggerated emphasis on national concerns in the Orthodox Church's self-understanding. Under the pressure of a totalitarian regime, the church was in danger of becoming distant, blind, and deaf in responding to the needs of the people and in defending human rights.⁹⁴

From here, Bria goes on to describe the elements of a certain "double polarity" found in Stăniloae's *Dogmatic* and characterizing his theological response to the danger posed by the social apostolate and the church's collaboration with the regime: "The first polarity is to define the *World* as the work of God's love destined to 'deification.' "⁹⁵ According to Stăniloae, the "World" is to be understood as both nature and humankind.⁹⁶ The Eastern Orthodox tradition defines "deification" as the process whereby believers grow in likeness to God, an idea that is termed *theosis* in the West.[97] Thus, Stăniloae describes a God who is active, and who calls humanity and creation to the fullness of life that can be experienced in imitating Christ to the point of achieving such "deification." This active call of God to the world is, according to Bria, Stăniloae's way of saying the church should not canonize any existing social system.[98]

There certainly is some validity in this first polarity in Stăniloae's theology. The church, constituted into a humanity striving to imitate Christ in view of the active role played by God in a world that is not preserved in a cyclic form but in which the intervention of God is a reality, may counter any attempts at totalitarianism by a regime. However, for Stăniloae, "deification" is the necessary and ultimate goal of humankind. "Deification" assumed a movement toward what the Orthodox tradition calls "synergy," that is the collaboration of God with the human will toward the sinner's newness or "deification."[99] Baptist pastor and theologian Emil Bartoş (b. 1957), having closely engaged with Stăniloae's concept of "deification," underlined the danger of such concept for the church:

> Human persons cannot conceivably be absorbed into God. This makes it difficult to understand how deification came to take centre stage in a theology so firmly constructed on a patristic foundation. What need have we to speak of human deification, when the principal aim of the Church is to worship a single God in three persons? Orthodox theology ought to correctly position its theology of deification in such a way that it can never constitute a danger to those essential Christian doctrines and concepts to which all its advocates adhere unreservedly.[100]

Although as a theological concept "deification" appears dynamic and offering hope for a church under political persecution, its ontological emphasis means that concrete evidence of that union with Christ is underplayed, and with it the role of social ethics and their political relevance. Therefore, it is difficult to see how exactly Stăniloae's whole emphasis on "deification" could have helped the church during Communism.

The second polarity offered by Bria as an example of the relevance of Stăniloae's theology for an Orthodox Church under Communism is the emphasis on a historical and pastoral sensitivity toward the "World."[101] The discussion in his *Dogmatic* that is brought to support this argument refers to Stăniloae's argument about "Human Responsibility toward the World," wherein he develops a positive view of history as the place of communication between God and man.[102] For Stăniloae, the Fall of man is not fatally tragic because evil, being ambiguous, cannot stand on its own, nor captivate anything by itself. Man remains in an ambivalent state, preserving the knowledge of evil within himself as "a complex understanding of this sad knowledge of good and evil."[103] In this state, however, man can also penetrate the opacity of the world by "another kind of knowledge."[104] Stăniloae thus offers here a very optimistic view of humanity, affirming the "indelible remnant" of good in the human person even after the Fall, something he refers to as that "minimum of good left in him."[105]

Lucian Turcescu (b. 1966), the past President of the Canadian Society for Patristic Studies, who has engaged Stăniloae's optimist view of history and positivist *Hamartology* (doctrine of sin) described in Bria's second polarity, finds a close link between Stăniloae's understanding of the Fall, its consequences for human nature, and the Law's role as a temporary corrective.[106] In his exposition of the Fall, Stăniloae insists that freedom was bestowed by God upon the first humans not merely as a gift, but as a responsibility that involved effort and led to maturity.[107] He quotes St. Basil of Caesarea who names the cause of the Fall to be *aboulia*, meaning "laziness of the will."[108] Refusing to respond to God by loving obedience, Stăniloae argues, humans thought they were affirming their freedom:

> In fact it was this very act that marked the beginning of the human's selfish confinement within himself. This was how he enslaved himself to himself. Reckoning on becoming his own lord, he became his own slave. The human person is free only if he is free also from himself for the sake of others, in love, and if he is free for God, who is the source of freedom because he is the source of love.[109]

Stăniloae thus equates freedom with a willing subject always choosing the good. Nevertheless, Stăniloae made a distinction, in line with Gregory of Nyssa, between freedom as the will to choose (*prohairesis*) and freedom as the will to be what one wishes to be (*boulesis*), and used the latter in his treatment of the Fall.[110] Having misused their freedom, humans now suffer the consequences of the Fall, such as estrangement from God, passionate impulses, domination, and corruption.[111] But still, even in the state of sin, what comes through is Stăniloae's optimist's affirmation of the "indelible remnant," the little good left in humans that is enough to enable them to contribute with God in synergy, which is combined action between God and humans toward newness or "deification."

The concept of synergy employed here by Stăniloae is where his reflection on the Law comes in. Thus, the newness of the work accomplished in synergy becomes the newness of life opposed to the oldness of the letter (the Law), in the Pauline exhortations (Rom. 6.4, 7.6).[112] Once identified with the Law of the Old Testament, Stăniloae condemns together the Old Testament Law and the laws of modern states. He writes: "The Law is repetition, according to an external form, within the monotonously confined horizon of egoism and death."[113] As Turcescu notes, the "newness of life" that Stăniloae opposes to the Law was inspired by Gregory of Nyssa who employed it in his theory of beatitude stages in the afterlife: "Stăniloae does not, however, elaborate Gregory's views. And it is not clear how, in his view, human society could survive without the Law. Not everybody shows or reaches that dimension of love that Stăniloae champions."[114]

Such a negative attitude toward the Law could have been a reaction to the Communist context with its oppressive system that characterized the times in which Stăniloae wrote his *Dogmatic*. If that is the case, then it has had a terrifying and long-term impact on his theology. When, in 1992, two years after the fall of Communism in Romania, Stăniloae was asked why human relations in the West are better regulated and more disciplined than in the East, he answered that these are misguided perceptions as long as interhuman relations in the West are characterized by a sense of distance and alienation, while the laws that "sustain the correctness" are secular and do not retain the element of hospitality pervasive in Romania.[115] Furthermore, in another interview, Stăniloae claimed that "without Christ everything is monotonous, legalistic, everything unfolds in a forced way," and through sin, the world "fell into monotony, in the prison of invariable laws and causal determinism."[116] The negative perception of the notion of Law apparent in Stăniloae's *Dogmatic* became evident to Pavel Chihaia (b. 1922), a dissident Romanian writer who observed that after 1990 Stăniloae stressed that Communism and its totalitarian ideology had been developed by intellectuals who had been cultivated by pagan Western civilization, and who now had to return to popular Orthodoxy.[117]

The discussion has come a long way from Fr. Bria's optimism concerning the contribution of the *Dogmatic* emphasizing a historical and pastoral sensitivity toward the "World" to see how the doctrine of sin and synergy lead to anti-legalistic and anti-Western concepts. The argument that the church's response to a Marxist ideology, like the social apostolate, is to emphasize deification has been unconvincing, emphasizing the risk of a loss of distinctiveness as church and as theologians.

Stăniloae's Disagreement with Karl Barth

One of the important contributions Stăniloae is said to have made was to bridge Eastern Orthodoxy and Western theology in his *Dogmatic* approach.[118] It is certainly true that Stăniloae engaged deeply with Western theology and was particularly indebted to Karl Barth's dialectical theology that generated such ferment in Germany with the publication of the second edition of the *Römerbrief*. Barth's dialectical theology seemed to contrast the stultifying academic theology of the age with a God who was not simply a theological premise but a Person who comes to man in judgment and challenges man's existence.[119] While studying in Munich, Stăniloae inevitably became acquainted with the theology of the *Zwischen den Zeiten* group (Friedrich Gogarten (1887–1967), Eduard Thurneysen (1888–1977), and Karl Barth). With the distancing of Barth from liberal theology after World War I, Stăniloae found in Barth's dialectical theology an insightful dialogue partner, which he continued to challenge for many years in his works. Stăniloae found in Barth's dialectical theology:

... the fundamental affirmation of the person, the personal contact with God, the awareness of sin, which although overemphasized, ... did imply the awareness of the fact that God is a Personal being who has something to say to the human being who is at fault.[120]

Sources of inspiration from Barth's theology included the existential approach to faith and the centrality of Christ, and in this respect Stăniloae continued to dialogue with dialectical theology throughout his life. Moreover, key Patristic doctrines, such as the centrality of Christ as both the subject and the object of revelation, as well as the affirmation of the personal character of God manifested in his love for the human person, came to be appropriated by Stăniloae through his encounter with Barth's theology.

Stăniloae became interested in the Barthian concept of diastasis (the wholly other), which the Swiss theologian used to emphasize the utter transcendence of God and His incomprehensibility. This dialogue was however as much creative as it was contradictory for Stăniloae, who was attempting to balance dialectical theology with Eastern Orthodox theological concepts, especially *Palamitan* "divine essence" theology. Steeped in the theology of Gregory of Palamas (1296–1359), Stăniloae was aiming to correlate between that which is communicable and that which is incommunicable in God's relationship to the world:

> I soon realised that it [dialectical theology] is not exactly the Christian truth. In this so called 'dialectical' theology the separation between God and man is too much emphasised. It is a theory of a 'diastasis'. However, from this theology I gained the affirmation of a living God, of the transcendence of God in relation to man. I combined this with the knowledge I had, according to Saint Gregory of Palamas, that God is in relationship with us through His energies.[121]

According to Gregory of Palamas, there is a distinction between God's incomprehensible "essence" and His accessible "energy."[122] Although initially comparing Barth's diastasis with Palamitan divine essence in an attempt to make an organic synthesis between God's transcendence and His reality in creation, Stăniloae became increasingly insistent on the experiential closeness that is realized between God and humanity in Stăniloae's conceptual framework.

Here there are hints of Stăniloae's incomplete familiarity with Western theology that could explain his discomfort with Barth's dialectical theology. Stăniloae's interest in Palamitical theology seemed to offer him a useful theological framework, presenting God as being personal and acting in the history and hearts of the people, a framework that enabled him to critique what he thought was a modern German theology that presented God as being only transcendental. This approach, he thought, was too rationalistic a relationship to God, which limited Him to a conceptual being. Stăniloae wrote:

> Both the dialectical theology and the theology of Saint Gregory Palamas made me see a living, personal God; but while in the dialectic one God was separated from man because he could free himself from his own sins, in the Palamitical theology God moves towards man called by prayer. In the dialectical theology I found the image of a separated and distant God, while in the Palamitical one I met a God who comes toward man, opens Himself to him like light, through prayer. He fills him with His energies, yet remaining incommunicable with respect to His essence, incomprehensibility, apophaticy.[123]

As the above passage indicates, Stăniloae reduced Barth's distinction between the "No!" of God's judgment and the "Yes!" of God's movement of grace to a distorted image of God as an alien and transcendental being, indifferent and removed from humankind.[124]

More influenced by the demythologizing project of Rudolf Bultmann (1884–1976) than by Karl Barth's theology, Stăniloae often referred to the "typical" example of the failure of the "purely rationalist tradition of the West."[125] Although perhaps accurately highlighting some of the limitations of liberal theology, Stăniloae's critical generalizations about Western theology may represent the most superficial aspects of his *Dogmatic* as a whole.[126] To note one example, Stăniloae was convinced the theological notion of "satisfaction" is central to a Western understanding of the atonement, and that this notion undermines the whole Western concept of the church and the sacraments.[127] However, the passages he cites from Barth, Karl Rahner, and Hans Urs von Balthasar to sustain this argument insist on the need to retain the notion of satisfaction against liberal understanding of atonement, rather than making it central to the doctrine of atonement.[128]

The evidence brought to bear here points to a lack of serious engagement with Western theology and to a readiness to point out its perceived deficiencies without fully understanding the complex Protestant and Catholic theological traditions. It also raises questions as to the quality of the synthesis Stăniloae has been able to achieve between neo-Patristic and Western dogmatic structures, and how this could be viewed as a basis for ecumenical dialogue between the two traditions. Such limitations could be ascribed to Stăniloae's scarce access to Western theological literature in the hermetically sealed world of Romanian Communism after 1947. However, the next section will focus on a certain continuity characterizing Stăniloae's thinking throughout his extensive theological career.

Stăniloae and Nationalism

The work of a true ecumenist, Stăniloae's *Dogmatic* represents, according to Bishop Kallistos, a bridge-building work written by one who is profoundly

Romanian in spirit and sensitive to the distinctive insights of Romanian poetry and folklore.[129] Whereas the ecumenical function of the *Dogmatic* remains a matter of debate, it is the second part of this statement that will concern us here. The previous chapters have pointed out that both interwar and Communist Romania were characterized by varying degrees of nationalism. During the decades from the 1920s to 1940s the force of nationalist ideology resulting from the so-called national debate has led to a radical form of nationalism known as ethnocracy. Spearheaded by the Iron Guard, this radical version of Romanian nationalism was richly Orthodox in content, and thus attracted and gained the support of numerous theologians of the day. Stăniloae, who was a good friend of the mystical-nationalist Nichifor Crainic, Gândirism's mastermind, worked on defining a theological framework that would incorporate the nationalist ideology pervading interwar Romania.[130]

During this period, Stăniloae is thought to have developed a practical understanding of the role of theologian as one who is to interpret the times for the benefit of his fellow Christians.[131] Having returned to Romania from his travels and studies across Europe, he devoted considerable publishing efforts in the Orthodox journal *Telegraful Român* (*Romanian Telegraph*), which he directed during the 1934–46 period, and in the secular press of the interwar period.[132] The topics he tackled ranged from current social and political aspects to commentaries addressing politics and nationalism from a theological viewpoint, as well as issues regarding other religious denominations. In particular, Stăniloae was interested in developing a theological basis for nationalism. Some of the ideas concretizing in this attempt were at the heart of his theological construct, fully developed later in his *Dogmatic*.[133]

Under the influence of the Gândirism ideology, which saw a close identification between Orthodoxy and the "Romanian soul," Stăniloae developed a theory of "Orthodox Romanianness," which basically argued for an intrinsic and deep unity between Romanian ethnicity and the Orthodox Church.[134] Although the ecumenical patriarchate (1872) had defined this tendency as phyletism and banned it as heresy, many Orthodox theologians continued to refer to the Apostolic Canon 34, written in the fourth century, which states that "the bishops of every nation (*ethnos*) must acknowledge him who is first among them and account him as their head, and do nothing of consequence without consent."[135] The Greek *ethnos* used here for nation has the same connotation with the biblical one in the Great Commandment (Mt. 28.19) "Go and make disciples of all the nations" (Greek *ethnos*), making reference to non-Jewish peoples living together regardless of their ethnic origins.[136] This meaning of *ethnos* complies with the modern concept of nation-state, which is ethnically diverse and bound together by allegiance to a set of common institutions and practices. Stăniloae, however, understood *ethnos* in a typically Orthodox fashion, that is to say, as defining an ethnic group characterized by a common language, history, race, and religion.[137]

There are two terms used in the Romanian language for "nation," namely *națiune* (nation, people) and *neam*. The second term indicates a people that is centered on an ethnic group and whose identities are rooted in a long-established history, in the case of Romania with Orthodoxy as part of that history. As Stăniloae makes it clear:

> The Romanian nation (*neam*) is a biological-spiritual synthesis which combines a number of elements. They are: the Dacian element, the Latin element and the Orthodox Christianity. It's a new synthesis, a unique individuality with a uniting principle that differs from each one component. The highest Law of our nation (*neam*) is a Law which describes the nation in the best way. . . . All components are stamped with a new, unifying and individualizing mark, which is Romanianness (*românitatea*). Therefore, we can say that the highest Law of our nation (*neam*) is the Romanianness. . . . The permanent national ideal of our nation can only be perceived in relation to Orthodoxy.[138]

Thus conceived, Romanian nationalism becomes a pervasive element of Stăniloae's theology and explains his negative view of the laws of modern states. For him, ethnic nations are something God desired and planned, and as part of the "World" all God's creation was good, and so was nationalism.[139]

From this perspective, Stăniloae's theology informed his ethnic nationalism, which could account for the other reflexes denoted during the interwar period, namely his ethnocratic tendencies and involvement with Gândirism, his opposition to Lucian Blaga's immanentism, which he perceived as a danger to Romanianness, and his criticism of Roman and Greek Catholicism, to name only a few.[140] The same could be said about the Communist period, when his ethnic nationalism informed his criticism of the Greek Catholic Church, even though this persecuted denomination had been disbanded by then, or his anti-Western critique that comes across in his *Dogmatic*.[141]

As Bielawski noted, Stăniloae continued to develop the subject of nationalism in conjunction with Orthodoxy until the end of his life.[142] After the fall of Communism in 1992, he revived the interest in Romanianness, publishing a volume entitled *Reflections on the Spirituality of the Romanian People*, wherein he denotes ample right-wing tendencies, blaming the West for the immanentism affecting post-1989 Romanian society; and he continues to expand on the intrinsic bond between Romanianness and Orthodoxy, expressed through its ethos, customs, and folklore.[143] It is revealing to note that rediscovered interest in Romanianness after 1989 was well received among Orthodox theologians like Ioan Leb (b. 1953) who found inspiration in Stăniloae's proposals for a rural version of popular Christianity as a solution to the pressure of modernity.[144]

Returning to Fr. Bria's earlier expressed convictions that the *Dogmatic* was a clear representation of the resistance shown by Stăniloae to the Marxist and atheist regime, it is difficult to be persuaded in that direction once the nooks and crannies within Stăniloae's theological architecture have been exposed.

This dilemma has been stressed by Orthodox voices who regard Stăniloae's loyalty to the nationalist Orthodox Church and his unshaken belief in the unique character of the Romanian Orthodoxy to represent a "grave limitation" of his theology.[145] The evidence examined here suggests that Stăniloae's otherwise open and dialogical style was limited by an ethnocentric and antimodern tendency.

Conclusion: Between Resistance and Collaboration

Stăniloae's affirmation of the link between Romanianness and Orthodoxy, evidenced throughout his life, is surprisingly similar to what Patriarch Justinian had to say in his social apostolate:

> From their very inception, the Romanian Orthodox Metropolitanates have supported the Romanian lands throughout the territory under their jurisdiction, helping them culturally, economically and patriotically, contributing to the physical and intellectual formation of the Romanian people. Orthodoxy has contributed to the shaping and preservation of the consciousness of our unity as a nation (*neam*).[146]

In the conclusion of his dissertation on Stăniloae's "ontology of love," Silviu Rogobete comments that the "possible political pressure exercised towards him [Stăniloae] may have led to his unilateral affirmation of the superiority of Romanian Orthodoxy compared with the other Christian traditions."[147] The investigation of these aspects leads to the only logical conclusion, namely that Stăniloae's theological opposition to Communism has been hampered by his preoccupation with Romanian nationalism. Perceived in such close proximity to the *ethnos*, his theological opposition had little to offer for an effective resistance to collaboration and compromise with the political religion represented by the Romanian Communist regime. The implications of this conclusion are not just personal, reflecting negatively on Stăniloae's otherwise mythologized persona, but also relate to the Orthodox Church, which lacked the prophetic leadership of its hierarchy and theologians. The organic unity envisaged between Orthodoxy and Romanianness made it difficult for Stăniloae to understand the crucial distinction between church and state in the way Barth understood it.

After the war, Barth returned to the topic of German nationalism in *Church Dogmatics*, where, in the final part of the "Doctrine of Creation," he described *Volk* as "the novel elevation of the term 'people' to the front rank of theological and ethical concepts ... one of the most curious and tragic events in the whole history of Protestant theology."[148] This consistent rejection of the total claims of German Nazism as having anything to do with theology or the church was Barth's way of resisting any theological compromise. It was possible because he saw the flawed understanding of natural theology that offered the church little potential for an uncompromising distancing of itself from the nationalist goals of the Third Reich. Barth's critical distance was based on a Christological understanding of the supremacy of Christ above any secondary, alternative social, political, or ideological loyalties. Showing awareness of the fact that "the Christ" of natural theology often becomes the relativized Christ of culture, Barth led the Confessing Church to distance itself from the German Christians and National Socialism.

After the fall of Communism, Stăniloae showed he was not prepared to relate his theology to the most sensitive aspects challenging the church in the public arena. Asked why the Orthodox Church had remained silent during Communism and whether it should at least now distinguish between those who had collaborated with the secret police and those who had suffered imprisonment, torture, and hardship because of opposition to the regime, Stăniloae retorted that the church preaches Christ and does not assign guilt in the public sphere.[149] Then he was asked whether the Christian theme of forgiveness of sin does not become "cheap grace" when politicians in post-Communist Romania are using it to evade responsibility and to cover up their own guilt, claiming exoneration because they deserved Christian forgiveness, in the same way that Hitler's officers claimed exoneration because they were simply following orders.[150] Stăniloae again insisted the church cannot condemn anybody, and reiterated the Orthodox teaching about individual confession of the penitent to a confessor. Stăniloae finally admitted the ROC did share some degree of culpability, which prevented it from proclaiming with a louder voice the need for justice in Romanian society.[151]

A theology that emphasizes God's collaborative work of synergy toward human deification, a non-biblical concept developed by the Greek Church Fathers, leads to what Barth described as an assimilated theology, a theology in which Christ is not the ultimate revelation and authority but where center stage is occupied by humanity. Such a theological basis is prone to compromise by aspects of the "World," like human culture and politics, which can replace the church's allegiance to Christ with other alternative allegiances to nation, *Volk*, race, or *neam*. Moreover, as showed by this analysis, such a theological concept, emphasizing ontological union at the expense of the experiential, leads to a diminishing of the importance of personal morality, social ethics, and political relevance.

Notes

[1] M. Burleigh, *Third Reich*, pp. 4–14.
[2] K. Barth, *Theological Existence Today*, p. 47.
[3] Mark R. Lindsay, *Covenanted Solidarity: The Theological Basis of Karl Barth's Opposition to Nazi Antisemitism and the Holocaust* (New York: Peter Lang, 2001), p. 63.

4 Ernst C. Helmreich, *The German Churches under Hitler: Background, Struggle, and Epilogue* (Detroit: Wayne State University Press, 1979), p. 34.
5 Eberhard Bethge, "Troubled Self-Interpretation and Uncertain Reception in the Church Struggle" in *The German Church Struggle* by Franklin H. Littell and Hubert G. Locke (Detroit: Wayne State University Press, 1974), p. 178.
6 Charles Villa-Vicencio, *A Theology of Reconstruction: Nation-Building and Human Rights* (Cambridge: Cambridge University Press, 1992), p. 229.
7 K. Barth, *Theological Existence Today*, p. 25.
8 Herrmann is usually described as Ritschlian but that is not accurate given that Hermann moved away from Ritschl's theological positivism. McCormack described Herrmann's theology as a kind of existentialized *Schleiermacherianism*. From Herrmann, Barth learned to disdain natural theology and apologetics and to oppose historicism. Bruce McCormack, *Karl Barth's Critically Realistic Dialectical Theology* (Oxford: Clarendon Press, 1997), pp. 31–72.
9 Albrecht Ritschl (d. 1889) was a dogmatic theologian characterized by a commitment to a churchly theology, oriented towards God's revelation in the historical person of Jesus Christ. Ernst Troeltsch followed a similar direction but focused more on the historical comparative studies, known for his *Religionsgeschichtliche Schule*.
10 Karl Barth, "Evangelical Theology in the Nineteenth Century" in K. Barth, *The Humanity of God* (Atlanta: John Knox Press, 1978), p. 14.
11 Barth's "Socialist speeches" to the local Worker's Union is where he develops his criticism of the prevailing view on religion in Germany, namely to be a personal matter between God and soul, soul and God. For Barth, the coming kingdom proclaimed by Jesus will make *all* things new including social and economic. The new themes emphasized by Barth are the judgment of God, depravity of human race, the wholly-otherness of God, and the criticism of religion. B. McCormack, *Karl Barth* pp. 78–111.
12 Karl Barth, quoted in D. Haddorff, *"Karl Barth's Theological Politics,"* p. vi.
13 This was the title of a lecture in 1916. See Karl Barth, *The Word of God and the Word of Man* (London: Hodder and Stoughton, 1928), pp. 28–50. B. McCormack, *Karl Barth*, pp. 129–83.
14 The commentary represents Barth's break with Hermann's liberalism. According to McCormack, Barth moves from Hermann's idealistic theology (where God is a necessary postulate for the sake of ethical activity) to a critically realistic theology (where God is a Reality complete, whole, and entire in itself, apart from and prior to entire human knowledge). B. McCormack, *Karl Barth*, p. 129.
15 *Diastasis* is a relationship in which the two members oppose each other with no possibility of a synthesis into a higher form of being. B. McCormack, *Karl Barth*, p. 129.
16 D. Haddorff, *"Karl Barth's Theological Politics,"* p. ix. Cf. Karl Barth, *The Epistle to the Romans* (Oxford: Oxford University Press, 1960), pp. 455–6.
17 Karl Barth, "The Christian's Place in Society" in *The Word of God and the Word of Man* (New York: Harper & Row, 1957).
18 Barth developed a *dialectical* approach which stressed that revelation is never identifiable with something given to human cognition but that God reveals himself by veiling himself in a creaturely medium. Revelation, thus understood, entails an unveiling in and through the veil. In the commentary, Barth localized

revelation in the cross, but later (Göttingen Lectures, 1924) he would come to see it in the whole complex of the life, death and resurrection of Jesus. B. McCormack, *Karl Barth*, p. 129.

19 Cf. Emil Brunner, "Nature and Grace" in Karl Barth, Emil Brunner, *Natural Theology: Comprising "Nature and Grace" by Professor Dr. Emil Brunner and the Reply "No!" by Dr. Karl Barth*, translated by Peter Fraenkel (Eugene, OR: Wipf & Stock Publishers, 2002).

20 Karl Barth, *The Göttingen Dogmatics: Instruction in the Christian Religion* (Grand Rapids: Eerdmans, 1990), p. 344.

21 K. Barth, *Göttingen Dogmatics*, pp. 345–6.

22 Aquinas, stresses Barth, "standing with both feet in revelation" developed the proofs as a work of supererogation, thinking they were worthwhile as pointers to the problem and necessity of the concept of God. K. Barth, *Göttingen Dogmatics* p. 347. For an elaborate discussion of Barth's development of the denial of natural theology, but in view of the possibility that he later developed a "theological metaphysics" as an alternative to natural revelation, see Stanley Hauerwas, *With the Grain of the Universe: The Church's Witness and Natural Theology* (London: SCM Press, 2002), pp. 141–204.

23 George Hunsinger, *Disruptive Grace: Studies in the Theology of Karl Barth* (Grand Rapids: Eerdmans, 2000), p. 80.

24 Karl Barth, *Church Dogmatics*, vol. I/1 (Edinburgh: T. & T. Clark, 1936), p. 60.

25 G. Hunsinger, *Disruptive Grace*, p. 80.

26 Karl Barth, *Church Dogmatics*, vol. II/1 (Edinburgh: T. & T. Clark, 1957), p. 163.

27 Karl Barth, *Ethics*, translated by Geoffrey Bromiley (Edinburgh: T & T Clark, 1981), p. 192.

28 K. Barth, *Ethics*, p. 192.

29 K. Barth, *Ethics*, p. 193.

30 Karl Barth, *God in Action* (Edinburgh: T & T Clark, 1937), p. 137.

31 K. Barth, *Theological Existence Today*, p. 46.

32 Timothy J. Gorringe, *Karl Barth: Against Hegemony* (Oxford: Oxford University Press, 1999), p. 21.

33 Karl Barth, *How I Changed my Mind* (Edinburgh: St. Andrew Press, 1969), p. 46.

34 K. Barth, *Theological Existence Today*, pp. 51–2.

35 K. Barth, *Theological Existence Today*, p. 52.

36 K. Barth, *Theological Existence Today*, p. 70.

37 K. Barth, *Theological Existence Today*, p. 84.

38 According to Cochrane, the pamphlet sold 30,000 copies in the first six months. A. Cochrane, *Church's Confession under Hitler*, p. 100.

39 Pastor's Emergency League (*Pharrernotbund*) was organized by Martin Niemöller in 1933 as a counterpoint to the German Christians' movement. The league merged into the Confessing Church a year later.

40 Bergen correctly noted that although counting among its members people like Barth or Bonhoeffer, the Confessing Church consisted of a majority of professed apoliticals, supporters of the National Socialist regime, and party members. The Confessing Church rallied less against National Socialism than against German Christian domination of institutionalized Protestantism. Doris L. Bergen, *Twisted Cross: The German Christian Movement in the Third Reich*, p. 12.

41 Like Bergen, Conway has underlined the complex situation of the Protestant churches during Nazism, which includes historical, hagiographical, apologetic,

political, as well as theological factors involved. His analysis points to the extent to which even some of the leaders of the Confessing Church have held the German Christians' movement in sympathy and expressed positive attitudes towards Hitler's ideology and policies. To this complex situation, he contrasts Nazis' rejection of Christianity. See J. S. Conway, *The Nazi Persecution of the Churches*, pp. 86–7. Cf. Robert Ericksen, *Theologians Under Hitler*; Richard Steigmann-Gall, *The Holy Reich*.

[42] The "Confessing Church" was perhaps a label expressing their claim to represent the true church of Christ over against the German Christians. The Confessing Church did however have their own national synods (1934, 35, 36) and had set up their provisional church leadership. D. Bergen, *Twisted Cross*, p.13.

[43] "The Barmen Theological Declaration: A New Translation," translated by Douglas S. Bax, in *Christ, Justice and Peace: Toward a Theology of the State in Dialogue with the Barmen Declaration* by Eberhard Jüngel, D. Bruce Hamill, Alan J. Torrance (Edinburgh: T. & T. Clark, 1992), p. xxii.

[44] R. Ericksen, *Theologians Under Hitler*, p. 116. Cf. Robert Ericksen, "The Political Theology of Paul Althaus: Nazi Supporter" in *German Studies Review*, vol. 9, No. 3 (October 1986), p. 558.

[45] P. Althaus, quoted in A. Cochrane, *Church's Confession under Hitler*, p. 191.

[46] P. Althaus, quoted from a lecture in 1937 by P. Ericksen, "The Political Theology of Paul Althaus," p. 558.

[47] "The Barmen Theological Declaration," pp. xxiv–v.

[48] "The Barmen Theological Declaration," pp. xxv–xxvi.

[49] G. Hunsinger, *Disruptive Grace*, pp. 80–1.

[50] "The Barmen Theological Declaration," pp. xxvi–vii.

[51] "The Barmen Theological Declaration," pp. xxvii–viii.

[52] The sixth thesis concludes the declaration by rejecting the "arbitrary chosen desired and plans" while affirming service to the "message of the free grace of God," implying that all political activity in which the church will engage will carry the basic statutes of a witness to grace. "The Barmen Theological Declaration," pp. xxviii–xxix.

[53] A. Cochrane, *Church's Confession under Hitler*, p. 190.

[54] In an article afterwards, Walter Elert brought this point home poignantly: "The proposition that apart from Christ no truth is to be acknowledged as God's revelation is a rejection of the divine authority of the divine Law *beside* that of the Gospel." A. Cochrane, *Church's Confession under Hitler*, p. 190.

[55] Althaus published the same year a book titled *Die deutsche Stunde der Kirche* (The Hour of the German Church).

[56] Other reactions blamed Barth for his stab-in-the-back theology, undermining the positive role played by the church during World War I with his theology, which wanted to separate the Kingdom of God from the state, and humanity from God. A. Cochrane, *Church's Confession under Hitler*, pp. 176ff.

[57] R. Steigmann-Gall, *Holy Reich*, pp. 128–9.

[58] K. Barth, E. Brunner, *Natural Theology*, p. v.

[59] K. Barth, E. Brunner, *Natural Theology*, vi. Barth's final words on natural theology are found in *Church Dogmatics* II/1 (1939), where he elaborates on how Brunner's "point of contact" leads to an alternative source of revelation.

[60] As Haddorff stressed, Brunner's respected theological position in the Reformed Church made Barth reject his deviation more poignantly, because "being closer

to the truth" he was "much more dangerous." D. Haddorff, *"Karl Barth's Theological Politics,"* p. xxvii.

[61] D. Bergen, *Twisted Cross*, p. 12.

[62] See Jürgen Moltmann, *Forgiveness and Politics: Forty Years after the Stuttgart Confession* (London: New World Publications, 1987).

[63] K. Barth, *Theological Existence Today*, p. 9.

[64] This accusation is set within the larger charge for a lack of rejection of the totalitarian regimes behind the Iron Curtain. See K. Barth, *Against the Stream: Shorter Post-War Writings, 1946–52* (London: SCM Press Ltd, 1954), p. 113.

[65] Karl Barth, *Church and State* (London: SCM Press, 1939), p. 82.

[66] As Frank Jehle noted, having voted unanimously for the theological declaration, the Confessing Church's chairman (1934–36) August Marahrens began opposing Barth as the "greatest danger" to the Protestant Church because he picked too many specific battles with National Socialism. Frank Jehle, *Ever Against the Stream: The Politics of Karl Barth 1906–1968* (Grand Rapids, Michigan: Eerdmans, 2002), p. 55. In 1935, having refused to take the Nazi oath of allegiance to Hitler, Barth was forced to leave Germany.

[67] Olivier Clément, "Prefazione" in *Dumitru Stăniloae, La Preghiera di gesu e lo Spirito Santo, Meditazioni Teologiche* (Rome, 1988), p.1.

[68] During his eightieth birthday celebrations, Barth said in an attempt to distance himself from his reputation: "As a theologian one can never be great, but at best one remains small in one's own way." "Karl Barth's speech on the occasion of his eightieth birthday celebrations" in *Fragments Grave and Gay* by Karl Barth (London: Collins, 1971), p. 112.

[69] John Meyendorff, "Foreword" in Dumitru Stăniloae, *Theology and the Church*, translated by Robert Barringer (New York: SVS Press, 1980), p. 7.

[70] Although written in 1978, Stăniloae's *"Dogmatic"* had yet to be translated into English as of 2010. The first of the three volumes was translated in two parts (1994 and 2000). Louth agrees that outside Orthodox ecumenical circles, Stăniloae is not yet well-known. Andrew Louth, "Review Essay: The Orthodox Dogmatic Theology of Dumitru Stăniloae," in *Modern Theology*, vol. 13, No. 2 (April 1997), p. 253.

[71] M. Păcurariu speaks of "Stăniloae's epoch in Romanian theology." M. Păcurariu, "Preotul Profesor și Academician Dumitru Stăniloae" in *Persoană și Comuniune*, by Mircea Păcurariu, Ioan Ică Jr., eds (Sibiu: Editura Arhiepiscopiei Ortodoxe, 1993), p. 13.

[72] Comprehensive critical analyses of Stăniloae's dogmatic theology are limited to the engagement of certain themes. What is more, most of the published dissertations listed below belong to Evangelicals, Anglicans, and Catholics. See Charles Miller, *The Gift of the World. An Introduction to the Theology of Dumitru Stăniloae* (Edinburgh: T & T Clark, 2000); Maciej Bielawski, *The Philocalical Vision of the World in the Theology of Dumitru Stăniloae* (Bydgoszcz: Homini, 1997); Emil Bartoș, *Deification in Eastern Orthodox Theology: An Evaluation and Critique of the Theology of Dumitru Stăniloae* (Carlisle: Paternoster, 1999); Silviu Eugen Rogobete, *O ontologie a iubirii. Subiect și Realitate personală supremă în gîndirea Părintelui Dumitru Stăniloae* (Iași: Editura Polirom, 2001); Dănuț Mănăstireanu, "A Perichoretic Model of the Church: The Trinitarian Ecclesiology of Dumitru Stăniloae," unpublished thesis (Brunel, London, 2005).

[73] M. Bielawski, *Philocalic Vision*, p. 9.
[74] An incomplete bibliography of his work lists 90 books, 33 translations, 275 theological articles, and 437 journalistic essays, in addition to published homilies, TV and radio interviews and so on. See Gheorghe Anghelescu, "Opera Păr. Prof. Dumitru Stăniloae. Bibliografie Sistematică" in *Persoană şi Comuniune*, pp. 16–59.
[75] Ion Bria, *Spaţiul Nemuririi sau Eternizarea Umanului în Dumnezeu* (Iaşi: Editura Trinitas, 1994), p. 43.
[76] Cf. Ion Bria, "Preface" in *The Experience of God* by Dumitru Stăniloae, vol. 2 (New York: SVS Press, 2000), p. xi. Concerning his silence about the imprisonment, Clément reported him saying: "when one simply carries his cross, which is the normal condition for any Christian: there is no need to talk about it." O. Clément, "Le Pére dr. D. Stăniloae et le genie de l'Orthodoxie roumaine" in *Persoană şi Comuniune*, pp. 82–3.
[77] Metropolitan Bălan took a special interest in Stăniloae, so after sending him to Western Europe to be exposed to the Western tradition, also awarded him a grant to study in Athens.
[78] Turcescu here makes reference to the negative picturing of *Palamitism* in the West by Catholic scholar Martin Jugie, who lived at the beginning of the twentieth century. Lucian Turcescu, "Dumitru Stăniloae," unpublished article.
[79] As a reaction to this Orthodox regeneration of Palamitism, Roman Catholic scholars like Andre de Halleux, Jacques Lison, and Robert Sinkewicz developed more academic and objective treatments of Palamitism. Lucian Turcescu, "Dumitru Stăniloae."
[80] The Greek Fathers central to Stăniloae, namely Athanasius, the Cappadocians, Cyril, Dionysius, Maximus, and finally Gregory Palamas, have been deeply engaged by the Russian neo-Patristic theologians. Cf. Vladimir Lossky, *Mystical Theology of the Eastern Church* (London: James Clarke, 1957).
[81] Fr. Bria devoted a study to the relationship between theology and philosophy as it emerged in Stăniloae's early thinking. Stăniloae debated the thought of theologian and metaphysician Lucian Blaga. Blaga sought to describe the impossibility of human beings to know God, and proposed a horizontal religious dimension that was more aesthetic and pantheistic due to the absence of the transcendence. Fr. Bria believed the novel philosophical system which Blaga developed needed more constructive interaction rather than the harsh criticism it instead received from Stăniloae. Nevertheless, Stăniloae's responses have been published in two compilation volumes. Dumitru Stăniloae, *Ortodoxie şi Românism* (1939); *Poziţia d-lui Lucian Blaga Faţă de Creştinism şi Ortodoxie* (Sibiu, 1942). Cf. Ion Bria, "Theology and the Bridge of Metaphysics" in *Ortodoxia*, vol. 9 (1990); *Spaţiul Nemuririi.*
[82] Dumitru Stăniloae, *Iisus Hristos sau Restaurarea Omului* (Craiova: Omniscop Press, 1993). A developed version of the Christology exposed in this book, but heavily influenced by the theology of Maximos the Confessor, can be found in Stăniloae's later works, including Dumitru Stăniloae, *Chipul Nemuritor al lui Dumnezeu* (Craiova: Mitropolia Olteniei, 1987) and in the chapter entitled "Omul şi Dumnezeu," in *Studii de Teologie Dogmatică Ortodoxă* (Craiova: Mitropolia Olteniei, 1991).
[83] D. Stăniloae, *Iisus Hristos*, p. 159.
[84] Maximus the Confessor is quoted as saying that "God's incarnation makes man like God only to the extent that He made himself man." Athanasius is also

reported stressing that "the Logos became man so that man might become god," to which Stăniloae adds, "not only that but also that man might become man." D. Stăniloae, *Iisus Hristos*, pp. 193ff.

[85] Andrew Louth, "The Orthodox Dogmatic Theology of Dumitru Stăniloae" in *Dumitru Stăniloae: Tradition and Modernity in Theology* (henceforth quoted as *Tradition and Modernity*) edited by Lucian Turcescu (Iaşi: Center for Romanian Studies, 2002), p. 57.

[86] Dumitru Stăniloae, TDO. First volume has been translated and published in English as *The Experience of God—Orthodox Dogmatic Theology*, 2 vols (Brookline: Holy Cross Orthodox Press, 1994–1998).

[87] Here he addresses in two chapters, the relationship between natural and supernatural revelation. This includes his discussion of revelation, ways of knowing God, the doctrine of God and his attributes, and the doctrine of the Trinity. He then proceeds to address the world and work of God's love. For Stăniloae, natural revelation is known and understood fully in the light of supernatural revelation. A crucial statement is the first sentence of the chapter: "The Orthodox Church makes no separation between natural and supernatural revelation." This view is in agreement with theologians of the Eastern Orthodox tradition who, like Maximus the Confessor, believe supernatural revelation is the embodiment of natural revelation in historical persons and actions. Although they are not to be separated, natural and supernatural revelation are distinguished from one another. According to Stăniloae, Orthodox theology only separates them in order to better explain and understand them while at the same time striving to express their continuity. TDO, vol. 1, pp. 7ff.

[88] TDO, vol.1, pp. 337ff.

[89] TDO, vol. 2, pp. 7ff., 201ff. respectively.

[90] TDO, vol. 3, pp. 7ff., 223ff. respectively.

[91] Dumitru Stăniloae, *Ascetica şi Mistica Bisericii Ortodoxe* (Bucureşti: Editura Institutului Biblic, 2002, 1981).

[92] Dumitru Stăniloae, *Spiritualitate şi Comuniune in Liturghia Ortodoxă* (Craiova: Mitropolia Olteniei, 1986).

[93] M. Bielawski, *Philocalic Vision*, p. 33.

[94] I. Bria, "Preface," pp. xi–xii.

[95] I. Bria, "Preface," p. xii. Bria summarizes here from Stăniloae's last section in vol. 1, entitled "Providence and the Deification of the World." TDO, vol.1, pp. 511–20.

[96] "The economy of God, that is, his plan with regard to the world, consists in the "deification" of the created things, which, as a consequence of sin, implies also its salvation. The salvation and the "deification" of the world presuppose, as primal divine act, its creation. Salvation and "deification" undoubtedly have humanity directly as their aim but not a humanity separated from nature, rather one that is ontologically united with it. . . . Thus, by *world* both nature and humanity are understood; or when the word world is used to indicate one of these realities, the other is always implied as well." TDO, vol.1, p. 337.

[97] Stăniloae did not change its meaning but rather preserved the essence of the concept as it had been formulated by the Greek Church Fathers. In history, "deification" has been associated with the idea of spiritual progress, or imitating Christ. Emil Bartoş, a Romanian Baptist, wrote a dissertation on Stăniloae's

concept of "deification" wherein he outlined its various functions in the *Dogmatic*, namely its making use of the ideas of imitation, resemblance, metaphor, ethic, adoption, sanctification, ontology, and so on. See E. Bartoş, "The dynamics of deification."

[98] I. Bria, "Preface," p.xii.
[99] TDO, vol. 1, p. 512.
[100] E. Bartoş, "The dynamics of deification," p. 246.
[101] I. Bria, "Preface," p. xii.
[102] TDO, vol. 1, pp. 374–80.
[103] TDO, vol. 1, p. 489.
[104] TDO, vol. 1, p. 495.
[105] TDO, vol. 1, p. 495.
[106] L. Turcescu, "Dumitru Stăniloae."
[107] TDO, vol. 1, p. 489.
[108] "By commanding man not to eat from the tree of consciousness before he was guided by freedom of spirit, God, in fact, commanded him to be strong, to remain free, and to grow in spirit, that is, in freedom. This very commandment made appeal to man's freedom." TDO, vol. 1, p. 488.
[109] TDO, vol. 1, p. 488.
[110] According to Turcescu, the Greek concept of the "will to choose" (*prohairesis*) and "the will to be what one wishes to be" (*boulesis*), coined by philosopher Plotinus, were borrowed by Gregory of Nyssa and applied to the Christian God. Stăniloae picks up the later emphasis and applies it to the Fall of humans. L. Turcescu, "Dumitru Stăniloae."
[111] TDO, vol. 1, pp. 494–5.
[112] "And this newness is not one that grows old, but one in which we must unceasingly be walking and growing: . . . so that we too may walk in newness of life . . . so that we might serve not under the old written code but in the newness of spirit." TDO, vol. 1, p. 514.
[113] TDO, vol. 1, p. 515.
[114] L. Turcescu, "Dumitru Stăniloae."
[115] See Sorin Dumitrescu, *Şapte Dimineţi cu Părintele Stăniloae* (Bucureşti: Editura Anastasia, 1992), p. 97.
[116] S. Dumitrescu, *Şapte Dimineţi*, p. 165.
[117] Pavel Chihaia, *Faţa cernită a libertăţii: 20 de convorbiri la Europa Liberă* (Bucureşti: Editura Jurnal Literar, 1991), pp. 41–9.
[118] In his introduction to the German translation of Stăniloae's *magnum opus*, Jürgen Moltmann calls Stăniloae a Pan-Orthodox theologian, assessing him as a bridge between two divides; between the Greek Orthodox and the Russian theological tradition on the one hand, and between Eastern Orthodox and Western theology on the other hand. Jürgen Moltmann, "Introduction" in *Orthodoxe Dogmatik*, German transl. by H. Pitters (Cologne: Gütersloh, 1985), p. 10.
[119] C. Miller, *The Gift of the World*, p. 14.
[120] D. Stăniloae, quoted in M.-A. Costa de Beauregard, *Dumitru Stăniloae: "Ose Comprendre que Je t'aime"* (Paris: Editions du CERF, 1983), p. 18.
[121] D. Stăniloae, *Ose Comprendre*, p. 18.
[122] Ion Bria, "The Creative Vision of Dumitru Stăniloae" in *The Ecumenical Review*, vol. 33 No. 1 (January, 1981), p. 55.

123 D. Stăniloae, *Ose Comprendre*, p. 108.
124 As Mănăstireanu has noted, Stăniloae rejects the natural-supernatural dichotomy in relation to revelation, salvation and the church, and criticizes Barth on this aspect, although generally agreeing with much else Barth taught. Dănuţ Mănăstireanu, "Dumitru Stăniloae's Theology of Ministry" in *Tradition and Modernity*, pp. 131–2.
125 Cf. Dumitru Stăniloae, *Theology and the Church* (New York: SVS Press, 1980), pp. 109ff.
126 Other inconsistencies in Stăniloae's rapport with Western theology have been indicated by Andrew Louth, who noted that he borrowed almost unknowingly Western theological concepts and deemed them Orthodox. Such was the case with Christ's work of redemption, which is presented in Stăniloae's *Dogmatic* in terms of the Calvinist threefold office of Christ as prophet, priest, and king but which he claims is patristic. Cf. A. Louth, "Orthodox Dogmatic," p. 62. These limitations have been conceded, though in a more veiled and somehow apologetic fashion, by his Orthodox disciple, Fr. Bria, cf. Ion Bria, *Spaţiul nemuririi*, p. 41.
127 Ronald Robertson, "Dumitru Stăniloae on Christian Unity" in *Tradition and Modernity*, p. 125.
128 R. Robertson, "Dumitru Stăniloae," p. 125.
129 Cf. T. Ware, "Foreword," p. x.
130 According to Păcurariu, Nichifor Crainic, the legionnaire director of *Gândirea* magazine, referred to Stăniloae as the "great religious thinker from Sibiu" and regarded him as the pioneer of a new and original phase in the evolution of Romanian theology. Cf. M. Păcurariu, "Preotul Profesor," p. 6.
131 A. Louth, "Orthodox Dogmatic," p. 54.
132 During this period Stăniloae wrote lesson fewer than 350 articles and essays in various publications and on different topics. Cf. G. Anghelescu, "Bibliografie Sistematică," pp. 38–49.
133 Most of the articles written on Romanian nationalism are contained in these two sources: D. Stăniloae, *Ortodoxie şi Românism*; *Naţiune şi Creştinism*.
134 In developing these ideas in *Gândirea*, Stăniloae was joined by other Orthodox voices, notably Vasile Voiculescu. See Dumitru Micu, *Gândirea şi Gândirismul* (Bucureşti: Editura Minerva, 1975), pp. 176–80, 183–5.
135 Henry Percival, ed., *The Seven Ecumenical Councils of the Undivided Church. Their Canons and Dogmatic Decrees*, Nicene and Post-Nicene Fathers (New York: Scribner's, 1990), p. 596. I am indebted to L. Turcescu for this reference. Cf. L. Turcescu, "Dumitru Stăniloae."
136 See Gillet's elaborate discussion on the relationship between Romanian Orthodoxy and nationalism. O. Gillet, *Religie şi Naţionalism*, pp. 134–78.
137 Dumitru Stăniloae, "Naţionalismul sub aspect moral" in *Ortodoxie şi Românism*, p. 97.
138 Dumitru Stăniloae, "Idealul Naţional Permanent" in D. Stăniloae, *Naţiune şi Creştinism*, pp. 103–4.
139 "Concerning man in particular, God created Adam and Eve in the beginning. In them they were virtually present all nations. . . . Every nation has an eternal divine archetype." Dumitru Stăniloae, "Scurtă interpretare teologică a naţiunii" in D. Stăniloae, *Ortodoxie şi Românism*, p. 22.

140 Cf. Dumitru Stăniloae, *Catolicismul de după Război* (Sibiu: Editura Arhidiecezană, 1933). See also the collection of articles on Roman Catholicism and Greek-Orthodox Catholicism in D. Stăniloae, *Naţiune şi Creştinism.*

141 Dumitru Stăniloae, *Uniatismul în Transilvania* (Sibiu: EIBMOR, 1973); "Problema uniatismului din perspectiva ecumenică" in *Ortodoxia*, vol. 4 (1969), pp. 347–77.

142 M. Bielawski, *Philocalic Vision*, p. 25.

143 In this work, Stăniloae advocated for a reverse dynamic concerning the influence of modernity to Romanian Orthodoxy, by suggesting some of the contributions that Orthodoxy could make to modernity. He, thus, advocated for the superior humanism of the popular Romanian Orthodoxy as an idyllic model for the political organization of the modern state, an ideal that would surpass the obsession with individualism brought about by the Renaissance. Cf. Dumitru Stăniloae, *Reflecţii despre Spiritualitatea Poporului Român* (Bucureşti: Editura Elion, 1992, 2001).

144 Ioan Vasile Leb, *Biserica în acţiune* (Cluj: Editura Limes, 2001), pp. 115–18.

145 Ioan Ică Jr., "Dumitru Stăniloae" in *Dictionary of Historical Theology*, edited by Trevor Hart (Grand Rapids: Paternoster Press, 2000), p. 530.

146 Patriarh Justinian Marina, *Apostolat Social*, vol. X (1971), p. 23.

147 Cf. Silviu E. Rogobete, *O Ontologie a Iubirii: Subiect şi Realitate Personală Supremă în Gândirea Părintelui Dumitru Stăniloae* (Iaşi: Editura Polirom, 2001), p. 261.

148 K. Barth, *Church Dogmatics* III/4, p. 305.

149 S. Dumitrescu, *Şapte Dimineţi*, p. 97.

150 S. Dumitrescu, *Şapte Dimineţi*, p. 55.

151 S. Dumitrescu, *Şapte Dimineţi*, p. 58.

Conclusion

Toward a Theology of 'Permanent Revolution'

From Resistance to Nation-building

The important role theology plays in religion and nationalism has been emphasized throughout this volume. Max Horkheimer stressed that "Without a theological moment, the space for critique, openness and renewal within secular debate, no matter how skilful, [politics] in the last analysis is mere business."[1] In addressing the problem of ideological compromise of the church under Communism, Barth's emphasis on the uniqueness of Christ has proved a useful challenge and basis for rejecting any human-centered ideological, social, or political construct. His uncompromising and prophetic "No!" uttered to nationalist ideologies made space for the "Yes!" of God's grace expressed only through the Gospel. For Barth, nothing that could be named, experienced, or conceived should ever be identified with God.[2] However, there are times when the theologian does not just have to say "No!" to totalitarianism and nationalism, but also a "Yes!" to political and social renewal.

So far in this volume, theology has figured only as what Paul Tillich called a "theology of resistance," which he thought was "a mighty weapon in warfare," but that once the crisis was over, becomes "an inconvenient tool for use in the building trade."[3] The "building trade" necessitated by Romanian post-Communist society requires the critical assistance of a theology that can make a positive contribution to this process. Tillich misinterpreted Barth's rejection of Nazism as a rejection of all political systems. Barth, however, wrote in his commentary on Romans: "Grace is the axe laid at the root of the good conscience which the politician and the civil servant always wish to enjoy."[4] Such a theology, which remains critically opposed to the sacralization or absolutization of any political ideology, whether Communism, nationalism, or liberalism, has been described by Paul Lehmann as Barth's theology of "permanent revolution."[5]

In the introduction, it was posited whether theologians could encourage political thinking that would contribute positively to the churches and to society as a whole. The contention of the author of this volume is that a theology of "permanent revolution" could assist the Orthodox Church in contemporary Romania to address the problems described by this study. What is more, such a theology would help prevent the identification of the church with nationalism.

Villa-Vicencio, speaking for the context in South Africa, notes: "It [permanent revolution] furthermore has a significant contribution to make in situations of political stability, militating against political complacency where the danger always exists of the nation being elevated to the level of an absolute."[6] Without surrendering its prophetic task or becoming yet another legitimizing theology such as the social apostolate, theology as permanent revolution against any tendency of absolutizing nationalism, democracy, human rights or secularism, can offer a significant contribution to consolidating Romania into becoming a tolerant and inclusive democratic society. In anticipation of the conclusion, the emphasis will now be on the Orthodox Church's affirmative "Yes!" in relation to some of its most difficult contemporary challenges.

Repentance and Justice

Much has been said in Romania about the issue of repentance for collaboration with Communist authorities. As in other countries of Eastern Europe, post-Communism has been the stage for dealing with the past as much as with the present and the future. Romania continues to struggle with its recent past, the legacy of which impacts as much the political as the social, economic, and spiritual life in important ways. In his study, Tzvetan Todorov argued that the twenty-first–century world has not taken Stalinism and Communism seriously enough.[7] The mockery of the Soviet show trials as well as the mockery of the condemnation of Communism in Romania underlines the reluctance to face honestly the Communist and Fascist past.[8] Such moral complacency has led over the past 20 years to much political and social extremism, if one considers the exacerbating nationalist and chauvinist sentiments, the lack of commitment to the strengthening of democratic institutions, and the discrediting of civil society. As stressed in the introduction of this volume, the general reaction to the findings of the "Commission for the Study of the Communist Dictatorship in Romania" (2006) has been symptomatic of the unconvincing break with the past of the political players.[9]

The Orthodox Church's refusal to acknowledge the findings of the report, which generically identified the collaborationist role played by the church and its clergy, underlined once more the ambivalent attitude to its own past and how its theology reflects on this issue.[10] This reaction takes us back to Stăniloae's contention, when asked whether the church should distinguish between the oppressors and the oppressed, that the church does not assign guilt in the public arena but preaches only Christ.[11] However, the justification by faith which the church preaches to the sinners should not obscure the public relevance of Christian notions of justice. In a volume written in 1939, Barth expressed this concern more poignantly when he asked:

> Is there a connection between the justification of the sinner through faith alone, completed once for all by God through Jesus Christ, and the problem

of justice, the problem of human law? Is there an inward and vital connection by means of which in any sense human justice (or law) as well as divine justification, becomes a concern of Christian faith and Christian responsibility, and therefore also a matter which concerns the Christian Church?[12]

Barth's answer to this rhetorical question was an uncompromising "Yes!" stressing once more the political relevance of a theology that is God-centered. The responsibility of the church cannot be limited to offering forgiveness of sins without stressing the implications for human responsibility because that would transform the Gospel of salvation into cheap grace.

Christian responsibility for justice also brings into discussion the relationship between theology and the laws that underpin human justice. If the church preaches a message that gives a negative connotation to the notion of Law, this has direct implications for human justice and responsibility. A theology that describes human law as repetitious, monotonous, and as part of a confined horizon of egoism and death, cannot bring an affirmative contribution to the building of a just democratic social and political climate.[13] Like God's Law for biblical Israel, human laws today are a positive incentive that reveals the presence of God in society and helps create in people a responsibility for justice and restitution.[14]

In the beginning of this volume, the "repossession saga" underlined certain mishandlings of the Orthodox Church regarding the restitution of worship places to the Greek Catholic Church. Without repeating what has already been discussed, there is an incompatibility between the Christian notion of justice and the attitudes and actions which have characterized the Orthodox Church and its Holy Synod in what remained a debated issue, 20 years after the fall of Communism. The process of reparations for the injustice perpetrated by the Communist regime against this denomination directly involves the Orthodox Church, which is not just the de facto adjudicating body controlling the return of their churches and places of worship, but the prior possessor of many of these Greek Catholic buildings. In most discourses concerning this repossession matter, outlined in chapter 1, the emphasis has been on "justice." However, this is as much a matter of repentance as it is an issue of Christian justice. Far from being a passive observer in the Greek Catholics' persecution during Communism, the ROC and its theologians made significant "contributions" by—at the regime's demand—supplying nationalist sermons and journal articles condemning this denomination.[15] As Barth noted: "The church acknowledges and promotes the state insofar as service of the neighbour, which is the purpose of the state, is necessarily included in its own message of reconciliation and is thus its own concern."[16] When the message of the theologians is identical with the message of the oppressor against the well-being of the neighbor, the church loses its distinctiveness and becomes another legitimizing agent of the political actor.

Nationalism and Post-Communism

Hobsbawm wrote that "nationalism precedes the historical construction of nation-states, but, unless critically checked, it leads to an obligation to the nation which overrides all other public obligations."[17] As illustrated throughout this volume, Romanian nationalism has exerted a powerful incentive for the Orthodox Church, particularly since the nineteenth century, and has proved detrimental to the church's critical distance from and prophetic witness to the state. The church ceases to be the church if it fails to remind the state of its responsibility to govern justly and within the boundaries of its power. Neamțu rightly expressed that there is a longing for the Orthodox Church in Romania to criticize the systemic corruption, laziness, and criminality that are characteristic of the Balkan state bureaucracy.[18]

The investigation of the church's relationship to Romanian nationalism has indicated that Orthodoxy has failed to overcome its political idolatry and to prevent the absolutization pressures of the state. The church's inability to remind the nationalist state of its responsibilities has led to Romanian totalitarianism becoming a political religion, taking a quasi-religious form, demanding unbending faith, and ultimately becoming utterly oppressive. Christian and political thinker Reinhold Niebuhr cautioned that, when left unchecked, "nationalism takes on the character of a religious faith and becomes one of the most destructive powers imaginable, undermining and inevitably destroying democracy."[19] Niebuhr's warning is a reminder that the nationalist inclination of the Orthodox Church since the fall of Communism can further affect negatively the development of Romanian society. The way in which the ROC relates to religious pluralism ultimately reflects on crucial elements at the foundation of democracy, namely unrestricted participation, human solidarity, and open debate. While churches are not alone in the responsibility to ensure these social practices are observed, they can nevertheless support social engagement by practicing it in dialogue with other denominations. Here, too, a theology of "permanent revolution" can ensure the Romanian state and civil society offer protection against the infringement of human rights and religious pluralism without absolutizing them. As has been pointed out, the church has to remain in awareness of the fact that there are two kinds of religious pluralism, namely the one desired by the state and the one desired by the minorities.[20] While the state will always be tempted to impose what is more accurately described as religious tolerance, the minorities will be tempted to seek religious pluralism which suits *their own* needs, with little concern for fairness toward *all* religious minorities.[21]

As the present study has argued, the most serious challenge the Orthodox Church in Romania is facing is its constant temptation toward nationalism. To this extent, this study has put forward an argument which suggests that a theology which is God-centered and is capable of saying "No!" to the church's identification with any political ideology will enable the Orthodox Church to maintain a critical distance from nationalist tendencies, while uttering its "Yes!" in support of a democratic society. By emphasizing a theology of affirmative and yet critical support, a theology of "permanent revolution," the ROC can make a significant contribution to the development of a democratic society in which religious pluralism, human rights, justice, and respect are observed, a society in which the ideological demons of nationalism are cast out once and for all.

Notes

[1] Max Horkheimer, quoted in C. Villa-Vicencio, *Theology of Reconstruction*, p. 3.
[2] K. Barth, *Epistle to the Romans*, p. 330.
[3] Paul Tillich, "What is wrong with dialectical theology?" in *Journal of Religion*, vol. 15, No. 2 (April, 1935), p. 135.
[4] K. Barth, *Epistle to the Romans*, p. 430.
[5] Paul Lehmann, "Karl Barth, the theologian of permanent revolution" in *Union Seminary Quarterly Review*, vol. 28 (1972), pp. 67–82.
[6] C. Villa-Vicencio, *Theology of Reconstruction*, p. 22.
[7] Tzvetan Todorov, *Hope and Memory*, p. 137.
[8] As stressed in the beginning of this volume, the official condemnation of Communism in December 2006 in Romania has been met with violent verbal reactions and has generated debates in society that have greatly reduced and undermined any significance of this symbolic act. Cf. Alexandru Macoveiciuc, "Condamnarea comunismului, balamucul furioșilor" in *Adevărul*, No. 5117 (19 December, 2006), p. 1.
[9] "Final Report of the Presidential Commission for the Study of the Communist Dictatorship in Romania." Read in the Romanian Parliament in the presence of Lech Walesa, Jelio Jelev, Romanian King Mihai, former Christian Democrat President Emil Constantinescu, and many others, the report was met with vehement shouting and whistling by the Romanian MPs and followed by a frenzy of defamatory articles and public statements aimed at discrediting both the efforts and the commission itself.
[10] "Contraatac al BOR la Raportul Tismăneanu."
[11] S. Dumitrescu, *Șapte Dimineți*, p. 95.
[12] K. Barth, *Church and State*, p. 1.
[13] TDO, vol. 1, p. 515.
[14] Cf. K. Barth, *Church Dogmatics* II/2, p. 572.
[15] Cf. S. Rogobete, *O Ontologie a Iubirii*, p. 261. Ioan Ică stressed that Stăniloae's polemical articles against the Greek Catholics, written during Communism, were "a price that he had to pay to be allowed to continue working on his *magnum opus*." Cf. I. Ică, "Dumitru Stăniloae," p. 530.
[16] K. Barth, *Ethics*, p. 521.
[17] E. J. Hobsbawm, *Nations and Nationalism Since 1780: Programme, Myth, Reality* (Cambridge: Cambridge University Press, 1992), p. 15.
[18] Mihai Neamțu, quoted in Corlățan and Voica, "Schimbarea la față a BOR."

[19] Reinhold Niebuhr, *Radical Monotheism and Western Culture* (New York: Harper and Row, 1970), p. 27.

[20] Steve Bruce, Chris Wright, "Law, Social Change, and Religious Toleration" in *Religious Liberty in Northern Europe in the Twenty-first Century*, by Derek David, ed. (Waco, TX: Baylor University, 2000), pp. 34–5.

[21] This situation was observed in relation to the Evangelical denominations in Romania, where the struggle for religious equality in the public sphere made clear that they pursued a distinct freedom, one that would ensure *their* freedom of action, with little concern for other, smaller denominations. Cf. Cristian G. Romocea, "Democracy" in *Dictionary of Mission Theology*, by John Corrie, ed. (Leicester: Inter-Varsity Press, 2007).

Bibliography

Albu, Corneliu. *Pe urmele lui Ion-Inocenţiu Micu-Klein.* Bucureşti: Editura Sport-Turism, 1983.
Alivisatos, Hamilcar. *Proces-Verbaux du Premier Congres de Théologie Orthodoxe à Athénes.* Athens, 1939.
Almond, Mark. *Decline without Fall: Romania under Ceauşescu.* London: Institute for European Defence and Strategic Studies, 1988.
Aloys, Evina. "Romania President Approves Europe's 'Worst Religion Law,'" *Journal Chretien* (4 January 2007). [Online] Available at: http://www.spcm.org/Journal/spip.php?article5250. Accessed January 2007.
"Am fost Turnător din Frică, Laşitate, Ignoranţă şi Disperare." *Evenimentul Zilei,* No. 2665 (26 March 2001).
Anania, Bartolomeu. "România şi Europa." *Renaşterea,* No. 9 (September 1998).
—. "File de Jurnal." *Renaşterea,* Cluj (2003).
Anania, Lidia, Cecilia Luminea, Livia Melinte, Ana-Nina Prosan, Lucia Stoica, and Neculai Ionescu-Ghinea. *Bisericile osândite de Ceauşescu: Bucureşti 1977–1989.* Bucureşti: Editura Anastasia, 1995.
Andreescu, Gabriel. *Naţionalişti, antinaţionalişti: O polemică în publicistica românească.* Iaşi: Editura Polirom, 1996.
—. "Relaţii internaţionale şi ortodoxie în estul şi sud-estul Europei." *Studii Internaţionale,* vol. 4 (1998).
—. *Extremismul de Dreapta în România.* Cluj-Napoca: Centrul de Resurse pentru Diversitate Etnoculturală, 2003.
Anghelescu, Gheorghe. "Opera Păr. Prof. Dumitru Stăniloae. Bibliografie Sistematică." *Persoană şi Comuniune: Prinos de Cinstire Părintelui Profesor Academician Dumitru Stăniloae la împlinirea vârstei de 90 de ani.* Sibiu: Editura Arhiepiscopiei Ortodoxe Sibiu, 1993.
Antonie, Bishop. "Church and State in Romania." *Church and State: Opening a New Ecumenical Discussion, Faith and Order Paper.* No. 85. Geneva: World Council of Churches, 1978.
APADOR-CH Press Release. "On Failure to Recognize Religious Denominations in Romania" (19 May 1997). [Online] Available at: http://www.apador.org /old/rapoarte/anuale/1997e.htm. Accessed March 2006.
Arendt, Hannah. *The Origins of Totalitarianism.* London: George Allen & Unwin, 1967.
—. *The Human Condition.* Chicago: University of Chicago Press, 1998.
Arieli, Yehoshua. "Jacob Talmon—An Intellectual Portrait." *Totalitarian Democracy and After: International Colloquium in Memory of Jacob L. Talmon.* By The Israel Academy of Sciences and Humanities. Jerusalem: Magnes Press, Hebrew University, 1984.

Armbruster, Adolf. *Romanitatea românilor: Istoria unei idei*. București: Editura Enciclopedică, 1993.
Aron, Raymond. *Democracy and Totalitarianism: A Theory of Political Systems*. New York: Frederick A. Praeger, 1969.
—. "On Totalitarianism." *Partisan Review*, vol. 60 (1993).
—. "The Essence of Totalitarianism According to Hannah Arendt." *Partisan Review*, vol. 60 (1993).
Ashworth, Pat. "Romania's Tough Law on Religion." *Church Times*, Issue 7504 (5 January 2007).
Augustine, Saint, Bishop of Hippo. "The City of God." *Nicene and Post-Nicene Fathers*. Edited by Alexander Roberts and James Donaldson. Revised edition. vol. II. Peabody, MA: Hendrickson, 1994.
Austin, H. W. *Moral Re-Armament: The Battle for Peace*. London: William Heinemann, 1938.
Baconsky, Teodor. *Lupta cu îngerul: 45 de ipostaze ale faptului religios*. București: Editura Anastasia, 1996.
—. "Sfada Elitelor." *Dilema*, vol. 183 (1996).
—. *Ispita Binelui: Eseuri despre Urbanitatea Credinței*. București: Editura Anastasia, 1999.
—. *Puterea Schismei: Un portret al creștinismului european*. București: Editura Anastasia, 2001.
—. "Dialog Amânat." *Dilema Veche*, vol. 43 (5–11 November 2004).
Bălan, Ioanichie. *Convorbiri duhovnicești*. 2 vols. Roman: Episcopia Romanului, 1984.
Bantaș, Andrei. *The Romanian Orthodox Church Yesterday and Today*. București: Editura IBMBOR, 1979.
Barbu, Daniel. *Șapte teme de politică românească*. București: Editura Antet, 1997.
—. *Republica absentă: Politică și societate în România postcomunistă*. București: Editura Nemira, 1999.
—. *Bizanț contra Bizanț*. București: Editura Nemira, 2001.
Barnett, Victoria J. *For the Soul of the People: Protestant Protest against Hitler*. New York, Oxford: Oxford University Press, 1998.
—. *Bystanders: Conscience and Complicity during the Holocaust*. Westport, CT; London: Praeger Publishers, 1999.
Baron, Nick. "History, Politics and Political Culture: Thoughts on the Role of Historiography in Contemporary Russia." *Cromohs*, vol. 5 (2000).
Barth, Karl. *The Word of God and the Word of Man*. London: Hodder and Stoughton, 1928.
—. *The Epistle to the Romans*. 2nd ed. Oxford: Oxford University Press, 1933.
—. *Theological Existence Today: A Plea for Theological Freedom*. London: Hodder & Stoughton, 1933.
—. *Church Dogmatics*. vol. I/1. Edinburgh: T. & T. Clark, 1936.
—. *God in Action*. Edinburgh: T & T Clark, 1937.
—. *The Church and the Political Problem of Our Day*. London: Hodder & Stoughton, 1939.
—. *Church and State*. London: SCM Press, 1939.
—. *Against the Stream: Shorter Post-War Writings, 1946–52*. London: SCM Press Ltd, 1954.

—. *Church Dogmatics*. vol. II/1. Edinburgh: T. & T. Clark, 1957.
—. "The Christian's Place in Society." *The Word of God and the Word of Man*. New York: Harper & Row, 1957.
—. *How I Changed My Mind*. Edinburgh: St. Andrew Press, 1969.
—. *Fragments Grave and Gay*. London: Collins, 1971.
—. *The Humanity of God*. Atlanta: John Knox Press, 1978.
—. *Ethics*. Translated by Geoffrey Bromiley. Edinburgh: T & T Clark, 1981.
—. *The Göttingen Dogmatics: Instruction in the Christian Religion*. Grand Rapids: Eerdmans, 1990.Barth, Karl and Emil Brunner. *Natural Theology: Comprising "Nature and Grace" by Professor Dr. Emil Brunner and the Reply "No!" by Dr. Karl Barth*. Translated by Peter Fraenkel. Eugene, OR: Wipf & Stock Publishers, 2002.
Bartholomew I, Ecumenical Patriarch. "L'apport de L'eglise Orthodoxe a la Construction de L'europe." *Service Orthodoxe de Presse* 190 (July–Aug 1994).
Bartoş, Emil. *Deification in Eastern Orthodox Theology: An Evaluation and Critique of the Theology of Dumitru Stăniloae*. Carlisle: Paternoster, 1999.
—. "The Dynamics of Deification." *Dumitru Stăniloae: Tradition and Modernity in Theology*. Edited by Lucian Turcescu. Iaşi: Center for Romanian Studies, 2002.
Baylor, Michael G., ed. *The Radical Reformation*. Cambridge: Cambridge University Press, 1991.
Beeson, T. *Discretion and Valour: Religious Conditions in Russia and Eastern Europe*. London: Fontana, 1974.
Bell, Daniel. *The End of Ideology: On the Exhaustion of Political Ideas in the Fifties*. New York: Free Press, 1962.
Benedict, Anderson. *Imagined Communities*. 2nd ed. London: Verso, 1991.
Berdyaev, Nicolas. *The Russian Revolution*. Ann Arbor: University of Michigan Press, 1966.
Bergen, Doris L. *Twisted Cross: The German Christian Movement in the Third Reich*. Chapel Hill and London: University of North Carolina Press, 1996.
Berger, Peter. *The Desecularisation of the World: Resurgent Religion and World Politics*. Grand Rapids: Eerdmans Publishing, 1999.
Berman, Paul. *Terror and Liberalism*. London: W.W. Norton & Company, Ltd., 2003.
Bernstein, Richard J. "The Origins of Totalitarianism: Not History but Politics." *New School of Social Research*, vol. 69, No.2 (Summer 2002).
Berry, Stephen. "No Tears for the Führer." *Libertarian Alliance*, No. 3 (5 April 2001).
Berstein, Serge and Pierre Milza. *Istoria Europei*. vol. 3. Iaşi: Institutul European, 1998.
Besancon, Alain. *Nenorocirea secolului. Despre comunism, nazism şi unicitatea Şoah-ului*. Bucureşti: Editura Nemira, 1999.
Bethge, Eberhard. "Troubled Self-Interpretation and Uncertain Reception in the Church Struggle." *The German Church Struggle and the Holocaust*. Edited by Franklin H. Littell and Hubert G. Locke. Detroit: Wayne State University Press, 1974.
Betts, Raymond F. *Europe in Retrospect: A Brief History of the Past Two Hundred Years*. D C Heath & Co, 1979.
Bielawski, Maciej. *The Philocalical Vision of the World in the Theology of Dumitru Stăniloae*. Bydgoszcz: Homini, 1997.
Billington, James. *Fire in the Minds of Men: Origins of the Revolutionary Faith*. New York: Basic Books, 1980.

Blackbourn, David and Geoff Eley. *The Peculiarities of German History: Bourgeois Society and the Politics of Nineteenth-Century Germany.* Oxford, New York: Oxford University Press, 1984.

Blaga, Roman and Gheorghe Calciu-Dumitreasa. "The Church in Romania under Communist Rule." *Solia,* vol. LI, no. 2 (February 1986).

Boari, Mircea. "Elitism maximal și mentalitate antidemocratică." *Polis,* vol. 4 (1995).

Bogdan, Cătălin. "Lupta pentru patriarhie. *ID,* vol II. No. 12(15) (December 2005).

—. "Insidioasa intoleranță." *ID,* vol. III, no. 1(16) (January 2006).

Bogomilova, Nonka. "Eastern Orthodoxy: The New Age and the Old Myths." *Orthodox Christianity and Contemporary Europe.* Edited by Jonathan Sutton and Wil Van den Berken. Leuven: Peeters Publishers, 2004.

Boia, Lucian. *Istorie și mit în conștiința românească.* București: Editura Humanitas, 2002.

—. *România: Țara de frontieră a Europei.* București: Editura Humanitas, 2002.

—. *Mitologia științifică a comunismului.* București: Editura Humanitas, 2005.

Bonhoeffer, Dietrich. *Letters and Papers from Prison.* New York: Macmillan, 1971.

Boobbyer, Philip. *S. L. Frank. The Life and Work of a Russian Philosopher 1877–1950.* Athens, OH: Ohio University Press, 1995.

Booth, Philip. "Romanian State Fears Too Much Believers' Independence." *Religion in Communist Lands,* vol. 12, no. 2 (1984).

Bozgan, Ovidiu. *Studii de istoria bisericii.* București: Universitatea din București, 2002.

Brands Jr., H.W. *Cold Warriors: Eisenhower's Generation and American Foreign Policy.* New York: Columbia University Press, 1988.

Brătianu, Gheorghe I. *Sfatul Domnesc și Adunarea Stărilor în Principatele Române.* Paris: Evry, 1977.

Bretall, Robert W. and Charles W. Kegley, eds. *The Theology of Paul Tillich.* New York: Macmillan, 1952.

Breuilly, John. *Nationalism and the State.* 2nd ed. Manchester: Manchester University Press, 1992.

Bria, Ion. "Confessing Christ Today." *International Review of Mission,* vol. LXIV (1975).

—. "The Creative Vision of Dumitru Stăniloae." *The Ecumenical Review,* vol. 33, No.1 (January 1981).

—. "Theology and the Bridge of Metaphysics." *Ortodoxia,* vol. 9 (1990).

—. "Romanian Orthodox Theological Education." *Catholic World,* No. 237 (January–February 1994).

—. *Spațiul nemuririi sau eternizarea umanului în Dumnezeu.* Iași: Editura Trinitas, 1994.

—. *Ortodoxia în Europa: Locul spiritualității române.* Iași: Editura Trinitas, 1995.

—. *Romania: Orthodox Identity at a Crossroads of Europe.* Geneva: AC Publications, 1995.

—. *Liturghia după Liturghie.* București: Atena, 1997.

—. "Evangelism, Proselytism, and Religious Freedom in Romania: An Orthodox Point of View." *Journal of Ecumenical Studies,* vol. 36, No. 1–2 (Winter–Spring 1999).

—. "Preface." *The Experience of God.* By Dumitru Stăniloae. vol. 2. New York: SVS Press, 2000.

Broun, Janice and Grazyna Sikorska. *Conscience and Captivity: Religion in Eastern Europe*. Washington: Ethics and Public Policy Center, 1988.

Bruce, Steve and Chris Wright. "Law, Social Change, and Religious Toleration." *Religious Liberty in Northern Europe in the Twenty-first Century*. Edited by Derek David. Waco: Baylor University, 2000.

Brunner, Emil. *The Divine Imperative*. Philadelphia: Westminster Press, 1947.

Bulgakov, Sergius. *The Orthodox Church*. New York: St. Vladimir's Seminary Press, 1988.

Bureau of Democracy, Human Rights, and Labor. "Country Reports on Human Rights Practices—2005" (8 March 2006). [Online] Available at: http://www.state.gov/g/drl/rls/hrrpt/2005/61670.htm. Accessed March 2006.

Burleigh, Michael. *The Third Reich: A New History*. London: Pan MacMillan, 2001.

—. *Earthly Powers*. London: Harper Perennial, 2006.

—. *Sacred Causes: Religion and Politics from the European Dictators to Al-Qaeda*. London, Harper Press, 2006.

Byassee, Jason. "Theologians and Nazis." *The Christian Century*, vol. 123, No. 11 (30 May 2006).

Cadzow, John, Andrew Ludanyi, Louis J. Elteto. *Transylvania: The Roots of Ethnic Conflict*. Kent: The Kent State University Press, 1983.

"Caesaropapism." *Oxford Dictionary of the Christian Church*. Edited by F.L. Cross & E.A. Livingstone. 2nd ed. Oxford: Oxford University Press, 1983.

Cajus, Fabricius. *Positive Christianity in the Third Reich*. Dresden: H. Poeschel, 1937.

Canovan, Margaret. "Arendt's Theory of Totalitarianism: A Reassessment." *The Cambridge Companion to Hannah Arendt*. Edited by Dana Villa. Cambridge: Cambridge University Press, 2000.

Carr, William. *Hitler: A Study in Personality and Politics*. London: Edward Arnold, 1986.

Cesereanu, Ruxandra, ed. *Imaginarul violent al românilor*. Bucureşti: Editura Humanitas, 2003.

—. *Comunism şi Represiune în România: Istoria Tematică a unui Fratricid Naţional*. Iaşi: Editura Polirom, 2006.

Chadwick, Henry. *East and West: The Making of a Rift in the Church: From Apostolic Times until the Council of Florence*. Oxford: Oxford University Press, 2003.

Chadwick, Owen. *A History of Christianity*. New York: St. Martin's Press, 1995.

Chernyshevsky, Nikolai. *What is to be Done?* Cornell: Cornell University Press, 1989.

Chihaia, Pavel. *Faţa cernită a libertăţii*. Bucureşti: Editura Jurnal Literar, 1991.

Ciachir, Dan. *Cronica ortodoxă*. Iaşi: Editura Timpul, 1994.

—. *Ofensivă Ortodoxă*. Bucureşti: Editura Anastasia, 2002.

Ciobotea, Daniel. *Confessing the Truth in Love: Orthodox Perceptions of Life, Mission and Unity*. Iaşi: Editura Trinitas, 2001.

Clark, John and Aaron Wildavsky. *The Moral Collapse of Communism: Poland as a Cautionary Tale*. San Francisco: ICS Press, 1990.

Clark, Victoria E. *Why Angels Fall: A Journey through Orthodox Europe from Byzantium to Kosovo* London: Picador, 2001.

Clément, Olivier. "Prefazione." *La Preghiera di gesu e lo Spirito Santo, Meditazioni Teologiche*. By Dumitru Stăniloae. Rome, 1988.

—. "Le Pére dr. D. Stăniloae et le genie de l'Orthodoxie roumaine." *Persoană şi Comuniune Prinos de Cinstire Părintelui Profesor Academician Dumitru Stăniloae la*

împlinirea vârstei de 90 de ani. Sibiu: Editura Arhiepiscopiei Ortodoxe Sibiu, 1993.
Cleopa, Ilie (Arhimandrite). "În dreapta credinţă a neamului românesc." *Scara*, vol. 1, No. 2 (1997).
"CNSAS: Patriarhul Daniel nu a colaborat cu Securitatea ca poliţie politică." *România Liberă* (17 October 2007).
"CNSAS: Patriarhul Daniel nu a făcut poliţie politică." *Realitatea.net* (16 October 2007).
Cochrane, Arthur. *The Church's Confession under Hitler*. Philadelphia: Westminster Press, 1962.
Codreanu, Corneliu Z. *Pentru Legionari*. Bucureşti: Totul pentru Ţară, 1937.
Cohn, Norman. *The Pursuit of the Millennium: Revolutionary Millenarians and Mystical Anarchists of the Middle Ages*. London: Secker and Warburg, 1957.
Collingwood, R.G. *The Idea of History*. Oxford: Oxford University Press, 1961.
Coman, Constantin, ed. *Ortodoxia sub presiunea istoriei*. Bucureşti: Editura Bizantină, 1995.
Comaroni, Bogdan. "Bătălia pentru Patriarhie." *Ziua* (7 November 2001).
Comisia Prezidenţială pentru Analiza Dictaturii Comuniste din România. *Raport Final*. Bucureşti, 2006. [Online] Available at: http://www.gardianul.ro/documente/capitolul2.pdf. Accessed December 2006.
Commission on Security and Cooperation in Europe, United States Helsinki Commission. "Religious Freedom Gains in Romania Threatened by Regressive Draft Law." *CSCE News Release* (9 June 2006). [Online] Available at: http://www.csce.gov/index.cfm?Fuseaction=ContentRecords.ViewDetail&ContentRecord_id=513&ContentRecordType=P&ContentType=P7CFID=21589297&CFTOKEN=26140635. Accessed June 2006.
"Communism." *Dictionary of the Social Sciences*. Edited by Craig Calhoun. Oxford: Oxford University Press, 2002.
Conovici, Iuliana. "L'orthodoxie roumaine et la modernité." *Studia Politica*, vol. IV, No. 2 (2004).
—. "Biserica Ortodoxă Română în spaţiul public postcomunist." *Akademia*, No. 1/20 (2006).
Constantinescu, Alexandru. "Contribuţii ale bisericii în justiţia Ţării Româneşti sub Alexandru Ipsilanti." *Biserica Ortodoxă Română*, vol. 97, Nos. 1–2 (1979).
Constantiniu, Florin. *O istorie sinceră a poporului român*. Bucureşti: Univers Enciclopedic, 1999.
Constituţia României din 1923. [Online] Available at: http://www.cdep.ro/pls/legis/legis_pck.htp_act_text?idt=1517. Accessed January 2004.
"Contraatac al BOR la Raportul Tismăneanu." *Ziua*, No. 3811 (20 December 2006).
Conway, J. S. *The Nazi Persecution of the Churches 1933–45*. New York: Basic Books, 1968.
—. Review of *Twisted Cross: The German Christian Movement in the Third Reich*. By Doris Bergen. *German Studies Review*, vol. 19, No.3 (October 1996).
Corlăţan, Mirela, Steluţa Voica. "Schimbarea la faţă a BOR: Patriarhul în blugi Daniel." *Cotidianul* (29 May 2009).
Corley, Felix. "Romania: Sudden Secretive Rush to Adopt Controversial Religion Law." *Forum 18 News Service*, Oslo, Norway (12 December 2006).
—. "Romania: Controversial Religion Law's Passing Violated Parliamentary Processes." *Forum 18 News Service*. Oslo, Norway (15 December 2006).

Corneanu, Nicolae. *În pas cu vremea*. Timişoara: Editura Mitropoliei Banatului, 2002.
Cotan, Claudiu. *Ortodoxia şi mişcările de emancipare naţională din sud-estul Europei în secolul al XIX-lea*. Bucureşti: Editura Bizantină, 2004.
Courtois, Stephane and Mark Kramer. *The Black Book of Communism: Crimes, Terror, Repression*. Cambridge, MA, London: Harvard University Press, 1999.
Crăciun, Oana. "Legea cultelor religioase, mai presus de legile societăţii." *Cotidianul* (13 December 2005).
Craig, Edward, ed. *The Routledge Encyclopedia of Philosophy*. London: Routledge, 2001.
Crainic, Nichifor. "Problema biblică." *Icoanele vremii*. Bucureşti, 1919.
—. *Punctele cardinale în haos*. Bucureşti: Editura Timpul, 1936.
—. *Ortodoxie şi Etnocraţie*. Bucureşti: Cugetarea, 1937.
—. "Transfigurarea românismului." *Ortodoxia*, vol. II, (1943).
—. *Ortodoxie şi Etnocraţie*. Bucureşti: Editura Albatros, 1997.
Culcer, Rodica. "Politica bisericii în campanie." *Revista 22*, No. 776 (11–18 November 2004).
Culianu, Ioan Petru. *Mircea Eliade*. Bucureşti: Editura Nemira, 1995.
Czeslaw, Milosz. *The Captive Mind*. London: Secker & Warburg 1953.
Dagron, Gilbert. *Emperor and Priest: The Imperial Office in Byzantium*. Translated by Jean Birrell. Cambridge: Cambridge University Press, 2003.
Davis, Derek H., ed. *Religious Liberty in Northern Europe in the Twenty-First Century*. Waco: Baylor University, 2000.
Davis, Nathaniel. *A Long Walk to Church*. Boulder, CO: Westview Press, 1995.
de Beauregard, M.-A. Costa. *Dumitru Stăniloae: "Ose Comprendre que Je t'aime."* Paris: Editions du CERF, 1983.
de Tocqueville, Alexis. *The Old Regime and the French Revolution*, translated by Stuard Gilbert. New York, London: Anchor Books, 1955.
"Decree No. 358." *Official Monitor*, Year CXVI, Part I–A, No. 281 (2 December 1948).
Deflem, Mathieu. "Ferdinand Tönnies (1855–1936)." *The Routledge Encyclopedia of Philosophy*. Edited by Edward Craig. London: Routledge, 2001.
Deletant, Dennis. *Ceauşescu and the Securitate: Coercion and Dissent in Romania, 1965–1989*. Armonk, New York: M.E. Sharpe, 1996.
Devi, Savitri. *Gold in the Furnace*. Uckfield, England: Historical Review Press, 2005.
Dobrincu, Dorin, ed. "Libertate religioasă şi contestare în România lui Nicolae Ceauşescu: Comitetul Creştin Român pentru Apărarea Libertăţii Religioase şi de Conştiinţă (ALRC)." *Analele Sighet*, vol. 10 (2003).
—. *Proba infernului: Personalul de cult în sistemul carceral din România potrivit documentelor Securităţii, 1959–1962*. Bucureşti: Editura Scriptorium, 2004.
Dobrolyubov, Nikolai. *Selected Philosophical Essays*, translated by J. Fineberg. Moscow: Foreign Language Publishing House, 1956.
Drummond, Andrew L. *German Protestantism since Luther*. London: The Epworth Press, 1951.
Dumitrescu, Sorin. *Şapte dimineţi cu Părintele Stăniloae*. Bucureşti: Editura Anastasia, 1992.
Dumitru-Snagov, Ioan. *Relaţiile Stat-Biserică*. Bucureşti: Editura Gnosis, 1996.
Duţu, Alexandru. *Coordonate ale culturii româneşti în secolul XVIII*. Bucureşti: Editura pentru Literatură, 1968.

—. "Traditional Toleration and Modern Pluralism: The Case of Orthodox Europe." *East European Quarterly,* vol. 29 (1995).
Eliade, Mircea. *Istoria credinţelor şi ideilor religioase.* vol. II. Bucureşti, Editura Ştiinţifica, 1978.
Enache, George. "Din arhiva rugului aprins: Daniil Sandu Tudor, un sfânt în gulagul românesc." *Clouds Magazine,* vol. 11 (Fall 2002).
—. *Ortodoxie şi putere politică în România contemporană.* Bucureşti: Editura Nemira, 2005.
Encyclopaedia Britannica. vol. 2. London: Encyclopaedia Britannica Inc., 1985.
Ericksen, Robert P. *Theologians under Hitler: Gerhard Kittel, Paul Althaus, and Emmanuel Hirsch.* New Haven: Yale University Press, 1985.
—. "The Political Theology of Paul Althaus: Nazi Supporter." *German Studies Review,* vol. 9, No. 3 (October 1986).
Evans, J. Richard. *The Coming of the Third Reich.* London: Penguin Books, 2003.
Fedotov, Georgii Petrovich. *A Treasury of Russian Spirituality: Reflections from the Revolutions.* London: Sheed and Ward, 1950.
Fergusson, David. *Church, State and Civil Society.* Cambridge: Cambridge University Press, 2004.
Fest, Joachim. *Hitler: Eine Biographie.* Ullstein Tb: Neuausg, 1998.
"Final Report of the International Commission on the Holocaust in Romania." Bucureşti, Romania (11 November 2004). [Online] Available at: http://www.ushmm.org/research/center/presentations/features/details/2005-03-10/#toc. Accessed August 2005.
"Final Report of the Presidential Commission for the Study of the Communist Dictatorship in Romania" (18 December 2006). [Online] Available at: http://www.presidency.ro/static/ordine/RAPORT%20FINAL_%20CADCR.pdf. Accessed December 2006.
Finger, Thomas. "Post-Chalcedonian Christology: Some Reflections on Oriental Orthodox Christology from a Mennonite Perspective." *Christ in East and West.* Edited by Paul Fries and Tiran Nersoyan. Macon, GA: Mercer University Press, 1987.
Florovsky, George. *Christianity and Culture.* vol. 2. Belmont: Nordland Publishing Co., 1974.
Friedrich, Carl J. and Zbigniew Brezinski. *Totalitarian Dictatorship and Autocracy.* 2nd ed. Cambridge, MA: Harvard University Press, 1965.
Frunză, Florin. "Biserica Ortodoxă Română şi laicizarea." *Un suflet pentru Europa: Dimensiunea religioasă a unui proiect politic.* Edited by Radu Carp. Bucureşti: Editura Anastasia, 2005.
Frunză, Sandu. "Statul naţional şi politicile multiculturale." *JSRI,* No. 5 (Summer 2003).
Galeriu, Constantin. "Biserici demolate, bisericii omorâte, biserici deplasate, biserici deportate din sânul odrăslirii sacre." *Biserici Osândite de Ceauşescu: Bucureşti, 1977–1989* by Lidia Anania, et al. Bucureşti: Editura Anastasia, 1995.
Gallagher, Tom. *Romania after Ceauşescu: The Politics of Intolerance.* Edinburgh: Edinburgh University Press, 1995.
—. *Democraţie şi naţionalism în România, 1989–1998.* Bucureşti: All Educational, 1999.
—. *Furtul unei naţiuni.* Bucureşti: Editura Humanitas, 2004.

Gavrilă, Letiția, Silvestru Augustin. *Credința noastră este viața noastră: Memoriile Cardinalului Iuliu Hossu*. Cluj: Casa de Editură Viața Creștină, 2003.

Geanakoplos, Deno. "Church and State in the Byzantine East: A Reconsideration of the Problem of Caesaropapism." *Church History*, vol. 34, No. 4 (December 1965).

Gellately, Robert. *The Gestapo and German Society: Enforcing Racial Policy, 1933–1945*. Oxford: Clarendon Press, 1991.

Gellner, Ernest. *Nations and Nationalism*. Oxford: Blackwell, 1983.

—. *Chosen People: Sacred Sources of National Identity*. Oxford: Oxford University Press, 2003.

George, Timothy. *The Theology of the Reformers*. Nashville: Broadman Press, 1988.

Georgescu, Valentin Al. *Bizanțul și instituțiile românești până la mijlocul sec. al XVIII-lea*. București, 1980.

Georgescu, Vlad. *The Romanians: A History*. London: I.B. Tauris & Co., 1991.

—. *Istoria românilor de la origini până în zilele noastre*. București: Editura Humanitas, 1995.

Georgiev A. and E. Tzenkov. "The Troubled Balkans." *Redefining Europe: New Patterns of Conflict and Co-operation*. Edited by Hugh Miall. London: Royal Institute of International Affairs, 1994.

GfK Custom Research Worldwide on behalf of *The Wall Street Journal Europe*. "Religion—A Personal Matter." Nuremberg/Frankfurt, 10 December 2004.

Gilberg, Trond. "Religion and Nationalism in Romania." *Religion and Nationalism in Soviet and Eastern European Politics*. Edited by Sabrina P. Ramet. Durham, NC; London: Duke University Press, 1989.

Gillet, Olivier. *Religie și naționalism: Ideologia Bisericii Ortodoxe Române sub regimul comunist*. București: Editura Compania, 2001.

Gilley, Sheridan, Brian Stanley, eds.. *World Christianities, c. 181 –c. 1914*. Cambridge: Cambridge University Press, 2006.

Giurescu, Constantin. *Istoria Românilor: Din cele mai vechi timpuri până la moartea regelui Ferdinand*. București: Editura Humanitas, 2000.

Giurescu, Dinu C. *Distrugerea trecutului României*. București: Editura Museion, 1994.

Glanzer Perry L., Konstantin Petrenko. "Religion and Education in Post-Communist Russia: Making Sense of Russia's New Church–state Paradigm," *International Symposium "Church and State in Eastern Europe"* Iași, Romania, September 2005.

Gleason, Abbott. *European and Muscovite: Ivan Kireevsky and the Origins of Slavophilism*. Cambridge, MA: Harvard University Press, 1972.

Goldhagen, J. Daniel. *Hitler's Willing Executioners: Ordinary Germans and the Holocaust*. New York: Knopf, 1996.

Golsan, B. Lucy, Henry Rousso, Peter Rogers, Richard J. Golsan, and Thomas Christian Hilde. *Stalinism and Nazism: History and Memory Compared*. Lincoln, NE: University of Nebraska Press, 2004.

Goodrick-Clarke, Nicholas. *The Occult Roots of Nazism*. New York: New York University Press, 1985.

Gorringe, Timothy J. *Karl Barth: Against Hegemony*. Oxford: Oxford University Press, 1999.

Greenfeld, Liah. *Nationalism: Five Roads to Modernity*. Cambridge, MA: Harvard University Press, 1992.

Gregor, A. James. *Giovanni Gentile: Philosopher of Fascism.* New Brunswick, NJ, London: Transaction Publishers, 2001.

Grossu, Sergiu. *Calvarul României creștine.* Iași: Editura Polirom, 1992.

Gurian, Waldemar. *Hitler and the Christians.* New York: Sheed & Ward, 1936.

Habermas, Jürgen. "Concerning the Public Use of History." *New German Critique,* No. 44 (Spring/Summer 1988).

Haddorff, David. "Karl Barth's Theological Politics." *Community, State and Church: Three Essays.* Eugene, Oregon: Wipf and Stock Publishers, 2004.

Hakeem, Michael. "The Protestant Reaction to the Nazi Holocaust." *Freethought Today* (March 1993).

Halliday, Fred. "The Perils of Community: Reason and Unreason in Nationalist Ideology." *Nations and Nationalism,* vol. 6 (February 2000).

Harakas, Stanley S. "Orthodox Church–state Theory and American Democracy." *Greek Orthodox Theological Review,* vol. XXI, No. 4 (Winter 1976).

Harrelson, Walter. Review of *Theologians under Hitler: Gerhard Kittel, Paul Althaus, and Emmanuel Hirsch.* By Robert P. Ericksen. *Theology Today,* vol. 43, No.1 (April 1986).

Hastings, Adrian. *Church and State: The English Experience.* Exeter: University of Exeter Press, 1991.

—. *The Construction of Nationhood.* Cambridge: Cambridge University Press, 1997.

Hauer, Jakob Wilhelm. *Germany's New Religion: the German Faith Movement.* London: Allen and Unwin, 1937.

Hauerwas, Stanley. *With the Grain of the Universe: The Church's Witness and Natural Theology.* London: SCM Press, 2002.

Hayes, Stephen. "Nationalism, Violence and Reconciliation." *Missionalia,* vol. 27, No.2 (August 1999).

Hegel, W.F. Georg. *Politische Schriften,* edited by Hans Blumenberg. Frankfurt am Main: Suhrkamp, 1966.

Helmreich, Ernst C. *The German Churches under Hitler: Background, Struggle, and Epilogue.* Detroit: Wayne State University Press, 1979.

Hitchins, Keith. "The Romanian Orthodox Church and the State." *Religion and Atheism in the USSR and Eastern Europe.* By Bohdan R. Bociurkiw and John W. Strong, eds. London: Macmillan Press, 1975.

—. *Orthodoxy and Nationality: Andreiu Șaguna and the Romanians of Transylvania 1846–1873.* Cambridge, MA: Harvard University Press, 1977.

—. *Conștiință națională și acțiune politică la românii din Transilvania, 1700–1868.* vol 1. Cluj: Editura Dacia, 1987.

—. *România, 1866–1947.* București: Editura Humanitas, 1994.

—. *The Romanians, 1774–1866.* Oxford: Clarendon Press, 1996.

Hitler, Adolf. *Mein Kampf.* Translated by Ralph Manheim. London: Hutchinson Press, 1974.

Hobbes, Thomas. *The Leviathan,* Oxford World's Classics. Oxford: Oxford University Press, 1996.

Hobsbawm, Eric J. *Nations and Nationalism since 1780.* Cambridge: Cambridge University Press, 1990.

Hobsbawm, Eric J. and Terence Ranger. eds. *The Invention of Tradition.* Cambridge: Cambridge University Press, 1983.

Hunsinger, George. *Disruptive Grace: Studies in the Theology of Karl Barth.* Grand Rapids: Eerdmans, 2000.
Huntington, Samuel P. *The Clash of Civilizations and the Remaking of World Order.* New York: Simon & Schuster, 1997.
—. *Ciocnirea civilizațiilor și refacerea ordinii mondiale.* Oradea: Editura Antet, 1998.
Hutchinson, John. *Modern Nationalism.* London: Fontana, 1994.
Ică Jr., Ioan. "Dumitru Stăniloae." *Dictionary of Historical Theology.* Edited by Trevor Hart. Grand Rapids: Paternoster Press, 2000.
—. "Dilema sociala a Bisericii Ortodoxe Romane: Radiografia unei probleme." *Gândirea Socială a Bisericii.* Edited by Ioan Ică Jr., Germano Marani. Sibiu: Deisis, 2002.
Ică Jr., Ioan and Germano Marani, eds. *Gândirea Socială a Bisericii: Fundamente, Documente, Analize, Perspective.* Sibiu: Editura Deisis, 2002.
Inglis, Tom and Zdzislaw Mach, ed. *Religion and Politics: East-West Contrasts from Contemporary Europe.* Dublin: University College Dublin Press, 2000.
Institute on Religion and Public Policy. "Institute Deeply Disappointed by Promulgation of Contentious Romanian Religion Law; Romania Now Identified with Worst Religion Law in Europe." Washington, D.C. (3 January 2007). [Online] Available at: http://www.religionandpolicy.org/show.php?p=1.1.1844. Accessed January 2007.
Institutul Național de Statistică. *Recensământul Populației și al Locuințelor.* vol.1. București, 2003.
Ioanid, Radu. *The Sword of the Archangel: Fascist Ideology in Romania.* Boulder, CO: Columbia University Press, 1990.
Iordachi, Constantin. *The Anatomy of a Historical Conflict: Romanian-Hungarian Diplomatic Conflict in the 1980's.* MA Thesis, Central European University, 1996.
Iorga, Nicolae. *În lupta cu absurdul revisionism maghiar.* București: Editura Globus, 1991.
—. *Bizanț după Bizanț.* București: Editura Gramar, 2005.
"Înnoiri în Biserica Ortodoxă." *România Liberă* (14 January 1990).
Jäckel, Eberhard. *Hitler's Worldview: A Blueprint for Power.* Cambridge, MA: Harvard University Press, 1972.
Jantzen, Kyle. Review of "Die Christlich-Deutsche Bewegung: Eine Studie zum Konservativen Protestantismus in der Weimarer Republik." by Christoph Weiling. *The Catholic Historical Review,* vol. 88, no. 3 (July 2002).
Jaspers, Karl. *Texte Filozofice.* Translated by G. Purdea. București: Editura Enciclopedică, 1986.
Jedin, Hubert, ed. *The History of the Church.* vol. 10. *The History of the Church in Modernity.* London: Burns and Oates, 1981.
Jehle, Frank. *Ever Against the Stream: The Politics of Karl Barth 1906–1968.* Grand Rapids: Eerdmans, 2002.
Journal of the Moscow Patriarchate, No. 4 (1987).
Judt, Tony. "Romania: Bottom of the Heap." *The New York Review of Books.* (1 November 2001).
—. *România: La fundul grămezii.* Iași: Editura Polirom, 2002.
Junction, Joy. "Romanian Religious Minorities Concerned About New Religion Law." *The American Daily: Political and Social Commentary* (10 August 2005).

Jüngel, Eberhard, D. Bruce Hamill, and Alan J. Torrance. *Christ, Justice and Peace: Toward a Theology of the State in Dialogue with the Barmen Declaration.* Edinburgh: T. & T. Clark, 1992.

Kedourie, Elie. ed. *Nationalism in Asia and Africa.* London: Weidenfeld and Nicolson, 1971.

Kershaw, Ian. *Hitler 1889–1936: Hubris.* London: W. W. Norton & Company, 1998.

— and Moshe Lewin, eds. *Stalinism and Nazism: Dictatorships in Comparison.* Cambridge: Cambridge University Press, 1997.

Khomyakov, Aleksei Stepanovich and Ivan Vasilevich Kireevskii. *On Spiritual Unity: A Slavophile Reader.* Hudson, NY: Lindisfarne Books, 1998.

Kittel, Gerhard. *Theological Dictionary of the New Testament,* translated by Geoffrey W. Bromiley, 10 vols. Grand Rapids: Eerdmans, 1965–76.

Klinghoffer, Arthur Jay. *Red Apocalypse: The Religious Evolution of Soviet Communism.* Lanham: University Press of America, 1996.

Koch, Stephen. *Sfârşitul inocenţei: Intelectualii din Occident şi tentaţia stalinistă; 30 de ani de război secret.* Bucureşti: Editura Albatros, 1997.

Kogălniceanu, Mihail. *Discursuri parlamentare din Epoca Unirii.* Bucureşti: Editura Ştiinţifică, 1959.

Kolarz, Walter. *Mituri şi realităţi în Europa de Est.* Iaşi: Editura Polirom, 2003.

"Ku Klux Klan Ortodox." *Meridian* (May–June 1990).

Lakatos, Peter. "Denominational and Cultural Models and a Possible Ecumenical Strategy from a Romanian Context." *Religion in Eastern Europe,* vol. XVIII, No. 5 (October 1998).

Layton, Geoff. *Germany: The Third Reich 1933–45.* London: Hodder and Stoughton, 2000.

Leb, Ioan Vasile. *Biserica în Acţiune.* Cluj: Editura Limes, 2001.

"Legea privind libertatea religioasă stârneşte controverse." *BBC Romanian* (11 Aprilie 2006). [Online] Available at: http://www.bbc.co.uk/Romanian/news/story/2006/04/printable/060411_libertate_religioasa.shtml. Accessed May 2006.

Lehmann, Paul. "Karl Barth, the Theologian of Permanent Revolution." *Union Seminary Quarterly Review,* vol. 28 (1972).

"Letter of Protest." Bucharest, 27 October 2005. [Online] Available at: http://www.areopagus.ro/index.php?option=content&task=view&id=144&Itemid=179. Accessed March 2006.

Leuştean, Lucian N. "Ethno-Symbolic Nationalism, Orthodoxy and the Installation of Communism in Romania: 23 August 1944 to 30 December 1947." *Nationalities Papers,* vol. 33, No. 4 (December 2005).

—. *Orthodoxy and the Cold War: Religion and Political Power in Romania, 1947–65.* Basingstoke: Palgrave, 2009.

"Libertatea religioasă în România." *BBC Romanian* (16 September 2004). [Online] Available at: http://www.bbc.co.uk/Romanian/news/story/2004/09/040916_religie_Romania.shtml . Accessed March 2006.

Lindsay, Mark. *Covenanted Solidarity: The Theological Basis of Karl Barth's Opposition to Nazi Antisemitism and the Holocaust.* New York: Peter Lang, 2001.

Lippmann, Walter. *The Good Society.* New Jersey: Transaction Publishers, 2005.

Lossky, Vladimir. *Mystical Theology of the Eastern Church.* London: James Clarke, 1957.

Louth, Andrew. "Review Essay: The Orthodox Dogmatic Theology of Dumitru Stăniloae." *Modern Theology*, vol. 13, No. 2 (April 1997).

—. "The Orthodox Dogmatic Theology of Dumitru Stăniloae." *Dumitru Stăniloae: Tradition and Modernity in Theology*. Edited by Lucian Turcescu. Iaşi: Center for Romanian Studies, 2002.

Lupaş, I. *Mitropolitul Andrei Şaguna: Monografie*. Sibiu: Editura Consistorului Mitropolitan, 1909.

Luther, Martin. "Of the Liberty of a Christian Man" (1520); "Of Temporal Authority" (1523). [Online] Available at: http://www.fordham.edu/halsall/mod/luther-freedomchristian.html . Accessed May 2004.

—. "To the Christian Nobility of the German Nation" (1520). [Online] Available at: http://www.iclnet.org/pub/resources/text/wittenberg/luther/web/nblty-01.html . Accessed May 2004.

Macoveiciuc, Alexandru. "Condamnarea comunismului, balamucul furioşilor." *Adevărul*, No. 5117 (19 December, 2006).

Magee, Bryan. *The Story of Philosophy*. New York: DK Publishing, 2001.

Magyari-Vincze, Eniko. "Politics of Multiculturalism and the Construction of Border Identities." Research in progress, Center for Comparative Social Analysis, (May 1999).

Maier, Charles. *The Unmasterable Past: History, Holocaust and German National Identity*. Cambridge, MA: Harvard University Press, 2003.

Maiorescu, Titu. *Critice*. vol. I. Bucureşti: Editura pentru literatura, 1967.

Mănăstireanu, Daniel. "Legea cultelor sau a cultului?" (2005). [Online] Available at: http://www.adoramus.ro/legeaCultelor.htm. Accessed January 2006.

Mănăstireanu, Dănuţ. "Dumitru Stăniloae's Theology of Ministry." *Dumitru Stăniloae: Tradition and Modernity in Theology*. Edited by Lucian Turcescu. Iaşi: Center for Romanian Studies, 2002.

—. "A Perichoretic Model of the Church: The Trinitarian Ecclesiology of Dumitru Stăniloae." Unpublished thesis. Brunel, London, 2005.

Manent, Pierre. *An Intellectual History of Liberalism*. Princeton: Princeton University Press, 1994.

Manolescu, Anca. "Grupul de Reflecţie pentru Înnoirea Bisericii 1990–1991." *Dilema*, No. 202 (22–28 November 1996).

Marina, Patriarh Iustinian. *Apostolat Social*. vol. I. Bucureşti: Editura Institutului Biblic, 1948.

—. *Apostolat Social*. vol. V. Bucureşti: Editura Institutului Biblic, 1955.

—. *Apostolat Social*. vol. VII. Bucureşti: Editura Institutului Biblic, 1962.

—. *Apostolat Social*. vol. VIII. Bucureşti: Editura Institutului Biblic, 1966.

—. *Apostolat Social*. vol. X. Bucureşti: Editura Institutului Biblic, 1971.

Marino, Adrian. *Pentru Europa. Integrarea României: Aspecte ideologice şi culturale*. Iaşi: Editura Polirom, 1995.

Markham, Reuben H. *România sub jugul sovietic*. Bucureşti: Editura Fundaţia Academia Civică, 1996.

Martin, David. *Does Christianity Cause War?* Oxford: Clarendon Press, 1997.

McCormack, Bruce. *Karl Barth's Critically Realistic Dialectical Theology*. Oxford: Clarendon Press. 1997.

McDonough, Frank. *Hitler and Nazi Germany*. Cambridge: Cambridge University Press, 1999.

Mehedinți-Soveja, Simion. *Creștinismul Românesc: Adaos la Caracterizarea Etnografică a Poporului Român*. București: Editura Anastasia, 1995.

Mestrovic, Stjepan. G. *Habits of the Balkan Heart: Social Character and the Fall of Communism*. College Station: Texas A& M University Press, 1993.

Meyendorff, John. *Byzantine Theology*. New York: Fordham University Press, 1974.

—. "Foreword." *Theology and the Church*. By Dumitru Stăniloae. Translated by Robert Barringer. New York: SVS Press, 1980.

—. *The Orthodox Church: Its Past and Its Role in the World Today*. 4th ed. Crestwood: St. Vladimir's Seminary Press, 1996.

—. *The Byzantine Legacy in the Orthodox Church*. New York: St. Vladimir Seminary Press, 2001.

Micu, Dumitru. *Gândirea și Gândirismul*.București: Editura Minerva, 1975.

Mihăieș, Mircea. *Masca de Fiere*. Iași: Editura Polirom, 2000.

Miller, Charles. *The Gift of the World. An Introduction to the Theology of Dumitru Stăniloae* Edinburgh: T & T Clark, 2000.

Milosz, Czeslaw. *Gândirea Captivă*, București: Editura Humanitas, 1999.

Moisin, Ioan. "Situația Bisericii Române Unite în primele opt luni din actuala guvernare." *Viața Creștină*, vol. 8 no. 16 (August 1997).

Mojzes, Paul. *Religion Liberty in Eastern Europe and the USSR Before and After the Great Transformation*. Boulder, CO, New York: Columbia University Press, 1992.

Moltmann, Jürgen. "Introduction." *Orthodoxe Dogmatik*. German translation by H. Pitters. Cologne: Gütersloh, 1985.

—. *Forgiveness and Politics: Forty Years after the Stuttgart Confession*. London: New World Publications, 1987.

Monsma, Stephen V., J. Christopher Soper, *The Challenge of Pluralism: Church and State in Five Democracies*. Lanham: Rowman & Littlefield, 1997.

Moraru, Mihaela. "Legea cultelor, fără formula biserică națională." *Evenimentul Zilei* (12 June 2006). [Online] Available at: http://www.evz.ro/article.php?artid=261843. Accessed June 2006.

Moses, John A. *The Politics of Illusion: The Fischer Controversy in German Historiography*. New York: Barnes & Noble Books, 1975.

Moss, Vladimir. "Sergianism as an Ecclesiological Heresy." *Monastery Press* (February–March 1999). [Online] Available at: http://www.monasterypress.com/sergianism.html . Accessed December 2005.

Mosse, George. *The Nationalization of the Masses: Political Symbolism and Mass Movements from the Napoleonic Wars through the Third Reich*. New York: Howard Fertig, 1975.

Mungiu, Alina. *Românii după '89: Istoria unei neînțelegeri*. București: Editura Humanitas, 1995.

Mungiu-Pippidi, Alina. "The Ruler and the Patriarch: The Romanian Eastern Orthodox Church in Transition." *East European Constitutional Review*, vol. 7, No. 2 (Spring 1998).

Mureșanu, Andrei. "Cât de catolici au fost corifeii 'Școlii Ardelene'?" *Vatra*, vol.1 (1998).

Namier, Lewis Bernstein, Sir. *In the Nazi Era*. London: Macmillan, 1952.

Năstase, Dorina. "Secularizare și religie în integrarea europeană." *Un suflet pentru Europa: Dimensiunea religioasă a unui proiect politic*. Edited by Radu Carp. București: Editura Anastasia, 2005.

National census conducted by the Gallup Organization, *Metromedia Transylvania*, 2002–4.

Negruț, Paul. *Biserica și Statul: O interogație asupra modelului simfoniei bizantine*. Oradea: Emanuel, 2000.

Nicodim, Patriarch of Romania. *Cuvântul Patriarhului pentru post, pentru oștire, pentru ogor*. București, 1942.

Niebuhr, Reinhold. *Radical Monotheism and Western Culture*. New York: Harper and Row, 1970.

Nistor, Vlad. "Echilibru nepărtinitor." *Dilema*, No. 284 (10–16 July 1998).

O'Donovan, Oliver. *The Desire of the Nations: Rediscovering the Roots of Political Theology*. Cambridge: Cambridge University Press, 1996.

— and Joan L. O'Donovan, eds. *From Irenaeus to Grotius: A Sourcebook of Christian Political Thought 100–1625*. Grand Rapids, Cambridge: Eerdmans, 1999.

Oprea, Marius. "Problema 132: Biserica Română Unită în atenția Securității." *Istoria Bisericii Greco-Catolice sub regimul comunist 1945–1989*. By Cristian Vasile. Iași: Editura Polirom, 2003.

—. "Securitatea și moștenirea sa." *Comunism și represiune în România: Istoria tematică a unui fratricid național*. Edited by Ruxandra Cesereanu. Iași: Editura Polirom, 2006.

Ornea, Zigu. *Anii Treizeci: Extrema Dreaptă Românească*. București: Editura Fundației Culturale Române, 1995.

Osborne, Basil. "Orthodoxy in a United Europe: The Future of Our Past." *Orthodox Christianity and Contemporary Europe*. Edited by Jonathan Sutton and Wil van den Bercken. Leuven: Uitgeverij Peeters, 2003.

Oțetea, Andrei, ed. *The History of the Romanian People*. New York: Twayne, 1970.

Overy, Richard. *The Dictators: Hitler's Germany and Stalin's Russia*. London: Penguin Books, 2004.

Pacepa, Ion Mihai. *Orizonturi roșii: Amintirile unui General de Securitate*. București: Editura Venus, 1992.

—. *Cartea neagră a Securității*. vol. 2: *Viața mea alături de Gheorghiu-Dej*. București: Editura Ziua, 1999.

Păcurariu, Mircea. *Istoria Bisericii Ortodoxe Române*. vol. 3. București: Editura Institutului Biblic și de Misiune Ortodoxă, 1981.

—. "Preotul Profesor și Academician Dumitru Stăniloae." *Persoană și Comuniune*. Edited by Mircea Păcurariu and Ioan Ică Jr. Sibiu: Editura Arhiepiscopiei Ortodoxe, 1993.

Pana, Georgetta. "Religious Anti-Semitism in Romanian Fascist Propaganda." *Religion in Eastern Europe*, vol. XXVI, No. 2 (May 2006).

Papacostea, Șerban. *Geneza statului în Evul Mediu românesc*. București: Editura Corint, 1998.

Paperno, Irina. *Chernyshevsky and the Age of Realism: A Study in the Semiotics of Behavior*. Stanford: Stanford University Press, 1988.

Pârvan, Vasile. *Contribuții epigrafice la istoria creștinismului Daco-Roman*. București: Socec and Company, 1911.

Patapievici, Horia-Roman. "Biserica Ortodoxă și Modernitatea I." *Dilema*, No. 331 (11–17 June 1999).

—. *Omul recent: O critică a modernității din perspectiva întrebării „Ce se pierde atunci când ceva se câștigă?"* București: Editura Humanitas, 2001.

—. *Politice.* Bucureşti: Editura Humanitas, 2002.
—. "Rugul Aprins." *ID,* vol. II, No.12 (15) (December 2005).
Patraşconiu, Cristian. "Sorin Antohi: Am turnat la Securitate." *Cotidianul* (5 September 2006).
"Patriarhul Daniel, managerul în sutană." *România Liberă* (14 September 2007).
"Patriarhul Daniel semnalează preşedintelui Băsescu eliminarea religiei din legile educaţiei." *Hotnews.ro* (19 August 2009).
Pavel, Dan. *Etica lui Adam: Sau de ce rescriem istoria.* Bucureşti: Editura Du Style, 1995.
—. *Cine, Ce şi De ce?: Interviuri despre politică şi alte tabuuri.* Iaşi: Editura Polirom, 1998.
—. *Leviathanul bizantin: Analize, atitudini şi studii politice.* Iaşi: Editura Polirom, 1998.
Peet, Garnet. "The Protestant Churches in Nazi Germany." *Clarion,* vol. 37, Nos. 22–24 (28 October 1988).
Percival, Henry, ed. *The Seven Ecumenical Councils of the Undivided Church. Their Canons and Dogmatic Decrees, Nicene and Post-Nicene Fathers.* New York: Charles Scribner's Sons, 1990.
Petrescu, Dragoş. "Biserica Ortodoxă Română sub regimul comunist." *Teologie şi Politică: De la Sfinţii Părinţi la Europa Unită.* Edited by Miruna Tătaru-Cazaban. Bucureşti: Editura Anastasia, 2004.
Petro, Nicolai N. "The EU: The Orthodox are Coming." *Transitions Online* (25 March 2005).
Pippidi, Andrei. *Tradiţia politică bizantină în Ţările Române în Sec. XVI-XVIII.* Bucureşti: Editura Corint, 2001.
Plămădeală, Antonie. "Biserica Slujitoare în Sfânta Scriptură, Sfânta Tradiţie şi în Teologia Contemporană." *Studii Teologice,* vol. 24, Nos. 5–8, (1972).
—. "Church and State in Romania." *Church and State: Opening a New Ecumenical Discussion.* Faith and Order Paper, no. 85. Geneva: World Council of Churches, 1978.
Pleşu, Andrei. *Chipuri şi măşti ale tranziţiei.* Bucureşti: Editura Humanitas, 1996.
—. "Poarta cea Largă." *Dilema,* No. 206 (20–26 December 1996).
Pleşu, Andrei, Petre Roman, and Elena Ştefoi. *Transformări, inerţii, dezordini: 22 de luni după 22 decembrie 1989.* Iaşi: Editura Polirom, 2002.
Poewe, Karla. *New Religions and the Nazis.* New York: Routledge, 2006.
Popa, Radu. *Ţara Maramureşului în secolul al XIV-lea.* Bucureşti: Editura Enciclopedica, 1997.
Pope Gelasius I, "Epistle 12." *Epistolae Romanorum pontificum genuinae.* vol. I. Edited by Andreas Thiel. Brunsbergae, 1868.
Pope Innocent III. "Letter to the prefect Acerbius and the nobles of Tuscany" (1198). [Online] Available at: http://www.fordham.edu/halsall/source/innIII-policies.html . Accessed April 2006.
"Pope John Paul II to Romania." *www.cathorth.hist.org* (26 March 2003). Available online: http://www.cathorth.hist.org/roma.html. Accessed January 2006.
Popescu, Alexandru. *Petre Ţuţea: Between Sacrifice and Suicide.* Oxford: Ashgate, 2004.
Popescu, Dumitru. *Hristos, Biserică, Societate.* Bucureşti: Editura IBMBOR, 1998.
Popper, Karl. *The Open Society and Its Enemies.* 2 vols. London: Routledge & Kegan Paul, 1945.

—. *The Poverty of Historicism.* London: Routledge & Kegan Paul, 1961.
"Positive Christianity." Louis L. Snyder, *Encyclopedia of the Third Reich.* London: Robert Hale, 1998.
Preda, Radu. *Biserica în stat: O invitație la dezbatere.* București: Editura Scripta, 1999.
—. "Cultura dialogului sau despre o altă relație biserică-stat." *Nostalgia Europei: Volum în onoarea lui Alexandru Paleologu.* Iași: Editura Polirom, 2003.
—. "Lupta pentru Patriarhie continuă." *ID,* Year II, No. 12(15) (December 2005).
"Proces-verbal al Adunării Eparhiale Extraordinare a Arhiepiscopiei Vadului, Feleacului și Clujului." *Renașterea* (25 November 2005).
Prodan, David. *Supplex Libellus Valachorum.* București: Editura Academiei, 1971.
—. *Transylvania and Again Transylvania.* Cluj Napoca: Romanian Cultural Foundation, 1992.
Rădulescu-Motru, Constantin. *Etnicul românesc. Naționalismul.* București: Editura Albatros, 1990.
Ramet, Pedro. "Autocephaly and National Identity in Church–state Relations in Eastern Christianity: An Introduction." *Eastern Christianity and Politics in the Twentieth Century.*
Ramet, Sabrina. P. *Nihil Obstat: Religion, Politics, and Social Change in East-Central Europe and Russia.* Durham, NC: Duke University Press, 1998.
Rămureanu, Ioan. *Istoria Ortodoxă Universală.* București: Editura Institutului Biblic, 1988.
—. *Istoria bisericească universală.* București: Editura Institutului Biblic și de Misiune Ortodoxă, 1993.
Rațiu, Alexandru. *Persecuția Bisericii Române Unite.* Oradea: Imprimaria de Vest, 1994.
Rauschning, Hermann. *Hitler Speaks.* London: Thorton Butterworth, 1939.
Reynalds, Jeremy. "Romania's Christian Minorities Protest Proposed New Legislation." *ASSIST News* (3 October 2005).
Rhodes, James. *The Hitler Movement. A Modern Millenarian Revolution.* Stanford: Hoover Institution Press, 1980.
Ritter, Gerhard. *Europa und die Deutsche Frage: Betrachtungen über die geschichtliche Eigenart des Deutschen Staatsdenkens.* München: Münchner Verlag, 1948.
Robertson, Ronald. *Contemporary Romanian Orthodox Ecclesiology.* Romae: Typis Pontificiae Universitatis Gregorianae, 1988.
—. "Dumitru Stăniloae on Christian Unity." *Dumitru Stăniloae: Tradition and Modernity in Theology.* Edited by Lucian Turcescu. Iași: Center for Romanian Studies, 2002.
Roest, Bert. "Franciscan Views on Papal and Royal Sovereignty: A Case for a Contextual Approach." *Franciscan Authors, 13th to 18th Century: A Catalogue in Progress.* (2006) [Online] Available at http://users.bart.nl/~roestb /franciscan/ GILLEEDS.html. Accessed August 2006.
Rogobete, Silviu. *O ontologie a iubirii. Subiect și realitate personală supremă în gîndirea Părintelui Dumitru Stăniloae.* Iași: Editura Polirom, 2001.
—. "Between Fundamentalism and Secularization." *Religion and Democracy in Moldova.* Edited by Silvo Devetak, et al. Timisoara: Brumar Publishing House, 2005.
Roman, Viorel and Hannes Hofbauer. *Transilvania: Românii la încrucișarea intereselor imperiale.* București: Editura Europa Nova, 1998.
Romanato, Gianpaolo. "Biserica și statul laic." *Religie și Putere.* Edited by Ioan Petru Culianu. București: Editura Nemira, 1996.

"România respectă dreptul la libertate religioasă" in *BBC Romanian* (10 November 2005). [Online] Available at: http://www.bbc.co.uk/Romanian/news/story /2005/11/printable/051110_libertate_religioasa.shtml. Accessed March 2006.

"Romanian Church Seeks to Cleanse Itself." *Christian Century* (3 April 1991).

Romanian Orthodox Church News. vol. IV, Nos. 1–2 (January–June 1974).

Romanian Orthodox Church News. vol. IV, No. 3 (July–September 1974).

Romanian Orthodox Church News. vol. XIII, No. 1 (January–March 1983).

Romanian Orthodox Church News. vol. XV, No. 1 (January–March 1985).

Romanian Orthodox Church News. vol. XVII, No. 5 (September 1987).

"Romanian Patriarch Asks for Forgiveness." *BBC News* (15 February 2000). [Online] Available at: http://news.bbc.co.uk/1/hi/world/europe/643898.stm. Accessed March 2006.

Romannides, John S. "The Orthodox Churches on Church–state Relations and Religious Liberty." *Readings on Church and State*. Edited by James E. Wood, Jr. Waco: J.M.D. Institute of Church–state Studies, 1989.

Romocea, Cristian G. "Forgiveness and Reconciliation between Hungarians and Romanians in Transylvania." Unpublished thesis. Osijek, 2001.

—. "Reconciliation in the Ethnic Conflict in Transylvania: Theological, Political and Social Aspects." *Religion, State & Society*, vol. 32. No. 2 (June 2004).

—. "Democracy." *Dictionary of Mission Theology*. Edited by John Corrie. Leicester: Inter-Varsity Press, 2007.

Rothfels, Hans. *The German Opposition to Hitler, An Appraisal*. Chicago, Ill.: Henry Regnery Company, 1948.

Rousso, Henry, ed. *Stalinism and Nazism: History and Memory Compared*. Lincoln, London: University of Nebraska Press, 2004.

Ruh, Ulrich. "Europa şi secularizarea: Trăsăturile principale ale unui proces cu multe faţete." *Un suflet pentru Europa: Dimensiunea religioasă a unui proiect politic*. Edited by Radu Carp. Bucureşti: Editura Anastasia, 2005.

Runciman, Steven. *The Orthodox Churches and the Secular State*. Auckland: Auckland Univ. Press, 1971.

Russell, Bertrand. *The Practice and Theory of Bolshevism*. New York: Harcourt, Brace and Howe, 1920.

Russett, Bruce, John R. Oneal, and Michaelene Cox. "Clash of Civilizations or Realism and Liberalism Déjà Vu? Some Evidence." *Journal of Peace Research*, vol. 37, No. 5 (2000).

Sacerdoţeanu, Aurelian. "Organizarea Bisericii Ortodoxe Române în Secolele al IX-lea–al XIII-lea." *Studii Teologice*, vol. 20, Nos. 3–4 (March–April 1968).

Saunders, Will. "Cross and Swastika: The Nazi Party and the German Churches: To What Extent Did Christians Support Hitler, and for What Reasons?" *History Review*, No. 46 (2003).

Sârbu, Daniel. "Legea cultelor: Proiect eşuat." *Ziua de Ardeal* (3 November, 2001). [Online] Available at: http://www.catholica.ro/stiri/show.asp?id=2079&lang=r. Accessed March 2003.

Scarfe, Alan. "The Evangelical Wing of the Orthodox Church in Romania." *Religion in Communist Lands*, vol. 3, No. 6 (November–December 1975).

—. "Patriarch Justinian of Romania: His Early Social Thought." *Religion in Communist Lands*, vol. 5, No. 3 (Autumn 1977).

—. "The Lord's Army Movement in the Romanian Orthodox Church." *Religion in Communist Lands*, vol. 8, No. 4 (1980).
—. "The Romanian Orthodox Church." *Eastern Christianity and Politics in the Twentieth Century*. vol. 1. Edited by Pedro Ramet. Durham, NC: Duke University Press, 1988.
Schaser, Angelika. *Reformele iosefine în Transilvania și urmările lor în viața socială*. Translated by Monica Vlaicu. Sibiu: Editura Hora, 2000.
Schifirneț, Constantin. "Studiu Introductiv." *Teoria lui Rösler: Studii asupra stăruinței românilor în Dacia Traiană*. By A.D. Xenopol. București: Editura Albatros, 1998.
Schmemann, Alexander. *The Historical Road of Eastern Orthodoxy*. London: Harvill Press, 1963.
Scrima, Andre. *Timpul rugului aprins*. București: Editura Humanitas, 2000.
Sereda, G. "De la Biserica Autocefală la Patriarhia Română." *Ortodoxia*, vol. 2, no. 2 (1950).
Sheehan, James J. *German Liberalism in the Nineteenth Century*. London: Methuen, 1982.
Shirer, William L. *The Rise and Fall of the Third Reich: A History of Nazi Germany*. New York: Simon & Schuster, 1960.
Smith, Anthony D. *The Ethnic Origins of Nations*. Oxford: Blackwell, 1986.
Smith, Helmut Walser. *German Nationalism and Religious Conflict: Culture, Ideology, Politics, 1870–1914*. Princeton: Princeton University Press, 1995.
"Soluții și direcții de acțiune necesare pentru însănătoșirea vieții morale și spirituale a societății românești contemporane." *Comunicat Oficial*, Simpozionul Național "Sfântul Andrei-Apostolul Românilor" (24–27 September 2002). [Online] Available at: http://www.rugulaprins.go.ro/ comunicat.htm . Accessed March 2005.
Song, Robert. *Christianity and Liberal Society*. Oxford: Clarendon Press, 1997.
Soulen, R.K. *The God of Israel and Christian Theology*. Minneapolis: Fortress Press, 1996.
Spengler, Oswald. *The Decline of the West*. London: Allen and Unwin, 1961.
Stan, Lavinia and Lucian Turcescu. *Religion and Politics in Post-communist Romania*. Oxford: Oxford University Press, 2007.
Stăniloae, Dumitru. *Catolicismul de după Razboi*. Sibiu: Editura Arhidiecezană, 1933.
—. *Poziția d-lui Lucian Blaga față de creștinism și ortodoxie*. Sibiu, 1942.
—. "Problema uniatismului din perspectiva ecumenică." *Ortodoxia*, vol. 4 (1969).
—. *Uniatismul în Transilvania*. Sibiu: IBMBOR, 1973.
—. *Teologia dogmatică ortodoxă*. 3 vols. (București: IBMBOR, 1978).
—. *Theology and the Church*. New York: SVS Press, 1980.
—. *Spiritualitate și comuniune în liturghia ortodoxă*. Craiova: Mitropolia Olteniei, 1986.
—. *Chipul Nemuritor al lui Dumnezeu*. Craiova: Mitropolia Olteniei, 1987.
—. *Studii de teologie dogmatică Ortodoxă*. By Dumitru Stăniloae. Craiova: Mitropolia Olteniei, 1991.
—. *Iisus Hristos sau Restaurarea Omului*. Craiova: Omniscop Press, 1993.
—. *The Experience of God: Orthodox Dogmatic Theology*. 2 vols. Brookline: Holy Cross Orthodox Press, 1994–8.
—. *Ortodoxie și românism*. București: Editura Albatros, 1998.
—. *Reflecții despre spiritualitatea poporului român*. București: Editura Elion, 2001.
—. *Ascetica și mistica Bisericii Ortodoxe*. București: Editura Institutului Biblic, 2002.

—. *Națiune și Creștinism*. București: Editura Elion, 2004.
Stăniloae, Lidia I. *Lumina faptei din lumina cuvântului. Împreună cu tatăl meu, Dumitru Stăniloae*. București: Editura Humanitas, 2000.
Stark, Rodney and Roger Finke. *Acts of Faith*. Berkeley: University of California Press, 2000.
Stayer, James M. *Martin Luther, German Saviour: German Evangelical Theological Factions and the Interpretation of Luther, 1917–1933*. Montreal and Kingston: McGill-Queen's University Press, 2000.
Steigmann-Gall, Richard. *The Holy Reich: Nazi Conceptions of Christianity*. Cambridge: Cambridge University Press, 2003.
Steinfels, Peter. "In Eastern Europe's Churches, Triumph Leads to Uncertainty." *The New York Times* (22 July 1990).
Steinhardt, Nicolae. *Jurnalul fericirii*. Cluj: Editura Dacia, 1991.
Stoicescu, Nicolae. *Continuitatea Românilor: Privire istoriografică*. București: Editura Științifică și Enciclopedică, 1980.
Strauss, D.F. *Der Alter und der Neue Glaube: Ein Bekenntnis*. Liepzig, 1872.
Stürmer, Michael. "Geschichte in Geschichtslosen Land." *"Historikerstreit': Die Dokumentation der Kontroverse um die Einzigartigkeit der nationalsozialistischen Judenvernichtung*. Munich: Piper Verlag, 1987.
Sturza, Dimitrie A. *Acte și documente relative la istoria renascerii române*. vol. 6. București: Academia Romana, 1909.
Tal, Uriel. *Faith, Politics, and Nazism: Selected Essays*. London: Frank Cass, 2003.
Talmon, Jacob. *Political Messianism: The Romantic Phase*. London: Secker and Warburg, 1960.
Tănase, Stelian. *Anatomia mistificării*. București: Editura Humanitas, 2003.
—. *Clientii lu" Tanti Varvara: Istorii clandestine*. București: Editura Humanitas, 2005.
Taylor, J.P. *The Course of German History*. London: H Hamilton, 1948.
Teleanu, Bogdan A. "Condamnarea comunismului de către biserică." *Ziua* (18 March 2006).
Teoctist Arăpașu. "Mărturisirea valorilor evanghelice." *Ortodoxia*, vol. LII, No. 304 (2001).
Teoctist, Patriarch. "Mărturisirea valorilor evanghelice." *Magazin Istoric*, vol. 6 (June 2001).
Teoteoi, Tudor. "O misiune a patriarhiei ecumenice la București în vremea lui Vlad Vintilă de la Slatina." *Revista Istorică*, vol. V, Nos. 1–2 (1994).
Tikhon, Bishop (Fitzgerald). "About Sergianism." *The Orthodox West* (Summer 1992).
Tillich, Paul. "Kritisches und Positives Paradox." *Theologische Blätter*, vol. XIII (1934).
—. "What is wrong with dialectical theology?" *Journal of Religion*, vol. 15, No. 2 (April 1935).
Timotin, Andrei. "Paleocreștinismul carpato-danubian." *Archaevs*, vol. II, No. 2 (1998).
Tismăneanu, Vladimir. "Byzantine Rites, Stalinist Follies: The Twilight of Dynastic Socialism in Romania." *Orbis*, vol. 30, No. 1 (Spring 1986).
—. "From Arrogance to Irrelevance: Avatars of Marxism in Romania." *The Road to Disillusion: From Critical Marxism to Post-Communism in Eastern Europe*. Edited by Raymond Taras. Armonk, NY: M.E. Sharpe, 1992.
—. *Reinventing Politics: Eastern Europe from Stalin to Havel*. New York: The Free Press, 1992.

—. *Stalinism pentru eternitate, O istorie politică a comunismului românesc.* Iași: Editura Polirom, 2005.
Tismăneanu, Vladimir and Mircea Mihăieș. *Încet, spre Europa.* Iași: Editura Polirom, 2000.
Tobias, Robert. *Communist-Christian Encounter in Eastern Europe.* Indianapolis: School of Religious Press, 1956.
Todorov, Tzvetan. *Hope and Memory: Lessons from the Twentieth Century*, translated by David Bellos. London: Atlantic Books, 2003.
Tönnies, Ferdinand. *Community and Society.* Translated and edited by Charles P. Looomis. New York: Harper & Row, 1963.
Toynbee, Arnold. *Studiu asupra istoriei.* Sinteză de D.C. Somervell. vol. 2. București: Editura Humanitas, 1997.
Treitschke, Heinrich, von. *Politics.* Translated from the German by Blanche Dugdale. vol. 1. New York: The MacMillan Company, 1916.
Trotsky, Leon. *The Revolution Betrayed.* London: Faber and Faber, 1937.
—. *Stalin: An Appraisal of the Man and His Influence.* London: Hollis and Carter, 1947.
Tudor, Sandu. "Veacul Ucigătorilor de Dumnezeu" quoted in "Rugul Aprins de la Mănăstirea Antim la Aiud." *Detenția.* [Online] Available at: http://www.literaturasidetentie.ro/detentia/carte_3.php . Accessed May 2006.
Turcescu, Lucian. "Dumitru Stăniloae." *The Teachings of Modern Christianity: Law, Politics, and Human Nature.* Edited by John Witte, Jr., and Frank Alexander. vol. 2. New York: Columbia University Press, 2006.
Tusicisny, Andrej. "Civilizational Conflicts: More Frequent, Longer, and Bloodier?" *Journal of Peace Research*, vol. 41, No. 4 (2004).
Țuțea, Petre. *Omul: Tratat de antropologie creștină.* Iași: Editura Timpul, 1992.
Vânău, Liviu. "The Easter Ball: Interaction between Secularism and Religion in Romania." *Religion in Eastern Europe*, vol. XVI, No. 6 (December 1996).
Vasilachi, Vasile. *Another world: Memories from Communist Prisons.* New York, 1987.
Vasile, Cristian. *Între Vatican și Kremlin: Biserica Greco-Catolică în timpul regimului Communist.* Editura Curtea Veche, 2003.
—. *Istoria Bisericii Greco-Catolice sub regimul comunist 1945–1989.* Iași: Editura Polirom, 2003.
—. "Comunismul și Biserica: Represiune, compromitere și instrumentalizare." *Comunism și represiune în România: Istoria tematică a unui fratricid național.* Edited by Ruxandra Cesereanu. Iași: Editura Polirom, 2006.
Verdely, Katherine. *Political Lives of Dead Bodies: Reburial and Postsocialist Change.* New York: Columbia University Press, 1999.
Villa-Vicencio, Charles. *A Theology of Reconstruction: Nation-Building and Human Rights.* Cambridge: Cambridge University Press, 1992.
Villers, Miranda. "The Romanian Orthodox Church Today." *Religion in Communist Lands*, vol. 1, No. 3 (May–June 1973).
Voegelin, Eric. *Die politische Religionen.* Munich: Wilhelm,1996.
Volovici, Leon. *Nationalist Ideology and Antisemitism: The Case of Romanian Intellectuals in the 1930s.* Oxford: Pergamon, 1991.
Von Harnack, Adolf. *Marcion: The Gospel of the Alien God.* Partial Translation. Durham, NC: Labyrinth, 1990.
Von Papen, Franz Joseph Hermann Michael Maria. *Memoirs.* New York: Dutton, 1953.

Von Treitschke, Heinrich. *Politics.* Translated by Blanche Dugdale. vol. 1. New York: The MacMillan Company, 1916.
Vondung, Klaus. *Magie und Manipulation: Ideologische Kultund politische Religion des Nationalsozialismus.* Göttingen: Vandenhoeck & Ruprecht, 1971.
Vulcănescu, Mircea. *Către fiinţa spiritualităţii Româneşti: Dimensiunea românească a existenţei.* vol. 3. *Dimensiunea românească a existenţei.* Bucureşti: Editura Eminescu, 1996.
—. *Bunul Dumnezeu cotidian: Studii despre religie.* Bucureşti: Editura Humanitas, 2004.
Walters, Philip. "Eastern Europe since the fifteenth century." A World *History of Christianity 1920–1985.* Edited by Adrian Hastings. London: SCM Press, 1991.
Ware, Timothy Kallistos. *The Orthodox Church.* Harmondsworth: Penguin, 1963.
Webster, Alexander F.C. *The Price of Prophecy: Orthodox Churches on Peace, Freedom and Security.* Washington, D.C: Ethics and Public Policy Center, 1993.
Wiener, Philip P. *Dictionary of the History of Ideas,* vol. 1. New York: Charles Scribner's Sons, 1973.
Wiesel, Elie. *One Generation After.* New York, Avon: Schoken Books, 1970.
Wogaman, Philip. "The Changing Role of Government and the Myth of Separation." *Journal of Church and State,* vol. 5, No. 1 (May 1963).
—. *Christian Perspectives on Politics.* Louisville: Westminster John Knox Press, 2000.
Wood, James, E. Bruce Thompson, and Robert T. Miller. *Church and State in Scripture, History and Constitutional Law.* Waco: Baylor University Press, 1958.
World Council of Churches. "Orthodox Church Admits Mistakes in Romania." *The Word* (April 1990).
Zizek, Slavoj. *Did Somebody Say Totalitarianism? Five Interventions in the (Mis)Use of a Notion.* London: Verso, 2001.
Zub, Alexandru and Sorin Antohi. *Oglinzi Retrovizoare: Istorie, memorie şi morală în România.* Iaşi: Editura Polirom, 2002.

Index

Acacian Schism 79–80
ALRC 170–1
Althaus, Paul 61–2, 187
Anania, Bartolomeu 21, 23–4, 31
Anderson, Benedict 87, 103
Andreescu, Gabriel 30
Antohi, Sorin 76
Aquinas, Thomas 80, 183
Arăpaşu, Teoctist 166–7
Arendt, Hannah 46, 58
Armbruster, Adolf 111
ASCOR 32

Baconsky, Teodor 20–1, 25–6, 30
Barbu, Daniel 18, 20
Bariţiu, George 118
Barmen Declaration 186–8
Barth, Karl 7
   and Barmen Declaration 186–8
   on German Christians 61
   on National Socialism 49
   rejection of natural theology 183–4
   rejection of *Volk* ideology 204
   resistance to German
     nationalism 181, 190
   Stăniloae's view of 198–200
   theological formation 182
   two kingdoms doctrine
     challenge 189
   on *Volk* 56
Bartoş, Emil 196
Băsescu, Traian 4, 32
Berdyaev, Nikolai 95
Bergen, Doris 57
Berger, Peter 1
Bernea, Horia 21
Birdaş, Emilian 15
Blaga, Lucian 193, 202
Blumhardt, Christoph 182
Bonhoeffer, Dietrich 59, 171

Breuilly, John 87, 103
Bria, Ion 27, 195, 202
Brunner, Emil 73, 190, 191
Bulgakov, Sergius 82
Bultmann, Rudolf 63, 200
Burleigh, Michael 45, 89, 150
Byzantium after Byzantium 77–8

caesaropapism
   definition 78–9
Calciu-Dumitreasa, Gheorghe 167
Carol I, King 128
Carol II, King 23
Ceauşescu, Nicolae 13, 24, 161–2
Chadwick, Owen 81
Chamberlain, Houston Stewart 58
Chrysostom, John 79
church–state typologies 73–4
Ciobotea, Daniel 21–3
Clément, Olivier 192
CNSAS 22
Codreanu, Corneliu Zelea 134
Coman, Constantin 27
Constantinescu, Emil 32
Corneanu, Nicolae 15, 17
Crainic, Nichifor 30, 135, 201
Cristea, Miron 31, 135
Culianu, Ioan P. 41
Cuza, King Alexander 128

Dagron, Gilbert 84
de Tocqueville, Alexis 48
Deletant, Dennis 179
Dobrincu, Dorin 173, 179
Dostoevsky, Fyodor 169
Dumitrescu, Sorin 21
Duţu, Alexandru 170

Eliade, Mircea 122
Enache, George 9, 158, 160, 170

European Union 1, 13, 30, 31, 32, 34, 74

Fergusson, David 101
Florovsky, George 92, 93, 193
French Revolution 29, 48, 74, 86, 88–90

Galeriu, Constantin 21
Gallagher, Tom x, 17, 111, 148
Gelasius I, Pope 79
Gellner, Ernest 87, 89
genocide ix, 3
Georgescu, Valentin 77
Germany
    Bekennende Kirche (Confessing Church) 54, 59, 185
    Deutsche Christen (German Christians) 3, 53–63, 181, 183, 187
    Führer 4, 51, 55, 63, 185
    Gemeinschaft 49–51
    National Socialism 2, 3–4, 44–63
    Positive Christianity 51–2
    racism 58–60
    Sonderweg 50
    Volk 4, 48, 52–3, 56–8
Gheorghiu-Dej, Gheorghe 152
Ghibu, Octavian 21
Ghiuş, Benedict 168
Gilberg, Trond 163
Gillet, Olivier 8, 75, 112, 158
Gogarten, Friedrich 198
Gorbachev, Mikhail 162
Greek Catholic Church 14
    Bartolomeu and 24
    buildings restitution 6, 16–18, 216
    Communist persecution 151–2
    Operation 132, 152
    origins in Transylvania 111
    reinstatement 14
    Stăniloae and 202
Greenfeld, Liah 87, 103
Group for Social Dialogue 24, 28

Habermas, Jürgen 8
Halliday, Fred 110
Harakas, Stanley 81

Hastings, Adrian 79, 87, 109
Hegel, Georg W.F. 45, 52, 89
Hirsch, Emmanuel 62, 190
Hitler, Adolf 54–6, 185
Hobbes, Thomas 88, 104
Hobsbawm, Eric 87, 103, 217
Hoxha, Enver 13
Hume, David 52
Huntington, Samuel 75
Hutchinson, John 87

Ică Jr., Ioan 38, 92, 163
Ilie, Cleopa 168
Iliescu, Ion 28
Il-Sung, Kim 13
Innocent III, Pope 80
Ionescu, Nae 30, 167
Iorga, Nicolae 77, 122
Iron Guard 24, 51, 133–7

Jaspers, Karl 18
Judt, Tony 13
Justinian I, Emperor 79

Kant, Immanuel 52, 182
Kedourie, Elie 89
Kittel, Gerhard 62–3
Koch, Stephen 95
Kulâghin, Ivan 169
Kutter, Hermann 182

Lakatos, Peter 160
Lenin, Vladimir I. 94
Leopold II, Emperor 112
Leuştean, Lucian 9, 22, 154, 156
Locke, John 52
Lord's Army 14
Lossky, Vladimir 93, 193
Louth, Andrew 194
Luther, Martin
    and racism 60
    two kingdoms doctrine 85, 189

Mănăstireanu, Daniel 42
Mănăstireanu, Dănuţ 208, 212
Marchiş, Iustin 21
Maria Theresa, Queen 111

Index

Marina, Justinian 24, 203
  social apostolate 155–61
Marino, Adrian 31
Meyendorff, John 81, 82, 192
Micu-Klein, Inocenţiu 111, 113–16
Mihăieş, Mircea 38
Milosz, Czeslaw 10, 157
Mineriade 28
Moisescu, Justin 163–5
Müller, Ludwig 54, 55
Mungiu-Pippidi, Alina 38

nationalism
  birth of 86–8
  Bolshevik 2, 93–5
  Fascist 2, 45, 49
  German 2, 3–4, 44–63
  Orthodox East 90–1
  religious 3, 109, 134, 138, 191
Neamţu, Mihai 22, 217
Negruţ, Paul 38
Niebuhr, Reinhold 217
Niemöller, Martin 59, 186
Noica, Constantin 28

O'Donovan, Oliver 81

Pacepa, Ion Mihai 10, 40, 162
papocaesarism 83
Pârvan, Vasile 121
Patapievici, Horia-Roman 26
Pavel, Dan 32, 95
Peter the Great, Tsar 91
Pippidi, Andrei 92
Plămădeală, Antonie 159
  Servant Church 165–6
Pleşu, Andrei 24–5
Political Religion 7
  Communism as 95–6
  National Socialism as 48, 49
Popescu, Dumitru 27
Popper, Karl 45
Positive Christianity 49
Preda, Radu 17, 19, 30, 74
Prodan, David 115
Protestant Reformation 84
  and caesaropapism 84–6

Rădulescu-Motru, Constantin 127
Ragaz, Leonard 182
Rahner, Karl 200
Ranger, Terence 103
Raţiu, Ioan 118
Revista 22 28
Robertson, Ronald 11
Rogobete, Silviu 5, 203
Romania
  church–state model 4, 122–37
  Communism 47
  Communist Party 15, 150
  corruption 5
  Evangelicals 32
  interwar 133–7
  Law on Religious Freedom 19, 33–4
  Marxism 2–3
  national debate 5, 29–31
  nationalism 122–37, 217–18
  păltinişani 28
  paşoptişti 127
  post-Communism 1, 4–6, 12–35,
    76–7, 202, 204, 215–18
  religiosity 5
  resistance movement 3, 167–71
  securitate 10, 22, 48, 162
  Vyshinsky Plan 152
Romanian Orthodox Church 1–3
  autocephaly 125–9, 131–3
  caesaropapism 6
  church and state 26, 122–37
  Communist Party 15
  Communist persecution 152
  Group for Reflection and Church
    Renewal 20–6
  Holy Synod 16, 20
  national cathedral 31–2
  Phanariot 124–5
  phyletism 19
  post-Communism 12–35
  post-Communist nationalism 31,
    217–18
  post-Communist reform 13–15
  religious freedom 32–4
  religious national heroes 113–19
  religious proselytizing 33
  renewal under Communism 154–6

Romanian Orthodox Church (Cont'd)
   Russian influence 152
   sanctification of origins 110–12
   secular intelligentsia and 28–32
   Servant Church 165–6
   social apostolate 3, 7, 28, 157–61
   social role of the clergy 120–2
   state autonomy 18–20, 92, 122–37
   Symphonia 77, 156
   threats to national identity 119–20
   in Transylvania 129–31
   in Wallachia and Moldavia 123–4
Rosenberg, Alfred 52, 54, 190
Rugul Aprins 168–70
Runciman, Steven 101
Russell, Bertrand 96
Russia
   Bolshevik Revolution 29, 93–5
   Communism 2, 45
   hesychasm 92, 105
   influence on Romania 152
   nationalism 91–3
   pseudomorphosis 92
   Sergianism 158
   slavophilism 92–3
   sobornost 93
   Stalinism 2

Șaguna, Andrei 116–19
Schifirneț, Constantin 111
Schmemman, Alexander 83
Scrima, André 169
Smith, Anthony D. 87, 103
Spengler, Oswald 75, 135
Stalin, Joseph 96, 154
Stan, Lavinia 9, 32, 74, 77, 161
Stăniloae, Dumitru 7, 20, 93, 122, 168, 192
   disagreement with Karl Barth 198–200
   on Greek Catholic Church 202
   nationalism 200–3
   and post-Communism 204

   resistance through dogmatic 195–8
   Teologia Dogmatică Ortodoxă 8, 194, 195–8
   theological formation 193–5
   view of Law 197
Steinhardt, Nicolae 167, 168
Strauss, David 58
Symphonia 78, 84

Talmon, Jacob 94
Theodorescu, Răzvan 31
Thurneysen, Eduard 198
Tillich, Paul 63, 214
Tismăneanu Commission 4, 215
Tismăneanu, Vladimir 4, 14, 162
Todorov, Tzvetan 215
Tönnies, Ferdinand 49
totalitarianism 44–5
Toynbee, Arnold 75
Transylvania 17, 24
   nationalism 129–31
Trifa, Iosif 137
Trotsky, Leon 45
Tudor, Sandu 168
Turcescu, Lucian 9, 32, 74, 77, 161, 197
Țuțea, Petre 122, 167

Vasile, Cristian 9, 23, 173
Verdery, Katherine 113
Villa-Vicencio, Charles 181, 215
Vladimirescu, Tudor 125
Voicescu, Constantin 21
Voiculescu, Vasile 169
Voinescu, Alice 169
von Balthasar, Hans Urs 200
von Harnack, Adolf 58, 182
Vulcănescu, Mircea 167

Ware, Timothy 82, 154, 200
Webster, Alexander 158
Wood, James 85

Zedong, Mao 13